Narratives in Black

"This is a timely, even crucial, an[d] ... [collectio]n of scholarly work revealing Africanis[t] ... [ut]ilized' in a European post-colonial world, a[nd] ... [th]e racism and xenophobic exclusionism. *Narratives* ... a rich and varied category and home base to embodied ... [perf]ormance, choreography and research by a cadre of gifted practitio[ners] ... a history. It has a present and a presence. It deserves this attention."
—Brenda Dixon-Gottschild, Professor Emerita of Dance Studies, Temple University, USA

"An important treaty to the significance of dance community challenging dominant stereotypes and structures that reproduce social inequalities, this book makes a vital and exciting contribution to the dance field, mapping humanizing possibilities dance can offer the 21st century."
—Doug Risner, Editor-in-Chief Emeritus of *Journal of Dance Education* and Associate Editor of *Research in Dance Education*

"This informative book is not just for scholarly research, but highlights the importance of artist discovery, journey development, and the understanding and practice of dance-art forms in Britain. Journeys we have witnessed in each other."
—Jackie Guy, MBE, CD, Teacher and Choreographer

"An urgent offering to the expanding field of Dance Studies! Exploring a range of artistic practices from a variety of research perspectives, this volume affirms the deep histories of the embodied arts in Black Britain. These potent essays demonstrate that the moving body makes meaning through experience. A vibrant animation of the *narrative turn* of dance scholarship, this book is required reading for everyone in dance and cultural studies."
—Thomas F. DeFrantz, Founding Director of the Collegium for African Diaspora Dance

Adesola Akinleye
Editor

Narratives in Black British Dance

Embodied Practices

palgrave
macmillan

Editor
Adesola Akinleye
Middlesex University
London, UK

ISBN 978-3-319-70313-8   ISBN 978-3-319-70314-5 (eBook)
https://doi.org/10.1007/978-3-319-70314-5

Library of Congress Control Number: 2017961566

© The Editor(s) (if applicable) and The Author(s) 2018
This work is subject to copyright. All rights are solely and exclusively licensed by the Publisher, whether the whole or part of the material is concerned, specifically the rights of translation, reprinting, reuse of illustrations, recitation, broadcasting, reproduction on microfilms or in any other physical way, and transmission or information storage and retrieval, electronic adaptation, computer software, or by similar or dissimilar methodology now known or hereafter developed.
The use of general descriptive names, registered names, trademarks, service marks, etc. in this publication does not imply, even in the absence of a specific statement, that such names are exempt from the relevant protective laws and regulations and therefore free for general use.
The publisher, the authors and the editors are safe to assume that the advice and information in this book are believed to be true and accurate at the date of publication. Neither the publisher nor the authors or the editors give a warranty, express or implied, with respect to the material contained herein or for any errors or omissions that may have been made. The publisher remains neutral with regard to jurisdictional claims in published maps and institutional affiliations.

Cover illustration: Image Source Plus / Alamy Stock Photo
Cover Design: Humanities / Performing Arts

Printed on acid-free paper

This Palgrave Macmillan imprint is published by Springer Nature
The registered company is Springer International Publishing AG
The registered company address is: Gewerbestrasse 11, 6330 Cham, Switzerland

To all the dancers who have often been nameless or remain nameless: dancers who have contributed to the dance community in Britain and world-wide through their love, enthusiasm and belief in movement for expression, be they on the dance floor, in the dance studio, on the stage, in the school gym or church hall, or in the streets.

Thank you

This book was seeded by the excitement and conversations initiated by the first Re:Generations Conference in UK in 2010. Special thanks to the that first conference's organising team Jeannette Bain-Burnett & Judith Palmer, (ADAD), Deborah Baddoo MBE (State of Emergency productions), Anne Hogan, Lucy Richardson & Jane Turner (London Metropolitan University), and Beverly Glean (Irie! dance theatre) for their vision in collaborating to organise the conference. Thank you to Mercy Nabirye and One Dance UK for their continued support of the project as the book developed over the subsequent years.

FOREWORDS

Black Britishness is so often contextualised through either an African or a North American lens, asking us to locate Blackness in Britain as "of another place"; or implying ownership of emotions and histories that originate outside the British experience. Despite the vibrancy of African and North American Blackness, Britain adds its own distinctive threads of colour to the fabric of dance-art. Threads that can contribute beyond its shores to contextualise the spaces and silences its quiet presence have left. These Forewords from US and Nigerian artist-scholars salute diasporic connectedness while acknowledging the importance of recognising the uniqueness of each other's stories – A. Akinleye

FOREWORD BY DR. THOMAS F. DEFRANTZ

Many researchers of African descent understand that to write about Black performance is to value the possibilities of Black people's creativity and lives. For us, the act of narrating performance and researching histories of dance is an act of affirmation and of group communion; an opportunity to extend shared pleasures and critiques beyond the moments of our encounters in theatres, at dance halls, in studios, or at feasts and family gatherings. Scholarship in this area serves to stabilise the possibilities of the live experience: to expand historical contexts and explain connections among people and their histories; to validate the theoretical assumptions already at play in the performance; and to share stories from the dance floor about where and when we entered.

Too often in the past, we were not allowed the opportunity to critically celebrate our achievements as embodied artists. For too many researchers, "Black" performance arrived as a dynamic cipher, an approach to action that demonstrated an 'otherness' far from a mainstream of art. In identifying its particularities, researchers constructed an impossible alterity for Black performance as a capacious space without logical boundary or intentionality. Black dance might be anything done by Black people in any circumstance, and it needn't have been artistic or engaged in any social ambition. Dozens of essays took on the unreasonable task of trying to define Black dance practice, as though one might be able to define "music" or "art" in a useful and coherent manner. Getting caught up in the losing game of defining creative behaviour stalled the study of Black dance.

NOW we do better, and this volume offers crucial evidence of a vibrant field in formation. Here, we read about Black dance practices and their effects in the world from people who are committed to their recovery, recitation, and well-being. Surely, it matters that the researchers telling the stories here *care* about social possibilities for the people whose dances they narrate. Here, more than in most scholarly accounts of Black dance, the authors value the potentials of personal revelation, and its place in research about Black people. In this, we encounter a communication of an experience of dance; the translation of action into narrative. In editing the book, Akinleye acknowledges that much is lost in this violent translation from dance to manuscript; the dance leaves its place in time and space to become fixed as figures on a page or screen. But the process of translation is approached with care and consideration, with an abiding respect and desire to **do right** by dancing itself. This is an urgent goal approached by the present volume.

But where is the Black British? Is it a place, bound to the islands and colonies that make up Great Britain? Does it exist in time or space, or, more rightly, as an experience of the imagination endured by some but not all? When does it come into being, and what might be gained by calling it forth? Is it conceived as an alternative to some sort of White Britishness? These speculative questions drive the need for engaged research in this important area. Of course, Black British life is best considered on its own terms, without an inevitable reference to Whiteness or the disavowal of, say, a lack of Black dancers being cast by the Royal

Ballet. Black British dance deserves explication on its own terms, not as the leftovers from a historical recounting of White trends in dance-making. The essays in this volume demonstrate that Europe and its complex colonial histories will always be present, to some extent, in any articulation of life in Britain, and yet Black British lives demand their own tellings and imaginings according to terms that centre their own experiences in the world.

Black British Dance does not arrive with the same concerns as Black American dance. There are overlaps, of course: aesthetic devices and the importance of rhythm as a foundational organising tool; the need to connect across geography and time through embodied practices of Black diasporas; the excitement at the usefulness of dance as a weapon of community actualization and self-definition. However, the differences matter as well. Black USA produces all manner of music, movement, and glossy commercial products for mass consumption alongside the private, experimental, spiritual, and resistant modes of dance. Black British Dance reveals itself within the context of a neoliberal economy driven by the overexposure of Black American forms. In this volume, authors affirm that the stories told by Black British artists reveal particular histories of dance unlike any other. Reading along, we are invited to wonder: "What was it like to imagine professional dance in 1960s Great Britain?"; "What have been the problems in recognising Black British dance?"; "What do dancers do in classes that are part of a matrix of Black British dance?"; "How do we make art?"

Scholarship in dance necessarily takes on these difficult queries, as it tries to align unpredictable, always-changing practice with the stability of narrative and language. Researching Black British dance adds layers of concern: "What is this scholarship for?"; "Whose philosophical traditions do you stand in?"; "What sorts of movements matter most to you, and why?"; "How do you feel dance?" And then there is more, of course: the shifting paradigms of race and culture; questions of funding and access to venues; the constructions of social time and community support through forms of dance and their memory. The authors in this volume emphatically tell stories of Black British dance so that others can learn their truths and their ways of understanding how dance *means*.

In all of this, we raise as many questions as we might answer along the way. Some ideas do become clear. It matters who creates the scholarship, and who they intend to encounter it. It matters who is talking, and to whom. These stories of dance, and its emergences, and its affects intend to construct a paradigm of discovery, one that places Black British experience at the centre of research in dance. In all, this volume pushes us all, dancing itself toward a series of "what if" propositions that I imagine as I read this remarkable book:

> "What if I tell you what I think about the dances I've done?
> What if I tell you who I think I am when I dance?
> What if I tell you my story in my own way?
> And what if I shift the ways that these stories might be narrated?
> Sometimes I write in theoretical academic writing, but sometimes in anecdotal truth-telling. Will you be able to hear me?"

To this end, this volume expertly cajoles us,

> "*What I write here is only part of the story. Come closer, I will dance the rest ...*"

Foreword by Peter Badejo, OBE

'The Walk Toward Legacy'
Metaphorically, dance, is a "corn seed" planted in a fertile human field (society), be it the dance-expressions of the people of colour, Black or whatever terminology you may give. Once it germinates, it continues to grow, feed and energise the body and soul of the living in that environment.

Black British Dance
There is no denying the fact that Britain has placed itself in a position of great influence in all the colonies and it continues to exert its concept of cultural and artistic superiority over its ex-colonies and the world at large. This has been made possible through its dominance and grip on the dissemination of information on socio-cultural, economic, and political developments. To enable a balanced understanding of existence, much broader explanations must be explored and made available. There has been a dearth of literature on Black British dance. Simply because we do not *write* our experiences and history, Georg Hegel (1830–31 Lectures) concluded *that "Africa has no history, and that the history of Africa is the history of Europeans living in Africa"*. While Hegel is guilty of both cultural myopism and inadequacy, dance practitioners of African descent or

inspiration and academics—especially in Britain today, are guilty of a greater crime of unchecked intellectual languorousness of unpardonable proportion.

Narratives in Black British dance as a concept in exploring, intellectualising, and documenting the experiences of artistes and their different stories is long overdue and this gallant and stimulating effort must be commended. The insufficient analytical and documented materials on Black British cultural development have led to misinterpretations of cultural and artistic expressions. Artistes need to tell their stories and given the varied background experiences of writers, artistes, researchers, arts managers, and dance students, there is a need for periodic debates and dialogues to capture and document emerging practices and influences to avoid misrepresentation and build a body of knowledge for Black British dance. Environments and cultural influences shape our expressions. Pre-colonial and post-colonial experiences still determine, to a large extent, how we perceive and comment on sociocultural activities of others.

There is an African aphorism that says if you fail to tell your story the way it actually is, someone else will tell it the way it suits them. One could be forgiven for concluding that perceptions on dance expressions of non-European origins have been deliberately derogatory and in some cases patronising. The playing field in the development of the arts in Britain has not been even, hence the slowness, if not stagnation in the development of some non-European art expressions in Britain.

Information is power and the capacity to analyse situations and work towards solutions cannot be underestimated. It has been recognised for a while that the knowledge base for capacity building in African and Diaspora arts has been very limited. Acute lack of resources, research materials, and the inconsistencies in funding policies over the past few decades have stultified the efforts and attempts made by individuals and organisations to create enduring institutions that could have developed the African and Diaspora arts in Britain.

I believe that this book will serve as a peep through the door of knowledge to explore further possibilities and legacies for artistes, researchers, commentators, and writers, who will contribute their stories to the continuum of dialogue that will change perceptions and help enhance the future creativity of artists. It will also free artists from the bondage of colour coding and labelling, which may have inhibited their identity as African and Diaspora artists. This book I hope will spur the continued dialogue that will empower the artists and educate the non-appreciation, assessment, and judgement of ignorance of a privileged few who have for too long classified dance expressions from African and Diaspora artists in many unsuitable terms.

Duke University   Thomas F. DeFrantz
Durham, NC, USA

Badejo Arts Independent Artist   Peter Badejo
Lagos / London, Nigeria / UK

Preface: Dancing Through This Book

The notion of dance from a British perspective consists of a number of untold stories, some of which converge in the territory of Blackness, Britishness and dance. This edited collection includes the work of a range of emerging and established scholars and artists who all present responses to the notion of Black British dance. The book's aim is to offer the reader theoretical possibilities for engaging with notions of Black British dance while also providing dance-artists, and those involved in dance, reflections on experiences they might have had or witnessed themselves.

As its title suggests the book takes inspiration from seeing Black Dance as a complex, broad socio-cultural network of relationships and rhythms that reach far and wide. The book is designed to be read in multiple ways: from cover to cover, tracing themes using the index, reading the Parts as independent sections, or picking out specific chapters to be read individually. It is hoped that the micro within the chapters are read alongside each other in order to construct larger critically reflective pictures of the notion of Black British dance. Chapters are grouped together under three sections: Paradigms, Processes and Products. Rather than attempting to be a comprehensive overview, the book offers possible entryways to discussing Blackness, Britishness and dance. As such it offers a rich archive of narratives crafted through testimony. These serve the multiple purposes of capturing key moments in personal and universal histories, as well as generating multi-layered portraits of the embodied practices of dance in Britain. The book also acts as a kind of resistance to the normative constrains of a single Grand Narrative for Black British dance by underlining the importance of telling the multiplicity of dancers' "own" stories. The book challenges the presumption that Blackness, Britishness or dance are monoliths. Instead, it suggests that all three descriptors (Blackness, Britishness, and dance) are living networks created by rich diverse histories, multiple faces, and infinite future possibilities, the significance of which suggests a widening of the constructs for what British dance looks like, where it appears, and who is involved in its creation.

The collection includes the work of scholars and artists from across the extended family of Blackness, Britishness, and dancers. Rooted in the somatic-based, embodied experience of dancing, our starting point is the belief that the moving body makes meaning through experience. Through the complexities of their personal histories, sensations, reflections, and experiences, contributors share their narratives from within the field of dance. Placed together in the book, these narratives create a mosaic of understandings and interpretations for the reader to explore. To this end, this book rejects the notion that we should (or even could) define "Black British dance" and instead submits that there are common threads, common experiences, and common expressions shared by those who identify, or are identified as, or have a relationship with the notions of British-ness, and Black-ness, and dancing. Holding to Africanist and Indigenous (K. Anderson, 2000; hooks, 1992; Smith, 1999) and postmodern (Burkitt, 1999; Desmond, 1997) values in which identity is multi-dimensional, transient, performed, and often projected, each chapter is an individual response to the idea of "Black", "British", and "Dance" while acknowledging that all three labels are contested and open to interpretation. The book recognises that being Black, being British, or being a dancer are personal stories and by no means amount to a narrative with a single voice, nor do the qualifiers of "Black", "British", or "dance" have defined borders and fixed meanings. Therefore, the chapters do not claim to speak to one experience but collaboratively sit together with the aim of contributing to wider contexts for the arts, culture, and what it means to create dance.

The non-dualist approach the book takes posits that phenomena (or things) do not need to correspond to fixed definitions. As such, we draw on the ethnographic (Clifford, 1997; Clifford, Marcus, & School of American, 1986) and narrative approaches (Riessman, 2008; Schiff, McKim, & Patron, 2017) to share a range of perspectives. Narrative inquiry has differing significance according to the theoretical framework from which it is written. Here the use of the *narrative turn* is used as a verb. To tell the story is valued as *"giving presence to"* the lived life of an individual (Schiff in Hatavara, Hyden, & Hyvarinen, 2013, pp. 245–264). Narrating reveals something of the constructed socio-cultural landscape in which the story takes place (the Black, British, and Dance landscapes). Following feminist theory (Butler, 1990, 1993), this provides a means to trouble constructed stereotypes through sharing (embodied) *felt*, lived experiences.

Here narrative inquiry provides a structure that allows for all communication to be representative, as story is the re-telling of experience (Clandinin & Connelly, 2000; Schiff, McKim, & Patron, 2017). Rather than an attempt to actually communicate sensation (for instance of the sensation of dancing), the writers attempt only to share what it means to them, leaving space for the reader to find their own relationship with the story. If we see dance as a site where understanding happens physically, then we can assume that dance communicates something. Dancers engage with multiple narratives because they are literate in multiple modes of communication, for instance, in verbal literacy but also in physical literacy (Whitehead, 2010) and visual literacy. The ethnographic nature of narrative allows for the rhythm of the transforming, relationship-ed "I" to be present and describe across its literacies. The ethnography of narrative is sensitive to the paradox of how embodied experience can be represented, communicated, and ultimately written about in text. Just as my Grandma told me stories that are revealed across the complexity of the many manifestations of my identity, the narrative turn…

> *'… moves from a singular, monolithic conception of social science towards a pluralism that promotes multiple forms of representation… away from facts and toward meanings… away from idolizing categorical thought and abstract theory and toward embracing the values of irony, emotionality, and activism; away from assuming the stance of disinterested spectator and toward assuming the posture of a feeling, embodied, and vulnerable observer…Each of us judges our lived experiences against the ethical, emotional, practical, and fateful demands of life as we come to understand them.'* (Bochner, 2001, p. 134)

This book values the personal real-world knowledge of practice alongside the theory of scholarship, underlining that at times, as we write as dancers, we are re-telling a discovery that originated and remains primarily *in movement*. Here the presence of embodied metaphor (Lakoff & Johnson, 1980) at home, resilient, and resonant in story, is also drawn upon by the dancer for understanding, perceiving, and communicating their moving body (Desmond, 1997). Acknowledging the act of moving (dancing) generates knowing in itself, and leads us to acknowledge that writing about dancing involves representation of that physical knowledge. Therefore, it is not a direct sharing of the knowledge (—come into the dance studio and dance with me for that), the story is a communication of an experience. As discussed above, the book shares stories from the field that reveal episodes of engagement with the idea of Black British dance. In this way, narrative inquiry imagines the construction of the artist and scholar as an on-going project and a shifting practice of transformations. The book suggests moving away from the "scientific" need to define and measure "who" or what Black British dance is, and moving toward asking "when, where and how" Black British dance? (Riessman, 2008). The Self is not trapped within the measurable shell of the body. Instead the Self is the embodied, narrativised, self-coordinated by the sensations, relationships and rhythms of lived day-to-day movement. These are shared here to give insights in to artistic practices.

Each contributor to the book tells their story from within the experience of Black, British and dance (whether it be as a dance teacher, choreographer, dance scholar, practicing artists or all of these). This is done in order to stimulate further conversation. Therefore, the book explores the multi-layered, multi-dimensional nature of artists and artistic work in order to reject the injustice of attempting to classify Black British dance as "one thing". The book also attempts to avoid simply responding to "White" representations of Black-ness (hooks, 1992). Rather, the book constructs the interwoven relationships of dance across the African and British Diasporas.

Accompanying the book, there is also a web-site that acts as an on-going collection of interviews and sharing of practices http://narrativesindance.com. The web-site acts as a doorway using interviews to look from *outside in to* the lived experiences of artists' practices. The book acts as a doorway from *inside* artists' practices to speaking *out* through sharing their own narratives about dance.

Middlesex University London, UK

Adesola Akinleye

REFERENCES

Anderson, K. (2000). *A Recognition of Being: Reconstructing Native Womanhood.* Toronto: Sumach Press.
Bochner, A. (2001). Narrative's Virtues. *Qualitative Inquiry, 7*(2), 131–157.
Burkitt, I. (1999). *Bodies of Thought: Embodiment, Identity, and Modernity.* London/Thousand Oaks, Calif.: Sage Publications.
Butler, J. (1990). *Gender Trouble: Feminism and the Subversion of Identity.* New York/London: Routledge.
Butler, J. (1993). *Bodies That Matter: On the Discursive Limits of "Sex".* New York: Routledge.
Clandinin, D. J., & Connelly, F. M. (2000). *Narrative Inquiry: Experience and Story in Qualitative Research* (1st ed.). San Francisco, Calif.: Jossey-Bass.
Clifford, J. (1997). *Routes: Travel and Translation in the Late Twentieth Century.* Cambridge, MA/London: Harvard University Press.
Clifford, J., Marcus, G. E., & School of American, R. (1986). *Writing Culture: The Poetics and Politics of Ethnography.* Berkeley, CA/London: University of California Press.
Desmond, J. (1997). *Meaning in Motion: New Cultural Studies of Dance.* Durham, NC./London: Duke University Press.
Hatavara, M., Hyden, L.-C., & Hyvarinen, M. (2013). *The Travelling Concepts of Narrative.* Amsterdam: John Benjamins Publishing Company.
hooks, B. (1992). *Black Looks: Race and Representation.* Boston, MA: South End Press.
Lakoff, G., & Johnson, M. (1980). *Metaphors We Live By.* Chicago: University of Chicago Press.
Riessman, C. K. (2008). *Narrative Methods for the Human Sciences.* London: SAGE.
Schiff, B., McKim, A. E., & Patron, S. (2017). *Life and Narrative: The Risks and Responsibilities of Storying Experience.* New York: Oxford University Press.
Smith, L. T. (1999). *Decolonizing Methodologies: Research and Indigenous Peoples.* London/New York/Dunedin, N.Z., New York: Zed Books, University of Otago Press, Distributed in the USA exclusively by St. Martin's Press.
Whitehead, M. (2010). *Physical Literacy: Throughout the Lifecourse* (1st ed.). London: Routledge

Contents

1 Narratives in Black British Dance: An Introduction 1
  Adesola Akinleye

Part I Paradigms 19

2 "I Don't Do Black-Dance, I Am a Black Dancer" 23
  Namron

3 Dance Britannia: The Impact of Global Shifts on Dance in Britain 31
  Christy Adair and Ramsay Burt

4 Negotiating African Diasporic Identity in Dance: Brown Bodies Creating and Existing in the British Dance Industry 37
  Tia-Monique Uzor

5 Tracing the Evolution of Black Representation in Ballet and the Impact on Black British Dancers Today 51
  Sandie Bourne

6   In-the-Between-ness: Decolonising and Re-inhabiting
     Our Dancing   65
     Adesola Akinleye and Helen Kindred

Part II   Processes   79

7   Trails of Ado: Kokuma's Cultural Self-Defence   83
     Thea Barnes

8   *Moving Tu Balance*: An African Holistic Dance as a
     Vehicle for Personal Development from a Black
     British Perspective   101
     Sandra Golding

9   'Why I Am Not a Fan of the Lion King': Ethically
     Informed Approaches to the Teaching and Learning of
     South African Dance Forms in Higher Education in
     the United Kingdom   115
     Sarahleigh Castelyn

10   Performativity of Body Painting: Symbolic Ritual as
     Diasporic Identity   131
     Chikukwango Cuxima-Zwa

11   Dancehall: A Continuity of Spiritual, Corporeal Practice
     in Jamaican Dance   167
     H. Patten

12   Our Ethiopian Connection: Embodied Ethiopian Culture
     as a Tool in Urban-Contemporary Choreography   187
     Ras Mikey (Michael) Courtney

13	Reflections: Snapshots of Dancing Home, 1985, 2010 and 2012 Hopal Romans	201
Part III	Products	213
14	Battling Under Britannia's Shadow: UK Jazz Dancing in the 1970s and 1980s Jane Carr	217
15	Caribfunk Technique: A New Feminist/Womanist Futuristic Technology in Black Dance Studies in Higher Education A'Keitha Carey	235
16	More Similarities than Differences: Searching for New Pathways Beverley Glean and Rosie Lehan	249
17	Epistemology of the Weekend: Youth Dance Theatre Hopal Romans, Adesola Akinleye, and Michael Joseph	265
18	Transatlantic Voyages: Then and Now Anita Gonzalez	277
Index		285

Notes on Contributors

Adesola Akinleye is a choreographer and artist-scholar. She trained at Rambert Academy and began her career as a dancer with Dance Theatre of Harlem later establishing her own company, Saltare (now Adesola Akinleye/DancingStrong), whilst living in New York, for which she was awarded the *1999 national Women's History Month award for Distinguished Achievement in the Field of Dance'* by Town of Islip, NY. She has been a part of Canadian nationwide artists-in-schools programmes as well as teaching at the University of Manitoba. She studied choreogry with Bessie Schönberg and her choreographic work has been commissioned and toured across the UK and North America. In the UK she has danced with Green Candle Dance Company, and Carol Straker Dance Company, among others. She has been awarded the *Association of Dance of the African Diaspora Trailblazers Fellowship 2005*, the *Bonnie Bird New Choreographers Award, 2006* and *One Dance UK's Champion Trailblazer Award, 2016*. She has taught and created work in universities in the UK, Canada and the USA, as well as being artist-in-residence for arts-in-education programmes such as Creative Partnerships (UK) and Learning Through The Arts (CA). She is a Senior Lecturer at Middlesex University and visiting lecturer at a number of universities in the USA. She holds a PhD from Canterbury Christ Church University and an MA (distinction) in Work-Based Learning: Dance in education and community from Middlesex University UK. She is a Fellow of the RSA.

Christy Adair Professor Emerita (Dance Studies) York St John University, wrote *Dancing the Black Question: the Phoenix Dance Company Phenomenon* (Dance Books: 2007). Her research interests, developed in *Women and*

Dance: sylphs and sirens (Macmillan: 1992), continue to focus on gender and ethnicity in relation to dance studies and performance. Her recent research investigates contemporary dance in Africa and the diaspora. She was Co-Investigator with Professor Ramsay Burt of the Arts and Humanities Research-funded project British Dance and the African Diaspora, 2012–2014, and is co-editor of *British Dance: Black Routes* (Routledge: 2016), which draws on material from this research project.

Thea Nerissa Barnes began her career with the Alvin Ailey American Dance Theater and then the Martha Graham Dance Company. Thea has Broadway/film production credits with The Wiz and the Broadway production of Treemonisha. She is a certified Stott Pilates mat instructor, sports conditioner and Ashtanga yoga instructor. Thea has taught, coached, choreographed and directed dancers aged 5 to 65, novices to professionals, in West End and Broadway musicals, concerts, community settings, elementary and high schools, universities, and professional schools in the USA, Britain and Europe. She has also published articles for web and traditional magazines including *Dancing Times, Dance Theatre Journal* and *Ballet Tanz*. She researched and was the presenter for the BBC Radio 3 broadcast *You Dance Because You Have To* which aired for the first time in September 2003 and again in October 2004, and she worked with Bedford Interactive Video (2003) to develop teaching CDs, and the British Arts Council to develop an educational documentary entitled *Not Just a Somersault* (1994). Thea holds a Bachelor of Fine Arts in Dance from the Juilliard School, New York, a Masters Degree in Dance Education from Columbia Teachers College in New York and a Master of Philosophy from City University, London.

Sandie Bourne completed her PhD in Dance Studies at Roehampton University. She has presented papers for ADAD's Re:Generations conference in 2012 and 2014. She also gave a paper on '*Representations of Black dancers in ballet*' at Trans.Form@Work, a postgraduate symposium at the University of Surrey in May 2012. She was a panellist for Dance and the Creative Case, which was part of the Arts England Council's 'Decibel', performing arts conference on diversity and equality in Manchester, in September 2011. Bourne trained for 3 years as a dancer at London Studio Centre, has a BA in Performing Arts, a major in Dance from Middlesex University, and an MA in Dance Studies from Surrey University.

Ramsay Burt is Professor of Dance History at De Montfort University, UK. His publications include *The Male Dancer: Bodies, Spectacle, Sexualities* (1995, revised 2007), *Alien Bodies: Representations of Modernity, 'Race' and Nation in Early Modern Dance* (1997), *Judson Dance Theater: Performative Traces* (2006), with Valerie Briginshaw, *Writing Dancing Together* (2009), and *Ungoverning Dance* (forthcoming). In 2013-2014, with Professor Christy Adair, he undertook a two-year funded research project into British Dance and the African Diaspora which culminated in an exhibition at the International Slavery Museum in Liverpool. With Susan Foster, he is founder editor of *Discourses in Dance*. In 1999 he was Visiting Professor at the Department of Performance Studies, New York University. Since 2008 he has been a regular visiting teacher at PARTS in Brussels. In 2010 he was Professeur Invité at l'Université de Nice Sophia-Antipolis.

A'Keitha Carey is a Bahamian artist, educator and scholar. She received her BA in Dance from Florida International University and an MFA in Dance from Florida State University. She also holds a Certificate in Women's Studies from Texas Woman's University. A'Keitha created CaribFunk dance technique, a fusion of Afro-Caribbean, ballet, modern, and fitness principles rooted in Africanist and Euro-American aesthetics and expressions. She researches Caribbean spaces, locating movements that are indigenous, contemporary, and fusion based, and investigates how Caribbean cultural performance (Bahamian Junkanoo, Trinidadian Carnival, and Jamaican Dancehall) can be viewed as praxis. She is the Department Chair of the Enrichment Program and the Performing Arts Teacher at Indian Ridge Middle School in Davie, Florida. She is also an Adjunct Professor in the Dance Program at Miami Dade College Kendall Campus and currently a member of Olujimi Dance Theatre in Miami, Florida.

Jane Carr worked as a ballet dancer before studying dance in higher education. She was a founding member of '*quiet*', an artists group that collaborated on multidisciplinary performance works during the 1990s. She also worked for many years at Morley College in Southeast London to develop opportunities for adults and young people to participate in dance. She received a BA and MA in Dance Studies from Laban and a PhD from Roehampton University, in 2008. Carr has been actively researching since May 2010, developing her doctoral research into embodiment in the context of dance practices. She has served as a member of the editorial board of the journal *Research in Dance Education* and serves as a member of the executive committee of The Society for Dance Research.

Sarahleigh Castelyn is an educator, researcher, performer, and choreographer. She is based at the School of Arts and Digital Industries, University of East London, where she teaches on the undergraduate BA (Hons) Dance: Urban Practice programme, and on postgraduate and research programmes. She has completed an Arts and Humanities Research Council-funded practice-based doctoral research project into the Body as a Site of Struggle in South African Dance Theatre at Queen Mary University of London. Castelyn has both performed in and choreographed dance works in the United Kingdom and South Africa. She is published in academic journals and dance magazines, such as *Dance Theatre* Journal, *Animated*, *African Performance Review*, *South African Theatre Journal*, and the *South African Dance Journal*. She serves on performance editorial and organisation boards, including The African Theatre Association and *South African Dance Journal*.

Michael 'RAS Mikey' Courtney holds a BFA in modern dance from the University of the Arts in Philadelphia and an advanced MA degree in ethnochoreology from the University of Limerick in Ireland where he recently completed his PhD in arts practice research. Courtney's postgraduate research explored Ethio-modern dance, his embodiment of Ethiopian and other world dance cultures, used as a tool in his urban contemporary choreographic process.

Chikukwango Cuxima-Zwa is a British/Angolan performance artist-scholar; he explores interdisciplinary theoretical approaches pertinent to the history, culture and identity of the African diaspora. In 2004 he completed his BA in fine arts and arts for community at Middlesex University; in 2005 his MA in art history and archaeology at SOAS, University of London; and in 2013 his PhD in performance arts and theatre studies at Brunel University, West London. Currently, he is an assistant teacher in theatre practice at Morley College.

Beverley Glean have been working together in partnership with Rosie Lehan, IRIE! dance theatre and City and Islington College since 1992. Since 2000 they have consolidated their work in a diverse range of projects. These include Connectingvibes Dance Company and the Dance and Diversity Project. The latter is an action-based research project originally funded by NESTA and Arts Council England to investigate the place of

African and Caribbean Dance, which in 2007 included a research trip to the USA, Jamaica, Cuba and Ghana. Since 2008 they have led the Foundation Degree in Dance delivered in partnership with IRIE! Dance Theatre, City and Islington College and London Metropolitan University.

Rosie Lehan have been working together in partnership with Beverley Glean, IRIE! dance theatre and City and Islington College since 1992. Since 2000 they have consolidated their work in a diverse range of projects. These include Connectingvibes Dance Company and the Dance and Diversity Project. The latter is an action-based research project originally funded by NESTA and Arts Council England to investigate the place of African and Caribbean Dance, which in 2007 included a research trip to the USA, Jamaica, Cuba and Ghana. Since 2008 they have led the Foundation Degree in Dance delivered in partnership with IRIE! Dance Theatre, City and Islington College and London Metropolitan University.

Sandra Golding is an African Holistic Dance practitioner, community artist, choreographer and performer. She trained at the London School of Classical Dance and West Street Studios. Golding specialises in African Caribbean dance, having had over 15 years experience in African Caribbean dance as principal dancer/teacher of Birmingham-based Kokuma Dance Theatre Company under the artistic direction of Jackie Guy, MBE. In 2009 Sandra graduated with an MA in Dance and somatic wellbeing and the living body from the University of Central Lancaster, and she continued her studies in 2010 at Worcester University on the MSc degree in the Integrative Dance Movement Psychotherapy programme designed by Terrence Wendell Brathwaite. Sandra has taught nationally and internationally, and she choreographed for Jamaica 50 celebration, Symphony Hall Birmingham in 2012. She has been guest teacher for L'acadco' Dance Company and Ashe Community Arts Company in Jamaica. In 2015 Golding delivered African holistic dance workshops for the Spiritual Living Consciousness Awakening retreat and conference at the Centre for Peace in Geneva. She performed in Dub Qalander an inter-cultural collaborative performance of Sufi and roots rock reggae music at Symphony Hall Birmingham. Golding regularly delivers African Holistic Dance, a complimentary therapeutic dance and movement education, in the community.

Anita Gonzalez heads the Global Theatre and Ethnic Studies minor in SMTD and LS&A at University of Michigan. Her research and publication interests are in the fields of ethnic performance, nineteenth-century theatre, maritime performance and the way in which performance reveals histories and identities in the Americas and in transnational contexts. Gonzalez is also a director and writer who has staged dozens of productions. Her directing and choreography has been broadcast on PBS and at Dixon Place, The Workshop Theatre, HereArts, Tribeca Performing Arts Center, Ballet Hispanico and other venues. She has been awarded a residency at Rockefeller's Bellagio Center (2003) and has received three Senior Scholar Fulbright grants. Gonzalez earned her Ph.D. in Theater/Performance Studies from the University of Wisconsin-Madison (1997). She is an Executive Board member of the National Theatre Conference, an Associate Member of Stage Directors and Choreographers, and a member of The Dramatists Guild, ATHE, ASTR and SDHS. Currently, Gonzalez is a member of the Executive Committee of the University of Michigan Press.

Michael Joseph since completing his training at The Rambert Academy and Dance Theatre of Harlem School, in the 1980s, has worked as a choreographer, dance artist, teacher and DSLR dance filmmaker – nationally and internationally. He danced with Union Dance for 23 years, a role that also included Assistant Artistic Director. He was an Associate Artist at the Hat Factory with Jean Abreu from 2009 to 2011. He currently works as a freelance dance artist with Comberton Village College, Cambridge and Barnwell School in Stevenage, teaching and choreographing. He has choreographed works for University of Bedfordshire, Union Dance, ADAD, Nubian Steps and State of Emergency: *The Mission Tour*, as well as for various youth companies at DanceDigital, Swindon Dance and Paddington Arts Centre. His choreographic piece created for Union Dance in 1997 '*Mass Equilibria in the Sea of Tranquility*' from Dance Tek Warriors is now a set piece on the GCSE Dance Syllabus.

Helen Kindred is a dancer, choreographer and movement practitioner-researcher. She has been performing and presenting work internationally and teaching extensively within and beyond formal education settings for over 20 years. Her work addresses some of the complexities of our embodied relationships with our selves and others explored through dance improvisation, text, music and touch. Kindred has created commissioned works for independent companies and community dance festivals, and faculty works for undergraduate dancers, and more recently she has worked within collaborative improvised performance. Kindred holds a BA in Dance Studies and an MFA in Choreography from Roehampton University

London, and has held Artistic Director posts both with her own company KindredDance and through Regional Dance Development Agencies. She is a Senior Lecturer in dance at Middlesex University London, co-curator and choreographer for the *trip* project (Turning Research Ideas into Practice) with Adesola Akinleye/DancingStrong, a founding member of TIN (TransDisciplinary Improvisation Network) and is engaged in doctoral studies, researching the conversations between practice, pedagogy and performance through dance improvisation.

Namron was a founding member of The Place, London Contemporary Dance School, opened in 1966. After finishing an illustrious career as a dance performer in 1983, Namron began teaching under the advice of Robert Cohan and Robin Howard having had previous experience teaching company class as an original member of the London Contemporary Dance Theatre. He was invited to Leeds by Nadine Senior to work with Harehills on an outreach programme for schools. In 1985 following this work, he became a founding member of the Northern School of Contemporary Dance. Namron proudly worked at the Northern School of Contemporary Dance for fifteen years. He continues to work as a freelance dance lecturer. In the past twelve years, he has worked with numerous dancers, groups, companies and organisations such as Mavin Khoo, Middlesex University and Jay Singha. In 2014 at age 70 he returned from retirement as a performer to dance at Sadler's Wells as part of the Elixir Festival and continues to perform to date. He was awarded the office of the Order of the British Empire (OBE) for services to dance in 2014.

H. Patten is the Artistic Director of Koromanti Arts. His career spans over 21 years, pioneering African and Caribbean music and dance. Trained in Ghana, 'H' has collaborated with many choreographers and producers including F. Nii-Yartey (Ghana), Monika Lawrence (Jamaica), Keith Khan (UK) and the British Council (UK, West, Central and Southern Africa). Obtaining his Masters in TV Documentary at Goldsmiths University College, 'H' has developed Dance for Camera techniques, and is currently on the PhD programme at Canterbury Christ Church University, researching the genealogy of Jamaican dancehall, with the working title of *The Spirituality of Reggae Dancehall Dance Vocabulary*.

Hopal Romans trained at the Laban Centre, London, while performing as a member of Extemporary Dance Theatre. After graduating from Laban, Hopal moved to New York where she studied with the Alvin Ailey

American Dance Theater as a scholarship student. She went on to work with US-based companies and choreographers such as Ulysses Dove, Rovan Deon, Mark Taylor & Friends, Andrew Jannetti & Dancers, and Ann Moradian's dance company. Returning to the United Kingdom, Hopal danced for The Kosh, Union Dance Company, Bill Louther and the company *Danza Libre* in Guantanamo, Cuba. She took part in the Arts Council England Fellowship Programme for Ethnic Minorities Arts Professionals. She was involved in arts management and music education for ten years. Hopal is currently a dance tutor working primarily in the teaching of contemporary dance in the Horton technique, infused with and influenced by Afro-Cuban dance. Hopal has a diploma in Dance Teaching and Learning – Children and Young People from Trinity Laban and an MA in Professional Practice: Dance Technique Pedagogy from Middlesex University.

Tia-Monique Uzor is a dance researcher. Her research explores issues of identity, cultural traffic, popular dance and sexuality within Dance of Africa and the African Diaspora. Tia-Monique has a Bachelor of Arts Honours degree in Dance and Drama and a Masters by Research degree in Dance, both awarded by De Montfort University. In 2012 whilst conducting her Masters by Research Degree, Tia-Monique presented her paper *The Evolving Face of the Iwa Akwa* based on her degree work at the Association of Dance of the African Diaspora's Re:Generations conference. Her recent work *Werking the Twerk: Empowerment of the Black Female Body* was presented at Serendipity's Blurring Boundaries conference in May 2015 and informed her chapter in *Blurring Boundaries: Urban street meets contemporary dance 2016* published by Serendipity. Tia-Monique has worked with Akram Khan Dance Company during the creation of *Vertical Road*. She has also worked with EC ARTS as an arts producer for a project within a local shopping centre. Tia-Monique currently teaches on the Understanding Dance module at De Montfort University.

List of Figures

Fig. 7.1	*Trails of Ado*. Choreography by Jackie Guy. Kokuma Performing Arts, 13 October 1987. Dress rehearsal of Revival Section from *Trails of Ado*. Left to right: Desmond Pusey, Doreen Forbes, Cecelin Johnson, Jacquline Bailey, Patricia Donaldson; Drummers behind dancers: Silbert Dormer, hidden behind Desmond-Tony Reid, Gladstone Foster, Kokuma Studio, 163 Gerrard Street, Lozells, Brimingham B19 2AH. Photographer Philip Grey	83
Fig. 7.2	Kokuma Performing Arts 1987. Left to right standing: Jackie Guy, Christine Seymour-costume seamtress, Desmond Pusey, Patricia Donaldson, Cecelin Johnson, Doreen Forbes, Jacqueline Bailey, Pete Barrett-stage management, Eky Charlery-administrator, Tracey Finch-clerical staff; Kneeling musicians: left to right: Silbert Dormer, Gladston Foster, Tony Reid. Kokuma Studio, 163 Gerrard Street, Lozells, Brimingham B19 2AH. Photographer Philip Grey	98
Fig. 10.1	Alberto Juliao during the Angolan carnival of victory in Luanda, 2013 (Alberto Juliao, 2013)	142
Fig. 10.2	Alberto Juliao during the Angolan carnival of victory in Luanda, 2013 (Alberto Juliao, 2013)	143
Fig. 10.3	Cuxima-Zwa, Area 10 performance Space, Peckham, London, 2007 (Savinien-Zuri Thomas, 2007)	146
Fig. 10.4	Cuxima-Zwa, Area 10 performance Space, Peckham, London, 2007 (Savinien-Zuri Thomas, 2007)	147

xxxii LIST OF FIGURES

Fig. 10.5	Cuxima-Zwa, Area 10 performance Space, Peckham, London, 2007 (Savinien-Zuri Thomas, 2007)	148
Fig. 10.6	Cuxima-Zwa, Parliament Square performance, London, 2009 (Simon Rendall, 2009)	151
Fig. 10.7	Cuxima-Zwa, Parliament Square performance, London, 2009 (Simon Rendall, 2009)	153
Fig. 10.8	Cuxima-Zwa, Parliament Square performance, London, 2009 (Simon Rendall, 2009)	154
Fig. 10.9	Cuxima-Zwa, Abney Park Cemetery performance, London, 2015 (Aguinaldo Vera Cruz, 2015)	155
Fig. 10.10	Cuxima-Zwa, Abney Park Cemetery performance, London, 2015 (Aguinaldo Vera Cruz, 2015)	156
Fig. 10.11	Cuxima-Zwa, Abney Park Cemetery performance, London, 2015 (Aguinaldo Vera Cruz, 2015)	158
Fig. 10.12	Cuxima-Zwa, Abney Park Cemetery performance, London, 2015 (Aguinaldo Vera Cruz, 2015)	162
Fig. 17.1	Romans' private collection: Pages from the first National Festival of Youth Dance programme, held in Leicester 14–21 September 1980 at De Montford Campus and performances shown at the Haymarket and Phoenix Theatres. Dame Ninette de Valois was the Guest of Honour (Hopal Romans, 2017)	272
Fig. 17.2	Romans' private collection: Pages from the first National Festival of Youth Dance programme, held in Leicester 14–21 September 1980 at De Montford Campus and performances shown at the Haymarket and Phoenix Theatres. Dame Ninette de Valois was the Guest of Honour (Hopal Romans, 2017)	273
Fig. 17.3	Romans' private collection: Pages from the first National Festival of Youth Dance programme, held in Leicester 14–21 September 1980 at De Montford Campus and performances shown at the Haymarket and Phoenix Theatres. Dame Ninette de Valois was the Guest of Honour (Hopal Romans, 2017)	274
Fig. 17.4	Romans' private collection: Pages from the first National Festival of Youth Dance programme, held in Leicester 14–21 September 1980 at De Montford Campus and performances shown at the Haymarket and Phoenix Theatres. Dame Ninette de Valois was the Guest of Honour (Hopal Romans, 2017)	275

CHAPTER 1

Narratives in Black British Dance: An Introduction

Adesola Akinleye

> ...*to live at the tense borders of the skin, to live in an uneasy truce of evolution and the molting of cultural identity into something unforeseen and new.*
> *(Wilson in Hereniko & Wilson, 1999, p. 3)*

Britain's colonial history has left a network of 'Black' family, particularly from Britain to the Caribbean, across Africa, and North America. While part of the legacy of colonialism exported Britain's mainstream aesthetic of whiteness around the world, these Commonwealth connections also underwrite the day-to-day, on the ground, multicultural face of Great Britain. Sitting on a London bus, the passengers and people we pass on the streets testify to the complex range of backgrounds and values that form the British population. The dance field is no exception—although its mainstream face may appear to reflect a mono-cultural pre-war whiteness, British dance artists hail from the same colourful range of cultures *over which the sun never set*. These artists contribute to a dance scene that is often invisibilised or suffers by being constructed as in a continual state of early emergence. This gives a sense that those identifying with 'Black' dance and dancers are *new* to Britain, (just emerging) rather than a contributing part

---

A. Akinleye (✉)
Middlesex University, London, UK

© The Author(s) 2018
A. Akinleye (ed.), *Narratives in Black British Dance*,
https://doi.org/10.1007/978-3-319-70314-5_1

across the expanse of British dance history. There is also a plethora of professional Black British dancers and choreographers who have influenced dance worldwide, ironically being identified as British outside Britain's borders but being 'othered' when they return home to her shores.

Therefore, despite a strong creative presence in the arts through a history of individual artists and companies identifying as 'Black', there is a distinct lack of acknowledgement regarding dance and dancers with a relationship to the African Diaspora from the twenty-first century perspective of 'being British'. To this end, this book presents narratives from across the UK and beyond with the aim of offering a (re)articulation of the physical and cultural mapping of the richness of British dance. In order to present the narratives in the chapters that follow, this introductory chapter discusses and challenges some of the contexts for talking about the *dancing body* to expose them as having concealed or drowned out Black, British dance stories in the past. I suggest that the context of blackness as 'otherness' contributes to this along with the context of what kinds of dance styles are valuable, particularly the notion of a divide in value between 'cultural' dance and 'high-art'. I consider how we talk about dance in the West and suggest that some non-Western concepts for understanding what dance *is* are lost because of a lack of interest or knowledge of them in the language of Western mainstream media. I draw attention to the context of the historical legacy of abuse to the Black body and the effects that this has on how Black dancers are audienced. I draw attention to the many contexts created by dualism's separation of mind from body and how this is contrary to many non-Western dance forms. This introduction therefore suggests that by starting to theorise the contexts that have invisibilised some dance artists we can start to create more fertile ground from which to hear them and in turn have a richer dance community in general. This book attempts to refresh contexts for future discussion of the work of dance artists through broadening the narratives heard about Black and British dancing bodies.

Challenging the Context of the 'Other'

In the context of the post-colonial globe, living in London of Nigerian and English descent, I have been privy to the distinct experience gained from being 'black' living outside of the 'Mother land' of Africa. This experience is given a particular focus for those who identify as black yet come from a Western country—to be African-American or to be

Black British. To be a part of the collective consciousness of where you live and yet experience it from the side-lines of being the 'other': not British but 'Black British'. Growing up my very existence as black and living in London seemed to contribute to my non-'black' neighbours confirming their own British-ness. In Chap. 7 Thea Barnes describes how for the artists in Kokuma Dance Company, dance became a safe haven to shelter from the daily experiences of being the black 'other' in their own local communities.

It is of course an interesting phenomenon to meet people whose role in a culture appears to be the 'other' within it. To this end, there is a mainstream interest in engaging with black artists in terms of how they can define their own *otherness*—what is 'Black Dance'? What is 'Black Britishness'? However, this interest in what it is like to be *outside* comes only from the perspective of those who consider themselves *inside*. In addressing the question, for instance of 'What is Black British dance?' there is an implication that there is something distinctly specific and universally describable about being 'black'. 'What is Black British dance?' implies that I could subtract the black from my experience of Britishness and of Dance and have a concept of what was left. The question infers that there will be something that I could recognise as 'not black' and be able to compare that to my 'blackness'.

When I was eight, a classmate asked me 'What is it like to be black?' I said 'I don't know I have never been not-black'. It is equally difficult to answer questions such as 'How have you addressed your whiteness in the choreography?' But such questions are rarely asked of artists. Similarly, I have not met a white dancer who has been asked to define what white British dance was and how their work contributed to it? But I have met many black dancers who have been asked 'What is Black British dance and how does your work contribute to it?' Such questions require artists to be willing to accept themselves as 'other' in terms of their own work. These questions imply the possibility that we can be the 'other' in our own narratives, and can explain how that otherness manifests. To respond to such questions is to suffer the burden of justifying oneself within someone else's story: it denies the artists the liberty of telling their own stories about their work.

I am not suggesting that artists identifying as Black have been complacently silent or not attempted to articulate their own narratives on their own terms. Rather, I am suggesting that this is a problem for the field of dance in general. The context within which we consider dance is often constrained by a lack of challenge to mainstream Western values for what dance is, how it manifests, and the processes that lead to dance. Dance's problem of marginalising people who identify outside its mainstream (and therefore losing the full potential of their contribution to the art form) extends beyond the marginalisation of black dancers and choreographers. However, in the case of artists identifying or identified as Black it has meant that before many can talk about their dance work, they are tasked with proving it is '*dance*' at all, worth the full prestige of the dance industry listening in the first place. To this end, in Chap. 4 Tia-Monique Uzor considers the projections of otherness on to 'brown bodies' as they create work within the British dance industry today. The question 'What is Black British dance?' is about defining a kind of *dance* as much as it is about defining a kind of *Blackness*—both are limiting. It is clear that the notion of *dance* from the full spectrum of the British experience consists of a number of un-listened stories, many of which converge in the territory of Blackness, Britishness, and Dance.

CHALLENGING THE CONTEXT IN WHICH DANCE IS GIVEN VALUE

A challenge of globalisation in the twenty-first century is how we engage with the spectrums we have created for identifying ourselves, others, and the world around. This challenge begins with us looking at the ontological context into which each other's narratives are received (Appiah, 1991; Smith, 1999). The constructs we have for *the truth of our dancing bodies* lead to frameworks for understanding the world. Dance technique training is often guilty of expecting students (and audiences) to have a tacit acceptance of a specific philosophical construct for dance, implicitly inherited from the teacher demonstrating the movement. Students are not only taught to strive to look like the teacher demonstrating but are expected to think like them in order to attain that same aesthetic. Across many codified dance forms, this leaves a lack of encouragement for critical thinking or philosophical inquiry into what dance means beyond its visual appeal (Akinleye & Payne, 2016; Ambrosio, 2015; Sheets-Johnstone, 1984). The inheritance of unquestioning acceptance of dance as mainly a set of physical skills rather than a philosophical approach to moving in the world has left Western dance institutions, such as schools, theatres and production houses, with a powerful uncompromising hierarchy for which dances and dancers are valued. This manifests as the juxtaposition of 'cultural' and communal dance, which is objectified and engaged with from an anthropological perspective, against dance as codified and 'High art', which is highly valued and seen as involving skills of articulation that enhance the art form (Dils & Albright, 2001).

> ...*this way of thinking implicitly sets up an evolutionary model of history in which dance developed from communal or tribal dancing to professional and technically virtuosic....* (Dils & Albright, 2001, p. 370)

The Western dance establishment seems to tacitly adhere to an inference that dance emanating from traditional African or Indigenous forms is locked in the past with the anthropological purpose of reminding us of nostalgic cultural history. Alongside this is the assumption that Modern and Postmodern dance is solely the work of skilled individual artists responding to their current Western experiences. It leaves little room for the narratives of artists that inhabit the space between the perceived polarities of traditional dances and Western High Art. This context of cultural nostalgia 'v' High-Art therefore acts as an echo chamber for some narratives to be heard while silencing other stories. For instance, it mutes the narratives of any contemporary dance movement that comes from the non-Western starting point of traditional or Indigenous dances, yet is the artist's own self-expression and creation (such as Contemporary African dancers). In Chap. 12, RAS Mikey Courtney discusses traditional Ethiopian cultural practices as tools for Urban contemporary dance, and in Chap. 10, Chikukwango Cuxima-Zwa describes the spiritual and traditional practices that inform the contemporary response of his performance work. The cultural nostalgia 'v' High Art polarity also leaves little room for the narratives of dance artists who associate with non-Western belief systems, experiences or philosophy yet dance mainstream Western styles, such as Black ballerinas. In Chap. 5, Sandie Bourne shares historically invisibilised stories of Black British dancers.

CHALLENGING THE CONTEXTS FOR TALKING ABOUT THE DANCING BODY

Growing-up in an Anglo-Nigerian household, and later with Lakota extended family, my gut reaction continually re-sets to '...is this what Mama said?', '...is this what Grandma told me?'. Values from Grandmas are real-*ised* for me by the feeling, sensation of my body that become ideas and thoughts that resonate within me. A process that therefore starts with my connection to my elders/ancestors manifests in my body and only then can become an identifiable verbal thought. This process is clear within the realisation of choreographic work (elders and ancestors can be inside us as we dance, inside the dance studio with us) but, within the more academic Western context of printed text, we are still exploring how we evidence historical knowledge, sensation and intuition—how we write the embodied. The means by which physical experience is described or captured remains the topic of on-going discussion (Foster, 1996; Silk, Andrews, & Thorpe, 2017; Sparkes, 2002; Wellard, 2016). There is a tension between the corporeal, embodied experience of dancing and the linear static experience of reading. In other words, a *book* about dance would appear to be a contradiction-in-terms for my Yoruba and Lakota Grandmas.

This is because moving bodies engage non-verbal ways of knowing (Sullivan, 2001). The 'knowing' in dance could be described as part of our 'felt sense' (Gendlin, 1992), or a 'bodily consciousness' (Foster in Desmond, 1997): an embodied knowing that 'speaks' the somatic 'language' of movement and sensation rather than verbal words. The perception of the embodied Self is in the *situation* of dance, whether in the engagement of executing dance or through the empathy of remembering the sensation of movement when watching dance. Through this book, each author approaches the communication of the dancing body differently, but across the chapters it is clear that the embodied (the responding, experiencing, remembering body) is a part of the terrain of Black-ness and dance.

Because dance involves sensations, the person experiencing the sensation is a part of the story. This is because while we are making, watching, reflecting and writing dance we are making meaning of it through the first reference point of our own bodies. The embodied nature of dance involves the Self, so when dance is written about there needs to be a place for the person experiencing it to be recognised. This is a place to recognise that the writer/dancer and reader/audience are constructing the meaning of dance through their exchanges. The story of dance is filtered through the body of the 'I' who is experiencing it.

We are crafting dance itself when we write about it: we are crafting something, wright-ing (crafting) dance through how we write the somatic. Therefore, the 'I' who is filtering the dance experience through their body in order to craft an understanding of it needs to be present in the text in the first person, and the reader who is interpreting the writing needs to be aware of them. Although the communication of this somatic understanding is addressed in a variety of ways across this book, in my role as editor I have encouraged the contributors to address where they 'are' in the stories told through taking an ethnographic (Clifford, 1997; Clifford, Marcus, & School of American, 1986) and narrative approach (Riessman, 2008; Schiff, McKim, & Patron, 2017; Silk et al., 2017). An ethnographic and narrative approach has been encouraged in order to honour the somatic, connected experience of the dancing body. Ethnography acknowledges a place for the sensing 'I' in the text, while, the *narrative turn* is used to mediate the difficulty of telling the story of one's own bodily-sensation in words (Sparkes, 2002). Narrative inquiry acknowledges the problem that ethnographers/writers encounter as they attempt to represent and communicate their '*embodied experience*'. It also mirrors the oral traditions of African and Indigenous Diasporas that address lived experience through story.

The ethnographic and narrative approaches allow for an acknowledgement of the difficulty of writing about dancing. They help to address awareness of the deficit left when European words alone are used to describe embodied experiences (Mahina, 2002). However, alongside this framework for writing about the dancing body is the need to acknowledge that embodiment is routed in non-Western world views. I do not mean to imply that Africanist or Indigenous values are one thing or even harmonious. But as a dancer, I find that there is a distinct separation between Western dualist-infused attitudes (that separate mind from body, bodied-Self from ancestors, time from space) and those non-Western philosophers and Elders around the world for whom the body is not an isolated separate 'thing'. This re-articulation of Self as embodied is often an important part of the process of de-colonisation for artists (Anderson, 2000; Hereniko & Wilson, 1999).

Challenging Contexts for Seeing the Dancing 'Body' and the Distraction of Representation

The dancing body urges us to consider what the 'body' *is*, what it represents and what role the body plays in terms of the knowledge that resides in the movement that dance renders. Echoing Doris Humphrey, Mark Morris notes that:

> *Dancing is never abstract. It's evocative, because it's being done by human beings. If a dancer looks at something, that means something, and if he looks away, it means something else.* (Morris in Gottlieb, 2008, p. 797)

In addition to the evocative meanings that we derive from seeing bodies moving, there are the connotations placed on black bodies specifically. hooks (1992) points out that compared to advances in acknowledgment of discrimination in education and employment, there is still a struggle to counteract representations of *blackness* in mass media that have barely changed since the height of colonialism. For centuries, European popular culture has projected social significance on to the performer's Black body (DeFrantz & Gonzalez, 2014; Young, 2010). For instance, the hyper-sexualisation of the black female body justifies the measure of certain body parts as a testimony to how 'Black' she is. This is exemplified by the treatment of the South African artist Saartjie Baartman in the 1800s, whose body was *London's most famous curiosity* (Holmes, 2008). Today, black female dance performers and choreographers who by their art form have their bodies on display step into the collective trauma of many historical injuries such as Baartman's (Young, 2006). It is important to recognise that the Black body challenges a Western audience that is yet to acknowledge the tacit all-encompassing narrative of the *curious Black female body*. In Chap. 11, H. Patten suggests that Dancehall, often dismissed as a valueless sexual titillation, is a form of affirmation of continued spirituality that manifests in the ecstatic body. In Chap. 15, A'Keitha Carey uses a feminist lens to relate the reclaiming of her dancing Black body in the *hip wine*.

> *To be black is to have accrued a subjectivity haunted by the spectral traces of a social, political and ideological history… The black body thus enacts a discursive politic, situated within a rubric of knowledge and power, injured and resistant.* (Young, 2006, pp. 25–26)

As Europeans come to terms with the legacies of colonialism, they place the Black body in a projected cycle of victim and aggressor. The Black male body is often cast as 'violent', 'native' and 'raw' (DeFrantz, 2001 in Dils & Albright, pp. 342–349). For the Black body (of the dancer or the choreographer) there is an added hindrance in the written language of English texts about dance, in that this national language itself assumes in its structure a colonial-gaze that projects onto the black body further meanings and renderings of history. Similarly, dance performance work is left grappling with the preoccupation of the objectified story of the black dancer's body rather than the narrative of the artistry of the work itself. In Chap. 2, Namron draws on his career of over 50 years as a professional dancer to narrate the importance of his artistry and what he has contributed to dance practice in the UK. In doing this, he also rejects the attention given to the *spectacle* of his black body as one of the first Contemporary dancers in the UK.

THE LACK OF CONTEXTS FOR TELLING NON-WESTERN TALES THROUGH DANCE

Looking at our own experiences as we spin, jump or even watch someone else dance, the dancing body tasks us with some kind of orientation to larger philosophical questions about the nature of being and the mapping of histories.

> *Anchor your feet to the earth and balance your weight on both legs. Now shift your pelvis to the right and then to the left…when you whirl or when you circle your pelvis, you are drawing the dot, the origins. From this shape all other movements are born…I was excited to know that I carried inside me a source from which everything was born….* (Al-Rawi, 1999, pp. 5–6)

Fundamental relationships between body and the world around are carried and taught through many traditional, Indigenous and African dances. In these cultures, dance is not just a series of movements but a way of remembering and experiencing deeper complex relationships with the world around, before and after us (Al-Rawi, 1999; Trask, 1993). Dance underlines some of the distinctive questions, problems and assumptions that the idea of the isolated 'body' raises in Western philosophy. However strongly you hear Grandma's voice within you, for those working in Anglo-American settings, there is no protection from the watershed of Descartes' articulation of a separation of body from mind (and environment)—*I think therefore I am*. It is a separation that privileges mind over body in terms of how we establish what is true, real and moral. In dance, this manifests in further support of the concept of the separation of 'High art' from 'cultural art' discussed above. Cartesian dualism is used to privilege bodies that dance 'sophisticated' codified, 'virtuoso' dances associated with a thinking mind, over bodies who dance 'primitive', improvised dances associated with an intuitive body (Kealiinohomoku, 2001 in Dils & Albright, pp. 33–43) Western separation of body from mind creates a historical narrative from which justifications for labelling 'developed' and 'un-developed' bodies are hung, and by which many African and Indigenous dances have been banned, lost or dislocated (Jonas, 1992). This is not to imply that this oppression of these dances has ever been fully successful; as Shea Murphy (2007) suggests 'the people have never stopped dancing'. Similarly, resistance to racialised legislation against dance practices has led to dancers developing dance forms in innovative ways (Thompson, 2014). However, it has left dance art work emanating from non-dualist belief systems with the burden of being performed in places where it can be misinterpreted and sometimes appropriated. This has led to space being provided for non-white artists to 'perform their thing' as a kind of fun entertainment but with no attempt to understand their work from the perspective of an artistic practice. Thus, the tale of the artwork is lost to the audience through the exhibitionary nature of the performance.

The Context that Dualism Creates

Dualist assumptions in the dance studio today are the legacy of European colonisers' world–wide encounters with dances, encounters that were punctuated by their need to give a single Grand Narrative of hierarchical development to all they discovered (Gould, 1996; Smith, 1999). Therefore, because of colonialism, when dancers talk about dance they take on the implications of what their *bodies* have meant in the West. This involves negotiating Western values and aesthetics for the 'body' and also requires positioning the lack of knowledge-currency the dancing body represents within dominant Western cultures. This dualist separation of mind and body is rampant across European societies and language. In Chap. 6, Helen Kindred and I discuss how we have started to re-inhabit and de-colonise the dance studio for ourselves through rejecting dualist assumptions in the language we use during our rehearsal processes.

For dance, Descartes and Darwin changed the dancing body. Together, Descartes' exaltation of the certainty of mind over sensing body, and Darwin's birthing of the concept of evolution paved the way for a modern science polarisation of mind and body. This was to move from a human/God polarity that many traditional dances inhabit, to one of ethereal mind/mechanical body, leaving dance to be more about accomplishing physical skills. Descartes' *body as a machine* allowed for a body that could be overhauled as we would a working tool. Darwin envisioned a body that had been developed and fine-tuned over an expanse of time (Synnott, 1993). This was a body that held the knowledge of generations but through its evolutionary structure, not through its sensing or inherited memory.

Darwin's theories and the colonialist Hegelian vision of human enhancement armed colonisers with the righteousness to extrapolate a dance-history tinged with a dualist hierarchy in which the moving body *disclosed* the superiority of its dancer's mind. As Western 'explorers' encountered dance, what they could not understand in the dances they witnessed, they attributed to a lack of intelligence in the dance. That aspect of the dance that could not be translated was (and still is) not recognised as knowledge. What was felt and could not be verbalised was seen as a dangerous lack of control of the Self. As such, the mind's control of the body was sought after and the 'uncontrolled' body was seen as sinful (Burkitt, 1999). This was not something assumed by many pre-colonised cultures where the sensing-body was not seen as corrupt or sinful, but a means through which to connect with the world around. Implications for how different types of dances are valued is clear, but for instance in Yoruba religion the entranced dancing body becomes sacred (not sinfully out of control) as it hosts the Orishas (Woods Valdes, 2012).

Darwin had also placed hierarchical privileges on the differences within body types (Burkitt, 1999; Synnott, 1993). The body was not a *site* of knowledge but the *evidence* of knowledge. For Europeans the differences in bodies were to be explained as differences in evolutionary and moral development (Gould, 1996; Synnott, 1993). As discussed above for instance the black female body took on specific meanings. Differences in bodies were put into hierarchical order, privileging some human bodies over others (Gould, 1996). Rather than celebrating difference, difference was seen as a sign of stages of development within a linear hierarchical construct for the perfect body of the future. Dance in the Western academy today still displays the legacy of earlier aspirations of dance training toward the perfect (White) body of the future (Karina & Kant, 2003).

Rather than a site of expression and communication the body was rendered as a place of betrayal, unable to hide the inadequacies of the person it 'houses'. As well as displaying evolutionary retardation, some parts of the body were seen as more corrupted than other parts (Synnott, 1993). Therefore, depending on what parts of the body they use or highlight, some kinds of dances were regarded as more sinful than others. The body and its sensory attributes and movements became something to be measured, assessed and modified (Bourdieu, 1984; Butler, 1990; Du Bois, 1989; Foucault & Sheridan, 1979; Shilling, 2003; Synnott, 1993). Through the industrial revolution, the body became the site of judgement in the construction of social order, being cited to legitimise a number of social constructions such as class, gender, race and what 'art' is (Synnott, 1993). The modern measure of 'science' was used.

> *the adult who retains the more numerous fetal, infantile or simian traits, is unquestionably inferior to him whose development has progressed beyond them... measured by these criteria, the European or white race stands at the head of the list, the African or negro at its foot...All parts of the body have been minutely scanned, measured and weighed, in order to erect a science of the comparative anatomy of the races D.G. Brinton 1890.* (Gould, 1996, p. 145)
>
> *we might ask if the small size of the female brain depends exclusively upon the size of her body... but we must not forget that women are, on the average, a little less intelligent than men, a difference which we should not exaggerate but is, nonetheless, real. We are therefore permitted to suppose that the relatively small size of the female brain depends in part upon her physical inferiority and in part upon her intellectual inferiority G. Herve 1881.* (Gould, 1996, p. 136)

In the West, before Descartes, the perceived inadequacies of an individual's body were taken as an indication of one's closeness to good or evil. However, the Cartesian *body* could be *consciously* developed using human creativity. This meant that inadequacies in the body now betrayed inabilities of the mind (within that body), which had the power to change and develop it's body but appeared to choose not to do so. So in the West's emergent scientific world, the body could be measured in order to indicate the quality of the mind it housed.

Black, British dancers are not only dealing with the prejudice that the dancing body could not be knowledgeable in general, but also that at some level their particular body stubbornly remains 'black-looking' despite the amount of tucking, straightening or weight loss tips they are given as advice. On a subconscious level, their bodies' persistent *blackness* is a reflection of a lack of mental ability to understand that the dancer should cease from attempting to engage with mainstream dance! In our dualist

Western inheritance, the body's structure and movement, perfection and beauty are still seen by some as illustrating the identity of the individual (Shilling, 2005; Synnott, 1993). In the mainstream, this disadvantages those whose bodies do not conform to ideals of beauty. Within the Western dance academy, there is still a sense that without the 'correct' body the person moving could not legitimately identify as a *dancer* or contribute meaningfully to those who *do* identify as dancers (for instance cannot choreograph for anyone but themselves) and therefore their stories are not of interest (Albright, 1997).

The assumption of a distinction between *concrete* (*body*) and *cognitive* experience (*mind*) returns us to the European mind/body divide and the problem of where knowledge is located. Most dancers do not acknowledge the mind/body distinction, and therefore the '*body*' is '*embodied*', part of the process through which knowledge is gained. Many dancers see dance, the reflective-action of 'my embodied experience', as what is assumed for the word 'mind'. For them mind is not a separate thing, mind is action, and is therefore a verb (Dewey, 2005). However, this oneness of mind and body is not widely articulated on a day-to-day basis in the dance studio. The study of dance often accepts an approach to the body that sees it as something to meld and work into shape (*no pain, no gain*). This is accompanied by an approach to the mind as something to overcome (*just do it*). The result of these approaches is something that looks like mainstream dance. For those who do not look like mainstream dancers, however, or for whom embodiment is ever present in their cultural practices, dance cannot be something that is presumed. Dance is something where the 'mind' exists in the actions and transactions of the body (Dewey, Boydston, & Lavine, 1989)—dance is in the reflective and spiritual response. It is at the edges of the skin (Deleuze & Guattari, 1987; Sullivan, 2001) in the tools used; and dance is beyond the skin, in the light, drum, earth, music and in what these together create. Dance becomes something created across the artist's wide expanse of ever-changing relationships and rhythms of sensation. The dance-artist's identity is a daily activity. Meaning is spread across what 'I' do and how 'I' engage and respond—this is how an artist's work becomes an extension of their Self-identity. Embodied, dance work comes from the nuances of a mind-ful-body responding to the many complexities of the world around. (Dewey et al., 1989). Therefore, the recognition or non-recognition of an artist's work can impact on the very foundation of their identity. If the work is only recognised as an on-going affirmation of the single identifier of being *Black*, the artist is stifled. In the face of dualism's legacies, this book responds to a need to tell of a fuller range of identities from the art practice of dance.

New Contexts

This book presents new contexts and stories in order to offer further modes to theorise dance, modes that are informed by the rich practices of artists that identify with Blackness and Britishness. These narratives are organised into three parts. Part One—*Paradigms* considers the perceptions/thought patterns/sets of ideas that scaffold the landscape of dance and give rise to notions like 'Black British Dance'. This section, therefore, underscores approaches, models and concepts that artists (within Blackness, Britishness, and Dance) appear to be drawn to or find they repeatedly challenge. Part Two—*Processes* looks at ways of perceiving, understanding/digesting experience, and expression that manifest as processes of art-making and identity-making within Black, British, and Dance. Part Three—*Products* explores phenomena that appear to have arisen from the experience of 'Black' 'British' Dance. At the start of each of these Parts, I have written a short introduction to the section and chapters included in that section. The book is organised into these three parts in order to give a three-dimensional look at the artists and work within the spectrums of Black, British and dance. Therefore, the book could be read chronologically but, in the spirit of disrupting frameworks, the book's individual chapters and sections can also be read independently.

References

Akinleye, A., & Payne, R. (2016). Transactional Space: Feedback, Critical Thinking and Learning Dance Technique. *Journal of Dance Education, 16*(4), 144–148. https://doi.org/10.1080/15290824.2016.1165821.

Albright, A. C. (1997). *Choreographing Difference: The Body and Identity in Contemporary Dance.* Hanover, NH/London: Wesleyan University Press.

Al-Rawi, R.-F. B. (1999). *Grandmother's Secrets: The Ancient Rituals and Healing Power of Belly Dancing.* New York: Interlink Books.

Ambrosio, N. (2015). Critical Thinking and the Teaching of Dance. *Dance Education in Practice, 1*(1), 7–11. https://doi.org/10.1080/23734833.2015.990341.

Anderson, K. (2000). *A Recognition of Being: Reconstructing Native Womanhood.* Toronto, ON: Sumach Press.

Appiah, K. (1991). Is the Post in Postmodernism the Post in Postcolonial? *Critcal Inquiry, 17*(2), 336–357.
Bourdieu, P. (1984). *Distinction: A Social Critique of the Judgement of Taste*. Cambridge, MA: Harvard University Press.
Burkitt, I. (1999). *Bodies of Thought : Embodiment, Identity, and Modernity*. London/Thousand Oaks, CA.: Sage Publications.
Butler, J. (1990). *Gender Trouble: Feminism and the Subversion of Identity*. New York/London: Routledge.
Clifford, J. (1997). *Routes: Travel and Translation in the Late Twentieth Century*. Cambridge, MA/London: Harvard University Press.
Clifford, J., Marcus, G. E., & School of American, R. (1986). *Writing Culture: The Poetics and Politics of Ethnography*. Berkeley, CA/London: University of California Press.
DeFrantz, T. F. (2001). Simmering Passivity: The Black Male Body in Concert Dance. In A. Dils & A. C. Albright (Eds.), *Moving History, Dancing Cultures: A Dance History Reader* (pp. 342–349). Middletown, CT: Wesleyn University Press.
DeFrantz, T. F., & Gonzalez, A. (2014). *Black Performance Theory*. Durham/London: Duke University Press.
Deleuze, G., & Guattari, F. l. (1987). *A Thousand Plateaus: Capitalism and Schizophrenia* (p. 1988). London: Athlone.
Desmond, J. (1997). *Meaning in Motion : New Cultural Studies of Dance*. Durham, NC/London: Duke University Press.
Dewey, J. (2005). *Art as Experience* (Perigee Paperback Edition ed.). New York: Berkley Publishing Group.
Dewey, J., Boydston, J. A., & Lavine, T. Z. (1989). *John Dewey: The Later Works, 1925–1953* (Vol. 16: 1949–1952, Essays, typescripts, and Knowing and the Known). Carbondale: Southern Illinois University Press.
Dils, A., & Albright, A. C. (2001). *Moving History, Dancing Cultures: A Dance History Reader*. Middletown, CT: Wesleyn University Press.
Du Bois, W. E. B. (1989). *The Souls of Black Folk* (Bantam Classic ed.). New York: Bantam Books.
Foster, S. L. (1996). *Corporealities: Dancing Knowledge, Culture and Power*. London: Routledge.
Foucault, M., & Sheridan, A. (1979). *Discipline and Punish: The Birth of the Prison*. Harmondsworth: Penguin.
Gendlin, E. T. (1992). *The Primacy of the Body, Not the Primacy of Perception*. Man and World, 25(3), 341–353. https://doi.org/10.1007/BF01252424.
Gottlieb, R. (2008). *Reading Dance: A Gathering of Memoirs, Reportage, Criticism, Profiles, Interviews, and Some Uncategorizable Extras* (1st ed.). New York: Pantheon Books.

Gould, S. J. (1996). *The Mismeasure of Man* (Rev. and Expanded ed.). New York/London: Norton.

Hereniko, V., & Wilson, R. (1999). *Inside Out: Literature, Cultural Politics, and Identity in the New Pacific*. Lanham, MD: Rowman & Littlefield.

Holmes, R. (2008). *The Hottentot Venus: The Life and Death of Saartjie Baartman: Born 1789–Buried 2002*. London: Bloomsbury.

hooks, B. (1992). *Black Looks: Race and Representation*. Boston, MA: South End Press.

Jonas, G. (1992). *Dancing: The Pleasure, Power, and Art of Movement*. New York: Harry N. Abrams in Association with Thirteen/WNET.

Karina, L., & Kant, M. (2003). *Hitler's Dancers: German Modern Dance and the Third Reich*. New York/Oxford: Berghahn.

Kealiinohomoku, J. (*2001*). An Anthropologist Looks at Ballet as a Form of Ethnic Dance. In A. Dils & A. C. Albright (Eds.), *Moving History, Dancing Cultures: A Dance History Reader* (pp. 33–43). Middletown, CT: Wesleyan University Press.

Mahina, 'O. (2002). Atamai, Fakakaukau and Vale: 'Mind', 'Thinking' and 'Mental Illness' in Tonga. *Pacific Health Dialog, 9*(2), 303–308.

Riessman, C. K. (2008). *Narrative Methods for the Human Sciences*. London: SAGE.

Schiff, B., McKim, A. E., & Patron, S. (2017). *Life and Narrative: The Risks and Responsibilities of Storying Experience*. New York: Oxford University Press.

Shea Murphy, J. (2007). *The People Have Never Stopped Dancing: Native American Modern Dance Histories*. Minneapolis, MN/Bristol: University of Minnesota Press/University Presses Marketing. [distributor].

Sheets-Johnstone, M. (1984). *Illuminating Dance*. Lewisburg, PA/London: Bucknell University Press/Associated University Presses.

Shilling, C. (2003). *The Body and Social Theory* (2nd ed.). London/Thousand Oaks, CA: SAGE.

Shilling, C. (2005). *The Body in Culture, Technology and Society*. London: SAGE.

Silk, M. L., Andrews, D. L., & Thorpe, H. (2017). *Routledge Handbook of Physical Cultural Studies*. London: Routledge.

Smith, L. T. (1999). *Decolonizing Methodologies: Research and Indigenous Peoples*. London/New York/Dunedin: Zed Books/University of Otago Press. Distributed in the USA Exclusively by St. Martin's Press.

Sparkes, A. C. (2002). *Telling Tales in Sport and Physical Activity: A Qualitative Journey*. Champaign, IL: Human Kinetics.

Sullivan, S. (2001). *Living Across and Through Skins: Transactional Bodies, Pragmatism and Feminism*. Bloomington: Indiana University Press.

Synnott, A. (1993). *The Body Social: Symbolism, Self and Society*. London: Routledge.

Thompson, K. D. (2014). *Ring Shout, Wheel About: The Racial Politics of Music and Dance in North American Slavery*. Urbana, IL: University of Illinois Press.

Trask, H.-K. (1993). *From a Native Daughter: Colonialism and Sovereignty in Hawai'i*. Monroe, LA.: Common Courage Press.

Wellard, I. (Ed.). (2016). *Researching Embodied Sport: Exploring Movement Cultures*. Abingdon/New York: Routledge.

Woods Valdes, A. E. (2012). Sacred Survuval: Orisha Dance and the Ring Shout, Performative Symbols of African Retentions in the New World. *Attitude: The Dancers' Magazine, 25*(1), 11–17.

Young, H. B. (2006). *Haunting Capital: Memory, Text and the Black Diasporic Body*. Hanover, NH/London: University Press of New England/Eurospan. [distributor].

Young, H. (2010). *Embodying Black Experience: Stillness, Critical Memory, and the Black body*. Ann Arbor, MI: University of Michigan Press.

PART I

Paradigms

I have called this section *Paradigms* because it seems clear that a better understanding of what 'Black British dance' can mean requires a paradigm shift which these chapters start to discuss. I am defining 'paradigm' as sets of ideas, patterns, theories and rhythms that contribute to the conception, construction and discourses of some *thing*: in this case the ideas, patterns, theories and rhythms that contribute to how we perceive dance in Britain and internationally today. This first section acknowledges that it is the presumed expectations of Blackness, Britishness and dance that will have most influence on how this book is read. These presumed expectations mean that it is not just who tells the story but how the story is heard that gives the book meaning. 'How it is heard' is translated through what is perceived as significant or important within the text. This first section is compiled as a collection of chapters that challenge the supposed contexts under which we start to discuss the notion of Black British dance within the larger field of dance. The chapters in this section suggest that, rather than a focus on defining Blackness, what emerges as significant within the paradigm comments more on the ontology of dance in general.

Therefore, the chapters in this first section are chosen to highlight some of the assumptions that can slip into the discussion of Black British dance unnoticed. For instance, as we think about the notion of Black British dance, how drawn are we to a normative history of dance that is informed by Western concert dance? As we think about Black British dance, how ready are we to assume that we are talking about Black artists; as if Black dance and Black artists were interchangeable descriptions. When we think about Black British dance, how ready are we to assume that the artists involved are newly emerging? How often has Black British dance been discussed as if it were a single art form? How do we construct a context for dance that is aware of normalising particular cultural stereotypes in order to define what dance is?

Part I challenges the reader to think about what emerges when we interrogate what should be most significant within the paradigm that Black British dance inhabits. I begin in this way in order to deconstruct the landscape and language in which the notion of Black British dance is located. As with so many attempts to trace what some *thing* is, or what it represents, we can be seduced into a fixed historical outline for how it came about or manifested. Then having established this kind of history, it is theorised into the current manifestation of the *thing* in terms of how it developed from its 'origins'. I want to avoid this Grand Narrative approach but I understand that it is also important to root subjects historically. Following Smith (1999), this first section therefore attempts to interrogate our methodology for understanding how Black British dance is given its place in history and in the present. The chapters in this section look at how challenging mainstream historical narratives for Blackness Britishness and dance also contributes to wider discourses in dance in general: such as the communication of dance (how we label and communicate dance discussed in Chap. 6), dance as a living art form (how dance forms are contributed to by artists over history discussed in Chap. 5), dance existing in collective memory (how as an embodied practice many artists have had to rely on collective memory rather than documented history to preserve their work discussed in Chap. 3), and identity (how a dancer's identity manifests personally but also through how their dance is responded to discussed in Chap. 4).

Part I opens with an acknowledgement of an Elder in the British dance community – Namron. In Chap. 2, '*I Don't Do Black Dance, I am a Black Dancer*', Namron describes how over the longevity of his career he has seen what is identified as '*Black dance*' shift as dance practices and techniques become more established and acceptable to the general public. Shifts that realign dance practices so that '*Black dance*' often moves to be attributed to whatever is less established in the mainstream. Reflecting on his career, he notes how Contemporary dance began as a cultural shift highly influenced by the melting-pot of the USA, to being the thing that the Black student would be expected to study over the well-established *Ballet* technique, to today when Contemporary dance has become more a part of the establishment and the Black student would be expected to study Street dance. All of these are assumptions about the capability of the Black dancer, and the assumption of what '*Black dance*' is, that are located in the time period the dance is happening rather than in any kind of attributes of the dancers themselves.

In Chap. 3, '*Dance Britannia: The Impact of Global Shifts on Dance in Britain*', Burt and Adair underline the distraction that discussing Black British dance as if it were one thing has on valuing individual artists' work.

Often I am asked 'Where are all the Black ballet dancers?', to which I reply 'They are busy out there dancing'. Bourne documents a brief history of ballet from a British perspective in Chap. 5, '*Tracing the Evolution of Black Representation in Ballet and the Impact on Black British Dancers Today*'. Bourne underlines the historical loss that a dance form can suffer when so many of its artists are invisibilised by a White Eurocentric Grand Narrative. Further addressing the navigation of a Grand Narrative for dance, Uzor reflects on conversations with dance artists who are identified as Black artists in Britain. In Chap. 4 '*Negotiating African Diasporic identity in Dance: Brown Bodies Creating and Existing in the British Dance Industry*', Uzor returns us to challenging the validity of labelling within the embodied, non-verbal medium of dance.

In Chap. 6, 'In-the-Between-ness: Decolonizing and Re-inhabiting our Dancing', Kindred and I discuss the importance of the language we use to engage with choreographic processes. We question how much of the discourse around dance is affected by the language we use to describe and locate ourselves within it. We suggest that taking an Africanist, Indigenous peoples and/or 'Black Dance' approach to creating work is a philosophical shift for how we understand the moving body as embodied rather than an aesthetic for the moving body.

As a whole, Part I suggests that within the *paradigm* of dance, significances that manifest when we consider the notion of Black British dance are in dance as a lived history, dance as a language of embodiment, dance as a home and dance as expression of identity and artistry. Throughout all the chapters, I cannot but notice that although the labelling of a thing called Black British dance is present, what it represents is shifts across time and personal experiences. Through this is a sense of a community of people that are created from the experience of toiling under and negotiating the impact of a label, rather than a label that summarises a community.

Reference

Smith, L. T. (1999). *Decolonizing Methodologies: Research and Indigenous Peoples.* London/New York, Dunedin, NZ/New York: Zed Books/University of Otago Press/Distributed in the USA Exclusively by St. Martin's Press.

CHAPTER 2

"I Don't Do Black-Dance, I Am a Black Dancer"

Namron

When we are talking about dance in today's world or historically, we are talking about something I fell in love with. I fell in love with dance and dance fell in love with me and I'm still in love with it. In this chapter, I am suggesting that the personal connection each dancer has with their dance is what contributes to dance as an art form, what it is and what it can be. The dance scene is created out of the personal contributions each dancer makes to the art form; not in terms of how they can be culturally identified but in terms of their personal history, their personal relationships with dance—their performance of dance. Each dancer brings their unique experiences, personality, cultural background and how they relate to the place they are in to the art form of dance. Essentially this gives dance its rich diversity, vital connection and impassioned expression of the experience of being human.

> *I feel that the essence of dance is the expression of man – the landscape of his soul. I hope that every dance I do reveals something of myself or some wonderful thing a human being can be.* (Graham, 1991, p. 6)

Created by Namron and written by Adesola Akinleye from conversations with Namron.

Namron (✉)
Independent dancer, London, UK

© The Author(s) 2018
A. Akinleye (ed.), *Narratives in Black British Dance*,
https://doi.org/10.1007/978-3-319-70314-5_2

Of course, there are cultural, social and economic differences between us but as dancers we are all fighting the same fight to express our inner reflections with the considered movement of our bodies. This is a shared understanding of what it is to be human. The physicality of dance tells both a personal history and a world history. But the Grand Narrative of world history can drown out the personal narratives of the dancers themselves. Dance is a living art form, it continues to develop and transform, unfolding in the bodies of the dancers. Dance is constructed and shared and handed down body to body. This underlines the importance of Elders in the dance community in terms of better understanding the shared historical narratives we create every time we take on a movement in our dancing-bodies. Elder dancers carry memory in their bodies and in their stories that are a navigation towards how the dance we do today has been formed. Better understanding this makes a young dancer's own technique and contribution to dance more meaningful. As an Elder myself, I can trace the recent history of dance in the UK within my own body, within my own personal archives, and within my construction of who I am.

Tracing a Personal History

My first performances were back in 1962. In summer 2014, aged 70, I performed at Sadler's Wells Theatre again as part of the Elixir Festival. I am still performing today. 1962 to 2017 is 55 years of performing dance. I was a founding member of *The Place*, London Contemporary Dance School opened by Robin Howard in 1966, and original member of *The Company*, London Contemporary Dance Theatre. Later, in 1985, I was a founding member at Northern School of Contemporary Dance, where I worked for 15 years. As a founding member of these organisations, I can attest to how the landscape of dance in the UK has undergone a revolution during my lifetime.

I began training over 50 years ago. I began training at the Willesden Jazz Ballet in my teens, and then I took my classes with Madame Rambert. Ballet was my first love and introduction to dance training. I remember seeing Alison Bentley (now Alison Beckett) dancing ballet in the studio. I was entranced by the physicality of ballet, the control of the limbs: the control, artistry and athleticism of movement drew me in. As I started to dance ballet I found my physical home, ballet is part of my dream. (Later, as I went on to dance other styles of dance, I was able to earn a living as a dancer.) When I started dancing, there were not as many books and resources to find out about movement as there are today. I read Nijinsky,

Isadora Duncan, and I managed to find ballet books by Arnold Heskell. I read these over and over, back to back and over again. I read those four or five books to get inspiration.

Dance centres did not offer training in the wide variety of dance styles you find today. I used to go to take extra classes at a place where all the West End Show performers took classes; it was called the Max Rivers Studios, in Leicester Square. This little place had lots of ballet teachers and jazz teachers. At that time in London, there were no available classes in 'Street Dance' or 'African', nor were there any contemporary classes. That range of movement was all new to us training as dancers in the UK at the time. As a ballet dancer, contemporary dance was new to me. The first performance I ever saw was Martha Graham at the Prince of Wales Theatre in the early 60s. I saw a mixture of black and white dancers standing holding spears and it was enough to encourage me. Six months' later, I attended a performance by Alvin Ailey and my whole world fell apart. Over the years, I went on to take classes with Martha Graham, Merce Cunningham, and Alvin Ailey.

A Revolution

Although ballet was my first love, I am not associated with ballet because people identify me as the *black* male dancer from the London Contemporary Dance Theatre. There is an implied logic that a black dancer would be doing contemporary dance rather than ballet, but as a young artist in the dance scene in the UK in the 1960s, the barefoot dancing of American contemporary dance was as foreign to me as the next person. Inspired by Graham and Ailey, I still had to find my way through to physically understanding the movement. It is hard to imagine British dance without the range of techniques that are available for artists to explore today. With so many approaches to practice, we assume that different dance styles are inherent to particular cultural groups of people but back when I started dancing we were all contributing to a new idea for the UK's dance scene: the idea of contemporary dance. I am not suggesting that UK dancers were not already engaging in contemporary dance but Graham, Cunningham, and Ailey brought a force of energy that demanded an authentic artistic response from us.

Our response was influenced by the place we were in, London. London was full of Welsh, Canadian, American, English, Caribbean, Irish, Indian, and African peoples. The Commonwealth reached back to London. It was inspiring in terms of culture. Place cannot be separated from body and where we were dancing had its own unique vibe and affected how we moved. Robert Cohan talks about this in terms of *style*. For instance, Cohan jokes that the British execution of a contraction (a Graham-based movement) is a very soft way and in New York you do a contraction in a very aggressive way: 'soft' meaning that the English are politer! All movement is reinterpreted at some level.

The changes to dance in the 1960s are documented in books, which gives them a neatness, even an ordered quality but at the time we were all contributing to something that we were creating together. The movement emerging in the UK in the 1960s that formed the foundations for contemporary dance for many years to come was subject to the multitude of voices that welcomed this style of dance from America to Britain. It arrived in the UK to a multi-cultural revolution in music, and across the arts. When we started to explore and create contemporary dance in the early days, we had lots of different influences. As dancers practising in the context of the Commonwealth of which London was still a centre, we re-imagined, re-shaped and made these new ideas our own together.

Leg Work

I felt that the London Contemporary Dance Theatre was an exciting development in contemporary dance in the UK and I felt very lucky to be living in London at the time it was emerging. When the London Contemporary Dance School and the London Contemporary Dance Theatre were formed, we brought *ourselves* including our individual cultural backgrounds to *The Company*, to The Place. It was very stimulating to have that mix. People brought new and different experiences to each other. As artists, when you work together you share and exchange who you are and part of that is your cultural background. For instance, sometimes I used to cook fry fish and bring it in for other company members. We would go to each other's houses and share each other's food heritages. We were working together, making something together—you cannot extract one person's influence from the overall culture of dance in London. There is no way to say where the 'black' is, where the 'white' is or where the 'Irish' is, where the 'Jamaican' is. We were influencing each other and in turn influencing the dance that was emerging.

We did a lot of leg work developing audiences for contemporary dance. We toured, performing in out of the way places. Sometimes there were no wooden floors, just concrete. Sometimes there were just three or four people in the audience. So we pioneered the making of contemporary dance accessible, where people were only familiar with ballet, introducing barefoot dances to them. However, I never left ballet behind, it is still a part of how I see myself as a dancer and how I understand my training and teaching. When *The Company* came back from being out on the road touring, we used to go in to do a class with the students at the London Contemporary Dance School. I used to go to Brenda Last's classes. I took her basic first-year ballet classes because I wanted to realign my body after the heavy work of touring. When I came back from tour, my body felt out of line and twisted, and I would do those ballet classes as my *own*. We found that a lot of *The Company* dancers used to go and do ballet classes and eventually the company had to bring in a ballet teacher. So when we were not on the road, we moved to alternating company class between ballet and contemporary.

In 1973, I was offered a job by Australian Dance Theatre. I knew a number of other dancers who were taking up job offers outside the UK in America. However, I had negotiated a good wage working as a dancer with Robin Howard at the London Contemporary Dance Theatre and I realised that a revolution was still happening in British dance. I also worried that if I went to Australia, I would not know how to defend my blackness. I was aware of the destructive history of the politics of Aboriginal blackness. I did not know how I would run into politics over there, so I stayed in UK. In London, I was in the *politics* of dance in general. My identity as a black man within the context of my London home was something I was more used to dealing with. My presence in the London Contemporary Dance Theatre made it 'mixed–race' and this did have an impact. For instance, we never went to South Africa because of their apartheid policy at the time. I was the only black dancer in the company. Robin said, 'If you cannot stay in the same hotel with the rest of the company, what's the point of going to South Africa?' So, we never went to South Africa during apartheid.

A Black British Dancer

We were breaking new ground in Europe taking dance to places and people who had not experienced anything but ballet and sharing dance in contexts it had not been shared before. London was a multi-cultural centre but outside London, on tour, not only had audiences not witnessed contemporary dance before, but they may have never seen a black man dance before either. As an accomplished dancer, I became a representative for Blackness. This has happened to many artists and as their careers develop the notion of Blackness starts to represent them also. Somewhere the detail of the artistry itself can be lost in the shadow of the duty of representation. This is an interesting relationship of projected identity to be caught up in. But I have always said I do not do 'Black-dance', I am a black dancer. I do not feel that 'Black' is a dance form. Even 'African Dance' is too broad; Africa is a big continent and there are lots of kinds of dance and lots of periods in history and lots of contemporary interpretations that could all fall under the term 'African'.

I feel that dance reflects the places it is done; it is influenced by the bodies, society, and environment of where it happens. There are some dance forms that document and archive dance from a particular time. There are some dance forms that are based in movement generated from a particular place. These styles of dance can come from across the African Diaspora such as Congolese dances, Afro/Caribbean styles, even hip-hop, locking, house. These might be dances you see dancers who are also black doing but you could not see them as one thing—Black-dance. Throughout my career, I have watched many performers of 'dance' originating from or taking inspiration from across the African Diaspora. One notable group was Adzido, whom I would later work for, teaching classes. But as I discussed above, every time dance is performed it is affected by its environment and the bodies of the people who are doing it. As a dancer you respond to choreography, what the choreographer wants and who you are as an artist—it is dance and dance is much richer and much wider than black or white. As a performer, I am a black dancer who draws on the ballet and contemporary styles I was trained in.

In terms of my identity as a Black British dancer, many of the dance forms now associated with 'Black-dance' do not have resonance with me. The Commonwealth, London, at the time I started dancing, and the arts revolution of the 1960s all shaped my movement and as such I am a Black British dancer. For me, those forms often called 'Black' today, such as hip-hop or street dance I see as American. Just as we were inspired by American dance 70 years ago, new dance artists are inspired today. There is a danger that rather than an individual response that includes where you live and what you experience, artists around the world are locked into attempting to copy the Americans as if these dance forms were representative of Blackness in general. Of course there are some similarities in terms of youth culture. However, I feel that UK artists today who are doing interesting work are the ones who have said '*we don't live in America, we don't live in Africa*'. 'We don't go through what the Americans or Africans go through in terms of where they live'. These artists have resisted buying into blanket statements of 'black cultural identity'. When you look at work in terms of the artists' own expression, you find fascinating art.

I have always maintained that I don't do '*Black-dance*' and that I am a black dancer doing contemporary and ballet and, in doing so, a lot of people look to me as a role model. Interestingly, many of the dancers who create what has been referred to as 'Black-dance' have said that they were influenced by me when they were starting as young dancers. Artist Jonzi D told me that he remembers we went to his school when he was 12 or 13. I recently went to the 30th anniversary of Phoenix Dance Company in Leeds. Founding member of the company Merville Jones came over to me and said 'Namron, did you realise I saw you dancing when I was 10 years old? It was you that made me want to dance'. In 1984, I was asked by Nadine Senior to be rehearsal director for Phoenix for their first six months, helping out and being a mentor as the first black man in the London Contemporary Dance Theatre. We had taken Phoenix on a schools' tour then too.

Wherever you go, you are involved in the lives of those around you and you influence those that come after you. It is an accumulated history of personal interaction and innovation. For my artistic practice, I am exploring dance rather than exploring being black. When I think of the pieces that we have done over the years with the London Contemporary Dance Theatre, I was most interested in dance, in performing dance. I was a black dancer working in a dance company, a British dance company. I had a difficult time because as the only black man on stage I could not afford to put a foot wrong. I would stick out like a sore thumb and my role as first black male dancer in the company left me with expectations I had to meet. It made it twice as hard for me to perform and work but that did not bother me too much. It was a challenge and in meeting that challenge I have contributed to the dance landscape.

So what could be called '*Black-dance*'? I feel that Black dance is about how other people identify you. Black-dance would basically be a group of people, whom others identify as Black, creating dance about themselves. For instance, in the early days of Phoenix Dance Company, they were creating work about themselves and they were all black men and so people called what they were doing '*Black-dance*' but this could also be called 'Leeds dance' or '1980s dance'. They were inspired to make work about where they lived, where they went to school, and subjects such as the music around them. There were one or two things that they did that were not related to that because they wanted to explore other subject matters. So, when does it become no longer Black-dance?

When we label dance as Black-dance as if it were a universal technique, we lose the nuances of inspiration, the influences, and spirit of the people dancing. This leads to not realising the universal artistic quest to express something of '*what it is to be human*'; as well as not recognising the value of the small individual revelations that dancers of many colours have contributed in general to British dance today. The body borrows and takes from many art forms, experiences, and histories. The hip-hop dancers take classes in ballet and take something from it in order to enhance what they are doing. All dancers can explore where they come from and what their connection with African-ness is. The exploration of world cultures and the exploration of personal cultures are responses that mix and create new physical understandings—new works in the dancers themselves. So maybe Black-dance is more about an identity as White-dance would also be about identity and *dance* is about the movement itself. In my own artistic exploration of dance, I have influenced many people because they saw me in terms of being a dancer. People say to me 'I don't do Black-dance either, I do contemporary' and I say 'well, no problem'.

Respect your elders, respect yourself, it is your body contributing to the dance of *here* and *now*, the dance of then, and the imagination of what dance can become.

Reference

Graham, M. (1991). *Blood Memory* (1st ed.). New York: Doubleday.

CHAPTER 3

Dance Britannia: The Impact of Global Shifts on Dance in Britain

Christy Adair and Ramsay Burt

The British Dance and the African Diaspora research project aimed to write Black British dance artists and their legacies back into history. It was not the first initiative that tried to do so. We wanted to consider what made it so difficult to acknowledge the contributions to British dance history that have been made by British-based dancers who are black and why they have not received the recognition they deserve. It tried to understand the nexus of aesthetic, institutional, and conceptual problems that have rendered these dancers invisible, and, in some cases, excluded them from most accounts of British dance history. A key factor, we believe, is the inadequacy of existing frameworks to provide a suitable basis for analysis. The term '*Black Dance*' suggests a singular style or genre of dance or

This article was first published in the Summer 2013 edition of Animated, the magazine of People Dancing. See www.communitydance.org.uk/animated for information.

An earlier version of this paper has been published in the CORD Conference Proceedings Vol. 2014, Fall 2014, pp. 1–13 published online by Cambridge University Press, 23 September 2014.

C. Adair (✉)
Leeds Beckett University, Leeds, UK

R. Burt
De Montfort University, Leicester, UK

movement that is separate from, for example, ballet or contemporary dance; by doing so, it makes it difficult to recognise the broad range of different approaches developed by British-based dancers who are black. We, therefore, held a series of events mapping histories and memories of dance in different parts of the country and connected younger dancers with dancers from older generations to reveal the continuities while at the same time acknowledging that the sector is dynamic and changes over time. We held three roadshows in Leeds, Liverpool, and Birmingham that were one-day events that each included an open professional class and public panel discussion. An exhibition at the International Slavery Museum in Liverpool, *British dance: Black routes*, drew on our findings.

In the Arts Council of England's Report, *Time for Change*, the authors noted that

> *there is not yet a body of work that can be labelled 'Black Dance'. However, it is evident that a new vocabulary is being born out of the Black British experience, which might well dominate the choreography of Black British artists in the future.* (McIntosh, 2000, p. 5)

Note here that the report hopes for 'a' new vocabulary, as if the broad diversity of vocabularies and approaches that are proliferating are a problem, rather than a strength. Since the 1970s, a number of British-based dancers who are black have been teaching and producing performance work in a variety of dance styles. Some drew on music and dance traditions from Ghana, Nigeria, Senegal, and other former African colonies and from the Caribbean. Others worked within the genres of ballet, jazz and contemporary dance from the US. Thus, for example, Peter Badejo, Felix Cobson, and George Dzikunu, among others, taught and initiated new forms of 'African dance' during the 1970s and 1980s leading to a vibrant artistic revival in Britain. Companies such as Adzido, Delado, Ekome, Kokuma, and Lanzel drew upon traditional African rhythms and patterns; others like Greta Mendez of MAAS Movers and Beverley Glean of Irie! drew upon Caribbean dance styles while artists such as Sheron Wray, Corrine Bougard and members of Phoenix and RJC Dance Companies explored styles of jazz and contemporary dance. Still others such as Jonzi D and Robert Hylton have, from the 1990s onwards, used hip-hop dance forms and techniques to create hybrid performance forms. In a field dominated by men, there are a number of female dancers and choreographers, some of whom are also artistic directors, whose contributions we celebrate including Corrine Bougard, Sharon Watson, Brenda Edwards, Beverley

Glean, Cathy Lewis, Bunty Matthais, Greta Mendez, Gail Parmell, Judith Palmer, Hopal Romans, Carol Straker, and Sheron Wray.

In attempting to map out new approaches in this research, we avoided the problematic term 'Black Dance' and instead talked about 'dancers who are black and/or dance and the African Diaspora'. In the latter term we indicated current dance practices and legacies from Africa and the Caribbean which have made an impact on the British dance landscape. Adair has argued in *Dancing the Black Question* that the dancers in Phoenix Dance Company were expected by the funding bodies, critics, and audiences to represent 'the black community'. They carried what Isaac Julien and Kobena Mercer identified as 'the burden of representation'. Their seminal paper, 'De Margin and De Centre' (Julien & Mercer, 1988), noted that political struggles and unrest in the 1980s led to the formulation of arts funding policies in the UK that encouraged multiculturalism. Black and Asian dancers were funded because of the social good it was believed they could do. This resulted in the expectation that their work would be representative of their ethnicities. It was as if they were expected to speak for their communities as a whole. This was not of course something that white artists were expected to do.

In our first Roadshow in Leeds, Namron taught a contemporary dance class in which he remembered the sorts of classes he used to teach to members of Phoenix Dance Company and other young dancers in Leeds during the 1980s. His publicity states that he 'was the first Black British contemporary dancer to be employed by a British company'. It is clear from this that he recognises the representative aspect of his position. He is an important role model for dancers who are black and his teaching and performing have had an impact on numerous dancers' careers. Francis Angol acknowledged during the second roadshow in Liverpool that African People's Dance was at the heart of everything he did although he considers his work to be contemporary. Gail and Ian Parmel, in their class during the Birmingham roadshow, worked with a fusion of the African Diasporic movement and rhythmic forms to explore Western contemporary dance material. All the dancers and choreographers who have been participating in the research project are working from the specificity of their own trainings and backgrounds. They do not create choreography to represent the black community. They make work in relation to their own concerns, some of which may speak directly to specific black communities in Britain or may not. They work from, but not for, black experiences in Britain.

If one looks at some of the often inadequate reviews that have been written over the years about performances by British-based dancers who are black, it often seems as if the critic is looking for the kinds of clear, clean, slightly understated aesthetic qualities valued in the work of many white British choreographers; or the reviewer assumes that the choreographer or company is trying to create a 'Black' work using 'traditional' African or Caribbean forms, and therefore misses the extent to which they may be working with structures or approaches from contemporary dance, reinterpreting these in ways that are informed by black culture. There is now a body of critical dance theory developed largely in the US – by Professors Brenda Dixon Gottschild, Kariamu Welsh-Asante, Thomas F. DeFrantz, Yvonne Daniels, Anita Gonzalez, Robert Farris Thompson, and others—that identifies African or Africanist aesthetic qualities. We believe that these can usefully be applied to the choreography and performance of black artists in Britain who are working in a broad range of different approaches. The two main areas in which discussions about Africanist movement qualities have developed are rhythm and spirituality.

Many scholars have investigated the way that rhythm is central to dance and music forms that have spread across the world from African roots. Barbara Browning, writing about the difficulties that white (and some black) dance students can have when learning the complicated polyrhythms of Samba, notes that sometimes teachers tell people to stop thinking and dance. However, she adds, it 'isn't to say that the body is incapable of understanding more things at once than can be articulated in language. One has no choice but to think with the body' (Browning, 1995, p. 13). Robert Farris Thompson, from his research in Ghana and Nigeria, has discussed the differences between European classical music and the complex polyrhythms of dance and drumming traditions. In West Africa, drummers do not play in unison but the master drummer generally '*creates pleasing clashes with the rhythmic structure of his helpers. He departs from their text, as it were, and improvises illuminations*' (Thompson, 1984, p. 105). Thompson calls this 'playing apart', and points out that dancers also 'play apart' from the rhythms. He contrasts this with the European classical music tradition where dancers and musicians follow the same rhythms although dance and music are seen as separate forms, while in Africa dancers 'play apart' but don't recognise any separation between dance and music.

Brenda Dixon Gottschild, following Thompson (1980), discusses the aesthetic of the cool where the dancer may be working fast, hard, and hot, but their face seems to remain cool. This rhythm and energy, she argues, gives African American dancers soul:

> *For African American performers, soul is the nitty-gritty personification of the energy and force that it takes to be black and survive. Rhythm, and the many textures and meanings implied in the concept (percussive drive, pulse, breath, and heart beat, for example) plays a pivotal role in generating and disseminating soul power.* (Gottschild, 2003, p. 223)

This is surely also something British-based Black dancers also know and use. During a public discussion of early rehearsal and performance footage from Phoenix's archives, at the Leeds Roadshow, Dr. Jean Johnson Jones noted that the young founders seemed to have a confidence that young black men in Britain aren't supposed to have. Where did that come from? she asked. Edward Lynch responded that for him it was the energy he got from dancing. For Dixon Gottschild, this is what soul power does. It is, she says, having something intangible that is an invaluable asset, when one has almost nothing of value that is tangible. For some dancers, soul is a spiritual quality. Merville Jones, a founder of Phoenix Dance Company, identified the work of the early Company saying, 'it comes from the heart, it has spirituality behind it'. H. Patten spoke at a study day at De Montfort University about the centrality of spirituality in his work and about the connections he is researching between dancehall moves and those performed in Jamaican church services.

To draw together our argument, what we are proposing is that a way to get beyond the problems created by the term 'Black Dance' is to shift the focus from styles, forms, and vocabularies towards the analysis of aesthetic qualities. Drawing on work by a number of dance scholars, we have outlined a broad range of qualities which, following Dixon Gottschild, we are calling Africanist. We are not necessarily claiming that polyrhythms are always present in the work of British-based dancers who are black, or that the dancers are all cool, or have soul, or are religious. What we are nevertheless arguing is that dance and music traditions which exemplify these qualities have spread around the world as a result of the African Diaspora. They persist because, faced with the dehumanising effects of racism, they offer powerful means for expressing a positive sense of what it is to be human. They can be found in British works that span the broad range of different approaches outlined earlier.

When we first invited Namron to teach an open class for the roadshow in Leeds, he was very insistent that there should be a live accompanist. We were fortunate that Dougie Thorpe, a former member of Phoenix, was able to play for Namron. At the start of the masterclass, Edward Lynch spontaneously joined Dougie and together they beat out a driving polyrhythmic accompaniment. In the open discussion later, people commented on the way that some of the dancers responded more openly to the energy of the drums than others. Someone noted that Namron never counted beats but talked the rhythm instead as *boom tiki tiki*. Namron said, a good musician is half of the class. Francis Angol, teaching his class in Liverpool, also vocalised rhythms as *shoom pah pah*. Not counting but talking the rhythm was a way of encouraging the class to think with their bodies, as Barbara Browning puts it. This is an Africanist quality, and the dancing that expresses this has soul and spirit. This is surely a much more useful topic for research than the question, 'What is "Black Dance"?'

References

Browning, B. (1995). *Samba: Resistance in Motion.* Bloomington: Indiana University Press.

Gottschild, B. D. (2003). *The Black Dancing Body: A Geography From Coon to Cool.* New York/Basingstoke: Palgrave Macmillan.

Julien, I., & Mercer, K. (1988). De margin and de centre. *Screen, 29*(4, Autumn), 2–10.

McIntosh, H. (2000). *Time for Change: A Framework for the Development of Africans People's Dance Forms.* London: Arts Council of England.

Thompson, R. F. (1980). An Aesthetic of the Cool: West African Dance. In E. Hill (Ed.), *The Theatre of Black Americans* (pp. 99–111). Englewood Cliffs, NJ: Prentice-Hall.

Thompson, R. F. (1984). *Flash of the Spirit: African and Afro-American Art and Philosophy* (1st ed.). New York: Vintage Book.

CHAPTER 4

Negotiating African Diasporic Identity in Dance: Brown Bodies Creating and Existing in the British Dance Industry

Tia-Monique Uzor

In this chapter I present a series of conversations that explore themes around African Diasporic identity. It specifically focuses on the negotiation of the complexity of identity, and how this can be problematic to artists of African Diasporic heritage working and creating in the British dance industry. The participating artists are Vicki Igbokwe, Alesandra Seutin, Freddie Opoku-Addaie, Jamila Johnson-Small and Alexandrina Hemsley. Vicki Igbokwe founded Uchenna Dance after she experienced a life-changing trip to New York City in 2009. Her aesthetic draws from a range of urban and contemporary dance forms. Alesandra Seutin founded Vocab Dance Company in 2007, with the vision of fusing African traditional dance, contemporary and urban dance forms (*Vocab Dance*, 2015). Freddie Opoku-Addaie is a London-based independent dance artist and educator who has been creating since 2003. He is interested in structured rules and games. Project O was founded in 2011 by Jamila Johnson-Small and Alexandrina Hemsley. It is a collaboration that seeks to 'talk about [and]

T.-M. Uzor (✉)
De Montfort University, Leicester, UK

© The Author(s) 2018
A. Akinleye (ed.), *Narratives in Black British Dance*,
https://doi.org/10.1007/978-3-319-70314-5_4

make visible, the awkward stuff of everyday oppression' (*A Contemporary Struggle*, 2015). These artists were chosen as they represent a range of artists of African Diasporic heritage, utilising a variety of African Diasporic forms and addressing a variety of African Diasporic issues within their work in the UK.

African Diasporic identity is complex in its nature, and a defined cultural African Diasporic identity is difficult to attain as it involves a displaced people from a *home*, described by Stuart Hall (1990) as the 'original' Africa that no longer exists. It also involves the cultural experiences those people accumulate along their journey to the West and beyond. As a consequence, a displaced African living in the West often has a plurality of identities existing in one African Diasporic body, which varies depending on their circumstance. In this sense African Diasporic identity is truly demonstrative of the multiplicity of identity, and in the case of British and European African Diasporic identities this is no exception. Both European and African cultures play a part in the creation an African Diasporic identity; this is further complicated by the societal hierarchies that African Diasporic people have been placed into within Western society. The complexities and contradictions of these cultures make it difficult to define what it means to be Black within the African Diaspora and can often cause tensions within African Diasporic individuals. Having this heritage can both be a hindrance and a blessing to those that carry it. Being a part of a society while having a sense of being *Othered* can lead to traumatic experiences. Contrary to this, it can offer unique insights into the society that those of African Diasporic heritage call their own, insights that are not available to the majority of the society (*See* James, 1984). The fluid nature of identity means that it is often hard to tangibly hold and articulate it in a way that can resonate beyond language. Dance artists have the ability, and opportunity, to communicate the complexities of this identity within their own historical experience through the body, communicating on a level that transcends literary comprehension, and goes to the heart of human interaction.

I will first present self-definitions from each choreographer. It was integral to our conversations that I allowed the choreographer to examine African Diasporic identity within their choreography from a personal starting point. This then allowed for further discussion of choreographic process and aesthetics to be explored in light of these self-definitions. I will then present and analyse two themes that were prominent within these four conversations; these being, firstly, expectations and the burden of representation and, secondly, double consciousness and existing in the in-between spaces. These two themes were not just identified as significant to the discourse of African Diasporic identity but also identified by the artists themselves. There is a substantial body of theoretical work that recognises these themes as being important (e.g. Bhabha, 1994; DeFrantz, 2001; Dubois, 1903; Fanon, 1967; Gilroy, 1993; Hall, 1990; Mercer, 1994; Pasura, 2014).

The definition of an identity is an ongoing development within oneself, and is an important distinction to make in a rhetoric which can be consumed by the facts and the circumstances in which you were born. The question of identity is a familiar question to those living in the African Diaspora, who are often asked to establish who they are in their everyday lives. When the question of defining their identity was put to the choreographers, a plethora of answers revealed the tensions in the expectations that surround such a frequently asked question.

Both Seutin and Igbokwe initially gave answers which pointed to their lineage and historical geographical placement. Alesandra described herself as Afro-pean, a mixture of African and European (her mother being South African and her father white European). Similarly, Vicki described herself as British and Nigerian:

> *Vicki* – It depends on how I am feeling… I will always acknowledge the fact that I am Nigerian, I will always acknowledge the fact that I am Black, I will always acknowledge the fact that I am British, because that's the mix I have in me, actually in terms of heritage and Nigeria… I have been there twice in my whole life… but because of the way I was brought up…. The Nigerian side is there and it's there strong. (Igbokwe, 2015)

They both spoke of the challenges of embodying all of these things at one time, Vicki stating it was complex. When probed on her seeming preference for her African heritage, Alesandra elaborated further:

> *Alesandra* – I'm of mixed heritage, and I feel that both of these identities are very much part of me…but I am very rooted in … African culture and at the same time I am very European… I find that both of these identities are a part of me. (Seutin, 2015)

Freddie also started with historical facts. He was born in East London to Ghanaian, Ashanti parents. With a sense of unease, he explained that identity was still something he was trying to understand:

Freddie – Identity... the way I usually define identity is through other people's eyes, I don't reflect on myself saying, 'Freddie, you are this or you are that'... because there are many other layers to me that will probably take a whole book... the question I usually get asked is, 'oh where are you from' and I go .... 'I'm from London... I'm from England', and they go, 'where are you from' ... and that always reminds me, it's not that simple... so that's when identity becomes an issue... apart from that I don't really question it ... (Opoku-Addaie, 2015)

Seutin, Igbokwe and Opoku-Addaie all use their historic circumstance as a means to define themselves to others. This in itself is indicative of the pluralities that exist within African Diasporic identities, and we can see the beginnings of multiple consciousnesses functioning together within their individual lives. Freddie's response is insightful to the tensions that questions surrounding identity have for those with an African Diasporic heritage. This is echoed further by Jamila Johnson-Small and Alexandrina Hemsley, who cautiously avoid having to pinpoint their identity, wary of the connotations that it may have.

Jamila – I probably wouldn't ... I would really attempt to resist having to describe my identity...it depends on the context and ... what it would do... or how it could provoke that space.

Alexandrina – ... I don't think I have ever tried to describe my identity apart from when I have been asked to ... when I've been asked to do so by... dance programmers or people on the street who want to know where I am from ... it always seems a question that other people ask me, then I try to formulate the language around it, and its succinct and quick so we can get the conversation onto something else ... and I'm also very aware of that question ... I can't imagine that being asked of a White British choreographer, I don't think that question would ever be asked ... so there is also something there of wanting to resist having to answer it ... (Hemsley & Johnson-Small, 2015)

EXPECTATIONS AND BURDEN OF REPRESENTATION

Jamila and Alexandrina make an important point of the underlying terms that this question of identity has when asked, whether socially or professionally. There can be a sense of pre-conceived judgement or expectation that may occur depending on how the question is asked. A problematic element of African Diasporic identities, and indeed all identities in general, is that they are not fixed, as stated above. This is further made complex by the historic narratives of the African Diasporic people, as Hall explains, for those that are *Othered*,

> ....cultural identity is not a fixed essence at all, lying unchanged outside history and culture. It is not some universal transcendental spirit inside us on which history has made no fundamental mark. It is not once-and-for-all. It is not a fixed origin to which we can make some final and absolute Return (Hall, 1990, p. 226)

I believe this is why Freddie was uneasy with the term—he accepts himself as himself within a given moment in time. The questioning of that is not merely a fact-finding exercise, but often a 'measuring' up to the asker's preconceived expectation. Freddie's statement reflects society's perception of the African Diasporic body. The feelings of doubt and uncertainty that are conjured up by its presence lead to the questioning of it. Kobena Mercer (1994) recognises this as a crisis point. This is especially true within the performing arts world, where all the artists expressed feelings indicative of Mercer's concept of the *burden of representation* being projected on them. This is the situation of being positioned as representatives and speaking for the entire African Diasporic community in Britain. As Jamila points out, they are careful as to how an answer could 'provoke the space'. Freddie illustrates this further:

> *Freddie* – So I don't necessarily struggle with my identity… but I think other people like to make an issue which is a challenge in itself … I mean I make the work I want to make … I reckon I would be a bit more successful if I made the work that people think I should make … some people think I'm Ghanaian some people think I am not so Ghanaian, 'oh Freddie is lost in his … quinoa world'. It becomes Post Its…, you're this, you are supposed to do that, you're Black so you are supposed to be doing this or that. (Opoku-Addaie, 2015)

This sense of expectation was echoed by both Vicki and Alesandra:

> *Vicki* – …I felt like before I had to be like a chameleon, you change the way you speak slightly or the way you do things. When I first started the company I called it *urban contemporary* and that was about me trying to validate, and you know make it seem like something, like this high art… You make a piece of work you've got an all-Black cast; the fact that you have an

all-Black cast is an issue. If I happen or chose to work with a team of Black people... why is that anything? We should be judged on the work that we are doing and not the colour of our skin. When I look at my White Caucasian counterparts this happens all the time and there is no question about it. (Igbokwe, 2015)

Alesandra – It is always about identity, but no one questions it because it's White. But when its Black, people always say, 'oh so you are exploring identity'. My identity is there, when I come on stage I am moving, that's my identity, that is me, that's it! Of course it's going to be questioned, but I feel like when I am working with dancers...it's like I was working with six female dancers about the theme of polygamy, through the research they explored their own identity in a way, because they were exploring whether they could become these women who were living in a couple... you know, living with three other co-wives... so somehow they were exploring their position in the world and identity, but it's not like, 'oh now we are exploring identity'. No because my work is quite visceral, and very about the inside out... I always work with a lot of intention, so you are going to definitely explore something about yourself, which is your identity, yourself as an individual, as a human... but I don't necessarily put that name behind it. (Seutin, 2015)

And Jamila and Alexandrina:

Alexandrina – I think you are right there is something about the connotations of being Other... there is such a historical tradition of the way that Black Dance has been written about in terms of...
Jamila – 'oh yeah they are making that piece about identity'... and also I think identity is just like race it belongs to us in a way that it doesn't belong to White people because we are just swimming in a sea of their identity all the time. So its manifest, it's present all the time. We don't need to talk about it anymore.
Alexandrina – We have to somehow define our space...
Jamila – Or our space is marked... we are marking a space that is different to other people...
Alexandrina – And the bracket is identity ...
Jamila – Which is hideous... I don't want identity.
(Hemsley & Johnson-Small, 2015)

These four separate conversations with these artists explicitly demonstrate the challenge of simply being artists of African Diasporic heritage working within the British dance industry. They all identify a discourse of expectation that is projected on them and their work. As Alesandra states, a lot of choreographic work is about identity, yet this is only overtly expected and even encouraged when it is produced by those of African Diasporic heritage. There is even an expectation to present a specific aesthetic in order to be seen as professional. As Vicki voiced, in the beginning of her practice, although she was trained she felt that she had to validate the forms she was interested in working with. There is something deeply harrowing in Freddie's statement about how he feels that if he adhered to these expectations he would be a lot more successful. These expectations conjure up questions on how and at what level minority artists are permitted to exist within the British dance industry. This is perfectly concluded by Alexandrina and Jamila's realisation through their conversation: 'I don't want identity'. The space that a lot of African Diasporic artists occupy is marked by identity, not by an intellectual, holistic degree of identity which embraces and recognises the multiplicity of any one individual who is of African Diasporic heritage, but by the melanin that exists within their skin.

However, these artists exist and produce through the burdens and expectations that are forced upon them, and this condition has driven them to define their practice and the parameters within which they want to create.

> *Vicki* – I realised actually no, I don't need that validation, and the work is contemporary because it is new and of the now. Changing the way I speak about the work, the type of work I am making now, is just actually going this is me… and if I don't start celebrating me then who will? … I just started to get bold … I stepped into my fear … the things that scared me … of being seen to be too Black… or too ethnic, but I am Black! … Once I freed myself of all of the other stuff … is it too this or too that… I was just flying. That change is really allowing me to really start to produce the best work, when I look at the stuff that I did … before 2011 and what I have done since 2013. For me the jump is incredible. And that is largely about just embracing who you are as an individual and how God made you… so in terms of my work now I am just taking bold steps and then just wanting to take as many people along with me. (Igbokwe, 2015)

Alesandra talks of her revelations that allowed her to explore traditional African forms further, and then use that as a tool.

> *Alesandra* – When I came to England [from Belgium] it opened me up to embracing my African heritage even more. And somehow in the way I live now, I really embrace it, I always highlight it … whatever I do it's always

there… My revelations started in 2010 when I first went to Africa and I first started training there for three months. It was with my mentor and now mother of dance [Germaine Acogny] that I realised that when you start from the roots that you have, when you use the vocabulary that is given to you in terms of … culturally. You have so many possibilities for creating new languages… and the word contemporary means new. A lot of people here [in England] refer to contemporary dance as something that is only Western, but once you displace a movement from its roots or heritage, it is already something that is new because it is not in its original form. But then you start playing with it and using different tools … because that's what I do… (Seutin, 2015)

Hemsley and Johnson-Small talk of giving themselves the room to freely create beyond the expectations of others.

Jamila – I think we are really aware that we don't want to fulfil expectations people may have based on a show they may have seen before … there is something about… again avoiding capture… or not being reduced, that is running through the different things that we do, that said us being two brown people dancing…

Alexandrina – With western contemporary dance training

Jamila – hmm… maybe that is an aesthetic… that is setting us apart from… all the White … people (laughter)

Alexandrina – Yeah … I think what Jamila said about avoiding capture is really… it's really important… especially in this … kind of game of dance… where everybody wants to define and kind of separate out … and even treat audiences like… you know that audience is for this … this audience is for that… these are really unhelpful distinctions… I want to say the word eclectic but I don't really mean that word. I mean a mixture of resources, and … giving ourselves permission to move in any which way… using improvisation in a way that anything can happen and if any movement that manifest itself feels a really important… way of increasing the range of … our aesthetic… again so that it's not easily definable. That feels like quite a political act in itself, like dance is super radical for that, because it can't be pinned down. (Hemsley & Johnson-Small, 2015)

This is reiterated by Freddie:

Freddie – To be honest, I think if you have that attitude of I want to make the kind of work I want to make, regardless of people telling you be Black in this work or not, something will filter through that is coming from your heritage. I have been told that my work is not very African, and I've been told that my work is not very Black and I just look at them and go… fair enough… and this is why we are in trouble… and I'm not saying we need more opportunities, I'm saying we need space just to be free and try stuff out. I find it hard because I know the form is always evolving … I've not avoided it [African Dance forms]… I've just done what work I've wanted to do… I've not explicitly danced with any African dance companies, not because I wasn't interested, because actually there is a major African dance teacher, and I go there whenever I want to get grounded again … It's how you want to use it, because to be honest I use it as a tool, I don't see it as I'm going to put that on stage. If anyone goes, this is Freddie's work because he is Black and that's what Black people do, I start to get worried because I think … you really do not understand what the work is. (Opoku-Addaie, 2015)

All of the artists have communicated a sense of embracing, or giving themselves the permission to step away from/use their embodied movement vocabularies in order to communicate and create in a way that fulfils their artistic intentions. This noticeably is not a given when it comes to artists of African Diasporic heritage creating within the British dance industry. There is a sense of allowing yourselves to function in realms that were not made for you to function in, and this can also be a psychological boundary that needs to be overcome.

Consciousness and Existing in-Between

African Diasporic people living in the West tend to exist in the in-between spaces. In the case of British African Diasporic individuals, they are not entirely British, although they live, function and relate to some aspects of British society. However, they are not African—both Freddie and Alesandra spoke of not being seen to be African to Africans, and not being seen to be European to Europeans. This is summed up perfectly by Homi Bhabha who says:

> *'you are continually positioned in the space between a range of contradictory places that coexist …'*. (Bhabha, 1994, p. 48)

This is the space in which African Diasporic people negotiate identity and this often leads to a multitude of consciousnesses. Hall signifies that diasporic identities by their nature are constantly producing and reproducing themselves anew, through transformation and difference (Hall, 1990, p. 235). This experience creates a wealth of resources from which these artists are able to draw from and utilise in order to produce exciting and unique work.

Freddie – One thing I am interested in are games and parameters. I mean… the reason I talk about Desert Island Discs [a BBC radio show] is that any person… of note… can fit into that structure, it's not just a White person or Black person… regardless, they can come in and select eight songs and pick their favourite song, and they are still going to be left on an island. And what I try to do in my choreographic work is try to find rules and parameters that give space for the individual to come through, and hopefully through that you will see the quirks. So you give them the space, the parameters, that lets them be free, and we … choreographically try and structure that and find a way to do that. Sometimes I might bring other tools in, which might be traditional Ghanaian *Adowa*… or Western forms that I have trained in… there is all that information… so it's to coax, kind of push the direction where I think it should go, but is mainly led by the individual … I really do like playing games … using rules and structure, because I think rules really shape how identities behave… [For example] *Set in Stone* (2008). It was a stone game and the beginning one guy would sit in the middle throwing a stone and behind him, there was one side and another side lined up facing him and if he caught the stone he would do one nice phrase, if he didn't catch the stone he would do… like a crazy work out plan like… Mr Motivator! So that breaks down the barrier[s] of you are this, you are that. It's about who caught it, who didn't catch it … So that's what I really try and negotiate within my work. It's not so explicit but it is in the process and the live work. (Opoku-Addaie, 2015)

Freddie's negotiation creates an environment where the individual can truly be treated as an individual on an equal playing ground, away from some of the discriminations that may be projected onto him as a choreographer. He has a Cunningham-esque approach to his work, that allows for even his own discriminations to be somewhat abandoned from the creative process. The awareness Freddie has of the multiplicity of his identity is creatively manifest during his choreographic process. He draws on his Ghanaian heritage and the African and Contemporary dance forms in which his body is fluent. As noted earlier, he has been told that his work is not representative of an African or of Blackness. Freddie's work, however, challenges this opinion, by existing in the in-between space and breaking down the barriers within movement. Both the process and the creative output is a bold statement to the ubiquitous nature of movement and dance. He clarifies:

Freddie – Form is more than shape, it is the gathering of things, and the [African] Diaspora, that's what we do, we gather… the navigating bit is the hardest part of it, it is the gathering of things... I realise that's connected to Kathak, and Bharatanatyam, Popping, Locking, Fresno... it's just finding a way to tell people, it's the same parameters...regardless of where we are coming from there is space to see the individual, the group and the outsider, without really going you are this, you are that, all those things can exist in one place. I can be a part of a group but I can still be an outsider, I can be an individual but I can also be a part of a group, that kind of navigating is something I find interesting. And the toughest thing is how to compose that, and I'm still trying to get towards that... (Opoku-addaie, 2015)

Project O is a very thought provoking, creative presentation created by the collaboration of Jamila and Alexandrina. Jamila and Alexandrina utilise their historic experiences and many other references in order to make some of the factions of an African Diasporic identity visible that may not be visible to the wider society. This forces the audience to address the African Diasporic experience in a way that they may have been ignorant of before. In addition to this, their work connects those that are *Othered* in society through performance.

Jamila – ...to go back to what you were saying about any movement can happen, yes any movement can happen, but any movement that is in our palate, that's in our bodies, that's in our education, that's been in our cultural social upbringing and experiences. So there is potential for many and that's also very much limited by our experiences of being people in a specific place at a specific time, in a specific context. But I think in a way, that the work speaks about identity. Rather than discussing it, it presents it ... and we try to present the multiplicities of our identities ... on stage through the moving, as well as through the choreographic framing and other considerations and details that fit into the work. It's this thing of acknowledging that we have many points of reference. Some show, some don't show. Some are shown to the audience, some are not shown to the audience. It changes in different spaces. Multiple reference points is something we try to throw in... and then mix it all up and then speak about identity in this way of blurgh here you go ... what do you make of that!

Alexandrina – Autobiographical references ... and a reference in a different way of wanting to invite the audience in, so a slow dance... wanting to be up close to them. To dissolve the separation.

Jamila – I think maybe we are making a world, that is crafted out of our experience ...presenting ... sometimes abstracted, sometimes more presentational, and direct ways... just making a world out of our experiences and references and shaping that.

Alexandrina – In ways my choreographic practice is so ...hopeful, things *can* work together, things *can* go alongside, things *can* be made visible, voices *can* be heard. People *can* have experiences, that maybe haven't happened yet, that aren't known... and also that by the end of my performance I will be in a place that I wouldn't have known about. (Hemsley & Johnson-Small, 2015)

Alexandrina talks of the audience response to their work:

Alexandrina – Someone once described a little thing we did in a café as really into her gut. And that made me really excited because that was her feeling, but it was a really sensation based experience of the work, and for me that made it feel very present... It was more like my gut feeling told me I was experiencing something. And that for me, that's the space *I* want to be in as an audience member. (Hemsley & Johnson-Small, 2015)

Alesandra also uses the sensation of feeling rooted within her dance vocabulary, as presented earlier when she spoke of working from the inside out. Being rooted within enables her to break down her training in African Dance forms and really explore the movement.

Alesandra... Let's say I may use one dance from South Africa... so I have the Zulu dance in its... own kind of pure form and then I will use different tools on the dancers, I will teach them the traditional form or if I am working on myself I will use the movement. Then I will start exploring different ways of using them, different rhythms... not the original spacing or placing in the space. I might start doing it on the floor, I might start doing it in reverse, I might start playing with the language of it... Then add different sound... the intention behind it will then completely transform what you started with. But what will be interesting is that you have started from a movement that was completely African but ... the more you play with it, the more distance you create from where it started. But at the same time when people look at it they might say oh this is a contemporary movement, but you say no it's not a contemporary Western movement, it's a movement that came from an African movement... it starts from a movement that is rooted in African dance or a movement from the diaspora. That's how I begin my movement. I think that if you are so strong in your ... roots and in your vocabulary it becomes the movement. It ... no longer refers to only one... class, or one culture. ... I think that will be the only way for us as Black, Mixed, whatever artists to be welcomed in this industry and rise above, is to be so strong and rooted in our vocabulary that it becomes part of us, that it becomes a language rather than always ... being referenced to a country, or to just Blackness, because the problem is, in this... Western world in which we are a minority, if you always place yourself as this minority and don't enter that world, I feel like the work won't transcend ... It will always stay separate... (Seutin, 2015)

Alesandra's work has begun to transcend the realms of the 'Black Dance' industry. Her solo *Ceci n'est pas Noire (2013)* has been identified by some as only contemporary art with no reference to her Blackness.

Alesandra... I showed a section of my solo they called it contemporary art and they didn't question identity. Which I loved, because I thought yes! And it's not the first time, because somewhere else in France they said that for them it was almost like contemporary art ... so I felt that it's quite interesting to have that as well... That to certain people they are not even referring to a race...And I like that... (Seutin, 2015)

For Vicki, negotiating the in-between space means allowing herself to relax and exist as the artist she wants to be. Shaking off these boundaries has transformed the way she works and her creative output,

Vicki – My first piece once I reinvented myself, the true me which was Our Mighty Groove created in 2013. One of the things I learnt ... in this transition and who I am ... outside of culturally, was leadership ... realising that I don't need to have all the answers... in the early days I was definitely feeling like I had to prove myself ... I had to have it all... I needed to have all this information. That is something that has definitely changed in terms of my choreographic process... I am more relaxed in who I am as a woman, as an artist. So I can go into [a dance] space with an idea, with a few moves and collaboratively work with performers and our rehearsal director to make these ideas a reality. It's weird because it's like a double talk. I think less but I am still conscious about the choices in terms of my styles ... House, Waacking, Vogue, African Dance[s] and Contemporary, those are the five that get me up in the morning, that really excites me ... in terms of the choreographic process ... just feeling really bold... and attacking the work in a way that I really want to. I feel like having these styles along with the way that I am now collaborating... with people has opened up new doors ... and the way that I use all this knowledge that I have acquired over the years. There is much more creativity in my work ... now I am really interested in telling stories. (Igbokwe, 2015)

For these artists, their African Diasporic heritage has allowed them to explore their choreographic concerns, and forced them to articulate their work in ways that maybe some of their Caucasian counterparts working within the British dance industry do not have to do. Embodying and being confident in their practice and their artistry results in a unique contribution to the contemporary dance world. Although African Diasporic identity comes with baggage, the four artists in this chapter demonstrate that dance is a non-verbal language where these complexities can be negotiated, presented, challenged, re-invented and made visible to the wider society.

References

A Contemporary Struggle. (2015). *About* [Online]. Available From: http://www.acontemporarystruggle.com/#!about/c1qdj. Accessed 04 Dec 15.

Bhabha, H. K. (1994). *The Location of Culture*. London: Routledge.

DeFrantz, T. F. (2001). Black Bodies Dancing Black Culture: Black Atlantic Transformations. In I. D. Fischer-Hornung & A. D. Goeller (Eds.), *Embodying Liberation: The Black body in American Dance* (pp. 11–16). Hamburg, LIT/Piscataway, NJ: Distributed in North America by Transaction Publishers.

Du Bois, W. E. B. (1903). *The Souls of Black Folk*. New York/London: Dover/Constable, 1994.

Fanon, F. (1967). *The Wretched of the Earth*. Harmondsworth: Penguin.

Gilroy, P. (1993). *The Black Atlantic: Modernity and Double Consciousness*. London: Verso.

Hall, S. (1990). Cultural Identity and Diaspora. In J. Rutherford (Ed.), *Identity: Community, Culture, Difference* (pp. 222–237). London: Lawrence & Wishart.

Hemsley, A., & Johnson-Small, J. (2015 October 8). *Interviewer: T.-M. Uzor*.

Igbokwe, V. (2015 September 8). *Interviewer: T.-M. Uzor*.

James, C. L. R. (1984). *Africans and Afro-Caribbean's: A Personal View*. Ten, 8(14), 55.

Mercer, K. (1994). *Welcome to the Jungle: New Positions in Black Cultural Studies*. New York: Routledge.

Opoku-Addaie, F. (2015 September 29). *Interviewer: T.-M. Uzor*.

Pasura, D. (2014). *African Transnational Diasporas: Fractured Communities and Plural Identities of Zimbabweans in Britain*. New York: Palgrave Macmillan.

Seutin, A. (2015 September 19). *Interviewer: T.-M. Uzor*.

Vocab Dance. (2015). *About Us* [Online]. Available From: http://vocabdance.co.uk/about/. Accessed 04 Dec 15.

CHAPTER 5

Tracing the Evolution of Black Representation in Ballet and the Impact on Black British Dancers Today

Sandie Bourne

INTRODUCTION

The focus of this chapter is to present an overview of the early Eurocentric representation of black people from the African diaspora in ballet. I then explore how these representations continue to negatively impact the career prospects of black British ballet dancers today. By following these dancers' progression towards acceptance and integration into British ballet institutions (from the 1970s onwards), it is possible to examine the extent to which the negative stereotypes associated with black African people have limited their inclusion in British ballet. It also highlights the role that key individuals have played in promoting the inclusion of black dancers and black dance forms in classical ballet. Finally, this chapter relays some of the experiences of contemporary black ballet dancers in British institutions in order to demonstrate how much progress remains to be made.

S. Bourne (✉)
University of Roehampton, London, UK

© The Author(s) 2018
A. Akinleye (ed.), *Narratives in Black British Dance*,
https://doi.org/10.1007/978-3-319-70314-5_5

Representation of Black People in Narrative Ballet

Since the sixteenth century, people from the African diaspora were mainly characterised in dance and theatre as Moors/Blackamoors. The word 'Blackamoor' (Black and Moor) means 'black African or a very dark-skinned person' (Stevenson, 2010, p. 173). The term originated and coincided with the European 'age of discovery' when the Portuguese began trading in Africa and Asia (Arnold, 2002, p. 3). Shakespearean scholar Anthony Gerard Barthelemy notes that:

> ...*much of this collective European experience with blacks and blackness is synopsized in the history of the word Moor [...] Moor became synonymous with black African.* (Barthelemy, 1987, p. 1)

The origins of ballet derived from the Italian renaissance courts of the fifteenth and sixteenth centuries. There are historical representations of Moors in theatre, ballets and plays, such as William Shakespeare's *Othello* (1604) (Thompson, 2001, p. 115; Bhattacharyya, 2007, p. 76). In theatrical productions, the parts of people from the African diaspora were often performed by white artists 'blacking up'. For example, the French King Louis XIV, the founder of the Académie Royale de Danse in 1661, performed as a variety of characters including slaves and Moors (Cowart, 2008, p. 33). Historian Georgia Cowart describes this:

> ...*the role of a Moor, a race associated in the seventeenth century with sexual prowess, hints at the sexual desirability of a king from whom procreation was expected.* (Cowart, 2008, p. 34)

Blacking up also occurred in Russian Sergei Diaghilev's (1872–1929) company Ballets Russes (established in 1911), 'there were Moors and slaves [...] played by whites in blackface' (Banes, 1998, p. 69). Other examples of blacked-up narrative characters in ballet include French choreographer Michael Fokine's *Schéhérazade* (1910), an 'Arabian Nights' story about an ancient Sultan of Persia who is told by his brother that his favourite wife, Zobeide, would be unfaithful. Cultural studies scholar Mica Nava describes the ethnicity and use of make-up in this ballet:

> *The Persian women are represented as white, or without colour, and the slaves as black. In the early ballet performances the dancers who played the part of slaves were blacked-up.* (Nava, 2007, p. 28)

The representation of the black Golden Slave Masud illustrates the stereotyping and sexualisation of the black male in this ballet. Nava explains:

> ... *the ballet narrative disrupted not only the dominant racial conventions of the period but also ideas about masculinity, femininity and sexual politics. [...] it emphasised the transgressive libidinal desire of women and eroticised the black male.* (Nava, 2007, p. 29)

Fokine continued to black-up dancers in the ballet *Petrouchka* (1911). The scene was set in a Russian fair in the late nineteenth century, and the story was based on three puppets—Petrouchka, a Ballerina and a Moor—who are brought to life by a magician. Petrouchka falls in love with the Ballerina, but the Ballerina is attracted to and seduced by the Moor. Petrouchka later tries to break up the couple, but the Moor fights and kills him with a blow to the head with a sword. The character of the Moor is usually blacked-up, and on occasion it has been known for the character to appear wearing blue-face make-up (Anderson, 2016, p. 90). The blacked-up Moor has many similarities with minstrel characters, including white make-up used to emphasise the eyes and the mouth, exaggerated red make-up to enlarge and emphasise the lips, and white gloves. The Moor also embodies the stereotypical caricature of a 'happy-go-lucky', wide-grinning character. In the 'The Moor's Room' scene, the Moor plays with a coconut. In another section, he makes sexual advances towards the Ballerina aimed at seducing her. Cultural theorist Stuart Hall describes the power and fantasy of such stereotypes:

> ...*when blacks act 'macho', [...], they confirm the fantasy which lies behind or is the 'deep structure' of the stereotype (that they are aggressive, oversexed and over-endowed).* (Hall, 1997, p. 263)

It can be argued that Hall's account of racial stereotypes is evident in the early representations of black people in narrative ballets, therefore producing a legacy of perceptions that twentieth-century black British ballet dancers would later encounter when performing traditional repertoire.

The African Diaspora and Depictions of Primitivism in Ballet

Black people from the African diaspora were often associated with performing 'primitive' or 'savage' dance forms. These ideologies date from the nineteenth century in the works of evolutionists such as Herbert Spencer and Charles Darwin, and of evolutionary anthropologists Edward Tylor and James Frazer (Buckland, 2014, p. 175). Their research influenced early dance writers such as Edward Scott and Lilly Grove, who were described by dance scholar Theresa Buckland as two prominent dance historians of the late nineteenth century. Other dance writers of the time were similarly influenced, including Ethel Urlin, Leo Frobenius, Wilfrid Dyson Hambly and Curt Sachs. Musicologist and writer Curt Sachs was not a dancer but his book *World History of Dance* (1937) became the 'encyclopedia of dance in its time' (Kassing, 2007, p. 36). Dance scholar Suzanne Youngerman explained how influential Sachs' book was and that:

> ...*many researchers still rely so heavily on Curt Sach's forty-year old* World History of the Dance *for guidance in analyzing the style and socio-cultural significance of specific dance cultures, especially those of so-called "primitive" societies.* (Youngerman, 1974, p. 6)

These writers were among the founders of dance history and contributors to the evolution of dance theory. Although the term 'primitive' can be considered a generic label for dances from non-literate societies, the label was more often applied as if synonymous with cultures from the African diaspora.

In 1970, dance anthropologist Joann Kealiinohomoku (1993, pp. 533–549) wrote about the depiction of ballet as an ethnic dance form and deliberates on the ideology of primitivism in dance, in relation to ballet. 'Primitive' themes for dance repertoire were popular from the turn of the century and Diaghilev was one of the main artists in ballet that utilised this style. Dance scholar Ramsay Burt notes that:

> ... *the exotic, Russian and 'oriental' settings of so many of the Ballets Russes productions accentuated the fact that the dancers were not entirely European, but in touch with the 'primitive' and 'oriental'.* (Burt, 1995, p. 78)

While studying law at the University of St Petersburg in 1890, Diaghilev became interested in social science, music and painting along with his socialite friends (Garafola, 2009, p. 150). He formed friendships and worked with modern artists such as the French painter/sculptor Henri Matisse, the Spanish painter Pablo Picasso and the French painter André Derain, among others, who were all inspired by 'primitivism' and had an interest in the visual arts of African sculpture and traditional African masks (Flam, 2003, pp. 3, 29–35). Enthused by these artists, Diaghilev sought to create a legacy for himself as an artist by incorporating various other art forms on the ballet stage. He wanted to change the early company repertoire, which was inspired by traditional Russian folk dances and mainly choreographed by Fokine, who worked with the company from 1909 until his departure in 1912 (Greskovic, 2005, pp. 51–56).

After Fokine left the company in 1912, Diaghilev invited principal Polish dancer Vaslav Nijinsky, who was already performing with the company, to choreograph new ballets. Nijinsky was inspired by the French painter Paul Gauguin (Burt, 1995, p. 91). Gauguin's interest in primitivism led him to create works of art depicting the 'native' Tahitians, who fascinated him with their 'innocent freedom of social and sexual relations', and in this way 'Gauguin contributed to the European myth of the "primitive"' (Burt, 1995, p. 91). Burt explains how Gauguin's work influenced Nijinsky's choreography. For instance:

> *Jeux was set in the present, and its theme was surely modern, uninhibited social and sexual relationships. His other ballets at the time, Faune and Sacre, deal with similar themes and are both set in the 'primitive' and mythic or mythological past.* (Burt, 1995, p. 91)

As a result, Nijinsky's choreographic contribution to the Ballets Russes introduced a 'new modern ballet' style based on primitivism, and through the influence of modern artists who shared similar interests, the company aligned itself with current trends.

In the late 1920s, the Ballets Russes embarked on another new style of ballet with a hint of jazz-inspired movements. The new style was created by Russian dancer and choreographer George Balanchine, who was hired by Diaghilev in 1924 (Scholl, 1994, p. 72). Balanchine was captivated by jazz dance and artists like Josephine Baker while working in Paris in the 1920s. Dance historian and musicologist Marion Kant explains:

> *Balanchine became fascinated with jazz dance [...]. There is evidence that Balanchine not only choreographed for, danced with and admired Baker, but [...] the two traded material, with Baker learning to dance en pointe and Balanchine absorbing her jazz style.* (Kant, 2007, p. 227)

Balanchine's merging of ballet and African-American jazz dance was not without its critics. Isadora Duncan, the early modern American dance pioneer, considered jazz dance to be a *primitive* form (Daly, 2002, p. 127). It is important to mention that she despised both jazz and ballet dance forms. While working at the Ballets Russes, Balanchine choreographed approximately nine ballets before Diaghilev's death in 1929 (Garafola, 2009, p. 376). The influence of jazz movements in Balanchine's ballet *Apollo* (1928) was noted by dance scholar and cultural historian Brenda Dixon Gottschild, who describes:

> *Balanchine's "Apollo," although choreographed in Paris before his emigration to America, is bathed in the Africanist aesthetic.* (Gottschild, 1998, p. 74)

Apollo was based on the mythological Greek god of music and his muse. Dance scholar Barbara Fisher (2006, p. 27) highlights Balanchine's Africanist influence in the ballet and describes *Apollo* as a piece that 'breathtakingly combined classical ballet and classical Greek images with modern jazz'. This ballet became the impetus for many of Balanchine's later works as Gottschild notes:

> 'Balanchine described "Apollo" as a turning point in his career, and so it was. Through it he appropriated Africanist conventions that were present in European popular performance, adapted them for use on the ballet stage, and imported (or exported) them to the United States where, with considerable additional input, he changed the face and shape of ballet. (Gottschild, 1998, pp. 68–69)

From the above examples of ballet's incorporation of primitivism and Africanist styles in Diaghilev's Ballets Russes, it is evident that Nijinsky and Balanchine's repertoire created success in a climate where artists of various genres (such as visual artists) also thrived on non-Western cultural influences.

This history is particularly relevant in this context because of the important role that Balanchine played in extending the traditional Eurocentric ideal of the ballet dancer. He went on to found and become the artistic director of the New York City Ballet with co-founder and American dance historian Lincoln Kirstein in 1934. Balanchine employed the African American dancer Arthur Mitchell, where he became a principal dancer in 1955 (Banes, 1994, p. 60). Mitchell went on to establish Dance Theatre of Harlem with American Karel Shook after the assassination of civil rights leader Dr Martin Luther King in 1968 (Greskovic, 2005, p. 137). They sought to create a dance school and an all-black ballet company in Harlem to demonstrate that blacks were equal in performing ballet to any company in the Western world (Allen, 1976, p. 65). Shook described their inspiration to form the company:

Neither Arthur nor I wanted to prove that black people could do ballet. [...] People said their backs were built the wrong way or that their behinds were too big. But black people can do ballet, because ballet is nonethnic. (Gruen, 1990, p. 44)

It was in the Dance Theatre of Harlem that many black British dancers first found employment in ballet.

Black British Dancers and Ballet Companies

African American dancers have been documented as performing in ballet companies since the 1930s. In Britain, black dancers are documented as having trained with renowned ballet teachers from at least the 1940s onwards. For example, Jamaicans Berto Pasuka and Richard Riley trained with well-known classical ballet teachers before founding Britain's first black dance company, Les Ballet Nègres, in 1946. Pasuka studied with Russian teacher Anna Northcote (Severskaya) (Thorpe, 1989, p. 172) while Riley took classes at the Astafievia School where famous dancers such as Antony Dolin, Frederick Ashton and Margot Fonteyn also trained (Craine and Mackrell, 2010, p. 27). One of the first persons of colour to train and work with a mainstream ballet company was Malaysian–South African Johaar Mosaval, who was born in 1928. He trained at the Royal Ballet School in 1951 and a year later joined the company (formerly known as the Sadler's Wells Theatre Ballet), where he was promoted to soloist in 1956 and was employed for 25 years (Wilkinson & Kragolsen-Kille, 2006, p. 95). Mosaval performed with notable artists like Fonteyn and Rudolf Nureyev, among others.

In the early 1970s, a few black British dancers who were interviewed like Brenda Garrett-Glassman, Julie Felix and Carol Straker were the first students to train in prominent ballet institutions. Garrett-Glassman studied at the Royal Ballet School (1971–1973); Felix attended the former Rambert School of Classical Ballet, (now known as the Rambert School of Ballet and Contemporary Dance) (1974–1977); and Straker trained at the Legat School of Russian Ballet (1974) and graduated from Urdang Academy (1979). Black dancers faced enormous challenges in finding employment with mainstream British ballet companies. Garrett-Glassman (2010) was told by the Royal Ballet School that they would train her, but that she would not be employed in the company because she was black. Felix had a similar experience with the former London Festival Ballet (now known as the English National Ballet) whose then-director Dame Beryl Grey informed Angela Ellis (Marie Rambert's daughter) that she could not employ Felix because she was black (Felix, 2015). White dance teachers sometimes suggested that openings were more likely in the USA with the Dance Theatre of Harlem or proposed the Ballet Nacional de Cuba as an option for black dancers to continue their career (Garrett-Glassman, 2010). These suggestions from 'white' mainstream ballet establishments highlighted their inability to see black ballet dancers employed in British companies.

From the 1970s, dancers like Garrett-Glassman and Felix went to join Dance Theatre of Harlem (DTH) because they were unable to find work in mainstream British companies. Writing for the Arts Council of Great Britain at the time, researcher Naseem Khan reported on the 'Arts of ethnic minorities in Britain'. She described the representation of West Indians/Africans and black British in ballet, and found that:

Even were the establishment British companies to build racially integrated companies (which we hope will happen), there is still a need for a new form, a form that accommodates the work at present being done. Such a growth could be as valuable as America's sturdy Harlem Dance Company. (Khan, 1976, p. 107)

Khan's observation on the DTH's stability would see a second wave of black dancers obtaining funding from local authorities and the Greater London Council to train and work with the company during the 1980s, because there were still no employment opportunities in British ballet companies. Carol Straker (2002) and Mark Elie (2011) also went to train with DTH during this period, receiving grants from local councils. In 1985, the Greater London Council and DTH assigned four dancers—Adesola Akinleye, Paul Bailey, Gregory James and Samantha Webb—to work with the company. The Greater London Council 'paid for travel and contributed to stipends through money given to Dance Theatre Harlem' (Akinleye, 2015). Black British dancers Adam James and Rachel Sekyi were working with the DTH at the time already. All dancers were hired 'as part of the DTH Workshop Ensemble' and performed with the corps-de-ballet of the main company. Akinleye and James stayed on for a number of years after the initial first year. Sekyi remains with DTH to date (Akinleye, 2015).

The on-going migration of black British dancers to DTH might have helped mainstream ballet companies to become aware of the racial exclusion at work within their organisations. Consequently, in 1985 Noel Wallace became the first black dancer to be employed with the English National Ballet (Taylor, 2003, online). Brenda Edwards joined the same company, becoming its first female black dancer in 1987. The flow of black British dancers to companies such as DTH exposed the need for integration within mainstream ballet companies. However, as mentioned above, it also gave British companies an excuse not to employ black dancers because there were already companies like the DTH that would employ them. In 1989, Graham Devlin published his report 'Stepping Forward: Some suggestions for the development of dance in England during the 1990s', which was commissioned by the Arts Council Dance Department. Similarly, to Khan's report 13 years earlier, Devlin explored the prospects of training black dancers in ballet and found that:

> ...*in areas of training, both the Royal Ballet School and the newly formed London Festival Ballet School recognise the need to attract black students.* (Devlin, 1989, p. 64)

It is important to note here that the schools' companies were the same institutions that refused to offer employment to Garrett-Glassman and Felix in the 1970s because they were black. He suggests:

> *Clearly, if the classical dance profession is to open up at all to the black communities, it needs both role models within it and an aggressively publicised equal opportunities policy in its recruitment and training practices.* (Devlin, 1989, p. 64)

Devlin's report implied that ballet schools should take affirmative action and offer training to prospective black students. Nevertheless, black students who entered the ballet profession were not taken seriously and, as a consequence, many of them left the UK. For example, when dancer Adesola Akinleye was working at DTH and met her former UK ballet teacher, who had come there to observe classes, the teacher exclaimed: 'Oh I didn't realise you were *serious* about ballet when you were training [in the UK]!' (Akinleye, 2015). Devlin's recommendations had an ultimate impact on employment and training opportunities: for example, principal dancers Ronald Perry and Christina Johnston from DTH were invited to perform with the Royal Ballet Company in their production of *The Nutcracker* at the Royal Opera House in 1990 (Pascal, 1990, p. 8). This collaboration began a process of integration in British ballet, opening the doors to international black dancers. In 1991, Evan Williams became the first black British dancer to join the Birmingham Royal Ballet (Barrowclough, 1991, p. 25) and journalist Anne Barrowclough disclosed in 1991 that:

> ...*the Royal Ballet are now trying to recruit people like him, and in October the company will go into inner London schools to search for talent from all ethnic backgrounds.* (Barrowclough, 1991, p. 25)

Royal Ballet made more changes that year and developed an outreach scheme called 'Chance to Dance'. Inspired by DTH's educational scheme, it encouraged talented children from diverse backgrounds to participate in free ballet classes across four boroughs of London (Jaffray, 1992, p. 749). Since the creation of Chance to Dance, Shevelle Dynott became a success story and the best-known example of the programme's aims (Dynott, 2010). He was raised in Brixton, South London and he was the first student to train on the scheme from the age of seven, achieving a scholarship for the Royal Ballet School in 1997. Though he was not employed by the Royal Ballet Company after graduating, he currently works for the English National Ballet. The results of this programme suggest that Chance to Dance was far more successful at promoting the inclusion of minority ethnic dancers in training.

In the late 1970s and 1980s, due to the lack of prospects in mainstream ballet, black British dancers went to train and work aboard, or, in the case of Cassa Pancho, they created their own. In 2001, artistic director Pancho founded a new company, Ballet Black. Inspired by Mitchell's example and the lack of opportunities and roles for black and Asian British dancers, Ballet Black continues to be at the forefront of the battle for the acceptance of these dancers (Ballet Black, 2012). Opportunities are arising, most notably in the casting of Trinidadian–Canadian Céline Gittens and black British Tyrone Singleton in the Birmingham Royal Ballet's programme of *Swan Lake* at the Birmingham Hippodrome in 2012 (Jennings, 2012, p. 29). Singleton performed the role of Prince Siegfried and Gittens danced the leading role of Odette and Odile in Britain's first black duet. However, these examples continue to be the exception rather than the rule.

Conclusion

People from the African diaspora were historically represented in ballet by white European dancers who blacked-up to perform Moors in narrative ballets. Although traditional dances from the African diaspora were not replicated in ballet, narrative themes and interpretations of non-Western culture or 'Africanism' began to emerge in the seventeenth century. In the early twentieth century, primitivism became fashionable in Western art and Diaghilev introduced this concept into his ballets through some of the works by Nijinsky and Balanchine.

African Americans led the way for black dancers in ballet and the DTH has had an enormous impact on Western ballet by providing training and a working environment for international black dancers. Although training schemes like Chance to Dance are well intentioned, employment of black dancers in British ballet companies remains lacking. British ballet companies need to actively work to reflect the diversity of modern society, which, as yet, has not been achieved. While black dancers are gradually making appearances in major roles, companies like DTH and Ballet Black still exist because of the lack of openings for black and Asian dancers. Their existence continues to highlight the invisibility of black artists in ballet, although they have unarguably generated greater visibility for talent from the African diaspora.

For anyone, regardless of skin colour, becoming a professional ballet dancer takes passion, training, finance and the right opportunities. Yet for black dancers, the odds are even more against them. Black dancers can achieve high levels of artistry, as has been proven time and time again. However, the fact that so few do manage to succeed is indicative of the sheer number of obstacles that are placed before them. Hopefully, it will not be a long time before mainstream companies' composition reflects Britain's diverse society.

REFERENCES

Allen, Z. D. (1976, July). Blacks in Ballet. *Dance Magazine*, pp. 65–70.
Anderson, Z. (2016). *The Ballet Lover's Companion*. London: Yale University Press.
Arnold, D. (2002). *The Age of Discovery, 1400–1600 (Lancaster Pamphlets)*. London: Routledge.
Barthelemy, A. G. (1987). *Black Face, Maligned Race*. Baton Rouge: Louisiana State University Press.
Banes, S. (1994). *Writing Dancing in the Age of Postmodernism*. Middletown Connecticut: Wesleyan University Press.
Banes, S. (1998). *Dancing Women: Female Bodies Onstage*. London: Routledge.
Barrowclough, A. (1991, July 2). Making a Splash in Swan Lake. *Daily Mail*, p. 25.
Bhattacharyya, J. (2007). *Othello (Atlantic Critical Studies)*. Delhi: Atlantic Publishers & Distributors Pvt Ltd.
Buckland, T. J. (2014). Dance and Evolutionary Thought in Late Victorian Discourse. In B. V. Lightman & B. Zon (Eds.), *Evolution and Victorian Culture*. Cambridge: Cambridge University Press.
Burt, R. (1995). *The Male Dancer: Bodies, Spectacle and Sexuality*. London: Routledge.
Craine, D., & Mackrell, J. (2010). *The Oxford Dictionary of Dance*. Oxford: Oxford University Press.
Cowart, G. J. (2008). *The Triumph of Pleasure: Louis XIV and the Politics of Spectacle (Heritage of Sociology)*. Chicago: University of Chicago Press.
Daly, A. (2002). *Done into Dance: Isadora Duncan in America*. Middletown Connecticut: Wesleyan University Press.
Devlin, G. (1989). *Stepping Forward*. London: Arts Council Dance Department.
Fisher, B. (2006). *In Balanchine's Company*. Middletown Connecticut: Wesleyan University Press.
Flam, J. (2003). *Primitivism and Twentieth-Century Art: A Documentary History (Documents of Twentieth-Century Art)*. Berkeley: University of California Press.
Garafola, L. (2009). *Diaghilev's Ballets Russes*. Boston: Da Capo Press.
Gottschild, B. D. (1998). *Digging the Africanist Presence in American Performance: Dance and Other Contexts*. Westport: Praeger Publishers.
Greskovic, R. (2005). *Ballet 101: A Complete Guide to Learning and Loving the Ballet*. New York: Limelight Editions.
Gruen, J. (1990). *People Who Dance*. Princeton: Princeton University Press.
Hall, S. (1997). *Representations and Cultural Signifying Practices*. London: SAGE.

Jaffray, D. (1992, May). A Chance to Dance – A Royal Ballet/Dance Theatre of Harlem Project. *The Dancing Times*. pp. 748–749.

Jennings, L. (2012, 23 September). Celine Gittens and Tyrone Singleton Interview: The First Mixed-race Leads in Swan Lake Say that Skin Colour Is Not Barrier in British Ballet. *The Observer. The New Review*, p. 29.

Kassing, G. (2007). *History of Dance: An Interactive Arts Approach.* Leeds: Human Kinetics Europe Ltd.

Kant, M. (2007). *The Cambridge Companion to Ballet (Cambridge Companions to Music)*. Cambridge: Cambridge University Press.

Kealiinohomoku, J. (1993). An Anthropologist Looks at Ballet As a Form of Ethnic Dance. In R. Copeland & M. Cohen (Eds.), *What Is Dance? Readings in Theory and Criticism.* Oxford: Oxford University Press.

Khan, N. (1976). *The Arts Britain Ignores: The Arts of Ethnic Minorities in Britain.* London: Community Relations Commission.

Nava, M. (2007). *Visceral Cosmopolitanism: Gender, Culture and the Normalisation of Difference.* Oxford: Berg Publishers.

Pascal, J. (1990, December). Black Swan Into Centre Stage – Two Black Dancers Are to Disturb the Royal Ballet's Thin, White Uniformity, Reports Julia Pascal. *The Guardian*, p. 8.

Scholl, T. (1994). *From Petipa to Balanchine: Classical Revival and the Modernisation of Ballet.* London: Routledge.

Stevenson, A. (2010). *Oxford Dictionary of English* (3rd ed.). Oxford: Oxford University Press.

Thompson, A. (2001). *Passing Strange: Shakespeare, Race, and Contemporary America.* Oxford: Oxford University Press.

Thorpe, E. (1989). *Black Dance.* London: Chatto & Windus.

Wilkinson, R., & Kragolsen-Kille, A. (2006). *Bo-Kaap.* Cape Town: Struik Publishers.

Youngerman, S. (1974, July). Curt Sachs and His Heritage: A Critical Review of World History of the Dance with a Survey of Recent Studies that Perpetuate His Ideas. *Congress on Research in Dance*, CORD News, 6(2), 6–19.

INTERNET SOURCES

Ballet Black. (2012). Available at: http://www.balletblack.co.uk. Accessed 14 Oct 12.

Taylor, J. (2003 April, 10). How the Life of One Barnardo's Boy Was Transformed by Dance. In *Herefordshire Archive.* Available at: www.archive.thisisherefordshire.co.uk. Accessed 08 June 10.

INTERVIEWS BY AUTHOR

Akinleye, A. I. (2015). Interviewed, 29 December.
Dynott, S. (2010). Interviewed, 14 April.
Felix, J. (2015). Interviewed, 24 August.
Garrett-Glassman, B. (2010). Interviewed, 25 May.
Straker, C. (2002). Interviewed, 16 July.
Elie, M. (2011). Interviewed, 24 September.

CHAPTER 6

In-the-Between-ness: Decolonising and Re-inhabiting Our Dancing

Adesola Akinleye and Helen Kindred

Tongue-tied

British born, our mother-tongue is English but we feel that the language itself does not communicate the cultural understanding of the world we have grown up in.

As dance artist-scholars, our sense of *reality* is in the transformation, transaction and interaction demonstrated by movement. Understanding the world through dance, we do not have a perception of stillness/fixedness because heartbeat rhythmically creates constant movement within us. Life is within and between the heartbeat, the breath: dance is within and between these rhythms. Our interest in the in-*betweeness* of things, (rather than seeking to pin down static identities) finds meaning *in* movement, meaning in the transitions between, in and through. However, as we write in English, it becomes clear that the words to which we have primary access do not adequately describe this '*in-betweenness*' (Mahina, 2002, 2004). For us both, tongue-tied by our spoken language, dance has been our preferred communication, becoming for us the language of our embodied experiences.

However, we cannot avoid talking (!). Working transnationally in studio exploration, in everyday discussions with each other and with collaborating dancers and musicians we use English as a common verbal

---

A. Akinleye (✉) • H. Kindred
Middlesex University, London, UK

© The Author(s) 2018
A. Akinleye (ed.), *Narratives in Black British Dance*,
https://doi.org/10.1007/978-3-319-70314-5_6

language. In doing this, we find that we need to look carefully at how we communicate our worldview. We need to be alert to how Western values we do not adhere to can creep into our processes through the language we use to discuss, describe and facilitate dance. Exploring how we extract our dancing bodies and our creative processes from the Imperialist language of Western binaries is the starting point for this chapter. As we work to decolonise the environment of creative exploration (Smith, 1999), it is important that we find ways to communicate that are liberatory and representative of our lived experiences (hooks, 1992).

Our history of collaborating together means that we have a familiarity with each other's practice, language and meanings that allows us to shortcut conversations through referencing many well-established African and Indigenous worldviews that embrace embodiment. This is also inferred in some of the familiarity of interactions we have with fellow artists. Nonethe-less, we have found that articulating embodied experience is made problematic by the use of English language frameworks. However vigilant we are, in the vernacular of everyday exchanges in the studio, the Western Cartesian dualist binaries of English becomes engrained in how we are talking to each other and in so doing seeps into how we are thinking. Despite our creative processes being informed by our multicultural, transnational life experiences, how we talk about, or describe our work is often limited by the necessity to describe it using Western mainstream terms. We see this as a continuing legacy of colonisation: the on-going processes through which a group imposes its values on another group. In this case, the central dominant Western construct for '*the body*', and what the '*dancing body*' represents dominates communicating our embodied experiences in the dance studio (Burkitt, 1999; Ehrenreich, 2007; Foster, 1996; Gould, 1996; Sullivan, 2001; Synnott, 1993). Therefore, how we engage with concepts for creating choreography is shackled by the language we use to communicate movement.

The Vulnerability of Meaning

Although spoken language is useful in communicating certain kinds of inner creative processes, the words, grammar and structure of a language impacts on how those processes become meaningful outside of our innerthoughts and sensations. Any language could be considered an outward communication of our inner reflective process, but in the translation of sensation to meaning, and on to communicatory language, *meaning* is more vulnerable than *language*. A language has the potential to shape expression of meaning through the limits of the vocabulary and grammar it can offer. *Language* fully shapes or even subtly changes meaning. Whereas *meaning* can only shape language to a small extent because the grammar and vocabulary of that language can only be manipulated a slight amount before what is being said loses structure and becomes incomprehensible (Dewey, 1958; Ogden & Richards, 1989).

As we communicate together in the studio using the vocabulary of English language, we encounter words (such as mind and body, time and space), which deny and cling to our meanings. These dualist assumptions shaped and given credence by English language can start to actualize in the physical context of the meaning of our movements. Locked into the spoken language of English, our verbal communication therefore also gives rise to tacit metaphors for the lived experience that we can habitually slip into accepting as '*true*' through the language we are using (Lakoff & Johnson, 1980). In the practicality of working together in the dance studio, this has meant developing a sensitivity to language, being attentive to moments when we implicitly return to Western polarities that separate the mind from the body, and deny our non-Western sensitivities. By challenging the language with which we communicate dance, we attempt to decolonise the lens through which dance is discussed and shared between people more generally. We see an urgency for dance artist-scholars to think about this communication of process at a wider level. How we as artists describe our own dance work and how this communication is understood, more broadly affects how we can challenge dance to be more than at the service of maintaining the political Western status quo of how different 'bodies' are perceived and valued.

Historically, there are numerous examples of dances being misunderstood or presented in ways that are not appropriate to the intent and meaning of the dance itself. This is because their meaning is often not successfully communicable outside of the language and context of the culture they hail from. The inheritance of this continues for contemporary dance choreographers who having been brought up in the knowledge of such cultures are inherently drawing on codes and signifiers from their upbringing which are not immediately accessible to mainstream Western dance. Work created by such artists is subject to notions of gender, sexuality and class, all of which are uniquely constructed within different cultures. Dance created outside of the cultural construct of the language of English is often identified as engaging with the politics of performance practice (Craighead, 2006). This leaves the work being identified as a political or personal statement on *difference* rather than being welcomed as part of a wider, richer canon of dance generated in the West. We are interested in how the finished work we make is understood and engaged with; but we are more concerned with not letting the climate our work emerges into limit our creative processes. Although we are largely creating work in our Western British home of England, we do not want to work only within the narrow confines of the concepts of Cartesian dualism that our Western English language affords us. Our decolonisation is therefore not just in the liberty to create, it is in being attentive to the practices that influence *how* we create.

Un-picking the Muzzle

Working in academia in the UK and USA often tasks us to bridge the inherently *personal* of our creative process with the Western canon that drives the perspectives of the institutions we work in. This involves being asked to articulate the paradigms we are working from in the language of the Academy. In doing this, we find non-western philosophies offer a more appropriate voice for discussing our work. We have searched for these philosophies. We have had to theorise our own contemporary contexts for the trajectory of our work—where it is rooted and where it is going. Often this can feel like a lonely search for 'location' or an indelicate cobbling together of ideas. We challenge the notion that, because of our ancestry, the means for alternatives to Western perspectives can manifest fully elaborated for us. In today's twenty-first century global community it is over-simplified to expect that being 'black' means that you inherently understand any given '*African*' culture or philosophy, just as it is over simplified to suggest that being 'white' means that you inherently conform to Western culture or philosophy. Exposed to non-Western, non-mainstream experiences through our personal lives, we have both encountered Indigenous and Africanist concepts that feel like a *relief* and have a sense of *home* in terms of giving our intrinsic creative processes a voice in the cacophony of the Academy.

Outside the Academy, our community-based (public pedagogy) approach to choreographic research has led us to further recognise a need to re-articulate the language through which we make, process and share dance-movement. This is because, as we find ourselves sharing in dance experiences through community settings, we do not want to re-enforce Western dualist separations through how we explain what we are doing to non-dancers. Sensitive to this, we have noticed our own frustrations at the limits for how we can talk about and engage from an embodied perspective, reflected in the experience of many of the participants in the community dance projects we have been involved in. We see this as a general lack of resources in the Western world to express experiences as embodied.

Tracing a journey of liberation from the Western language we are using here to the lived experience of the British multiculturalism we have been born and brought up in, we have been exploring two bridges out of the established Western canon towards our worldviews. Phenomenology and pragmatism offer routes and possibilities for translating across from the Euro-American settings we work in to the Africanist/Indigenous worldviews we adhere to. Although Western phenomenology and pragmatism differ fundamentally in some areas,[1] they share the theme of the lived experience as a fully embodied aesthetic. They place the sensing body as central to the lived experience while both being acknowledged within the Western canon of philosophy. Helen has drawn on Martin Heidegger to describe a journey to embodiment, while Adesola draws on John Dewey. Both Heidegger and Dewey work to offer lexicons that tackle the paradigm of mainstream Western binaries.

Our Murmuring in University Halls

Within a Western inward facing academic frameworks, Heidegger's theory of *Dasein* and Dewey's notion of *transaction* give credence to notions of *in*-between-ness (embodiment) that our work sits in. Although these ideas do not need legitimacy by being recognised in the Western Canon, we are seeing Dewey and Heidegger as useful translators, or bridges out of the Western academy. Helen foregrounds questions of embodied knowledge as a platform for us to explore the embodied *self*—a fluid combination of mind, body and reflective thought, further encouraging exploration of the self's relation to environment. For Helen, Heidegger's work (1996) offers a point of departure for discussions of the *betweeness*, the liminal space between conscious and unconscious self, experienced in the responsiveness of dance (Kindred, 2017). The movement *between* things interpreted through Heidegger's theory of *Dasein* is fundamental for Helen's experience of exploring moving. *Dasein*, translated *Da-sein*—'the site – *Da*, for the disclosure of being – *Sein*' (Heidegger, 1996), resonates within an embodied framework as it appears to offer room for exploring the site/the body in the *betweeness* (time/space/place) of being – *Sein*. Heidegger's theory of *Dasein* (about the being of *beings*) is particularly pertinent in articulating that there are pluralities of being rather than one being, one way, one knowing. Helen interprets the relationship between *Da* and *Sein* as the *betweeness*, the relationship between dancing *self* and *other* (people, environment). *Dasein* is already in existence, but its presence as a particular kind of *being* is only revealed through choices made in each moment. From this embodied perspective, the knowledge and experiences of the self are within the body—the lived, moving reflective, sensing body (Bartenieff & Lewis, 1980). Heidegger's *Dasein* hence offers a philosophical framework for articulating our embodied experiences in movement. It bridges the gap between our sensations of moving and the language of the Western canon to an extent. *Dasein* can, therefore, be used to position the dancing body within a broader context, which resists a singular narrative.

For Adesola, Dewey's work articulates some of the in-between-ness of being. Dewey (Dewey & Boydston, 2008) sees the lived experience as a matrix between mind, body and environment creating each other through the transaction between them. Dewey's pragmatism tackles the Cartesian proposition that certainty manifests as fixed and that change is not to be trusted. English language assumes the mantle that truth and knowing are static defined points of Subject and object. For Dewey, knowledge is experience that becomes registered, remembered and made meaningful both through immediate physical sensation (empirical experience) and reflective thought (the experience of recalling). These are not different *kinds* of knowledge but merely different temporal entry points. We are embodied through the interaction (transaction) of experience, which involves a mind-full body of sensation, and reflection and action (no dualist mind or body, subject or object, but instead response and interaction). It is the interaction—between-ness that creates the experience of being alive. In transaction, we create each other through how we experience each other/ourselves. There is a flow of interaction which forms sensation, understanding and interest—self as world around (Dewey & Boydston, 2008; Hildebrand, 2003; Jackson, 1998; James, Dewey, Capps, & Capps, 2005; Thayer, 1981).

Dance exemplifies this interconnectedness. The artist is both the dancer (perceiver) and the dance (perceived) and, as such, dancers are engaged across and through the reflective process of responding with knowing mind-full bodies in order to dance. Dance is both what the dancer is doing and what they are being. As we consider Dewey, however, his very concepts of 'interaction' and 'transaction' force us to acknowledge that he must have been shaped by experiences he was having in the community and natural world around him. Dewey's wider community consisted of a range of *pragmatists* such as Native Americans—Black Elk,[2] African Americans Du Bois and women such as Charlotte Perkins Gilman (Pratt, 2002; Sullivan, 2001). We feel that it is these influences of Africanist, Indigenous and female perspectives that resound in Dewey's work that resonate with us.

Dewey and Heidegger are established within the Western canon and are therefore useful because they offer methods for articulating the embodied within Western frames. However, in order to do so, both have needed to first develop extensive re-articulations of the existing Western-based languages they used. In explaining our practice through these philosophers, our dance work can become shrouded or overshadowed in theoretical frameworks that leave our physical dance seeming like a theoretical exercise rather than a movement practice. Although they help us position our work within the Western Academy, explaining this also leads us down a complex maze of Western concepts that detracts from the practicality of 'doing' our practice in the dance studio. We have found that improvisation provides a movement language that also challenges dualist assumptions within the context of the Western Academy of dance. Improvisation moves beyond the named Subject, creating the *situation* of dancing through the response and interaction of moving together. Defying the singular definition that dualist communication rests on, improvisation allows for plurality of meaning and multiple movement possibilities. With its ambiguity and reliance on individual interpretation, improvisation often sits outside Western mainstream dance. Movement improvisation allows for interpretation that is outside the codes or signifiers of mainstream Western dance theatre forms. Already present in many non-Western forms, improvisation in the Western Dance Academy has historically been borne out of artists' wishes to explore 'alternative' practices of moving (Claid, 2006). Improvisation in the Western Dance Academy studios creates bridges to other contexts, in the same way as Dewey and Heidegger do for the Western philosophical library.

Much of the literature on improvisation in dance comes from a dominant Western ideology, written largely from a White-European perspective. Tensions between Western and non-Western approaches to communicating dance and its validity are particularly highlighted in these instances. The interaction of dance improvisation calls for a constant reconsidering of self and an awareness of relationship with others. When improvising, we tune into a heightened sensorial awareness (transcendence/universal connection), a way of *arriving* and *being present, being a part of it all*. Heightened sensorial awareness is a process discussed through much of the literature on dance improvisation and somatic movement practices in the West (Fraleigh, 1996, 2015; Fraleigh, Calamoneri, & Eddy, 2004; Tufnell & Crickmay, 1998, 2004; Cooper-Albright & Gere, 2003; Nelson, 2003, 2006; Olsen & McHose, 2004; De Spain, 2014). Improvisation's deep level of listening through the senses is enhanced by a process of being in rhythm and relationship with… The dancer is attuned to the rhythm of the internal breath and the external environment. This is the *in-between-ness*, the movement between conscious and unconscious being. The integrity of an awareness of shared and created community, of environment, poly-rhythms, and relationships aligns our perception of improvisation with articulating our non-Western frameworks for choreographing (Black, Neihardt, & DeMallie, 2008; Thompson, 2011). If we consider key figures in twentieth-century Western dance improvisation such as Anna Halprin, Hilde Holger, Steve Paxton, Yvonne Rainer, and the Judson Church/Grand Union, practice-based improvisation appears to value making and being with others. When dance performance is participatory, there is no separation between spectator and spectacle (no dualist subject /object, mind/body, time/space), the dance is created as it is revealed through the experienced transactions of all involved. The sense of family, community, between-ness, togetherness and sharing, common to improvisation and also to participatory dance cultures is not common in the dominant mainstream. Within dance texts, this often leaves them as constructed as 'other' practices. Improvisation is often problematized as *other* by the very artists practising and writing about it (De Spain, 2014; Zaporah, 1995; Koteen, Smith, & Paxton, 2008; Nelson, 2006). The lack of a Western language to engage with the 'betweeness' of *doer* and *done* (no dualist Subject and object) contributes to a perpetuation of the invisibility of some practices.

Margaret Thompson Drewal writes about dance in the Yoruba tradition in relation to 'Improvisation as Participatory Performance' (Drewal, 2003). Drewal highlights the lack of writing on improvisation by Western dance critics, pointing to the differences between improvisation and Western theatre dance in terms of Subject/object in the distanced gaze of the viewer. She points out that situating the improvized dances of the Yoruba people within a participatory context, while relevant in terms of the nature of the dance itself, once translated through Western dance frameworks, negates the value of these dances. The means in which communication of the work is discussed is already hijacked by Western dualist values (of Subject/object) that do not have a perception of the meaning of the dances. Due to their apparent lack of Western form or codified rules, many dance practices maintain an ambiguous presence, outside of mainstream Western culture yet are invisibilized responses to Western society. Similarly, many contemporary dance-works are ignored by Western dance critics and left out of critical discussion about rigour in artistic practice. A lack of willingness to find language to discuss the dance limits the potential for it to be taken 'seriously' within Western dance literature and performance presentation. Wider literature referring to dances outside of a Western framework is overly concerned with situating these dances within a largely anthropological context. *Ritualistic* dances performed in non-Western societies are principally viewed by the Western dance canon through a cultural-movement lens in order to be read and legitimised rather than being seen as part of the wealth of the dance canon. There is often a distinction drawn between *moving* and *dancing*, and between *ritual* and *rigour* as if these were not able to co-exist in the same experience (De Spain, 2014). A lack of language leaves a lack of awareness that stifles artists' progression artistically, economically, politically and professionally. A widening of the Western language for what is dance would be useful for the richness and credibility of dance in general. However, we are also concerned with protecting the liberty to develop and grow our personal practices. This has meant that at times we are often tasked to trace a heritage from within the Western canon as well as from without. Pragmatism, phenomenology and improvisation allow us to demonstrate that our hybrid otherness (our between-ness) is not concocted; it has always quietly existed in and out of the halls of the Western mainstream.

Within our practices we have come to terms with being-out-of-context, not quite aligning to dominant thought, shifting the boundaries and accepting uncertainty as the landscape for our experiences. Part of the art of our practice, then, becomes about translating our work yet not compromising the *otherness or alternative narratives* we are perceived as working within. The decolonisation of our practice is not to find a way to justify ourselves within the Western canons but to find ways to maintain, communicate and work within our own contexts. For artists like ourselves making contemporary work from non-Western starting points, there is a danger of being stereotyped into a culturally historical Western representation of what *was*. While honouring what has come before, we need to affirm the visibility, currency, language and authenticity of the *nowness* that is the result of our own multicultural interactions. Our trans-national artistic experiences move away from a fixedness of this or that, a whitewashing of non-Western influences to come into the twenty-first century. We end this chapter by giving an example of how we continue to challenge ourselves to emancipate our creative processes, our methodologies and languages.

Finding the Language of the Decolonised Dancing Body

We have been looking at how we defy fundamental dualist concepts that manifest in the way we talk about dancing. We are particularly interested in negating a separation between time and space, the separation of which is mono-dimensional and denies the between-ness or transaction which is so central to our art practice (Dewey, Boydston, & Lavine, 1989; Mahina, 2004). For the embodied being, time and space can be no more separate than mind and body, dancer and dance. From an embodied perspective, when we are talking about space we have to be located in time—we could be at 36 Strode Road (space) but to understand the meaning of this we must be located in *time* also—36 Strode Road when it was a field, or when it was a building site, or when it was a house we lived in, or when it was a house someone else lived in? Similarly, we could talk about 4pm, but for this to be meaningful we must know 4pm in *space*, New York, Wamblee, Lagos or London? When we talk to each other about dance in terms of time or in terms of space (as if they are different from each other) fundamental concepts of the dimensions of *being*, of what embodiment *is* are lost, along with our valued availability of perception of mind-full bodies in harmony with each other and our environment.

Yet collaborating in the dance studio, we talk about time *and* space. Of course, within the dance studio when we use the word *space* we imply *time* too. But our concern is that by limiting our language to only tacitly explaining what we really mean while also evoking the presence of dualism in the room through our speech, we limit the possibility for where our movement can go. We started to reflect on Oceanic concepts of Ta-Va (rhythm-relationship) as a way to better describe the movement intentions that we are referring to when we had used the words 'time' and 'space'. We do not mean to suggest that Ta-Va replaces 'time' and 'space'. We question the validity of time/space as concepts altogether and would argue rather that they are merely products of a colonial worldview that needs to unnecessarily measure in order to understand things (Smith, 1999). However, having the articulation of Ta-Va helps us deal with the tensions that the notions of time/space have imposed on us. In the dancing body, *time* and *space* are combined: the proposition of *time* manifests through the sensation of rhythm (Ta), the proposition of *space* manifests in the relationships (Va). These also resonate meaningfully with the deeper rhythms of artists' lives and wider relationships that locate the self and form the identity which the artists bring to the creative process. The lived experience, therefore, becomes conceived of through the transaction of interaction, the between-ness of…

Oceanic philosophies ask us to engage with the notions of balance and harmony suggested through Tongan society. Mahina (2004) talks about this harmony in Oceanic philosophies in relation to how we find balance in our lives through the movement of the rhythms and relationships we weave. To construct dance within the terms of rhythms (Ta) and relationships (Va) rather than time and space is not just a theoretical need to position ourselves or an exercise in navel-gazing semantics. It is an example of how we desire to contribute to a shift that rejects dualism and the separations and power structures it nurtures in wider society through our work in dance—to contribute to our own decolonisation. The concept of Ta-Va rather than time and space has also encouraged us to address the implications of the separation of time and space from the person experiencing them, which has implications for notions of participation and community in our work. Ta-Va carries far wider-reaching implications about the body, spirit and cultural identity than we are able to discuss here. It is this depth of meaning that is liberatory. It is this that challenges ingrained colonised thinking in our processes.

Decolonising our micro personal dancing practices challenges macro worldviews and constructs of the body. In the studio, as we talk it is important that we develop a lexicon that does not tacitly return us to Western binaries, expectations and aesthetics. Through attempting to decolonise our approaches choreographically, we are defying constructs that limit our articulation and understanding of our relationships with the world around. Blackness, Whiteness, Britishness, dance: we are aware of the identities we are expected to embrace but in a twenty-first century global world these are interwoven with each other. We are living between them. While we might intrinsically feel a rejection of many Western values, being born into and living in a Western society part of our artistic practice becomes questioning *how* we interact within the world around us in order to create our own voice in our work. Part of our practice becomes untying our tongues to dance the stories of our *being*.

Notes

1. Heidegger's Phenomenology still sees a divide between subject and object but positions them as affecting each other, while Dewey's Pragmatist work does not see a separation at all.
2. Dewey was alive 1859 to 1952, Black Elk 1863 to 1950 (Black & Neihardt, 1932) Peirce lived 1839 to 1914, William Frederick "Buffalo Bill" Cody was born in 1846 and died 1917.

References

Bartenieff, I., & Lewis, D. (1980). *Body Movement: Coping with the Environment*. Hove: Psychology Press.

Black, E., Neihardt, J. G., & DeMallie, R. J. (2008). *Black Elk Speaks : Being the Life Story of a Holy Man of the Oglala Sioux* (Premier ed.). Albany, NY: Excelsior Editions, State University Press of New York Press.

Burkitt, I. (1999). *Bodies of Thought : Embodiment, Identity, and Modernity*. London/Thousand Oaks, CA: Sage Publications.

Claid, E. (2006). *Yes? No! Maybe...: Seductive Ambiguity in Dance*. London: Routledge.

Cooper-Albright, A., & Gere, D. (2003). *Taken by Surprise. A Dance Improvisation Reader*. Middletown: Wesleyan University Press.

Craighead, C. (2006). 'Black Dance': Navigating the Politics of 'Black' in Relation to 'The Dance Object' and the Body as Discourse. *Critical Arts: A Journal of South-North Cultural and Media Studies, 20*(2), 20–33.

De Spain, K. (2014). *Landscape of the Now: A Topography of Movement Improvisation.* Oxford, NY: Oxford University Press.

Dewey, J. (1958). *Experience and Nature.* New York: Dover Publications.

Dewey, J., & Boydston, J. A. (2008). *The Later Works of John Dewey, 1925–1953.* Carbondale: Southern Illinois University Press.

Dewey, J., Boydston, J. A., & Lavine, T. Z. (1989). *John Dewey: The Later Works, 1925–1953* (Vol. 16: 1949–1952, Essays, Typescripts, and Knowing and the Known). Carbondale, IL: Southern Illinois University Press.

Drewal, M. T. (2003). Improvisation as Participatory Performance. In A. Cooper-Albright & D. Gere (Eds.), *Taken by Surprise* (pp. 119–132). Middletown: Wesleyan University Press.

Ehrenreich, B. (2007). *Dancing in the Streets: A History of Collective Joy.* London: Granta.

Foster, S. L. (1996). *Corporealities : Dancing Knowledge, Culture and Power.* London: Routledge.

Fraleigh, S. H. (1996). *Dance and the Lived Body: A Descriptive Aesthetics.* Pittsburgh: University of Pittsburgh Press.

Fraleigh, S. (Ed.). (2015). *Moving Consciously: Somatic Transformations Through Dance, Yoga, and Touch.* Urbana: University of Illinois Press.

Fraleigh, S., Calamoneri, T., & Eddy, M. (2004). *Dancing Identity: Metaphysics in Motion.* Pittsburgh: University of Pittsburgh Press.

Gould, S. J. (1996). *The Mismeasure of Man* (Rev. and expanded. ed.). New York/London: Norton.

Heidegger, M. (1996). *Being and Time: A Translation of Sein und Zeit.* New York: SUNY Press.

Hildebrand, D. L. (2003). *Beyond Realism and Antirealism: John Dewey and the Neopragmatists.* Nashville: Vanderbilt University Press.

hooks, b. (1992). *Black Looks: Race and Representation.* Boston, MA: South End Press.

Jackson, P. W. (1998). *John Dewey and the Lessons of Art.* New Haven/London: Yale University Press.

James, W., Dewey, J., Capps, J. M., & Capps, D. (2005). *James and Dewey on Belief and Experience.* Urbana: University of Illinois Press.

Kindred, H. (2017, April 20). *KnowingUnknowing Through Improvised Movement Practices.* Conference Paper: Dance Fields, Roehampton University London.

Koteen, D., Smith, N. S., & Paxton, S. (2008). *Caught Falling: The Confluence of Contact Improvisation, Nancy Stark Smith, and Other Moving Ideas.* Toronto, Canada: Contact Editions.

Lakoff, G., & Johnson, M. (1980). *Metaphors We Live By.* Chicago: University of Chicago Press.

Mahina, 'O. (2002). Atamai, Fakakaukau and Vale: 'Mind', 'Thinking' and 'Mental Illness' in Tonga. *Pacific Health Dialog, 9*(2), 303–308.

Mahina, 'O. (2004). Art as Ta-va 'Time-Space' Transformation. In T. Baba et al. (Eds.), *Researching the Pacific and Indigenous Peoples: Issues and Perspectives* (pp. 86–93). Auckland, New Zealand: Center for Pacific Studies, University of Auckland.

Nelson, L. (2003). Before Your Eyes. Seeds of a Dance Practice. *Contact Quarterly Dance Journal, 29*(1), 20–26.

Nelson, L. (2006). Composition, Communication, and the Sense of Imagination: Lisa Nelson on Her Pre-Technique of Dance, the Tuning Scores. *Self Interview. Ballet Tanz. Critical Correspondence.*

Ogden, C. K., & Richards, I. A. (1989). *The Meaning of Meaning : A Study of the Influence of Language Upon Thought and of the Science of Symbolism.* San Diego: Harcourt Brace Jovanovich.

Olsen, A., & McHose, C. (2004). *Bodystories: A Guide to Experiential Anatomy.* Hanover, NH: UPNE.

Pratt, S. L. (2002). *Native Pragmatism : Rethinking the Roots of American Philosophy.* Bloomington, IN: Indiana University Press.

Smith, L. T. (1999). *Decolonizing Methodologies : Research and Indigenous Peoples.* London/New York/Dunedin, NZ: Zed Books/University of Otago Press/ Distributed in the USA Exclusively by St. Martin's Press.

Sullivan, S. (2001). *Living Across and Through Skins: Transactional Bodies, Pragmatism, and Feminism.* Bloomington: Indiana University Press.

Synnott, A. (1993). *The Body Social : Symbolism, Self and Society.* London: Routledge.

Thayer, H. S. (1981). *Meaning and Action: A Critical History of Pragmatism* (2d ed.). Indianapolis: Hackett Publishing Company.

Thompson, R. F. (2011). *Aesthetic of the Cool: Afro-Atlantic Art and Music.* Pittsburgh, PA: Periscope.

Tufnell, M., & Crickmay, C. (1998). *Body, Space, Image.* London: Dance Books.

Tufnell, M., & Crickmay, C. (2004). *A Widening Field.* Hampshire: Dance Books.

Zaporah, R. (1995). *Action Theatre; The Improvisation of Presence.* Berkeley, CA: North Atlantic Books.

PART II

Processes

In Part II – *Processes*, we look at the processes that surface for dance within the experience of Black British dance. For many artists, the process of dancing is part of a spiritual awakening to the moving body as a conduit for connecting with the world around. For some dancers marginalised by dance in the '*Academy*', or familiar with informal movements through family socialisation, the formal learning of African dances has left a significant impact on their artistic process. This section, therefore, acknowledges a history of the powerful experiential learning that dances from Africa have had on the creative processes of some British dancers. However, the chapters also warn against minimalising '*African dance*' or '*African dancers*' into merely the process of watching Black artists' self-realisation. The chapters in this section ask us to problematise the conflation of Black dance with African Dance, which not only homogenises African dance into one thing, but is also a reductionist approach to understanding individual artistic processes and contributions (thus underlined in Namron's Chap. 2. '*I don't do Black Dance, I am a Black Dancer*' in Part I). Through presenting the varied experiences of individual artists, Part II also warns the reader to be vigilant in noticing the Grand Narrative of mainstream attempts to simplify an understanding of Africa's relationship with dance as a single cathartic experience.

Over history, audiences have had the privilege and exciting experience of witnessing Black artists' engaging directly with internal tensions around belonging, from a British context. There is an interesting assumption articulated in Barnes' Chap. 7 '*Trials of Ado: Kokuma's cultural self-defence*', that engagement with these performances was with empathy. It seems clear that for some audience members this is true. We can recognise and appreciate the artist's complicated processes of understanding of Self, movement and environment through witnessing artists develop a somatic language for meaning-making. There are a number of individual artistic processes that address notions of belonging, home, authenticity and self-identity among dance artists who identify with Black, British and dance. Some of these are described in the following chapters. However, some personal historical-narratives within the book also bear witness to the UK dance establishment inferring a comfortable overly-simplified precedent that processes for Black artists are about exploring and finding a place of 'home' with their own Blackness. This assumed precedent denies empathy and betrays a voyeuristic obsession for seeing the toils and despondency and final realisation of *Otherness* told again and again. The expectation then becomes that every Black artist is contributing to the same narrative of loss and self-realisation in African/Blackness.

If we idealise 'African' derived dances as vehicles for 'Black' realisation, we do a disservice to dance in general. Rather, it seems important to note that commonly across art forms, cultures and time periods the process of maturity within an artist is a process of self-reflection and realisation. Artists who identify with any group—Black, Indigenous, working class, male, female, disabled, queer—explore their affiliations and the marginalisations that have manifested in their lives through association with these groups. In doing so, art is created. However, it is the process of exploration (for instance exploring tensions in identity) that creates work from artists. The marginalisations themselves are not inherently tools for manifesting art, they merely give a focus, intensity and sometimes aesthetic to the artist. Therefore, to focus on the signifiers of marginalisation (for instance colour of skin) in the artists rather than the art process itself implies a subtly racist assumption that art work was birthed from the situation rather than from the artistry of the people themselves.

Read together, the variety of experiences and analysis within the chapters starts to highlight how problematic reductionist constructs for '*Black dance*' are in terms of acknowledging individual artists' creative processes. Across the book, artists express how their artistic process includes tactics for navigating '*Black dance*' constructed as the return to a single fixed relic in the past (as African dance is often constructed as); or alternatively constructed as a social response to current urban marginalisation (as Street dance is often constructed as). Anything that does not fit into these two-temporal fixed but polar points is either consider not '*Black dance*' or is considered to be a not yet fully realised exploration of one or other of those imagined fixed points – *it will get to the point once it is completed*! However, dance is a living, moving art form and neither of these points for 'Black dance' are recognisable within the narratives of the lived experiences of dancers. In order to *recognise* artists' creative processes, we must start to insist on articulating the existence of the creative processes of artists who draw on non-Western dance forms to understand their movement practices. In a reductionist approach where 'Black dance' constitutes only one process (the process of understanding Blackness), we do a disservice to dance as an art form by invisibilising the practices where a myriad of creative processes are happening.

Part II begins with Barnes' chapter, '*Trials of Ado: Kokuma's Cultural Self-defence*'. Kokuma Dance Theatre Company (1978–2000) was one of the first dance companies in the UK to have an African dance repertoire. Considering the experiences of two dancers of Caribbean descent, Barnes traces how for some dancers who found themselves marginalised by racist stereotypes the repertoire of Kokuma opened up a vocabulary of movement into which they could find a sense of belonging, leading to a sense of defending their own artistic processes. In Chap. 8 '*Moving tu Balance: An African Holistic Dance as a Vehicle for Personal Development from a Black British Perspective*', Golding, a former principal dancer with Kokuma, gives testimony to how African dance practice has help her develop her own artistic processes. She traces how belonging to a community of dancers who studied African Dances in Birmingham contributed to a spiritual awakening of valuing somatic-based philosophy within her work. She describes how her personal process to find her own authentic artistic movement has developed into holistic-healing therapeutic movement workshops that she facilitates for other women.

In Chap. 9 Castelyn considers her pedagogical processes as a dance lecturer in a British University. In '*Why I am Not a Fan of The Lion King: Ethically-informed Approaches to the Teaching and Learning of South African Dance Forms in Higher Education in the United Kingdom*', Castelyn interrogates her ethical responsibilities as she begins to teach a class of British dance students about South African dance. A native of South Africa herself, she problematises the juxtaposition of her knowledge of the many dance forms, genres and creative processes that constitute the dance scene in South Africa in the twenty-first century, with her awareness of the expectation of her British students (some of them descendants of

African countries) that African dance will be a process for understanding a kind of general Black identity.

In Chap. 10 '*Performativity of Body Painting: Symbolic Ritual as Diasporic Identity*', Cuxima-Zwa traces his artistic process as an artist having grown up in Angola and moved to UK as a refugee. He describes his performance-ritual process using three site-specific works he has performed in London. In the chapter, he uses these performances as examples of his use of his body as a medium for constructing a personal ritual of healing and environmental connection through movement. Cuxima-Zwa explores how his dancing painted body becomes a vehicle for the process of transgressing perceived cultural and geographic boundaries.

In Chap. 11 '*Dancehall: A Continuity of Spiritual, Corporeal Practice in Jamaican Dance*', Patten asks us to further consider the dance space as a transformative space where dance can become a spiritual self-expression. He suggests that throughout the spectrum of African diasporic dance spaces, the moving body has been a part of the dance artist's spiritual meaning-making practice. This is a meaning-making that plays an essential role in how dancers have found an empowered response to socio-political discourses that would otherwise marginalise them. In Chap. 12 '*Our Ethiopian Connection: Embodied Ethiopian Culture as a Tool in Urban-Contemporary Choreography*', Courtney describes how his artistic process has been informed and enlightened by his experiences relocating to Ethiopia. Part II ends with Roman's retrospective chapter on finding artistic authenticity in her dance practice. In Chap. 13 '*Reflections: Snapshots of Dancing Home, 1985, 2010 and 2012*' Romans looks at how finding a *home* in and through dance has led to a lifelong process of journeying, including having to leave Britain at points in her career in order to continue the trajectory of her creative development.

This section – *Processes*, suggests that it is the processes for understanding the lived experience through the moving body that Black, British, dance artists contribute to in general. However, it is clear from the Black, British, and dance spectrums that there are a number of artistic processes that have been overshadowed by a focus on how their artistic outcomes fit within a mainstream Grand Narrative about cultural identity and Blackness and/or who and what dance is. Responding to this loss the chapters in this section present a range of processes and processings of dance.

CHAPTER 7

Trails of Ado: Kokuma's Cultural Self-Defence

Thea Barnes

Fig. 7.1 *Trails of Ado.* Choreography by Jackie Guy. Kokuma Performing Arts, 13 October 1987. Dress rehearsal of Revival Section from *Trails of Ado*. Left to right: Desmond Pusey, Doreen Forbes, Cecelin Johnson, Jacquline Bailey, Patricia Donaldson; Drummers behind dancers: Silbert Dormer, hidden behind Desmond-Tony Reid, Gladstone Foster, Kokuma Studio, 163 Gerrard Street, Lozells, Brimingham B19 2AH. Photographer Philip Grey

T. Barnes (✉)
Independent dance researcher, London, UK

© The Author(s) 2018
A. Akinleye (ed.), *Narratives in Black British Dance*,
https://doi.org/10.1007/978-3-319-70314-5_7

Cultural Self-Defence

This chapter seeks to illustrate how a group of dancers, members of Kokuma Performing Arts (Kokuma), achieved self-realisation through a dance, "*Trails of Ado*," choreographed by Jackie Guy (Fig. 7.1). The embodiment of this dance empowered the dancers who, through its creative process, gathered strategies for 'cultural self-defence' by affirming pride, admiration, and respect for themselves and their ethnic heritage. I offer descriptions and perspectives of this dance, performed in Birmingham during the early 1980s. Personal insights describe how these dancers achieved a level of personal self-realisation fortified with an evolving authentic self through the embodiment of *Trails of Ado*.

I begin by defining some of the terms I will be using: the word "authenticity" and its adjectives, "authentic" and "inauthentic," have many applications and can draw on several fields of knowledge including philosophic, psychological, and spiritual given the inquiry (Steiner & Reisinger, 2006). As a modifier, authentic or inauthentic clarifies whether something or someone is an imitation or an original and genuine. If the discussion is regarding an object or a dance, authentic and inauthentic can be used to appraise it and would comprise prescriptions held by practitioners and patrons of the art form. Appraisals by practitioners and patrons of the form invariably use social and cultural parameters to assist in authenticating the quality of an object (Filitz & Saris, 2013). Authentic and inauthentic can also indicate the degree to which one is true to one's self, personality, character, creativity, aesthetic preference, or one's perception of and relation to the world (Yacobi, 2012).

Becoming the person one seeks to be is a dynamic process ongoing everyday throughout one's life. Becoming the dancer one dreams to be is simultaneous with this everydayness of being in the world as time goes by coupled with where and how the dancer lives. "Like a dance, our being-in-the-world is of motion, time, and becoming" (Fraleigh, 1987, p. 164). It is the dancer's prerogative to devise a chosen genuine, authentic self and livelihood. The ability for an individual to evolve an authentic self in life and in dance performance is enabled or disabled by the situation in which she lives. Forming a synthetic whole with her situation, a person is an assemblage of probabilities: cultural allegiance, social and political notions paired with ethnicity, class, education, extent of economic stability, physicality, kinesthetic awareness, some of which are not chosen but given at birth (Sartre, 1976). Efforts to achieve a desired life, to become one's own idea of self, of life, or aesthetic preference in dance-making and performance is affected and limited by the situation one lives in. This lived experience shapes and moulds an individual as much as the choices one makes impact how one moves through the world and dances on stage. One can, though, given the circumstance, devise a way to transcend the situation one inhabits through alternative choices and attitudes also gleaned from the situation. This assemblage, unique to each individual, characterises and determines possibilities of who she is in relation to others in the situation in which she lives. Ultimately an assemblage of choices and possibilities affect one's quest to achieve a chosen life and a cherished livelihood (Birt, 2002, pp. 265–273).

> *No attempt must be made to encase man, for it is his destiny to be set free. The body of history does not determine a single one of my actions. I am my own foundation.* (Fanon & Markmann, 1967, pp. 230–231)

Here, Frantz Fanon as translated by Charles Lam Markmann (1967) writes defiantly of an unequivocal personal choice to circumvent those cultural and social mechanisms and failings which impede an individual's progression to self-realisation. There is a resolve in Fanon's words. An individual should be free to move through life with fluidity, to fulfil potentiality with chosen allegiances and be the architect of one's own life. The quote implies an agentic approach to self, society, and humanity given the situation one lives in. Fanon's words suggest an individual's quest for a more genuine and satisfying life will be pursued even when situational difficulties seek to deny self-realisation.

> *Consequently, the majority of Jamaicans discover a flexibility in coping with a society that is yet to be organized in the interests of that majority. A hold on any activity beyond the control of a cynical power structure is a valuable weapon of cultural self-defence. The art of dance, comprising the dancer's own body movements informed by his own spiritual and emotional states is such a weapon. Allied with music—which utilizes various African-derived drums and idiophones as well as European instruments such as piano and strings—the dance takes on compounded energy as a source for survival.* (Nettleford, 1985, p. 20)

In this quote, Rex Nettleford (1985) suggest cultural self-defence is a means to survive intolerable social situations by cultivating self-realisation in dance and ultimately in life. If a situation is intolerant and opposes or suppresses opportunities to achieve self-realisation, cultural self-defence will assist in securing self-realisation. The development of personal potential would manifest in dance when a person deliberately utilises their physicality, with its particular movement experiences, spirituality, and emotions to effect a revised more authentic self. For Nettleford, dance would comprise strategies to unite communities, provide opportunities to share histories, counter alienation while building strong bodies, exemplary work modes, patriotic commitment, and self-respect. Nettleford's choreography mirrored Jamaica's life-world providing visions of their subjectivity through historical and contemporaneous renditions portrayed through traditional gestures and modern dance. Dance performance became an opportunity to transcend everydayness while simultaneously vivifying Jamaica's varied ethnicities and their dance forms. Transcendence from lived life while one dances is a cherished experience, especially if each gesture refines artistry as well as identity. By aspiring to fathom the dancer one imagines to be, one is free to be the person one chooses to be.

Brimingham, UK 1980's

Civil disturbances occurred in Birmingham, UK in the Handsworth and Lozells area in July 1981 and September 1985. These disturbances coincided with those occurring in London, Leeds, and Liverpool. Home Secretary at the time, William Whitelaw, appointed Leslie George Scarman on April 14, 1981 to hold an enquiry into the disturbances two days after they ended in Brixton, London. The Scarman Report received mixed reviews but cited complicated social, political, and economic factors with inappropriate policing strategies contributing to the discord and violence (Scarman, 1982). Racial disadvantage and inner-city decline also figured in the dissatisfaction turned vehemence within these communities that resulted in death, injury, and destruction of property. Writing in 1984, Russell Profitt explained that racialism affected the consciousness of Britain's population so profusely that more than just better policing in the inner city would be needed to eradicate it (Profitt, 1984). Improved employment and educational opportunities, economic advancement, improved living conditions, and purposeful social and recreational facilities would be needed to circumvent racial oppression and its effect on the perception of self and community felt among the peoples of the Handsworth and Lozells communities in Birmingham.

At the time of the civil disturbances in Birmingham, Kokuma was a group of young people interested in dance as a means for cultural affirmation.

I interviewed two former members of Kokuma, Doreen Forbes and Cecelin Johnson, regarding Kokuma's dance- making and in particular the choreographing of *Trails of Ado* during the social turbulence of the 1980s. A brief history of Kokuma is given below but the individual experiences of Forbes and Johnson reveals how the embodiment of ethnically specific dance gestures within *Trails of Ado* was key to achieving self-realisation. Forbes joined the dance company Mystic and the Israelites (M&I, which later became Kokuma Dance Company) in 1978 and remained through the development of the company for 26 years. Forbes was born in Britain but her father and mother immigrated to Britain for amelioration working in Imperial Metal Industries and the Nursing Auxiliary respectively. Johnson, whose parents were from St Kitts, started dancing in 1981 with Danse de L'Afrique in Birmingham and joined Kokuma in 1985. Johnson, giving her perspective of the civil disorders in Handsworth in 1981 and 1985 states that the disorders were a result of the people in the community being dissatisfied: 'The Caribbean community, black women, black men, were not happy with the way society portrayed *them*' (Johnson, 2015). Johnson spoke of racialized impressions and expectations that impeded educational and economic access and advancement. These racialized perspectives disabled acceptance of Caribbean and African peoples and their cultures. The Scarman Report revealed that police checks provoked the violence already inflamed by racial myths, injustices, and intolerance. The unrest was a manifestation of the disillusionment felt by members of the community.

> *Below the schema I had sketched a historico-racial schema. The elements that I used had been provided for me not by "residual sensations and perceptions primarily of a tactile, vestibular, kinesthetic, and visual character," but by the other, the white man, who had woven me out of a thousand details, anecdotes, stories.* (Fanon & Markmann, 1967, p. 11)

Here Fanon describes how derogatory, disparaging ethnic appraisals devalue and threaten a person's sense of self on multiple levels. Everyday living, casual interactions and encounters substantiate or impede an individual's quest to achieve a genuine, authentic self. In *The Souls of Black Folk*, W. E. B. DuBois (1903) describes the psychological challenge of American Negroes in the nineteenth and early twentieth century struggle to secure self-realisation:

It is a peculiar sensation, this double consciousness, this sense of always looking at one's self through the eyes of others, of measuring one's soul by the tape of a world that looks on in amused contempt and pity. The history of the American Negro is the history of this strife—this longing to attain self-conscious manhood, to merge his double self into a better and truer self... He simply wishes to make it possible for a man to be both a Negro and an American, without being cursed and spat upon by his fellows, without having the doors of Opportunity closed roughly in his face. (DuBois, 1903, p. 3)

Johnson's and Forbes' descriptions of their experience at the time of the Handsworth riots is not the same situation which DuBois discusses but there are similarities. Many residents' heritage in the Handsworth and Lozells urban areas were from Bangladesh, Pakistan, the Caribbean, and Africa. The issues of race, longing, and belonging figured strongly in the civil disturbances in the Handsworth and Lozells community whose belief in themselves and their communities was challenged by social failures and racialized tensions. Britain, at first a land of promise, had become disingenuous for some members of the community who were denied dignity, a desired livelihood, and, as Dubois (1903) relates, the right to be a man or woman among other men and women. There were, though, efforts before and after these events that sought to inspire enrichment and fortitude in the community's root cultures.

A Brief History of Kokuma

Originally, Kokuma developed out of a dance project known as Mystic and the Israelites (M&I) that met informally at the offices of the Probation Service in Perry Barr, Birmingham. Bob Ramdhanie, Senior Probation Officer at the time, sought to develop the dance project for community development within the Probation Service. Cultivated within British social services, M&I facilitated activities to instill a sense of empowerment and agency for disenfranchized members of this community. Clients and non-clients of the Probation Service danced with M&I for personal enjoyment and activities that promoted self-esteem. In the 1970s, M&I was part of a burgeoning community of African and Asian writers, sculptors, photographers, musicians, film-makers, and dancers who utilised Handsworth Community Centre (HCC) as the location for their creative renaissance. HCC also began through the efforts of Ramdhanie, to provide a base for national and international exchange of artistic practices that enabled participants to develop creative and credible performance works for mainstream venues. At HCC, M&I members were encouraged to use dance to reclaim an invisibilized heritage as well as resistance against those social and cultural mechanisms that disparaged African diasporic cultural practices and identities.

Facing increasing responsibilities at HCC, Ramdhanie resigned and in response, M&I closed. In May 1978 former M&I members, Pat Donaldson and Hugh Watson, visited Ramdhanie to propose a new beginning for the company (Ramdhanie, 2003, p. 251). It was at this juncture that M&I metaphorically died and formed into the co-operative Kokuma Dance Company, and then Kokuma Performing Arts, in the years between 1978 and 1987 (Ramdhanie, 2003, p. 264). Jackie Guy was artistic director from 1988 to 1995. In conversation, Guy described "Kokuma" as a Ghanaian word meaning "this one will never die" (Guy, 2004). It was in this spirit that Kokuma was reborn with the mandate to become a professional dance company. Kokuma became the site to renew confidence in a cultural heritage and history that its members felt were valuable, more authentic components of who they were.

Both Ramdhanie and Guy's impressions of Kokuma in the 1980s were of a company of young performers with limited professional training opportunities. Both believed that Kokuma's dancers would benefit from activities that encouraged discipline and technical training in Caribbean and African forms and performance (Ramdhanie, 2003). I have been speaking with Guy about his tenure with Kokuma for many years. In reflection in 2015, Guy related that, during the making of *Trails of Ado*, the dancer's cultural politics were responsive to "a wider political context, consciousness, curiosity, yearning and openness" which inspired him to choreograph *Trails of Ado* (Guy, 2015).

The dance works of Kokuma in the early 1980s were of West African origin, particularly Ghana, with lesser influences from the Caribbean and usually presented in display form, meaning that one dance was done after another without an apparent story line. The dances were ethnically relevant to Caribbean and African people while being also universally significant as entertaining. Even with this inclusive artistic vision, the opportunity to perform in mainstream venues proved challenging. Regardless, Ramdhanie states "African Dance nonetheless and the assertion of '*who I am*' found expression and its own niche market amongst black communities within inner city areas" (Ramdhanie, 2003, p. 223).

Ramdhanie was Kokuma's artistic director from 1978 to 1981, Derrick Anderson, from 1981 to 1986, Jackie Guy, from 1988 to 1995 and Patrick Acogny, from 1996 till it closed in 2000. During Anderson's tenure, the late Francis Nii Yartey (1946–2015) choreographed *Abibrimma* along with Barry Moncrieffe's contribution to the production of *Backraman*. These works toured in the 1983–1984 season and initiated Kokuma's progression from display presentations towards dance theatre. *Abibrimma* and *Backraman* used Ghanaian and Caribbean forms respectively to enliven these cultural heritages. Nii-Yartey was a prolific Ghanaian dance practitioner who spoke and wrote of the importance of dance for social and cultural rejuvenation. *Abibrimma* used ethnically specific dance and songs integrated with contemporary poems. It featured a griot who offered anecdotes from the past to encourage individual and community strategies to uplift social and cultural life (Anderson, 2015) Barry Moncrieffe, founder member of National Dance Theatre Company of Jamaica (NDTC) worked closely with Rex Nettleford and shared Nettleford's vision to select ethnically specific gestures as source material to construct modern dance works that reinforced the efficacy of Jamaica's performing arts. In interview, Moncrieffe related that the sessions he led with Kokuma dancers provided the foundational techniques for Jamaican forms like Kumina, Gerreh, and Jonkonnu from which *Backraman* was built (Moncrieffe, 2015). Anderson's *Unwanted Prince* (1984–1985), was the first full-length dance theatre production shared with Watu Wazuri, an African Dance company also based in Birmingham. *Nine Nights* (1985–1986) written by Derrick Anderson continued Kokuma's progression to full-length dance theatre productions.

Ann Fitzgerald writing in *The Stage* and *Television Today* commented that in 1984 Kokuma made history by being "the first British-based Afro-Caribbean company to stage a dance theatre show" (Fitzgerald, 1992). Nii-Yartey, Moncrieffe, and Anderson's choreography utilised African and Caribbean dance, music and song, to embody and perform a preferred, authentic sense of self. Using selected ethnic gestures to fortify Kokuma's repertory became cultural self-defence. This strategy of affirmation enabled self-realisation in dance and ultimately in life.

Forbes comments that Kokuma members found "through dance we could express ourselves." Forbes' experience with Kokuma played a vital part in her growth as an artist as well as her growth as a confident and resourceful human being stating:

The dance had shaped me, the person that I am today; the discipline that I have in my life, it's from those early years. Because if I wasn't dancing I wonder what would have happened to me. (Fordes, 2015)

Forbes also expressed gratitude for the work that Ramdhanie did with Kokuma because Kokuma played such an important role in its members' lives. Kokuma enabled them to shape the livelihood they aspired to. Kokuma for Johnson was a chance, an opportunity for her to take an active part in reclaiming cultural value and self-worth:

We were already Caribbean, we already knew it was a blessing to be Caribbean; our food, our literature, we qualified like any other culture as nurses, actors, right down to cleaners whoever it is, we are equally valued as any other culture. (Johnson, 2015)

Kokuma practitioners devised an artistic vision to actively seek aesthetic clarity in their dance work. Those chosen aesthetic characterisations offered a means to satisfy personal and cultural aspirations in performance on stage and in life. Kokuma dancers evolved a cultural self-defence through dance by changing how people saw and thought about them individually and as a people, as much as the substantiation of the value of Africanist dance practices.

In these early years, every effort was made to provide the resources Kokuma would use to reclaim and refine its identity, collectively and individually. Guy's creative process for *Trails of Ado* was central to this purpose. As a member of National Dance Theatre of Jamaica for 15 years before arriving in Britain in 1985, Guy, like Nettleford, utilised Jamaica's ethnic dance practices as inspiration for dance choreography to assist dancers to fortify self and belief in ethnic heritages. Guy was aware of Kokuma's work in Britain in the early 1980s and, with encouragement from Barry Moncrieffe, Guy accepted the invitation to work with Kokuma to achieve its artistic vision.

TRAILS OF ADO

Trails of Ado (1987) was Guy's first production with Kokuma and arose out of his impressions of Kokuma's potential when he was travelling between Jamaica and Britain in 1985 and 1986. Guy worked with Kokuma to refine their practice of Caribbean traditional ethnic forms. Forbes relates that in 1985 Kokuma already had experience with Caribbean forms taught by Kokuma members, Derrick Anderson and Nicki Reid, who travelled to Jamaica to learn them first hand (Fordes, 2015). Guy relates that, through his efforts, Kokuma's dancers and drummers reinforced and clarified rhythmical sensitivity and significant Caribbean essences (Guy, 2004).

In 1987, Guy developed with Ramdhanie a syllabus for the Black Dance Development Trust (BDDT) 2nd Black Dance Summer School. The theme for the summer school was 'Religion and Religious Rituals'. It was at this summer school that members of Kokuma continued to embody Caribbean and African dance with a focus on sacred gestures. BDDT summer school presented an opportunity for Kokuma members to clarify their Jamaican authenticity, individually and collectively. The gestures learned and performed by the dancers and drummers marked their bodies in specific ways. Gestures learned, muscles and ligaments were recast to become manifestations of what envisioned thoughts apprehended. Corporeality recast, an anatomy for mindful agency was encouraged. With this experience, Guy began work on *Trails of Ado*:

> *The image of Kokuma when I came in was the part I was about to shift. I wrote a production called the Trails of Ado (1987) and basically it was telling about a Jamaican woman who rooted in her cultural life style, came to England, felt alienated in the community. 'Each season she would have a visitation of an ancestor who would remind her of her roots. And so I developed that story'.* (Guy, 2004)

Refining bodily awareness through the inscription of formalised Jamaican dance gestures, movement material gathered from Guy and other master teachers, would mould and shape, and effectively transform the mind, body, and spirit of Kokuma performers. Martha Graham believed:

> *…movement is the most powerful and dangerous art medium known. This is because it is the speech of the basic instrument, the body, which is an instinctive, intuitive, inevitable mirror revealing man as he is.* (Graham, 1941, p. 181)

Training and technique were for Graham a means to spontaneity, strength, and freedom but also training and technique "frees the body to become its ultimate self" (Graham in Rogers, 1941, p. 179). The practice of Jamaican gestures would inspire growth and restructure mind and body to assist performers in Kokuma to realise an ultimate self by illuminating who they were and dreamed of being.

For *Trails of Ado*, Guy used six female dancers, one male and three drummers playing twenty-one different rhythms interspersed with spoken word and ambient music. The theatrical space for *Trails of Ado* was a proscenium arch with the upstage centre cyclorama having a drawing of Queen Nanny and the stage left cyclorama capturing aspirants in the throes of baptism. The work began with a ceremonial procession for the drummers, then a quartet of ancestral female spirits incorporating yanvalou gestures moved across the stage and then exited. They danced barefoot and were dressed in white with arms, hands, and head covered in mesh. A solo figure, Anansi portrayed by Patricia Donaldson, entered the space. This dancer was dressed in a black unitard with a stencil of a spider web on the front and back, with mesh on her face. The movement in arms, torso, and legs was wave-like with balances on one leg between runs and stylized walking. Behind the mesh was a wide grin. Anansi is a Caribbean folk tale trickster figure originating from the West African Akan people (Nehusi, 2015). The Akan people brought Anansi with his knowledge and significances to Jamaica during the times of slavery. Anansi is a conduit for survival techniques and wisdom in difficult circumstances posed and understood through folk tales. The folk tales contained anecdotes and allegory illustrating strategies for living life on one's own terms given the situation. In Jamaica, Anansi works to secure his own goals, sometimes at the expense of friend and foe but his strategies for survival made him a symbol for resistance and ways for defining identity and culture linked to an African past (Zobel, 2012).

Four characters, a working woman, a hysterical woman, a young woman with clenched fist, and a surly man, assume postures indicative of their lifeworld. The drummers engage in a mimed game of dice upstage. The characters gather in a circle holding hands, indicating that they are members of the same community. It is during these movements that Ado, portrayed by Cecelin Forbes, enters. Ado carries a suitcase walking a circuitous path. She is apprehensive while moving through this unfamiliar space, meandering through the characters but not looking at any of them. Ado is searching for her connection to this new place but these people do not help her. As the people leave, Ado runs after them stopping abruptly, a gesture that establishes her disjunctive relationship with this community. Always looking upward, she finally notices something in the distance and exits the stage. The movement for each character is improvised and devised to illustrate different subjectivities. This scene marks Ado as dissimilar and conflicted in this situation.

A dance of traditional Caribbean movements occurs with four women. Ado enters during this dance and introduces herself to the group. The dancers make similar salutations and she joins in their frolic. The group exits and Ado dances a solo. After Ado's solo dance, she sings a sacred hymn. Four characters enter, tease, and laugh at Ado. She castigates them in return while they ignore her and retreat. Ado's danced reactions are a mixture of vehemence and frustration with gestures striking with fists to her side and reaching out and above before collapsing to the floor. Physically and figuratively, Ado has been rejected by the people of this new community. While feeling alone, Ado is visited by an ancestral spirit. The spirit's yanvalou gestures, undulations in arms and torso, encourage Ado to rise from the floor. Ado spins and runs rejuvenated by this apparition, then exits. Ado returns with an altar displaying a white cross. Ado's reverent gestures around the altar beckon followers who enter and position themselves around the altar. Ado has created her own *Revival Band*. Hymns are sung, a sermon delivered accompanied by spiritual possession with full body rhythmical gestures performed individually and in a circle. According to Guy's description, Ado was a member of a Revival band in Jamaica. Revival bands were groups of worshippers connected by their sacred practice.

As the dance continues, Ado attends a wake. Dressed in white and draped in black mesh, she joins the congregation in mourning gestures. The dead person is lifted and carried off stage. In the aftermath, Gerreh dance is staged in ensemble form with group, solo, and duets. Gerreh, as well as the Dinki Mini dance performed afterwards, is of African origin and is traditionally done when someone dies, in the following nine nights after death. The dance is intended to bring cheerfulness to bereaved family and friends. The dance, a deliberate performative act, is in defiance of death and its provocative gestures, rotational pelvic movements with fast feet and pumping action in the chest and arms, suggest the power of procreation as stronger than extinction. In this instance, Gerreh and Dinki Mini are movement metaphors for rejuvenation and resurrection.

The following two dances, Riverside Cass Cass and Warwick Play, illustrate Ado's relationship with her new community. Comfortable in this revised situation, Ado interacts as friend and messenger accompanying others in work and play, advising and offering conciliation and enlightenment. After a member of this community is stricken with illness, Ado administers solace and revives this person. Kumina dance is then performed. Kumina is a traditional Jamaican folk form involving dance, music, and religious practices and beliefs which are derived from Kongo-Angloan, Bantu forms re-imagined for use in the Jamaican context. Kumina, like Gerreh and Dinki Mini serve as a conduit from an African source, strengthening a specific body of gestures to shape a distinct way of being in the world. Kumina rituals, the dance, and music, is embodied specifically to express a range of human experiences. It prominently uses gestures, music, and song as a form of religious and cultural expression to invoke ancestral spirits for possession. The Kokuma dancers were earthy and grounded, even bodacious and articulate, in their performance of Kumina.

As the performance ends Ado has settled into her community as together they take up the mantle of Jamaican ritual and play. Seasonal celebrations are represented in the performance of Burru Masquerade and Jonkonnu Procession. Burru Masquerade is usually enacted during Christmas time. Burru is a fertility rite with provocative rotating action in the hips, enabled with bending of the knees to facilitate the circumduction motion of the pelvis. Jonkonnu Procession is also a Christmas event linking music, dance, mime, and symbolism. According to Cheryl Ryman (1984), Jonkonnu indicates the survival of an African aesthetic in content and context that fostered cultural unity. It is also a medium for reconstructing Africanisms for cultural survival in Jamaica.

It is during the Christmas Day Jonkonnu celebration that Ado disappears. The dancers move around the stage calling "ADO!!" Anansi enters and shifts the mood from desolation to gaiety:

This sudden disappearance frightens and shocks her friends who hail her as "Mother Earth", some feel she is possessed by the spirit of Compong Nanny a legendary Maroon of Jamaica. (Anonymous, ca. 1987/88)[1]

As mentioned above, Queen Nanny is prominently featured as a stencil on the cyclorama and likely a metaphor for Ado. It is appropriate that Ado would be resurrected as Queen Nanny, a female Jamaican national hero immortalised in songs and legends. Queen Nanny was a leader and instrumental in staving off the British with her methods of guerrilla warfare and spiritual cunning in the first Maroon War in Jamaica in the early 1700s. The Maroons traced their roots to West Africa. Isolated in the mountains of Jamaica, Queen Nanny became the personae and symbol of African resilience for Maroon people and the Jamaican populace because her legend kept the oral traditions and history of Africa alive. Recalling her roots by the visitation of spiritual ancestors, and practicing Jamaican rites and rituals in Britain, Ado becomes the embodiment of Jamaican culture. Ado's beliefs in her ethnic heritage assist her to build a tenable existence in her newfound community in Britain. Then she disappears. Ado's disappearance becomes an affirmation for her British community encouraging individual and collective cultural revitalization.

Jackie Guy is quoted as saying in 1989 "You can't do dance and music outside of a culture so history is quite important." Guy indicates that ethnic specific gestures have a space inclusive of time and situation that fosters their existence. Any endeavour to use ethnic specific gestures removed from space of origin must consider the root source and how those configurations will benefit a new space. Guy believed that dancers of Kokuma "have to use what they learn from the Caribbean and make it meaningful to their environment because the cosmic energies in Africa and the Caribbean are different from here in England" (Adjoe, 1989, pp. 7–8). Guy knew that Kokuma's collective diasporic experiences combined Caribbean and British permutations. *Trails of Ado* was created to illustrate this dialectical societal reality. It placed varied encounters and interactions, Caribbean and British, in an imagined space to describe a challenging life- world. The storytelling is episodic, revealing the seemingly insurmountable tensions that Ado endures to keep her traditional beliefs and identifications alongside the urban, secularised modernity proposed in the dance. Ado wants to fit in, with her ethnicity and authentic self intact, but her transition from Jamaica to Britain is disjunctive and intolerable. Ado guards her beliefs as she re-inscribes memory, symbol, myth, and ancestral teachings into her present situation. Searching for a community of likeminded citizens in her new British context, Ado seeks, defines, and sets the parameters for her situation.

Ado becomes a window into an imagined life world. Mimed situations enact varied subjectivities and assist the narration to illustrate alienation, desolation, fortitude, and rejuvenation as Ado passes through each scene. Authentic ethnic gestures situate each experience as they prepare and sustain Ado marking each occasion; worshiping, death, seasonal festivity, and then resurrection. The process of making and performing *Trails of Ado* provides a view and a reflection which enables a desired manifestation of the self; a subjectivity actively appraising itself and its circumstance. The Jamaican attributes, gestures, music, and song, are in the dancers and drummers who comprise Kokuma because those attributes are embodied and believed in. To learn these dances, embody these gestures with significance, is to become a cultural manifestation; to become Ado, affirming her culture, her imagined self aligned with Jamaican authenticity, physically, kinesthetically, and mindfully immersed.

It was Guy's intention to not only choreograph a dance work with high production values but also of significance for the dancers and the community they performed for. Writing in the *Birmingham Post* regarding Kokuma and Guy's choreography, *Trails of Ado*, Terry Grimley (1987) stated that the dancers are all British-born and attracted to dance as a means of exploring their cultural roots. Guy was quoted as saying:

> *it's not just doing the movements, it's understanding the story and uniting all the elements to communicate to the audience.* (Grimley, 1987)

Trails of Ado allowed dancers to investigate their personal histories and offered some audience members a reflection of themselves.

As mentioned above, in 1984 Kokuma was producing dance theatre that had multiple resonances for performers and audiences alike. Ann Fitzgerald states that the choreography for Kokuma benefited from Guy's expertise of African and Caribbean dance forms gained from NDTC but he tapped both forms to build cultural identity:

> *His (Guy's) choreography uses both, and grafts on to their roots what he calls "the Black-British experience" to create a unique style of dance which has earned Kokuma ecstatic reviews and enthusiastic audiences.* (Fitzgerald, 1992)

The dancing body embodied an imagined identity sought for in the British context but allusive for these individuals in their lived experiences. *Trails of Ado* moved Kokuma towards a modern dance theatre expression by using authentic Jamaican forms to rejuvenate British subjectivity.

> *Bodies that dance and move feelings in others are "modern," if not always "modernist," bodies—shapers of identities whose political stakes emerged with the help of ideological analysis. Although the history of the relation of bodies to ideologies is a long one, feelings themselves, when set into motion, are the ideologies of modern bodies, and their dance exposes ideology itself at work on embodied subjects.* (Franko, 1997, p. 491)

Mark Franko's words indicate that the dancing body's ability to comment on ideals regarding subjectivity is a modern approach to dance-making. Guy's approach to making *Trails of Ado* is similarly used by other modern dance choreographers, such as Dr Pearl Primus, who privileged

Fig. 7.2 Kokuma Performing Arts 1987. Left to right standing: Jackie Guy, Christine Seymour-costume seamstress, Desmond Pusey, Patricia Donaldson, Cecelin Johnson, Doreen Forbes, Jacqueline Bailey, Pete Barrett-stage management, Eky Charley-administrator, Tracey Finch-clerical staff; Kneeling musicians: left to right: Silbert Dormer, Gladston Foster, Tony Reid. Kokuma Studio, 163 Gerrard Street, Lozells, Brimingham B19 2AH. Photographer Philip Grey

authentic ethnic source material to construct alternative visions of or comment on modern living. Myth, symbols, memories, and ancestral connection exposed and re-inscribed identities. Performers as well as audience members recognised these theatrical manifestations as re-definitions for nationalism, statehood, ethnic, and racial identity (Fig. 7.2).

Conclusion

Kokuma dancers through their performance of *Trails of Ado* reclaimed an authenticity in dance practice that was diffused and disbursed but not lost. The movements seen in the dancers marked their bodies in specific ways. Gestures learned, muscles and ligaments recast, became manifestations of what thoughts apprehended. Lived experience and performance shaped agency, encouraged through classes and rehearsals where company members clarified an authentic self.

It is of immense value to perform or to see an authentic dance in its circumstance. A theatricalized rendition composed to enrich identity with its root culture in a differing society is of immeasurable benefit also. In Britain, in the 1980s, the use of authentic Jamaican dance forms as a storytelling device was exceptional and, for some, revolutionary. The use of authentic ethnic gestures in the manner utilised in *Trails of Ado* empowered Kokuma members' sense of self and heritage. This enrichment extended to the Jamaican British citizens and all populations that Kokuma performed for. As an effective means for cultural self-defence, the process of choreographing *Trails of Ado* allowed Kokuma members, dancers, and drummers, to investigate their own personal histories in a fulfilling way on the quest to self-realisation. Guy's modern approach to using authentic Jamaican gestures, music, and song was the means to this goal. The characters portrayed in different situations demonstrated how the discovery or recollection of root sources enabled cultural self-defence.

Note

1. Notes found at the University of Surrey Archives & Special Collections, offer this summation.

References

Adjoe. (1989, August 31). Homage to Caribbean Dance on the Southbank. *Caribbean Times Incorporating African Times, 31*, 7–8.

Anderson, D. (2015, December 15). *About Kokuma's First Efforts Towards Dance Theatre/Interviewer: T. Barnes*.

Anonymous. (1987/88). *Papers found in Kokuma Collection* [KO/E/42/17]. Archives and Special Collections. University of Surrey, University Library, George Edwards Building, Guildford, Surrey GU2 7XH, United Kingdom.

Birt, R. E. (2002). *The Quest for Community and Identity : Critical Essays in Africana Social Philosophy*. Lanham, MD: Rowman & Littlefield Publishers.

DuBois, W. E. B. (1903/2016, April 20). *The Souls of Black Folk*. Irvine, CA: Xist Publishing. Coterie Classics.

Fanon, F., & Markmann, C. L. (1967). *Black Skin, White Masks*. New York: Grove Press.

Filitz, T., & Saris, A. J. (2013). *Debating Authenticity: Concepts of Modernity in Anthropological Perspective*. New York: Berghahn Books.

Fitzgerald, A. (1992, June 4). The Toast of Many Colours. *The Stage and Television Today*, (5799), p. 26.

Fordes, D. (2015, August 26). *Kokuma/Interviewer: T. Barnes*.
Fraleigh, S. H. (1987). *Dance and the Lived Body*. Pittsburgh, PA: University of Pittsburgh Press.
Franko, M. (1997). Nation, Class, and Ethnicities in Modern Dance of the 1930s. *Theatre Journal, 49*(4), 475–491. https://doi.org/10.1353/tj.1997.0102.
Graham, M. (1941). *Dance: A Basic Educational Technique*. (F. R. Rogers, Ed. [*With Plates*]). New York: Macmillan.
Grimley, T. (1987, October 24). Handsworth Troupe Give Black Dance a Big Boost, Review. *The Birmingham Post*.
Guy, J. (2004, November). *Southbank Centre Interview/Interviewer: T. Barnes*.
Guy, J. (2015, May 23). Questions Regarding Kokuma [E-mail]. Message to Guy, J.
Johnson, C. (2015, October 30). *About Kokuma/Interviewer: T. Barnes*.
Moncrieffe, B. (2015, December 16). *About Backra Man/Interviewer: T. Barnes*.
Nehusi, K. S. K. (2015). Animal Folk Tales. In M. J. Shujaa & K. J. Shujaa (Eds.), *The Sage Encyclopedia of African Cultural Heritage in North America* (pp. 310–314). Thousand Oaks, CA: Sage Publications.
Nettleford, R. M. (1985). *Dance Jamaica: Cultural Definition and Artistic Discovery: The National Dance Theatre Company of Jamaica, 1962–1983*. New York: Grove.
Profitt, R. (1984). Equal Respect, Equal Treatment and Equal Opportunity. In J. Benyon (Ed.), *Scarman and After* (pp. 200–206). Oxford, UK: Pergamon.
Ramdhanie, R. (2003). *African Dance in England – Spirituality and Continuity*. Doctor of Philosophy, University of Warwick.
Ryman, C. (1984). Jonkonnu: A Neo-African Form, Part II. *Jamaica Journal, 17*(2), 50–61.
Sartre, J. -P. (1948; renewed 1976). *Anti-Semite and Jew*. New York: Schocken, 1995.
Scarman, L. S. B. (1982). *The Scarman Report : The Brixton Disorders 10–12 April 1981: Report of an Inquiry*. Harmondsworth: Penguin.
Steiner, C. J., & Reisinger, Y. (2006). Understanding Existential Authenticity. *Annals of Tourism, 33*(2), 299–318.
Yacobi, B. G. (2012). The Limits of Authenticity. *Philosophy Now, 92*, 28–30.
Zobel Marshall, E. (2012). *Anansi's Journey: A Story of Jamaican Cultural Resistance*. Kingston, Jamaica: University of the West Indies Press.

CHAPTER 8

Moving Tu Balance: An African Holistic Dance as a Vehicle for Personal Development from a Black British Perspective

Sandra Golding

> It is the desire to know one's body, to live in the body, to obey it and its natural experiences, in full awareness, without the use of drugs. It is to have the courage to respect laws which are not always of logic, the irrational being one of the privileged languages of the body.
> (Tierou, 1992, p. 12)

In traditional dance training, the body is often something that needs to be mastered. However, the symbolic nature of movement, the relationship with land and water and the survival of ancient cultural ceremonial dances from the Caribbean and Africa has enabled me to embody a deeper dance. I would like to present this chapter as a biography and testimony to my experiences as a performer, practitioner and instructor in the creative aspects of African and Caribbean traditional dance forms, starting at the very beginnings of my journey with dance as a child. The embodiment of my moving experience has evolved over many years. As a first generation Black British Jamaican, I have been strongly influenced by my rediscovery of the ancient wisdom, symbolism, spirituality and history of African and

S. Golding (✉)
Independent artist, Birmingham, UK

Caribbean culture—all of which has shaped my embodiment of dance, and has been consolidated through my undertaking of an academic study of Somatic Movement Education.

My Journey into Dance

I was born and raised in Birmingham, where there is a strong Caribbean community that arrived in Britain from the 1950s onwards to become a vital part of the British workforce. Of course, they brought their rich cultural traditions with them. As a first generation Black British Jamaican, I grew up in an environment where music and dance played a very important role in everyone's life through weddings, christenings, funerals and any other celebratory event, be it religious or secular. My parents once told me that when I was a young child they were specifically advised that I should engage in formal dance training, under doctors' orders, which my parents and I believe assisted my recovery from varying health issues that I had developed. Thus, I feel that I can locate the beginnings of my journey through the therapeutic aspects of dance at a very early age. Some of my fondest memories are of my early dance classes when we got to dance to live piano. I felt so inspired and to this day I try to incorporate live music as much as possible into my teaching.

Reflecting on these memories I can see how dance has been my medicine, my doctor/therapist and my nurturer. I am so grateful to all of my dance teachers who used movement to assist me through my earliest therapeutic experience of healing through dance.

My love of dance continued throughout my secondary education both inside and outside of school where I was involved in tap, ballet and freestyle. I joined a local dance group for children and we performed at various church events and numerous celebrations within the African-Caribbean community.

The African Dance Class

I worked hard on my ballet dance technique as a young person and in January 1980 I had the opportunity to set up my own ballet classes at the Handsworth Cultural Centre in Birmingham in order to give young people, particularly but not exclusively young people from my community, the opportunity to get involved in the arts. One day, after attending a meeting with a man called Bob Ramdhanie who worked at the Handsworth

Cultural Centre, I was drawn to the sound of drumming upstairs on the first floor. I went up and looked through the small window in the door to the dance studio and saw a group of African drummers and dancers. I was immediately awestruck by what I witnessed. I watched the dancers move with such energy, power and grace. Their passion was infectious and I could feel the energy coursing through my mind and body. I felt the energy and the rhythm of the drums literally vibrating through my bones. One of the dancers was so moved that for quite a few minutes she seemed to be standing in a heightened state of awareness. She reminded me of the Pentecostal Christians, when building up energy through ecstatic song and dance, waiting for the Holy Spirit to fall and fill their bodies and souls! Something at the core of me was woken up that day! There and then I tried performing a sequence of steps that I saw. But it was quite challenging because my body seemed stiff and clumsy in its movement. At that time in my life, I wanted to be a professional ballet dancer and yet at that very moment I felt more than I could physically do. I found that despite my training in a variety of dance styles my body lacked a sense of coordination. Yet I felt an instant connection with this dance and, although it was new to me, it changed my dance practice forever.

I was invited to watch the dancers and musicians rehearse a range of traditional African and Caribbean dances, where they played drums with their hands and as well as sticks while singing. On entering the room, I remember the smell of incense, seeing a small bottle of white rum on the floor, along with a white candle and a glass of water on a shelf in the corner of the room—which I learned were the ritual aspect of purification of the space and honour to ancestors. I remember that they were Rastafarian men who drummed and the women's heads were wrapped with African fabric which was also tied around their waists. They told me they had just come back from Jamaica where they went to learn about their culture through the music and dance. Fortunately, they were warm-hearted and radiated a friendly vibe towards me—it was easy to feel a connection with them as most of them, like myself, were the first Black British generation. One dance that they performed was the '*Kumina*'—a Congo-derived traditional folk dance form that involves ritual and is played on specially made Kumina drums made by the Maroons. Stories of being descendants of St Thomas Maroons have been part of my family oral history, where they fought in the Morant Bay rebellion, then moving up into the hills of the Blue Mountain. I feel a particular affinity with Kumina because of my family history—this expresses itself and comes alive connecting with earthy dance movements. I was invited to attend a dance workshop and evening performance the following week. I was very excited as I was going to learn the original dance of my ancestors and maybe find out which part of Africa my ancestors were from, as I didn't know at the time. In reflection, I now see this first session as my initiation and the beginning of my decolonisation through African music and dance.

During the workshop I felt that when we danced to the music of the drums we became spiritually and culturally enriched. This was the start of learning about my root culture and heritage through traditional West Africa dances and those from Jamaica. In 1980, I auditioned and became a member of Kokuma Dance Theatre Company, who specialised in the retention of African and Caribbean culture through music and dance in Birmingham, first under the Artistic direction of Bob Ramdhanie and then, after his departure in 1981, Derrick Anderson and Isaac Banda. The company became my extended family. It instilled very strong principles and values, giving us a sense of purpose and identity. Through the medium of African-Caribbean dance, we were given artistic tools to become ambassadors and positive role models within the community and throughout the West Midlands.

I performed with the company for a further two years, then left in 1983, after which I enrolled on a three-year training programme at a classical dance school in London. I was introduced to Classical Ballet, Traditional European English folkdances, Modern Contemporary and Jazz dance forms. After completing training, I auditioned for a contemporary dance school but was rejected because of my body type. I also auditioned for Jazz dance jobs and was rejected sometimes because of the colour of my skin. These things hurt me a lot especially as I had invested so much time and energy to become accepted into the UK performing arts industry. It seemed like a world that was not providing many opportunities for people from my cultural background, let alone a woman. To compound this, having learned a variety of dance forms, I began to experience a cultural conflict in my physical movement identity, which left me feeling confused and frustrated.

My next step forward began when I became involved in a community dance theatre company that worked in special needs schools, where I began to get more experience of teaching within the community. I also became involved with several other Black dance companies and organisations based in London with the aim of raising the awareness of the contribution of the African diaspora to world civilisation and the arts. I eventually returned to Birmingham as there were fantastic training opportunities with the Black Dance Development Trust. I re-joined Kokuma Dance Theatre Company in 1988, under the direction of Jackie Guy and had a flourishing performing career. This was an incredibly empowering time for me as I became the principle dance performer.

We worked hard to maintain the community spirit of the dance company and were inspired by current social themes within the Black British community—which were well received. This time in my life reminds me of the documentary film *Rize* (2005), about young people in Los Angeles, USA, where the young people's dance is both therapeutic and healing as it manifests creatively through ritual, and artistically expressed through movement, rhythm and music. These ritualistic dance styles were seen as a constructive outlet and alternative form of expression to channel the anger, aggression and frustration of young people in a non-violent way instead of engaging in drugs, violence or gang activity.

This was also evident in Kokuma's productions whose themes were always silently political. In the rise of African dance in the black communities in the UK, communicating through music, song and dance theatre was a creative way of tackling issues that were effecting the youth and people of the African and Caribbean community. The performances at the time incorporated elements of ritual, symbolism, spirituality, celebration, conflict and resolution in order to educate audiences about the Black British experience.

When I danced, I occasionally had what could be described as 'out of body experiences', where I felt as though my spirit came out of my body and I could see myself dancing from above—such was my spiritual connection to the dance that allowed the release of the stresses of balancing family life and that of work as a performing artist.

In 1994, Kokuma represented Birmingham in a festival in Leipzig when we performed at the Schauspielhaus Theatre. The review *'Endless Pleasure of Movement'* encapsulated the essence and the energy of the company when it recognised the retention of traditional dance forms within an integrated, intercultural experience.

> *The artists originate from the English industrial city and the communication between the drums and the bodies of the dancers reveal their African roots, the mixture of mime and body language and a varying amount of dance forms mixed with some ritualised patterns verging on the dramatic. They proved that Black dance in Birmingham had preserved its authenticity and had not*

sacrificed itself to the 'European norm. (Micheal Hametner Buhne Leipzig Newspaper May, 1994)

After many years of successful performances and outreach work, the company funding and contracts were not renewed and the company was finally dissolved a few years later. The funding priorities of the Arts Council had changed. The two major flagship companies for African Dance practice closed and there seemed to be no longer any support for the cultural dance forms of the Black British community. This was the end of an era for me and such a difficult time.

However, it propelled me to strike out on my own as an outreach dance artist, performer and community worker. I set up my own regular dance classes in and around Birmingham to encourage women of all ages, ethnicities and abilities to find their strength and cultural ground through African-Caribbean dance. This was when I embarked on an even deeper journey to find more balance and depth in my dance; one that embraced and reflected living in a multicultural and diverse community and one that I could use to support women in their own personal development.

In order to find and maintain a balance during my own artistic development, it was important for me to reconnect with the elders and cultural activists in my community. In 2004 in Birmingham, there was an open panel discussion with a gathering of African scholars from around the world speaking about spirituality verses religion. The only African female on the panel from a shamanic background sat very quietly. She spoke about bringing African spirituality into the twenty-first century to make it relevant by using our creativity, skills and tools that we had around us to foster change and growth in our communities. She talked about work that needed to take place as many had not gone through rites of passage because of loss of culture and traditions caused by enslavement. Her words vibrated with my own values within my dance and heritage. I resonated with her instantly as she spoke of connecting to our ancestors to connect us to nature; through ritual choreography, releasing energetic blocks in our lives and that of our descendants, to realign our ancestral line and heal DNA on a cellular level. She had a vision that healing villages were set up outside major cities throughout the UK where families could meet away from the inner city in countryside and coastal areas. The activities in the healing villages would involve dancing, chanting and singing for extended periods of time to traditional drumming. This is similar to retreats that I have organised over the years in the Wye forest, on the border of England

and Wales, where women came to temporarily escape manic city life to find grounding within themselves through Africanist healing dance and drumming.

I went on to complete a Masters of Arts in Somatic Movement Education at University of Central Lancashire (UCLAN) in Preston. Through that training, I began to learn academically the therapeutic use and value of dance. Although I identified with its concepts, I struggled because of the lack of acknowledgement to Africa and its place in this field. I felt that everything had been taught from an Eastern and Western philosophical perspective. However, I had lectures by Martha Eddy. After sharing some of my background with her, my passion and vision of working with women using the power of movement to improve health and wellbeing grew even stronger. Martha Eddy confirmed that what I'd described was somatic and she then brought my attention to the African influence in the development of 'Continuum'; a somatic practice by Emily Conrad who focused on biological experiences in movement and had written about her African-Caribbean experience in Haiti in order for Westerners to understand somatic movement from an African-Caribbean perspective. Knowing this gave me great hope, as I realised I was not alone in developing a somatic movement programme as an African concept.

My technique of 'African Healing Dance', is a synthesis of African and Caribbean dance and Somatic Movement Education through movement processes that allow individuals the opportunity to creatively discover healthier ways of wellbeing through the reconnection and understanding of the body, was born out of my studies at UCLAN. I realised that the fundamental movement activities and theory within somatic movement and dance therapy are often rooted in different African dance ideologies, and yet they are not always accredited as such. For example: the importance of ritual to maintain a safe therapeutic space, catharsis, purification, witnessing, 'holding' the space, movement reflection, early development movements to establish coordination and balance, stories through movement, honouring ancestors, community, circle dances, rhythm, chanting, breath work and group leader using observation and instinct to address the needs of the participants.

> *The entire repertoire of our life experiences can be accessed and activated through the body in movement. Since movement is the primary language of the body, moving brings us to deeper feelings and memories. The way in which we move also reveals disabling and repetitive patterns. Whatever resides in our*

body, despair, confusion, fear, anger, joy—will come up when we express ourselves in movement. (Halprin, 2003, pp. 17–18)

Thus I found that I already had the practical tools I needed to be a somatic movement practitioner!

In 2009, during my studies in UCLAN, I conducted research into African somatic movement on a physical level with a group of women in Birmingham in the UK. It was a chance for me to find a somatic context for the development of 'African Healing Dance' rooted in African and Caribbean culture. I also saw it as my official start in introducing the concept of Somatic Movement Education into my community through the medium of African and Caribbean dance. African Healing Dance (as it was named at the time) was aimed at connecting women and communities, in order to rediscover the healing qualities of movements that naturally lie within every woman. I worked to create a safe space; an important ritual aspect of African and Caribbean dances and one that serves to give the individuals the opportunity to rediscover an awareness of the potential and power of their movement.

During this time, I developed the concept of 'Ankh Ku Maat—life moving tu balance' in my practice, which was inspired by my research into ancient Egyptian mythology, Kundalini. I discovered in my body a system of movement by exploring releasing movements within the shape of the ancient Egyptian symbol of the 'Ankh' (key of life) combined with that of the snake. It involves meditation, breath work and undulating movements of the spine with a focus on the heart area of the body—which in ancient Egyptian belief is the seat of the mind. Also at this time, I explored the concept of 'Continuum', as mentioned earlier, which is based on the theory that as humans we carry memory of our ancient primordial selves in our DNA. This was interesting work as the women in my study explored early developmental movements such as crawling, wriggling and undulating the spine.

My participants fed back to me that they felt engaged with their inner core and felt strengthened by the work. One lady even declared that her usual backache had subsided. Once making the connection to the power of undulating movements in the body of the Yenvalou and the rhythmic patterns and movements of the Kumina, I found it was very organic and consolidated the creative-transformative aspect of African and Caribbean dance in my sessions. It focused specifically on the essence quality and embodiment of the dance forms to further develop the practice.

I also incorporated into my practice the theoretical influences of Bonnie Bainbridge Cohen, an art and movement therapist. In her words:

The explorer is the mind, our thoughts, feelings, energy, soul and spirit. Through this journey we are led to an understanding of how the mind is expressed through the body of movement. (Cohen, 1993, p. 1)

This inspired me to explore how our bodies can express inner stories through movement. Through this, I discovered the power of self-actualisation by what is known in Western movement therapy forms as Authentic Movement, accredited to Mary Starks Whitehouse. Thus 'African Healing Dance' at the time was not just a physical dance; it worked to engage the entire being. At this point in the development of the practice, 'African Healing Dance' changed to 'African Holistic Dance'.

This holistic, synthesised, somatic movement approach allowed the individual to embrace the spirit of dance in community as well as a space to 'just be' in a supportive environment. It involved opportunities to create, share and witness movement experiences within the sacred space of the circle. It was a chance for catharsis and telling individual stories through movement.

It was important that a safe and positive space was created and this normally takes the shape of a circle where the dancer/s were invited to move in the middle. Circle dancing is a prevalent feature in my sessions as a circle symbolises the world, the village and the connection of life in many African cultures. In Egyptian mythology and philosophy, the symbol of the circle is shown with a dot in the centre representing the creator that 'Projects itself onto itself; at the time of creation the outer circle, the cosmos is created.' (Ashby, 1996, p. 52).

Moving Tu Balance: Standing in Your Cultural Ground—A Sacred Space

'African Holistic Dance' began to emerge as a spiritual practice, a vehicle for inner change with the potential to support one's personal growth and a tool for liberation. This practice has now evolved into '*Moving Tu Balance*'. It is still evolving out of ancient wisdom; drawing from the vibrant and subtle energies of Africa, while sustaining a deep and strong connection to the earth and the universe through movement, music, ritual and visualisation. 'Standing in your cultural ground' is a more recent concept that I have nurtured in my practice and one that strongly defines *Moving Tu Balance*. This takes place through songs, chants and moving freely in the space. Its purpose is learning the importance of having a sense of really being grounded and remembering to walk with energy, depth and purpose. The empowerment of standing in your cultural ground comes from being aware of the connection to our ancestors, our culture, our personal beliefs and values, knowing who we really are, knowing what we really want, not being afraid of what we are truly capable of, and standing firmly on that ground. Standing in your cultural ground can also be a literal feeling of being 'grounded' or connected to the earth through the feet.

Moving Tu Balance uses traditional African movements to connect the body specifically with the elements of the earth. This universal relationship of the body with the earth aligns itself well with the somatic work of grounding at both the beginning and end of my somatic sessions in *Moving Tu Balance*. Drawing on traditional African movements to ground and connect specifically promotes our sense of grounded movement quite literally on the earth as we move through our daily lives. The dancer is at one with the earth mother and the whole world (Tierou, 1992, p. 53)

> *This love and respect for the earth is one of the main factors of African dance. It gives a certain vitality and dynamic strength, for it draws up into the dancer the unlimited force and ecstasy of the earth.* (Primus, 1996, p 7)

This experience reaffirms the connection and is at the core of Moving Tu Balance, as my aim is to help people to stand in their truth, find their feet in the world and stand in their cultural ground.

The African Diaspora and Development of New Dances

Between the sixteenth and nineteenth century the slave trade, driven by Europeans at that time of world history, forced the migration of groups of Africans who became displaced from their native cultural groups and found themselves in the company of African peoples from other areas of Africa. These displaced people were forced to disown their music (through the banning of the drum) rituals and traditional cultural practices for a new religion of Christianity, which had a value system very different to their traditional beliefs. Initially the suppression of dance in many cultures resulted in an imbalance in those spiritual, communal and interpersonal qualities that regulate the individual and societies (Monteiro & Wall, 2001, p. 237). However, both in the Caribbean and the Americas, the influences of Europe crossing with those of Africa gave rise to new dances that expressed their history along with traditional dances and rituals that survived the middle passage. Gaining an awareness of European and African culture and the history of the slave trade has enabled the development of my clinical practice of *Moving Tu Balance* because I carry the personal belief that many women in the modern Western world are experiencing a type of slavery. Slaves to the idea of being a 'superwoman' who is physically beautiful, young looking, well educated, has a well-paid career, is a perfect mother, has a perfect marriage, manages completely independently or even puts off having a family for the sake of a career.

Moving Tu Balance aims to provide an opportunity for us to connect to and nurture our feminine self with other women in a strong, grounded, proud and passionate way.

I want to highlight aspects of what I referred to earlier as 'ancient wisdom' and 'cross-culture', to further frame *Moving Tu Balance* within a cultural and historical context. I have learned that in order to understand the origin of dance, as well as the roots and the benefits of dance therapy/therapeutic experience, we have to look back to move forward. This reminds me of the West African image and symbol of Sankofa; a bird whose body is facing forward with its head looking back to its tail. It is described (by Willis, 1998, p. 189) as a realisation of self and spirit. It is said to symbolise self-identity, redefinition and an understanding our own destiny and the collective identity of the cultural group we are in. Sankofa also relates to the Ghanaian proverb 'Se wo were fi no wo sankofa a yenki', which means 'It is not wrong to go back for that which you have forgotten'. I incorporated the Sankofa principle as an aid in my clinical practice because I aim to be like the Sankofa bird by delving backwards in order to reach out to all women in particular. I found it important to look back cross-culturally, seeing how other cultures have contributed to dance movement through the ages and use this history to enhance my life and the lives of others.

The healing aspects of dance can even be seen in the ceremonial dances of Ancient Egypt, Greece, and many other Indigenous cultures. These dances, along with the movements of yoga from India, Chi gong and Ti Chi from China integrate the heart, mind, body and spirit. Many of these dances and movement practices have a strong connection to nature and the cosmos, which works to provide healing and cohesion within communities and an understanding of the environments that people live in. Ritual aspects of dance were (and still are in some indigenous communities) part of inspiring spiritual voyages and gaining strength for important events within the community and dance was usually integrated with music, song, storytelling and painting; all of which have existed as a form of communication and expression that has been passed down through the generations of human knowledge, wisdom and traditions within most cultures.

In order to create a balanced approach to the work, it is important to gain more of an understanding of the cultural experience of others. Modern dance can be seen as a form of communication, healing and therapy for young people in deprived communities. Today we have hip hop, Krumping, break dancing and other urban dance cultures have been assimilated and this continuously evolving style can now be seen in cultures all over the world and practised in diverse communities. This genre of movement expression, originating in the African American community, has its roots from practices of the West African culture. According to Monteiro & Wall (2001, p. 248), this physical expression of emotion lessens feelings of vulnerability and offers a channel to release negative emotions and work through feelings of deprivation and pain. This cathartic experience is particularly beneficial given the traumatic social context of these communities. Through this I see the importance in understanding how the mind, body and spirit work with the culture of the client group, while working cross-culturally in African somatic movement. I believe that this is therapeutic at a community level as it has been an essential part of many communities' daily life in all cultures throughout the world in the past. For me, it is important to integrate the *Moving Tu Balance* form into our various cultures. The relevance today is how it can be used to positively assist the healing of our minds and bodies in a busy urban context.

I feel that it is an innate human desire and a deep-seated need for people to find healing and identity through dance. Since the beginning of time, both the healing process and artistic expression albeit through dance, has enabled us to experience, connect and express on varying levels of emotions and feelings. Dance can be seen as a universal language and has assisted in the shaping and reshaping the history of different cultures around the world.

> ... dance is human, and humanity almost universally expresses itself in dance. (Hanna, 1987, p. 3)

I feel that this statement truly encapsulates what my practice of *Moving Tu Balance* is about. It's about creating a space where people can learn how to safely release and express their emotions, give physical form to their inner self within a supportive community. How to use dance, movement and music to express inner-self and even safely find catharsis is something so lacking in modern British culture. The fact that the movements are African-derived offers people of all ethnicities a route, the same direct path to the core that I have found. A route that many people sense in dance: to find the universal language of dance as a meaningful form of communication. It is why dance has formed part of human existence and co-existence, social interactions and wellbeing since ancient times. Dance helps us in understanding and accepting the human condition as belonging to both the earth and spirit.

REFERENCES

Ashby, M. (1996). *Egyptian Yoga. The Philosophy of Enlightenment* (p. 52). Miami, FL: Cruzian Mystic Books.

Cohen, B. B. (1993). *Sensing Feeling and Action: The Experimental Anatomy of Body- Mind Centering.* Northhampton, MA: Contact Editions.

Halprin, D. (2003). *The Expressive Body in Life, Art and Therapy: Working with Movement* (pp. 17–18). London: Jessica Kingsley Publishers.

Hametner, M. (1994). *Buhne Leipzig Newspaper* (p. 5).

Hanna, J. (1987). *To Dance Is Human: A Theory of Nonverbal Communication* (p. 3). Chicago: The University of Chicago Press.

Monteiro, N. M., & Wall, D. J. (2001, September). African Dance as Healing Modality Throughout the Diaspora: The Use of Ritual and Movement to Work Through Trauma. *The Journal of Pan African Studies, 4*(6), 237–248.

Primus, P. (1996). *African Dance: An Artistic Historical and Philosophical Inquiry* (Kariamu Welsh Asante, Ed., p. 7). Trenton, NJ: Africa World Press.

Tierou, A. (1992). *Dooplé: The Eternal Law of African Dance* (pp. 12–53). Philadelphia, PA, Harwood Academic Publishers.

Willis, W. B. (1998). *The Adikra Dictionary: Visual Primer on the Language of a Adinkra* (p. 189). Washington, DC: The Pyramid Complex Publishers.

CHAPTER 9

'Why I Am Not a Fan of the Lion King': Ethically Informed Approaches to the Teaching and Learning of South African Dance Forms in Higher Education in the United Kingdom

Sarahleigh Castelyn

INTRODUCTION

I teach on a university programme in London that requires students to explore popular and social dance practices. Whenever I introduce myself to students studying on a module that includes South African dance styles as its focus, I start the session by projecting a Peters world map, particularly as it attempts to portray 'countries and thereof in more correct size perspective' (Johnson, 2007, p. 60). I point out the routes I have taken that have led me to standing at that moment in front of them as a lecturer. I show how we are here—London—and I am from there—Pietermaritzburg, a small town in South Africa—and I left there to come here—London—

A version of this essay originally appeared in the *South African Dance Journal*, Vol. 2, Issue 1, Winter 2013, 1–19. Thank you to the editor of the said journal for copyright permission to publish this adaptation.

S. Castelyn (✉)
University of East London, London, UK

and I danced there—Durban, a major port in South Africa—and how now I dance here—London—and how I will be teaching about dance from there—South Africa, a country at the bottom-end of Africa—and they will be learning it here—in Great Britain, an island off the western coast of Europe. The university's dance studios are based in the East End of London that historically has—and is still—a location for immigrant communities. All of this makes the site of the dance studios an evocative location to study popular and social dance and related concerns such as 'cultural appropriation' (Glasser, 1993, p. 183) especially African and African Diasporic dance practices, and their relationship to and with dominant cultures from predominantly North American and Western Europe. Moreover, academic study of dance has over-privileged theatre/art dance, but particularly theatre/art dance from North America and Western Europe: '[i]n terms of dance practice, it is the serious endeavour of art dance that is awarded high levels of cultural values and, as several dance scholars reflect, the discipline of dance studies has perpetuated the hegemony of the canon' (Dodds, 2011, p. 19). Dodds' book is on popular dance and aims to 'show how and why popular dance exists within a system of values' (Dodds, 2011, p. 4) and her exploration of the value systems could be adopted and extended to consider all dance forms that have been excluded from the canon, such as the 'wide variety of dance genres and styles' (Friedman, 2009, p. 139) from South Africa. 'South Africa's dancescape has a rich cultural diversity, spanning traditional forms in African ritual dances as well as Western or European dance forms such as ballroom and ballet' (Craighead, 2006, pp. 22–23).

I am committed to opening up the academic study of dance to include all forms and practices and this includes my desire to introduce students in the United Kingdom to a diversity of dances from South Africa because, to understand South African culture, students need to study South African dances from not only the stages, but also dances from the screens and the streets of South Africa. Dance forms in South Africa are as diverse as its people are. There are traditional dance practices, such as Ingoma, that draws on Zulu warrior training with its 'high frontal kick' (Meintjies, 2004, p. 174) and is 'a style of competitive display' (Meintjies, 2004, p. 78). There is langarm, an Afrikaans dance style that has its roots in European folk dances, sometimes accompanied by musicians playing guitars and concertinas, or 'mainstream and "golden oldie" songs that

[...are...] danced as a two-step or quick-step' (Visser, 2010, p. 180). There are contemporary dance companies such as Flatfoot Dance Company that '[work] from a contemporary based training that includes Graham, Hawkins and Release Technique [...] ballet [...and] traditional African dance' (Flatfoot Dance Company, 2013). There are popular dances from the streets and social gatherings, for example, isipantsula and kwasa-kwasa with 'Hip Hop workshops [...] offered weekly to large groups of skilled as well as unskilled young people' (Friedman, 2009, p. 138). 'Salsa dance is also popular' (Gibson, 2008, p. 116) and there is 'Cape Jazz Social Dance that 'may have evolved from langarm [...] from swing [...] from jive' (Gibson, 2008, p. 114) or other dance forms or combinations. Smitha Radhakrishan states that Indian '[c]lassical dance has enjoyed a tremendous resurgence in South Africa in recent years, reflecting a new emphasis on dance as an authentication of Indianness and, generally, a new interest in performing culture' (Radhakrishnan, 2005, p. 265). There are many other dance forms too, including Greek dance, Irish dance, Spanish dance; it was in South Africa that Spanish Dance was '[i]n 1965 [...] for the first time ever codified into a teaching method, graded according to age and ability' (Spanish Dance Society, 2007). As I prepare to teach my university class, I find myself asking 'whose dance should be taught?' (Friedman, 2009, p. 131). I too understand that these dance forms and styles are often competing for funding, venues, and audiences.

I could follow an investigative path with the students and explore the semantics of the term 'South African dance', and what is understood by contemporary dance, traditional dance, popular, and social dance in South Africa. In his article 'State of Dance in South Africa' (2011, p. 98), Rob Baum raises a number of questions around this terminology asking,

> '[h]ow are we (or who [author's emphasis] are we) to separate South Africa from modern discourses in dance?' and '[c]an a form of dance (such as ballet or contemporary) extant in other parts of the world be considered South African, and what lends the form such regional, national or, for that matter, political categorisation'? (Baum, 2011, p. 98)

Nonetheless, before the students and I can ask these questions, I think it is extremely important that I have a sound ethical base from which to start this discussion with students in the United Kingdom. To teach any dance form in any tertiary institution across the globe, pedagogy must have an ethical foundation. This chapter focuses on how my pedagogical practice is shaped by three ethically informed approaches I draw on to teach South Africa dance forms in a British University.

Hybridity

The first approach is concerned with looking at the individual and the dance form, and thereby recognising that South Africa is composed of many diverse cultures, and a nation of various peoples who dance many dances for a number of reasons. Early on, the students and I discuss what Clive Kellner (1997, p. 29) might be suggesting in his statement 'to be South African is to be hybrid, from which no singular origin is evident'. This hybridity, and I draw on Homi K. Bhabha's (1994) work on hybridity here, resonates and is represented by the students I have in this British institution. Their demographic background ranges from first-generation to umpteenth-generation British born, to coming to study from an Eastern European state, North American exchange students, to those that have experience of growing up in both the United Kingdom and in an African state. The second approach is that to study South African dance, the relationship between the cultural and political landscape and the dance form must be analysed. To understand South African dance, the students have to engage with the social landscape of South Africa. This means that these British students need to understand that the body in South African politics and day-to-day life was—and remains—a site of struggle, the site where the discourses of race, gender, sexuality, nationality, and many others have a very real effect on the life of a South African. The majority of the students have a limited understanding of British colonialism and its negative effects. This is primarily due to how the history of the British empire is taught in schools (Owen, 2016). Furthermore, there is tokenistic coverage of the history and culture of Black and Minority Groups in the United Kingdom with Black history relegated to but a month a year. I feel that the students cannot study South African dance without studying the history of colonialism, Apartheid and contemporary Post-Apartheid South Africa. Therefore, it is imperative that I anchor my dance pedagogy in careful contextual study, and this applies to the teaching and study of all dance styles.

What is important to note is that I need to resist a drive to follow 'essentialist notions of culturally responsive pedagogy' and to acknowledge 'that their [student] identities are not solely based on their race or ethnicity. Rather, their identities are complex because of the experiences and relationships they create with others' (Irizarry, 2007, p. 22). Therefore, the first ethical approach of looking at the individual and the dance form is not only focused on a South African individual and the dance form, but what it means to be a student studying South African dance in a British university, and their relationship to other students in the classroom. These ethical approaches that inform my teaching of dance from South Africa are always under review and are not finite or closed, and I am keen to listen to other dance colleagues, and thereby develop my teaching. These three approaches are not static, nor do they operate as individual categories, and perhaps it might be better to think about them as choreographic approaches that I use to shape and direct my pedagogic practice. I strongly believe that to teach dance cultures in universities, there are ethics involved, and these three choreographic strategies are my building blocks, my starting points, for my pedagogy, which must be informed by good ethical practice. Furthermore, these approaches are not simply about ensuring that I have a good sense of integrity, honesty, and ethics that are central to my teaching, but I hope that my conduct is a good model for my students, and in so doing helps them think through their own ethics, and their personal interaction with dance cultures from outside the United Kingdom. I am committed to educating dance students who critically reflect on the unequal power relations that unfortunately still exist globally, and how they might *not* add to or perpetuate this inequality any further.

Audiences of South African dance are growing in number, and there is international recognition of South African dance cultural practices and a number of South African dance-makers, such as Vincent Mantsoe, Nelisiwe Xaba, and Gregory Maqoma, have performed internationally. Moreover, dance is used as a marketing tool for South Africa, from the adverts aired in the British cinemas promoting holidays in South Africa laden with images of gumboot dancers and Zulu warriors, to the idiski dance of the 2010 Football World Cup. Many dance productions like *Umoja* or *Gumboot* have toured South Africa and across the globe to large audiences. Productions such as these draw on dancers with both formal and informal training. Subsequently, my last, the third, approach, is that there must be close study of South African dance forms and the relationship between the street and the stage. It is integral that my students at the university where I teach, study examples of cultural tourism, and its problems and promises, how South African national identity is constructed through dance performance, and of course, how political and social ideologies are represented and at times questioned through the cultural practice of dance.

Back in the dance studio, after a discussion of the Peters map, I then project a map of South Africa, and try to make the students aware that there are a majority of people who speak Xhosa here, and Tswana there, and Afrikaans speakers here, and isiZulu there, which is near my birthplace Pietermaritzburg, where there are some people who do not speak isiZulu at all, and that I only speak a little and do they know why that might be? I point out where the Khoesan used to dance...and that dance from the east of South Africa is different to dance from west of South Africa... We then consider the Africanist aesthetic aspects that Brenda Dixon Gottschild proposes in her influential book *Digging the Africanist Presence in American Performance Dance and Other Contexts* (1998) and is further summarised in her article 'Crossroads, Continuities, and Contradictions: The Afro-Euro-Caribbean Triangle' (2005). Dixon Gottschild's aspects of Africanist aesthetics are helpful if used as a paradigm to introduce dance from Africa, or of the African Diaspora, to students in higher education who are based outside of South Africa, or Africa in general. Nevertheless, these aspects must be unpacked as it is important that students do not presuppose an original and essential African culture.

Like many involved with all aspects of the South African dance industry, and my colleagues working in the theme of dance with links to Africa, I am continuously frustrated by the homogenising of dance from the African continent, in both its form and its content. I am not alone. Dance academic Maxwell Xolani Rani stresses the 'challenge today for people living in South African townships to override western stereotypes of Africa' (Rani, 2012, p. 84). Choreographer Gregory Vuyani Maqoma in 'A Response: Beyond Ethnicity' (Maquoma, 2006, p. 36) states that '[w]e have to override other perceptions and stereotypes set out by the outside world in view of work coming from the continent.'

Later in his article, Maqoma (2006, p. 37) remarks on how African contemporary dance is also distorted 'on the continent itself'. In 2004, dance critic Adrienne Sichel chaired a panel discussion on 'Defining a Contemporary African Dance Aesthetic – Can It Be Done?' at the conference held at the seventh Jomba! Contemporary Dance Experience in Durban, South Africa. On the panel were Gilbert Douglas, Adedayo Liadi,

Kettly Noël, Reginald Danster, and Augosto Cuvilas; all key choreographers who work in the idiom of African contemporary dance across the African continent and tour internationally. Sichel opened the session observing that she was 'pretty sure that every choreographer sitting at this table – at some time or another – has been told that their work is not African or African enough and that's part of the cultural conundrum that creative and performing artists in Africa face' (Young-Jahangeer, Loots, Rorvik, Oosthuysen, & Rorvik, 2004, p. 37).

Sharon Friedman explores this frustration in 'The Impact of the Tourist Gaze on the Voice of South African Contemporary Dance' (Friedman, 2012, pp. 89–90) highlighting that this take on dance from Africa is not only a 'North American or West European perception' by citing an incident involving the South African choreographer Sifiso Kweyama at a dance event in Angola where he was informed that his 'piece was not African enough'. Friedman (2012, p. 89) outlines the development of 'a popular form of "African" dance which was defined by the tourist gaze' drawing on an interview with Lliane Loots, the Artistic Director of Flatfoot Dance Company in 2010, where Loots refers to this type of African dance as an 'imagined dance [that] makes reference to a cultural tradition that many foreign based audiences believe is authentic and thus will pay to consume it.' (Friedman, 2012, p. 90). This then poses an important decision for me in my role as a senior dance lecturer in the United Kingdom. What do I include in the curriculum? Do I exclude the productions of *Umoja* and *African Footprint* that take advantage of the tourist gaze and portray an imagined representation of South Africa? In spite of the fact that these are the shows that tour London dance venues and therefore students will have access to see dance from South Africa live? Besides, these productions do include a variety of South African dance forms that do reflect the diversity of dance practices in South Africa, and they do offer rich material to support class discussions around culture appropriation, performance of nationality, Benedict Anderson's concept of 'imagined communities' (1983), and spur an interesting discussion around what these dance productions 'claim to do' (Friedman, 2012, p. 98).

In addition to the above, there is the constant conflation of African dance with Black dance. It is important to encourage students to problematise the term 'African' and 'Black' helping them think through the relationship of their British location to Africa, and the terms 'European' and 'White', whereby hopefully the invisibility of privilege is exposed. Clare Craighead (2006) troubles the concept of Black dance in her article '"Black Dance": Navigating the Politics of "Black" in Relation to "the Dance Object" and the Body as Discourse.' Craighead critiques 'notions of reductionism and essentialism in order to engage the diversity of work that the label constitutes' (Craighead, 2006, p. 28) The constant conflation of 'African' dance with 'Black' dance reveals a simplistic understanding of the history of the continent of Africa, and ignores the complex, and at times contested, flows of migration of people to and from this geographical area. For example, the people from the Oman who have influenced East African culture in Kenya and Tanzania, or those with their roots/routes in Indian indentured labour who have had an effect on South African culture. There are many examples of movement of communities and their effect on culture that I can draw on, and yes, much of this migration is directly related to colonialism with many of its negative and oppressive aspects. This is not to dismiss the very real effect that colonialism and Apartheid has had on either South African dance nor dance forms from other parts of Africa and the African Diaspora. Rather, this is a call to unpack the categories that were instated often by way of colonialism and imperialism, and in South Africa's case Apartheid too; a call to dismantle these terms and expose their foundations that draw on notions of ownership and non-ownership, belonging and not-belonging, hegemony and binary systems of thought. It is necessary to state here, before I continue, that many of these students have their own personal history with aspects of British colonialism. For example, a number of students are first-generation British nationals of Nigerian parents. Or, they might be students who are third-generation British nationals who have great-grandparents from Jamaica who came to the United Kingdom, for instance, on the ship *The Empire Windrush* in 1948. Or, they might have great-great grandparents who fought in the South African War (1899–1902). Or, there might be students who have no known direct links to Africa, but nevertheless they are studying dance in a city that is built on the profits of trade, and often-imperialist trade with Africa. Akin to the traces of the British in Africa, there are very real instances of Africa in Britain, both historical and contemporary.

Returning to the terms of 'African dance' and 'Black dance', in his address at the Seventh Jomba! Contemporary Dance Experience Conference, Jay Pather, the Artistic Director of Siwela Sonke Dance

Theatre, calls for ownership of what he terms a 'response-aesthetic, [and that] this self consciousness may force us to unpack received notions' (2006, p. 14). Consequently, it is important to encourage students to problematise the terms 'African' and 'Black', helping them think through the relationship of their British location to Africa, and the terms 'European' and 'White'. Clare Craighead (2006) troubles the concept of Black Dance in her article "Black Dance": Navigating the Politics of "Black" in Relation to "the Dance Object" and the Body as Discourse'. Craighead critiques 'notions of reductionism and essentialism in order to engage the diversity of work that the label constitutes'. (Craighead, 2006, p. 28). I adopt a similar position in my teaching and I begin to disrupt the term 'South African dance' by showing the students a variety of images and clips from the Internet of as much dance from South Africa as I can. This shows the multitude of dance forms in South Africa and, most importantly, the diversity of its people. To organise this material, I attempt to illustrate what Lliane Loots, the Artistic Director of Flatfoot Dance Company, stated at the 2005 Opening Night of Jomba Contemporary Dance Festival in Durban; in South Africa 'we dance when we protest, we dance when we bury the dead, and we dance to celebrate new life'. By highlighting the relationship of the dance forms with the individual, I aim to help students make connections with the people of South Africa on a personal level, and hopefully, limit an othering, or a marginalisation, or a type of orientalisation of South African culture.

Nor do I ignore the cultural backgrounds of my students as to do so is dangerous; 'culture must be conceptualized more broadly in order to be responsive to students' identities' (Irizarry, 2007, p. 21). I try to balance the concept of self and other, not only when teaching my students in other modules, but especially when focusing on dance from South Africa in a British university context. This undertaking, of attempting to balance the self and the other, is an extension of an observation by Ninetta Santoro in 'Teaching in Culturally Diverse Contexts: What Knowledge about "Self" and "Others" do Teachers Need?' (2009). In this article in which she studies teacher education, specifically in Australia, Santoro (2009, p. 34) argues 'that knowing the "ethnic self" and the "ethnic other" are inextricably connected and are crucial to developing multicultural pedagogies and effective classroom practice'. Therefore, by focusing on the individual and their connection to the dance form, I seek to disrupt the binary of us versus them, or the North versus the South, or the

East versus the West, or the First World versus the Third World, or the notions of developed and developing. This type of polarity thinking reinforces stereotypes and homogenises cultural groups and as a result ignores the intricacies at play. Santoro captures this importance of recognising the complex interplay of self and other when she also draws on Homi Bahaba's concept of hybridity (1994). It is in this process of the students identifying what they might share with young people in South Africa, such as a passion for dancing or aspects of youth culture, and what they might not, for instance the access to travel that holding a British passport allows, that hopefully does not 'silence debates about the inequalities that do exist *because* of racial and ethnic difference' (Santoro, 2009, p. 38). Santoro (2009, p. 38) stresses how individuals 'can identify with a number of ethnic and cultural groups' and this is the case for many of the British students I teach.

I make use of as much visual material that the students can easily access themselves, as I try to approach any topic from a student's point of view, and by using the tools available to them, such as social media networks and various search engines on the Internet. Using this material, we then work together to discover more about the topic. As an example, the students and I have focused on Beyoncé's music video 'Run the World (Girls)' (2011) and her work with Tofu Tofu, a Mozambican isipantsula group. We discuss cultural borrowing of the dance forms kwasa-kwasa and isipantsula, the reinforcement or subversion of African stereotypes, and the appropriation of contemporary African art and cultural practices by dominant cultural praxes such as American popular music. I try very hard not to let my pedagogy be informed by an out-dated notion that the academic is a gatekeeper of a particular research area. In 'The Politics of Personal Pedagogy: Examining Teacher Identities', Doug Risner in his section titled 'The Politics of Gender in Dance Pedagogy' (Kerr-Berry, Clemente, & Risner, 2008, p. 95) highlights the problem of the 'traditional "banking method" in which a student is viewed as an empty vessel to be filled by the teacher's expert deposits of information.' Risner's essay draws heavily on Paulo Freire's *Pedagogy of the Oppressed* (1970) and his notion of the traditional 'banking method' and, like Risner, I too am *not* a supporter of this type of pedagogic system. As an academic, I research dance, and therefore am also a student of dance studies, and much like the students I teach, sometimes I do not know the answer. What I can do is share with the students a variety of research skills, and thereby hopefully help them develop their own set of critical skills in the study of dance. 'Pedagogy needs to be transformative rather than transmissive, and organised so that students are trusted to be involved in decision-making and jointly steer the direction of the learning (Whitburn & Yemoh, 2012, p. 24).

Risner writes about his own pedagogy, and outlines 'three significant power shifts that occur'. First is the 'Student-Directed Approaches' where the 'key [...] is balancing student input and direction with faculty guidance in a dialogical approach' (Kerr-Berry, Clemente & Risner, 2008, p. 96). The second shift is 'Learning from Shared Experience, that is that all knowledge is socially constructed. To really know something is to know it in relation to others – others' perspectives, experiences, thinking contexts, and histories' (Risner in Kerr-Berry, Clemente, & Risner, 2008, p. 96). Many of the students at the British university where I am based have had historically limited access to the diversity of dances practised on the African continent. Consequently, we start by collaboratively researching the South African dance practices available online via the Internet and social networks; for many young adults today, this approach tends to be their first tactic for obtaining information about dance styles. We watch a number of clips on YouTube, and almost as an accident by design, and as a shared experience, this then leads the students and I into a short discussion of the reasons why certain videos have better recorded quality, and what similarities or differences they noticed when looking at this visual material.

We also examine what the factors or reasons might be for some of the comments left on YouTube, and why I might not be a fan of the Disney musical *The Lion King*. This always becomes a heated but most enjoyable discussion, especially because a number of the students have seen the show, and are now being asked to think through issues around stereotyping and orientalism. At an external examiner's event at another university in the United Kingdom, I had an informal discussion with a dance academic who raised an important point about *The Lion King* musical and I must acknowledge this here. They noted that the British version of the musical offered many 'Black' dancers an opportunity to perform in a major production and many in leading roles. The colleague added that *The Lion King* enabled a number of these dancers to think through notions of identity and community. I understand that this might be the case but, nonetheless, I am concerned with the hegemonic representation of African culture in the musical, specifically Disney's representation of Africa, and the reinforcement and normalisation of an imagined and nostalgic Africa. Disney is guilty of similar acts, such as orientalism with the films of *Mulan* (1998) and historical revisionism in *Pocahontas* (1995).

Finally, Risner (2008) writes of 'Imperfection and Risk Taking' (p. 96) drawing on bell hooks' *Engaged Pedagogy* (2006) in which

> hooks advocates, [that] teachers must take the first risk by showing their lack of knowledge, their incomplete understanding of the worlds, the ways in which they struggle, and most importantly, that asking questions is not only acceptable, but also valid and valuable in allowing students to see teachers as people who are human, vulnerable, and not "always right". (Risner in Kerr-Berry et al., 2008, p. 96)

These power shifts are at the core of my pedagogic practice and ethical stances too, and I argue lead to 'genuine conversation' (Conquergood, 2007, p. 65). As a dance researcher, I use ethnography as one of my research methods, and my pedagogy is heavily influenced by this method too. I often make use of Conquergood's (2007, p. 61) concept of 'Dialogical Performance' as a teaching strategy, especially as it is 'a way of finding the moral center [*sic*] as much as it is an indicator that one is ethically grounded' (Conquergood, 2007, p. 67).

After a most enjoyable discussion about *The Lion King*, I introduce the students to a selection of South African choreographers and dance companies. Over the past decade, I have built a small library of DVD materials, and I am extremely thankful to the many choreographers and companies who have contributed material to this collection. It is rather obvious to make the case for students watching as much dance as possible. Yet, it is so important to underline this necessity. The more dances from other countries that the students engage with, not only is their understanding of dance in its multifarious forms developed, but hopefully this knowledge will broaden their understanding of dance from other countries. For instance, this might limit a reductionist understanding of dance from the African continent. Not only do the students study South African dance in a seminar setting, but over the last few years I have invited a few South African choreographers and companies, who are on tour, to work with the students, such as Vincent Mantsoe and Via Volcano, an isipantsula group. Regrettably, with the ruthless cuts across the United Kingdom and European arts sector, and the current changes taking place in British higher education, the arts have witnessed a massive reduction in support for teaching and research. The opportunity for these workshops and the importance of ensuring that a diverse range of cultural practices are represented in the curriculum, through seminars, workshops, and performances, is at risk. Ultimately, this will add to the ignorance of the diversity of dance from countries outside of the United Kingdom such as South Africa, and thereby reinforce dangerous and simplistic stereotypes.

In conclusion, I would like to build on a comment by Lliane Loots in her conclusion of her article 'Post-Colonial Visitations: A South African's Dance and Choreographic Journey that Faces Up to the Spectres of "Development" and Globalisation' (2006). In this text, Loots carefully unpacks the power and value systems at play in international dance exchanges, notions of inter-culturalism, globalisation and its market economy, and the danger and outcomes of a somewhat flawed politics of development (Loots, 2006, pp. 89–101). At the end of this personal and enlightening article, Loots writes about how she is 'yet to find solutions to many of the problems' she raises, 'but [an] awareness is a good beginning' (Loots, 2006, p. 99). It is this awareness that I am committed to embedding in my pedagogic practice, and it is this awareness that I hope the British students I teach have after studying dances from South Africa.

References

Anderson, B. R. O. G. (1983). *Imagined Communities: Reflections on the Origin and Spread of Nationalism*. London: Verso.

Baum, R. (2011). State of Dance in South Africa. *South African Dance Journal*, *1*(1), 97–101.

Bhabha, H. K. (1994). *The Location of Culture*. London/New York: Routledge.

Conquergood, D. (2007). Performing as a Moral Act: Ethical Dimensions of the Ethnography of Performance. In P. Kuppers & G. Robertson (Eds.), *The Community Performance Reader* (pp. 57–70). London/New york: Roughtledge.

Craighead, C. (2006). 'Black Dance': Navigating the Politics of 'Black' in Relation to 'The Dance Object' and the Body as Discourse. *Critical Arts: A Journal of South-North Cultural and Media Studies*, *20*(2), 20–33.

Dodds, S. (2011). *Dancing on the Canon: Embodiments of Value in Popular Dance*. Houndmills, Basingstoke Hampshire/New York: Palgrave Macmillan.

Flatfoot Dance Company. (2013). Retrieved February 28, 2017, from http://www.flatfootdancecompany.webs.com/

Friedman, S. (2009). Navigating the Byways of Polyculturalism – Whose Dance Are We Teaching in South African Schools. *Research in Dance Education*, *10*(2), 131–144.

Friedman, S. (2012). The Impact of the Tourist Gaze on the Voice of South African Contemporary Dance. In S. Friedman (Ed.), *Post-Apartheid Dance: Many Bodies Many Voices Many Stories* (pp. 89–105). Newcastle Upon Tyne: Cambridge Scholars.

Friere, P. (1970). *Pedagogy of the Oppressed*. London: Continuum.

Gibson, J. (2008). Short Steps to Freedom: Interfaces, Spaces and Imaginaries within Cape Jazz Social Dance and the Emerging Salsa Scene in Cape Town. In Friedman, S. & N. Lock (Eds.) *Confluences 5: High Culture, Mass Culture, Urban Culture – Whose Dance?* Proceedings of the Fifth South African Dance Conference (113–122). Cape Town: University of Cape Town.

Glasser, S. (1993). On the Notion of 'Primitive Dance'. *Journal for the Anthropological Study of Human Movement*, 7(3), 183–196.

Gottschild, B. D. (1998). *Digging the Africanist Presence in American Performance Dance and Other Contexts*. Westport/London: Praeger.

Gottschild, B. D. (2005). Crossroads, Continuities, and Contradictions: The Afro-Euro-Caribbean Triangle. In S. Sloat (Ed.), *Caribbean Dance from Abakuá: How Movement Shapes Identity* (pp. 3–10). Gainesville: University Press of Florida.

Irizarry, J. G. (2007). Ethnic and Urban Intersections in the Classroom: Latino Students, Hybrid Identities, and Culturally Responsive Pedagogy. *Multicultural Perspectives*, 9(3), 21–28.

Johnson, M. L. (2007). Review of Seeing Through Maps: Many Ways to See the World by Denis Wood, Ward L. Kaiser and Bob Abramms, and Many Ways to See the World (Companion DVD) by Dr. Bob Abramms. *Cartographic Perspectives*, 56(Winter), 60–62.

Kellner, C. (1997). Cultural Production in Post-Apartheid South Africa. In Enwezor, O. & C. Richards, *Trade Routes: History and Geography: 2nd Johannesburg Biennale 1997*. Johannesburg, South Africa/Den Haag, Netherlands: Greater Johannesburg Metropolitan Council/Prince Claus Fund for Culture and Development.

Kerr-Berry, J., Clemente, K., & Risner, D. (2008). The Politics of Personal Pedagogy: Examining Teacher Identities. *Journal of Dance Education*, 8(3), 94–101.

Loots, L. (2005, August 17). *Eighth Jomba! Contemporary Dance Experience*. Speech Presented at The Elizabeth Sneddon Theatre, Durban, South Africa.

Loots, L. (2006). Post-Colonial Visitations: A South African's Dance and Choreographic Journey that Faces Up to the Spectres of 'Development' and Globalisation. *Critical Arts: A Journal of South-North Cultural and Media Studies*, 20(2), 89–101.

Maqoma, G. V. (2006). A Response: Beyond Ethnicity. *Critical Arts: A Journal of South-North Cultural and Media Studies*, 20(2), 34–38.

Meintjes, L. (2004). Shoot the Sergeant, Shatter the Mountain: The Production of Masculinity in Zulu Ngoma Song and Dance in Post-Apartheid South Africa. *Ethnomusicology Forum, 13*(2), 173–201.

Mulan. (1998). *Directed by Tony Bancroft and Barry Cook.* USA: Walt Disney Pictures.

Owen, J. (2016, January 22). British Empire: Students Should Be Taught Colonialism "Not All Good" Say Historians. *The Independent.* Retrieved from http://www.independent.co.uk/news/education/education-news/british-empire-students-should-be-taught-colonialism-not-all-good-say-historians-a6828266.html

Pather, J. (2006). A Response: African Contemporary Dance? Questioning Issues of a Performance Aesthetic for a Developing Continent. *Critical Arts: A Journal of South-North Cultrual and Media Studies, 20*(2), 9–15.

Pocahontas. (1995). *Directed by Mike Gabriel and Eric Goldberg.* USA: Walt Disney Pictures.

Radhakrishan, S. (2005). "Time to Show Our True Colors": The Gendered Politics of "Indianness" in Post-Apartheid South Africa. *Gender and Society, 19*(2), 262–281.

Rani, M. X. (2012). Lost Meaning-New Traditions: Shaping Identity in the "New" South Africa: An Overview of Social Traditional African Dance in South African Townships. In S. Friedman (Ed.), *Post-Apartheid Dance: Many Bodies Many Voices Many Stories* (pp. 73–88). Newcastle upon Tyne: Cambridge Scholars.

Santoro, N. (2009). Teaching in Culturally Diverse Contexts: What Knowledge About "Self" and "Others" Do Teachers Need? *Journal of Education for Teaching: International Research and Pedagogy, 35*(1), 33–45.

Sichel, A., Douglas, G., Liadi, A., Noël, K., Danster, R., & Cuvilas, A. (2004). Defining a Contemporary African Dance Aesthetic – Can it be Done? In M. Young-Jahangeer, L. Loots, P. Rorvik, C. Oosthuysen, & M. Rorvik (Eds.), *African Contemporary Dance? Questioning Issues of a Performance Aesthetic for a Developing and Independent Continent. Proceedings of the Seventh Jomba Contemporary Dance Conference* (pp. 36–57). Durban: University of KwaZulu-Natal Press and Artworks Communication.

Spanish Dance Society. (2007). Retrieved April 8, 2013, from http://www.spanishdancesociety.org/main/history.htm

Visser, G. (2010). Leisurely Lesbians in a Small City in South Africa. *Urban Forum, 21*(2), 171–185.

Whitburn, R., & Yemoh, S. (2012). "My People Struggled Too": Hidden Histories and Heroism – A School Designed Post-14 Course on Multi-Cultural Britain Since 1945. *Teaching History, 147*, 16–25.

CHAPTER 10

Performativity of Body Painting: Symbolic Ritual as Diasporic Identity

Chikukwango Cuxima-Zwa

INTRODUCTION

In this chapter I will look at how the performativity of body painting, symbolic ritual and dance with movements and gestures has helped me better understand my black diasporic identity in Britain. I do this from the African perspective of having lived in Angola and England. I focus on the range of ideas and concepts, (ways of thinking and creating) that scaffold my practice. For me, body painting and ritual as creative and aesthetic forms of identity are important elements in the narrative of black British culture. It establishes a mental and physical connection with my roots in the motherland of Africa and has an imperative in practices I was introduced do growing up there.

The impact of the Angolan civil war and the political history and culture played an important part in my creation of three live performances in relation to my hybrid experiences of becoming to London as a refugee. Through using my body I translated those experiences artistically, metaphorically and symbolically to communicate and narrate personal concerns

C. Cuxima-Zwa (✉)
Brunel University London, London, UK

© The Author(s) 2018
A. Akinleye (ed.), *Narratives in Black British Dance*,
https://doi.org/10.1007/978-3-319-70314-5_10

131

about the intersection of Angolan and British cultures. Growing up in Luanda in the 1980s was an interesting period in the Angolan postcolonial situation, with modern urbanisation and migration of people from the rural parts of the country. This brought a new social and cultural dynamic of creative dance, music and fashion which influenced my diaspora creative fabric and identity of body painting and ritual.

As the nature of my work is pioneering, I use my experiences of dislocation and displacement in London to contextualise and challenge my practice. In this context, I explore body painting to re-create my identity and to validate African cultural traditions as an Afrocentric approach to the body. Through my performance works, I embrace Afrocentric principles as an ideology for liberation and cultural significance through self-determination (Asante, 1988, p. 2). One of the objectives of this chapter is to explain how I developed my work as a strategic necessity to position my unique creative perspective and contribution to the dance community based on my Lusophone worldview. My work is characterised and defined through the diasporic complexities and circumstances of migration, trauma and memory. Using photography to capture images of work is part of my creative methodology. Photography is an important medium I utilise to visually convey my ideas and creative processes. In a sense, I use photography as one of the broader aspects of methodology in my practice. My work in the diaspora is deeply rooted in African traditions of religion and philosophy and I utilise the medium of photography as a narrative methodology to capture and record my painted body in live performances. This is to create awareness of my symbolic and imaginary ideas of Africa and spiritual consciousness.

The challenges I faced living in Britain as a diaspora artist has led me to look at other contemporary and more established artists as a frame of reference for my own creative processes. For this reason, the works of Rotimi Fani-Kayode and Fela Kuti became my primary sources of influence. Their creativity played a great part in the formation of my performances and choreographic symbolic rituals. Fani-Kayode's photographic exploration of the black male body in the studio and Kuti's celebration of the African tradition of ritual and spirituality as subtexts of national and diaspora identity gave significance to the composition of my work at its earlier stages.

African religions are an important aspect in my practice as a black British performance artist creating contemporary works. The influence of African religions and philosophies manifests in my work through the use of cultural iconography. My body becomes a creative medium exploring symbolic ritual, movements and gestures to bring awareness of African spiritual consciousness. In a way, my body becomes the centre around which I narrate my personal trajectory and cultural history. In other words, in this context my body characterises my different sentiments and experiences in the British diaspora as an African navigating, exploring and creating spaces through performativity.

As a performance artist exploring symbolic ritual through body painting in the diaspora, my use of photography captures the imprint moments of my performances and interaction with an audience. Photography becomes a documentation of memory that traces the composition of my live performances and at the same time disseminates multiple information about audience behaviour, my body presence, and the characters and actions in the performative spaces I inhabit. The recorded photographic activity becomes incorporated into the realm of tradition and narrative. However, in this chapter, I use the photographic images to give a visual understanding of my artistic ideas and concepts.

Within the creative process of making art, I find, there is an importance to the theoretical works surrounding the discourse of the black experience and identity in the diaspora. The postcolonial and post-slavery African diaspora writers and historians have shaped and influenced my use of symbolic ritual and critical analysis in the work I have made since living in Britain. My work is an embodiment of Angolan cultural tradition, which reflects on my sense of origin and roots. The writers and historians provide structure and framework for my work to be theoretically situated in a broader academic context. Particularly, Benedict Anderson in his work *Imagined Communities* (2006) provides a context for my experience of displacement and re-invention of the self with ideas of national consciousness. Robert Farris Thompson in his text *Flash of the Spirit* (1984) informs the aesthetic of my performance making processes in the new world. It made me understand that as an Angolan artist I am not isolated in my experiences in Britain; but I am intimately connected to particular rich ancient cultures, traditions and societies in West Africa and the African diaspora. Thompson's copious and conducive research on religion and spirituality gave me an essential reading in reference to the African cosmology, philosophy and art in relation to Africa and the African diaspora, particularly in the Americas and the Caribbean. Molefi Kete Asante's work *Afrocentricity* and its philosophy is a victorious step in raising consciousness about the traditional culture and identity of African people in the diaspora. Asante created academic definitions of "Afrocentricity" and brilliantly made references to the black experiences in world history based on the black perspective. "Afrocentricity" theoretical concepts give structures to the African diaspora intellectual scholarship and creative practice as an ideological renaissance notion of origin and belonging.

Thus, later in the chapter I discuss aspects of the African diaspora religion and ritual of Voodoo from Haiti as a dynamic and consistent historical, cultural and spiritual practice in the Caribbean, which has its roots in the tradition of African ancestral religion. The Haitian Voodoo is directly related to the people of Congo and Angola as a transnational signifier of identity, because of the way they explore ritual, relating with god, cosmos and universe. By the same token, I cannot understate the impact and influence of the literary works of the African American folklorist Zora Neale Hurston (2009, 1990). Her writings on Hoodoo folk magic and Voodoo religious practice from New Orleans and Haiti gave me a visual understanding in my artistic and diasporic configuration. When I write about the performance piece *Abney Park Cemetery*, later in the chapter, I will discuss how I was influenced by the Hurston's literary works, which explored mystical ideas of folklore and ceremonies of Hoodoo and Voodoo in New Orleans and Haiti. I particularly draw references from her resourceful works of symbolism of anthropology to visually construct a personal narrative of ritual in an open space of the cemetery as a connection with my ancestors in Africa and to create expressive dramatic dialogue between body and spirit in a manner of ethnographic performance production. It is important to point out that, in the context of this chapter, I am spelling the word 'Voodoo', as written by the Louisiana Voodoo, also known as New Orleans Voodoo; a set of spiritual folkways that developed from the traditions of the African diaspora and the Louisiana Creole people also known as the servants of the spirits. Although, I am writing about Haitian Voodoo, I am using the Louisiana written spelling. This is to avoid confusion and as a way to stay with one type of spelling.

Growing Up in Luanda in 1980s

I grew up in Luanda, Angola during the time of the nationalists' struggle for independence from the repressive blood-soaked Portuguese colonial regime. During this period, the country was in massive turbulence with the progressive nationalists and anti-colonial movements mobilising the nation for change through rebellion by armed struggle, demanding that the brutal colonial regime come to an end. During the struggle, the nationalists had the ideological visions and ambitions to better control the nation from their own perspective of self-governance as indigenous Africans and proponents of culture and tradition (Somerville, 1986, p. 46). However, it was on 11 November 1975, in the streets of Luanda, the capital city, that the Portuguese government officially granted independence to the nation, through the speech of the newly elected political president Agostinho Neto (MPLA). This manifested through a creation of a transitional government based on the existing three main nationalist political parties (Hodges, 2004, pp. 6–7).

In my formative years in the 1980s, the country was embedded in devastating war and social upheaval. Although the war was mainly affected outside Luanda, there was still a sense of insecurity among the population around the metropolis. At the time Luanda was the sprawling centre of prosperity and modern life, but the city experienced an influx of internal refugees fleeing war and conflict in affected rural areas and villages in the country (Birmingham, 2006, p. 140). In the environment I grew up in, I was influenced by my neighbours who came from different parts of the country who were from the north, south and central regions of the country and ethnic groups as indigenous nationals. Creatively they brought with them innovative expressions of dance, music, ritual, dress code and religion, centred on body nativity as a vehicle of communication in the suburb areas. My neighbours, particularly the younger generation, brought with them a fascinating ways of dressing as a cosmopolitan cultural practice and production. For me, the new comers to Luanda in 1980s responded to postcolonial identity and representation of life through dressing. They were very creative in their dressing styles, which asserted their difference as active participants in the new postcolonial, social power construction and imagination. In other words, the way they dressed was a statement to assert their identity and difference in the city, which was characterised by symbols of their rural expression juxtaposing modernity in their new context. Their rural experiences, moralities and worldviews became the point of departure and possibilities in the new fabric of the culture and social activities in Luanda. Within this, they utilised the body as the primary object to convey ideas of liberation and nationalistic ideologies as an African manifesto. According to Carol Tulloch,

> *dress is a fundamental aspect of the black identity as a signifier of black popular culture and difference, which highlight collective existence and experiences of oppression and trauma.* (Tulloch, 2004a, pp. 86–88)

The impact of the Portuguese colonial legacy was a massive inheritance. Colonialism created damage in the roots of the cultural existence and African vernacular, and the psychic and conscious reality of the people was dominated by the Western hegemonic imperialism that devalued and alienated what was native in its origins. This was manifested with created stigmas such as "primitivism" and "tribalism" implemented as a control mechanism to legitimise European modernism, civilization and political power. In this way, Portugal wanted to maintain its colonial power as a sign of continuing perpetuation of imperial supremacy for economic and financial gain, even after the struggle for independence and during the decolonisation process. Portugal was one of the last European colonial regimes to hold on to colonial ideologies as opportunists for financial and material acquisition. David Birmingham points out that:

> *In most African countries the 'paleo-colonial' power became the neo-colonial economic patron. Portugal delayed its decolonisation for over a decade in the hope that it could develop a sufficiently powerful European manufacturing and financial base to serve that role when its colonies were given flag independence in the French style.* (Birmingham, 1999, p. 156)

During this period in Luanda, the cultural value was centred in Portugal as the "ideal" imperial point of prestige and civilization based on the structure of the colonial legacy and European hierarchy and race superiority, which places Europeans at the top and native black Africans at the very bottom, as described by Charles Darwin's theories of racial supremacy in his influential text *The Origin of Species* (1998). In this context, what I am arguing is that Portugal colonial legacy in Luanda gave credit to and was part of the European expansionist project and the evolution of the white race. Frances Cress Welsing explains that:

> *…The goal of the white supremacy system is none other than the establishment, maintenance, expansion and refinement of world domination by members of a group that classifies itself as the white "race"…Impressed that the concept of a "system" of white domination over the world's "non-white" peoples could explain the seeming predicament and dilemma of "non-white" social reality….* (Welsing, 1991, p. 3)

The cultural development that took place in Luanda was like most capital cities in Africa—the population from the countryside and rural areas gravitated into the city in order to create a new urban discourse, life and reality. Particularly, for my neighbours to live in Luanda was also to be part of the colonial structure, labour market and the consequences of capitalist enterprise (Moorman, 2008, p. 28). Although some of my neighbours had less contact with the Portuguese, this set them apart as innovative and producers of culture in an environment constructed and dictated by colonial dominance and influence. One of the main aspects that made my neighbours stand out was the way that they dressed with traditional garments, garb and attire made by African textile materials. In other words, their dress was a visual reference that depicted cultural resistance and the representation of rural communities, through dress and body practice. Adebayo Oyebade elucidates that:

> *Although Angolans have a rich dress culture that has been significantly modernized, some remote rural communities have resisted change in their form of dress and have stuck to their ancient ways of dressing. This is true of the Ovahimba, a seminomadic pastoral people of southern Angola (and also of northern Namibia). These people have retained the old ways; their women still go bare breast, and they coat their bodies with red ocher and fat as protection against the sweltering desert sun.* (Oyebade, 2007, p. 105)

I am arguing that their dress was a reinvention of identity of the body as social politics of resistance to colonial rule, because through this the dress was the medium which made them feel proud of their past realities, it connected them with their forefathers and ancestors. Furthermore, it was a representative signifier of their origin in a deeper sense, correlating their cultural inheritance and memory of past traditions with the body as locality in space and time (Picton, 2004, p. 41). Their dress and fabric wrapped around the body was very distinctive with colourful design, pattern and aesthetic depicting nature and the surrounding environment, which created a spiritual relationship between the physical bodies and the African cosmological principles of the universe. In this way, the physical body plays an important part in the cosmological relation with the sun, moon, earth and meteorites. With this in mind, looking at the universe in the context of some African belief systems and religiosity, John Mbiti explains that:

> *Their views are expressed in myths, legends, proverbs, rituals, symbols, beliefs and wise saying. There is no formal or systematized view of the universe, but when these various ideas are put together, a picture emerges. There are many*

> *mysteries in the universe and whenever possible people try to find an explanation for them, whether or not the explanation is final.* (Mbiti, 1991, p. 34)

Growing up and seeing my neighbours was inspirational. In my neighbourhood, I grew up learning traditional dance with local dance groups. In these dance classes, my neighbours (the migrants from rural areas of the country) trained the group of dancers in the principles and techniques of traditional Angolan dance, gestures and movements. During my formative years, the dance classes gave me an understanding of the diversity of national ethnicity and social relation, which was an exposure to the culture and customs of the people of Angola. The choreography and constructed genealogy of traditional dance styles was created and produced in the practice of rural and "tribal" articulations and iconographies that came from all parts of the country from south to north as an expression of the people (Moorman, 2008, p. 16). Although, in this context, Marissa Moorman in her book *Intonations: A Social History of Music and Nation in Luanda* (2008) makes references to the Angolan music and dance in the 1960s and 1970s, she elucidates to an extent the popular experiences of traditional dance in the suburban areas of Luanda with the influence of "tribal" and rural dance practice as a socio-cultural and socio-political struggle for nationalistic liberation (1–27). In this manner, certain "tribal" and ethnic groups played an influential role, (such as Chokwe, Mumuila, Ovimbundu, Bakongo, Kimbundu, Herero, Ambundu, Kikongo and Ngangela). The purpose of the dance rehearsal and training I did was a preparation to showcase at different local recreation centres and club scenes and to compete with other local and municipal dance groups. However, because of the influences and complexities of movement and dance practice, the cultural display and elaboration brought by my neighbours from rural habits and folklores, our group differentiated in its approach and creative skills (Bourgault, 2003, p. 178).

In Angolan society religion constitutes an important aspect in people's lives, and at the time among my neighbours I saw that they were influenced by "...their religion, their beliefs and ideas about life, human existence..." the universe, cultural tradition and habits (Oyebade, 2007, p. 33). Moreover, some of my neighbours practised traditional religion; which for them manifested in the way they dressed and lived in their day-to-day activities and decision-making processes. One of the important aspects of my formative years in Luanda was the influence of the Chokwe cultural tradition of masquerade. The Chokwe ethnic group is located in the hinterland in the north/east of Angola in the border with the Republic of Zambia and the Democratic Republic of Congo. Although I was not training among the Chokwe people, I have a family relation and lineage. My dad was a Chokwe, and through him I developed an understanding of their cultural practices.

In the postcolonial and post-civil war Angola, Chokwe art and culture is regarded with great prestige as higher art, and its art represents a national cultural symbol. However, because of its geographical location within Angola, the Chokwe did not have lots of contact with the Portuguese during colonialism. For this reason their culture, habits, customs and worldview was preserved, as a national heritage and cultural patrimony of the state. In this manner, their cultural tradition, cosmology and worldview has a great influence in the country; particularly their oral history, which plays an important role in the understanding of the Angolan history of the pre-colonial era. Their relation with the universe and the supreme god, and their myths, parables, riddles and folktales gives an insight into the characteristic of Angolan ancient cultural production as indigenous peoples and creators. Furthermore, the Chokwe culture is unique in the context of Angolan ethnic groups, because of their deep and sophisticated creation of cultural production reflecting their surrounding and environment (Cordell, 2004, p. 239).

In addition, oral history is a methodology of gathering information that has been used at great research level in recent times in Angola. In other words, oral history has been used significantly in the context of research practice to add value to the culture and historical narrative; considering the fact that because of the internal civil war much has not been written from an Angolan perspective and oral history helps to preserve this history as a collective identity and memory for future generations to come, through using audiotapes, videotapes, transcriptions and planned interviews.

For the most part, my interaction with my neighbours took place in the streets and social events. This was to do with the social differences that were prevalent and inherited through colonialism that made us look at each other as strangers in our own country because of the ethnic and geographical situation and characterisation, created by the Portuguese empire through boundaries and localised divisions (Maier, 2007, p. 14).

The use of ritual was very strong and visible in the day-to-day life in the streets; because ritual was an easy manifestation that my neighbours did individually and communally as a ceremony or divinatory rites. For example, funeral and wedding rituals made more impact on us because of the large participation of family members and people in the community, which attracted massive attention from people nearby. Particularly, in rituals of the dead and departed relative, there was a special importance and sensitivity in the way they treated the dead body, as a result of the spiritual and physical separation of the individual from the family. John Mbiti writes that:

African peoples believe that death is not the end of human life. A person continues to exist in the hereafter. This continuation of life beyond death is recognized through a very widespread practice of remembering the departed, which is found throughout Africa. (Mbiti, 1991, p. 128)

The funeral rites and ceremonies for my neighbours were conducted intentionally to draw attention to the permanent separation between the visible and invisible worlds and the spiritual and physical realities. They conducted funeral rites very carefully to avoid absenting or causing any offence to the departed family or ancestors and to successfully continue the divine connection and veneration.

Carnival and Ritual Influences of Luanda

In the 1980s, I was influenced by the magnificent dynamic of the ritual ceremony of carnival and masquerade as a popular culture practice celebrated by large crowds of people in the streets. The parade carnival groups were mainly from Luanda and the neighbourhoods and suburban areas. The carnival became popular and innovative after independence (in 1975) as a modern cultural event "rooted in the customs" and traditions of the fishing population together with the emerging postcolonial elite (Birmingham, 2006, p. 131). In the same manner, the native fishing population of the Island of Luanda, which predominately came from the north of the country as migrants and descendants of the Congo kingdom, created the ritual of the seaside called Kianda, which every year honoured the female witch and queen of the waters by throwing foods and drinks (beer, wine and traditional alcohol drinks) as an offer in a form of libation and veneration for protection against atrocities and natural disasters. Nonetheless, some of the elite were very influential people and part of the ruling party's political bureau and descendants of the historic Creole families, who had migrated to the country in about 1850s (Birmingham, 2006, p. 124). The majority of the Creole families came particularly from the Portuguese colonial territories of the Islands of Cabe Verde and St. Tome and Principe, as a result of the slave trade and the plantation industry located on these Islands in the Atlantic Ocean.

They monopolised the leadership and destiny of the nation, because of their direct assimilated connection with the Portuguese colonial master, through their notions of "...indigenous class of black bourgeois families..." (Hodges, 2004, p. 42); and these gave them pride and sense of superiority and as a result they looked down on the native African population. Because of the Creole elite's contact with the Portuguese, they were able to inherit the cultural legacy of Europe while they rose to prominence and created wealth (Birmingham, 1995, p. 91). However, the majority of those who embraced the concept of the carnival were the rural-urban migrant population, descendants of the north of the country and the kingdom of Congo, who settled in the shores of Luanda Island during the colonial struggle and the fight for independence as a postcolonial process of finding a better life and stable opportunities for work (Oyebade, 2007, p. 11).

By the same token, the content of the carnival as a public display and celebration of freedom "...was inherited from the Portuguese with much infusion of African culture through costume and music" according to Oyebade (2007, p. 157). On the other hand, I suggest that the carnival is an attempt to come to terms with the impact of colonisation and is a representation derived from a syncretism encounter of African pagan rituals and the European religiosity and practice of Catholic rituals of Christianity (Protestant and Evangelist). The carnival centred on the African way of life and according to Marissa Moorman "...carnival groups were predominant form of such cultural activity in the musseques (Moorman, 2008, p. 61). The word "musseques" is a colloquial terminology used in ordinary or familiar conversation, not formal or literary. It means small town or shantytowns in Angola and also a suburb of the capital Luanda, a place inhabited by descendants of the population from the rural areas of the country (Oyebade, 2007, p. 90) (Fig. 10.1).

In addition, I saw that the carnival ritual and worship was the most expressive experience people manifested in the streets, through their dresses, costumes and dances. Moreover, in Luanda I witnessed the carnival in my neighbourhood with the people gathering together in the evenings in the months prior to the celebration to rehearse the steps of traditional music and dance with bands in order to compete at the national level. This was an exciting experience which impacted on my creative practice. Seeing

Fig. 10.1 Alberto Juliao during the Angolan carnival of victory in Luanda, 2013 (Alberto Juliao, 2013)

and experiencing the variety of dance choreographies, drum techniques and adornment of the bodies and costumes are the foundation and roots of how I construct my current work in the British environment. David Birmingham (2006) gives an important account of the carnival history in

Fig. 10.2 Alberto Juliao during the Angolan carnival of victory in Luanda, 2013 (Alberto Juliao, 2013)

postcolonial Angola, which resonates with my experience during my formative years and the impact of the Portuguese colonisation (Fig. 10.2).

My Performance Practice in London

It is crucial to point out that, in this section, I intend to provide a comprehensive overview and interpretation of my performances, their origin and the ideas and concepts behind the making processes that draws references on the basis of my experiences of hybridity, fluidity, ambiguity, adaptability, mixing of cultural identity and syncretism. In this context, in London as a black British artist my work draws reference from my background of living in Luanda as well as my experiences of being a refugee in London: a displaced and dislocated individual. In the same way, the concept of hybridity reflects the holistic forms of experiences I have of the two cultural and political spaces, presented in an art form of body painting and body practicing. The hybrid experiences I had helped me to apostolate the visual aspect of my practice, drawing references to the Angolan traditions of iconography of ritual and spirit. In this process, my work represents the recording of my body as a vehicle creating and questioning identity in the city as Afropolitan. My individual experience through performance arts, ritual and dance gives special attention to the understanding of the black body and history in the African diaspora.

I am taking into account that hybridity in this context is utilised as a theoretical frame that gives possibilities to incorporate in my practice as relevant cultural values and performance appropriations that I encounter in Britain. Inevitably, by creating performance works in Britain, I am directly or indirectly influenced by the diversity of artists, arts and cultural productions, as a result of the conscious shared space and locality in a capital city (Gilroy, 2000b, p. 308). The multitude of artists shifting reality by producing and recognising difference practices which influences my perception of the self and creativity. In this process, through hybridity and representation, other postcolonial and ethnic practices, ideas and visions are allowed to be incorporated into my work as a creative agency that forges the idea of what it means to be black in Britain. In this light, hybridity operates through the body as a signifier of the social and cultural medium of communication and voice. Hybridity allows and celebrates cultural differences and intersections of identity and knowledge as a source of play, which makes important different narratives in the creation of the alternative third spaces of the performances, spaces that merge different pasts, perspectives and histories as "theoretical influences" (Doy, 2000, p. 23). John Akomfrah in his nonlinear documentary film *The Stuart Hall Project* (2013) shows the portrait of Hall as an influential and heroic black British figure in the fields of culture and media studies in the academic landscape and critical analysis. This work on Hall explores the kaleidoscopic of ideas of memory in relation to race and identity within the wide dialogue of political and social representation that constitutes our collective experiences and historical events that shaped the production of twentieth-century multiculturalism and postmodernism as a diaspora discourse in Britain.

In London, I began making performances in 2001 as a result of my exploration of ancient "primitive" and "tribal" traditions, through using my body painted as a result of my experiences of cultural intersection and hybridity, which seemed to be a challenge to some audience members of both the African diaspora community and Western culture. During that time, I was a refugee and a displaced individual without a sense of belonging and identification. I felt that I was lost without a location. In analysing three solo performances, all of them performed in London in the past eight years, I offer an understanding of my work in relation to the exploration of each particular site-specific space that I re-created through the performance. Below, I critically discuss and describe some of my primary concerns as a performance artist using the body as a vehicle of expression and communication in the British context. The performances are organised chronologically, and reflect the principles and issues I had set to explore at the time. As I have mentioned above, my past is the central point and the roots of my creativity. For this reason, I use my postcolonial experience and condition as a critical lens to analyse the performances of my fragmented body. I am doing this because of the impact colonialism made upon me and my generation.

Transformation

The following two performances were symbolic ritualistic activities and processes that were based on similar ideas and principles as those which explored community and gallery space. One of my intentions was to create a ritual practice and aesthetic of the body expressed by the Haitian people as part of their culture, customs and ceremonies of Voodoo. Essentially, their cultural tradition and divine practice influenced me to do these works as a symbolic idea and performance of diaspora experiences (Gilroy, 2000a, p. 490) (Fig. 10.3).

Haiti has a very rich ritualistic expression and ancestral worship based on West African (Benin, Nigeria, Senegal and Congo) traditional religion and cosmology (Deren, 2004, p. 58). In this case, my particular interest in looking at the Haitian cultural tradition as an inter-cultural and transcultural method to create performance in England does not mean that I lost my own sense of origin and integrity, but because the Haitian cultural and religious practice constitute one of the important aspects of the continuum of the African religion in the diaspora. This includes acknowledging the African diasporic religious practices of Brazil, Cuba, Jamaica, Dominican Republic and North America. According to Thompson the Kongo (which is where Angola is located now) has a direct link with the religion practised in Haiti, Brazil, Cuba and North America (1984, pp. 127–29). This demonstrates the communality with my practice and processes that I am currently looking into, as a quest for ancient connections derived from Africa.

Fig. 10.3 Cuxima-Zwa, Area 10 performance Space, Peckham, London, 2007 (Savinien-Zuri Thomas, 2007)

The reason I have chosen to include some reference to these pieces is because they are very significant and important visual representations of my practice. They represent the first time that I expressed a ritual practice and character beyond the Angolan cultural tradition and my personal trajectories in the diaspora world. In other words, in these pieces I demonstrated the direct link that I made in a form of a symbolic ritual based on the Haitian cultural expression of contemporary religion and iconography. It is important to state at this point that, through the devel-

Fig. 10.4 Cuxima-Zwa, Area 10 performance Space, Peckham, London, 2007 (Savinien-Zuri Thomas, 2007)

opment of my practice the Haitian cultural tradition and religion became an important diasporic source of information and inspiration because I wanted to integrate the experiences of my new British-self in relation to their cultural practice (Murphy, 1994, p. 14) (Fig. 10.4).

In these pieces, one of my objectives was to translate into a performative work my interpretation of the Haitian ritual presented through the extensive works of Maya Deren's *Divine Horsemen: The Living Gods of Haiti* (2004) a book and DVD with the same title. It is important to emphasise that I did these pieces based on my research of her works because of the accuracy and analysis she gives to Haitian rituals and ceremonies. In the performance, it was important to have the space dark, so then I could transform it and symbolically manifest the power of the ancestral spirits and deities in a connection expressed and mediated through the actions, movements and ephemeral gestures of my body inventing a ritual.

The space of the performance was deliberately configured and devised in a way so that the audience formed a circle to create a ritual approach and atmosphere, with the visibility of the space and my body placed in the centre. I consciously decided to set up the space to be this way. I was the focus of attention and through this setting I wanted possibilities to occur through my body as the medium constructing a personal ritual of healing and connection in the dark space. In these works my body was painted white, black, blue and red; and I used the following props: a "divine"

Fig. 10.5 Cuxima-Zwa, Area 10 performance Space, Peckham, London, 2007 (Savinien-Zuri Thomas, 2007)

basket, white powder and water to symbolically create a ritual that suggested both sacred and surreal worship and a point of access between the physical and the metaphysical world as expressed in the Haitian ceremonial religion (Thompson, 1984, pp. 179–80) (Fig. 10.5).

These pieces were constructed as an act of offering and veneration; I knelt and touched my lips to the ground as a gesture to express my devotion to the Angolan ancestors and the spiritual power of the Haitian deities. The candle light was used as a metaphysical point of contact and interfusion; at the same time, the body served to naturalise and establish a bond and unity between the physical and spiritual world. In addition, my props were placed in the middle of the space. My exploration of the cross-roads ritual was the visible aspect which represented the Haitian culture and religion. What is more, the use of the cross-roads was fundamental because symbolically it indicated the communion and traffic between the two worlds. These works were performed in a way that Haitians express the cultural tradition of Voodoo ceremonies. That is to say, my actions symbolically made reference to interlocking link between life, transfiguration and the Haitian gods and the cosmic world.

Identity, Parliament Square and the Houses of Parliament

In this site-specific performance, my idea was to explore notions of location in my body through performing in Parliament Square and in front of the iconic symbol of the Houses of Parliament in Westminster, London; where my body created a visual and imaginary past as a reflection of my postcolonial experience of social struggle and being a refugee. In this particular piece, the Houses of Parliament and the buildings surrounding it shaped and played an important part in the composition of the performance. The buildings helped my narration of the (my)self and the "primitive" and "other". It affected how I positioned my body as a vehicle of diasporic cultural production and identity. By positioning myself in Westminster Square in front of the Houses of Parliament I wanted to use the site-specific space to make a statement of performance of body painting as a representation of the aesthetic of my ancestral spiritual values. Painted as I was, I created an imaginary connection with home because of the contrast I created between "primitivism" and British ideas of civilization, past and present history and modernity. In this work, my body was a tool which connected the two cultures through the process of diaspora, displacement, dysfunction, trauma and migration as pointed out and broadly described by

Braziel and Mannur (2003, pp. 1–3). In this text *Theorising Diaspora*, they offer a source that offers an understanding of diaspora studies as a multicultural and theoretical emergency of identities.

This performance is a bodily representation of my strategy as a diaspora individual re-inventing and redefining the self and identity (Hall & Sealy, 2001, p. 35). It is my act of negotiating the space with the dominant culture portrayed by the Houses of Parliament. In this piece, ideas of space and visibility were a concern expressed through my body in a symbolic ritual. Furthermore, I posed a challenge by being visible and claiming my space in Westminster Square, where I shifted notions of home by positioning myself as the painted "other" constructing a representation of diaspora imagination and vision. In this case, diaspora experience becomes the focus of expression intersecting with ideas of home and origin, while the body claims the space. Notions of home are expressed by idealising the process of diaspora experience. In this context, I claim my space and occupy my position through my painted body making my diaspora experience exposed as a product of the inter-culturalism phenomenon in Britain. Through the process, my cultural tradition and performance became visible in the space of the colonial and imperial cultures. According to Daryl Chin:

> *Interculturalism is one of the ways of bringing previously suppressed material into the artistic arena, by admitting into a general discourse other cultures, cultures which had previously been ignored or suppressed or unknown.* (Chin, 1991, p. 95)

In this manner, inter-culturalism allowed my cultural tradition to manifest publically as an open option of cultural representation; it made expressive the meaningful perspectives of the perception and reading of the black body in public as material culture, transient art, and an autonomous tool of empowerment of identity and cultural tradition exploring the British space. Inter-culturalism, exchange and synthesis are a tool that I utilised, which promoted my cultural origin and artistic tradition through performance arts and ritual practice in the global world characterised by transnationalism (Fig. 10.6).

Notwithstanding, during the performance the statue of Nelson Mandela positioned in one of the corners of the square was the place where I narrated my diaspora experience and claimed my space. For the purpose of the performance, Mandela's statue connected me with home and Africa. It represented a site to express and elaborate my origins, the struggle of my

PERFORMATIVITY OF BODY PAINTING: SYMBOLIC RITUAL AS DIASPORIC... 151

Fig. 10.6 Cuxima-Zwa, Parliament Square performance, London, 2009 (Simon Rendall, 2009)

diaspora experience and what it means to be an African in the postcolonial and post-apartheid era, in Britain (Cohen-Cruz, 1998, pp. 286–287). The performance in front of the statue was an attempt to relate with Mandela's social struggle for justice, validation and the independent existence of African people in a way that shared a sense of the interconnectedness of diaspora and transnational experience. Empathy with the political struggle of African people in South Africa was symbolically eluded to through the performance in front of the statue. My body was a diaspora instrument to create a new reality and "...new ways of thinking and feeling" about the past and present in a new environment (Nicholson, 2009, p. 268). In this case, the statue served to trigger the link or relationship between diaspora and Africa (Hall, 1994, p. 394) as an important memorial moment for the construction of an alternative perspective on identity and history (Gilroy, 1996, pp. 225–227).

My body functioned as an agent that spoke out in the Westminster Square about my existence and experiences of national identity, hybridity and the impact of globalisation in the London metropolis (Enwezor, 1999, p. 245). In this piece, my presence was my way of contesting the position of the dominant culture that dismisses, subsumes and de-legitimates African "tribal" and "primitive" traditions and cultural practice. By presenting myself in this way, it was my intention to put forward my African origins, cultural heritage, legacies and ideologies in a symbolic ritual in front of the Houses of Parliament; an iconic British imperialist building. The Houses of Parliament reminded me of where I have come from and my history. It created in me a deep feeling of an outsider returning home through the process of encounter. In this context, The Houses of Parliament represented the central point of dialogue, whereby my ideas of identity with home and origin (Angola) became visible because of the contrast my body created and offered in the British imperial space in relation to culture, civilization, race, heritage and sense of belonging. What the building represents to the British people I did not feel I was part of. In a way I felt like an outsider invading the imperial space and culture. The encounter illustrated to me the beginning of coming to terms with the self in relation to notions of home and belonging (Matzke and Okagbue, 2009, p. xviii).

The structure and rigidity of the Houses of Parliament intimidated and created a division between the "us and them" of the social order, which de-authorises the "other's" existence and social realities in the British political and parliamentary discourse and hegemony. It created in me a feeling of separation between two worlds and cultures. The police and the gate keepers of the building restricted my approach and made me feel intimidated; it was safer to perform far away from the building, in case of any trouble or confrontations. The performance situation was appropriated to some distance from the building (especially when one was presented painted and half naked). My presence in front of the Houses of Parliament was unpredictable and it created a contrast against the hard solidity of concrete and the rigid architectural infrastructure, which displayed power and control in the city, assisted by the presence of the police and other gate keepers (Fig. 10.7).

Performing in front of the Houses of Parliament encouraged me to accentuate my cultural history and subjectivity in opposition to postcolonial modernism and institutional production, which constantly imperils the creativity of the "other" as a control mechanism. By performing in

Fig. 10.7 Cuxima-Zwa, Parliament Square performance, London, 2009 (Simon Rendall, 2009)

front of the Houses of Parliament, my work suffered the consequence of alienation within the constraints of the Western well-regulated establishment, which operated from a distance because of my appearance of being different and perhaps "inappropriate" in the centre of the city. In this case, the Houses of Parliament represents a symbolic site of the "axis of power" in a city where people gather and transit as a product of an environment very much embedded in modernism and capitalism to use Judith Rugg's terminology (Rugg, 2010, p. 54). Despite the fact that the piece was a self-articulation of experience of different localities and a narration of my culture in a re-fashioned manner, it also transgressed the boundaries of the Western power encoded by the legacy of the colonial condition perpetuated by the authority symbolised in the Houses of Parliament. In this case, the building symbolically represents imperial power and exposes the cultural hegemony of the West.

One of the main reasons I wanted to perform in front of the Houses of Parliament was because of the history of the British Empire associated with the building and the political power the building holds in correlation to colonial history and practice. The building represents the modern era, evolution, the contact with 'other' cultures through slavery, colonialism

Fig. 10.8 Cuxima-Zwa, Parliament Square performance, London, 2009 (Simon Rendall, 2009)

and the historical and social memory derived from it (Christian, 2002, p. 71) (Fig. 10.8).

Above all, my body painted with a mask in this site-specific performance posed a question and challenged what it means to be a black person and artist living in Britain in the twenty-first century; where the impact of hybridity, multiculturalism and globalisation very much alters black identity and confuses its realities in the development of notions of the self/group (Tulloch, 2004b, p. 11).

Abney Park Cemetery

I gave this performance during the end of the summer of 2015 at the historical park and cemetery in north London in the borough of Hackney, in Stoke Newington. The cemetery is one of the most important cemeteries in London. I wanted to make and explore my ideas for this performance for a long time, and this finally came to realisation with much effort and determination on my part, because I believed it was important to do this work in an environment considered by the public as abnormal for a

Fig. 10.9 Cuxima-Zwa, Abney Park Cemetery performance, London, 2015 (Aguinaldo Vera Cruz, 2015)

performance ritual in an open space during the daytime. However, initially I planned to do this performance ritual with Li Keegan, an artist and researcher who was studying at Morley College, where I was assistant teacher in the drama and theatre department. Sadly she could not physically perform and take part in the ritual but wanted to collaborate by being present at the space. The good news was that she suggested that Jackie Townsend, a colleague of hers, was interested in collaborating (Fig. 10.9).

Fig. 10.10 Cuxima-Zwa, Abney Park Cemetery performance, London, 2015 (Aguinaldo Vera Cruz, 2015)

One week before the actual collaboration, Jackie and I met at the college and did a brainstorm of ideas. The conversation went well, I had a good sense of her approach; she suggested bringing costumes and dressing up. She had conceptual ideas of merging the painted body with English modern cosmopolitan dress. The week before, I met with Aguinaldo Vera Cruz (Capela) on sight at the cemetery. I also spoke with Christopher Wilson, a friend I wanted to take part in the collaboration (Fig. 10.10).

The morning of the day of the performance, it was a beautiful sunny day. I met with Chris at Stoke Newington station and we walked to the cemetery. Two hours later, as expected, Capela arrived and as soon as he saw us he started recording with photographs, while Chris was painting my body. The surrounding environment of nature and the spirituality in the cemetery created a ritual ground. Together with my props, I wanted to use the background to link my body with my diasporic experience of identity and religion in a site-specific space. My presence at the cemetery was a deep reconnection with black people and their history with the space. Many black people were buried there such as Thomas Canry Caulker, son of the Sierra Leone King of Bompey, Joanna Vassa, daughter of Olaudah Equiano and Eric Wolrand, African American Harlem Renaissance writer. It was significant to be around people who fought for emancipation and freedom in the Caribbean, North America and Britain (Fig. 10.11).

During the performance, I walked to different parts of cemetery, finding particular spots to explore ideas through symbolic ritual and by making body movements, gestures and using props as a creative medium, interconnecting notions of diaspora with the African ancestors and religious iconography as a process of embedded cultural practice. During the performance, I used an African sculpture as a prop to give a spiritual and physical symbolism to my connection with the African tradition of ritual. In this devotional piece and re-enactment, I wanted to symbolically give meaning and value to the past. In other words, I utilised the process of symbolic ritual and performance as a powerful way for the ancestral spirits to manifest as a point of entry into the present. In this way, the piece symbolically allowed the ancestral spirits to enter as a creative entity engaged in the surrounding space, enticed by the adornment of my body, the choreographic ritual as a revelation of my thoughts, actions and identity. Benedict Anderson's, argument gives meaning and contextualises this piece in the new world as "imagined communities" and my idealised relationship with my ancestral spirit as transformative and transnational method of finding "cultural roots" (Anderson, 2006, p. 6). My approach of a creative narrative with the ancestral spirits reconnected and reconstructed past and present as a source and continuing validity of divine wisdom.

The referenced ritual works of the artists Rotimi Fani-Kayode and Fela Kuti were catalysts in the production of this piece. They made it possible for my ideas to flow and provided strands for aesthetic and derivative forms of rituals for my performance practice. They provided cultural codes of interpretation for the diaspora creative body. Fani-Kayode's photographic

Fig. 10.11 Cuxima-Zwa, Abney Park Cemetery performance, London, 2015 (Aguinaldo Vera Cruz, 2015)

works of popular culture and explorations of the symbolic matrix of the black male body in the studio influenced my process. At the centre, his subject matter comments on the religiosity of Yoruba, in which the use of masks and masquerade presents a sophisticated aesthetic that Fani-Kayode uses to discuss his experience of activism, politics of race, desire and sexuality in Britain as a means of connecting the diaspora and Africa. Kuti's, artistic practice and performance was an inspiration too. It made me realise the potential of my creativity. His outspoken hedonistic, rebel acts of art and voice promoted a revolutionary consciousness of liberation, justice and Pan-African postcolonial production of collective black identity (Tenaille, 2002, p. 72). His pioneering artistic endeavour on the African and African American traditions of iconography and spirituality manifested through Afrobeat music and dance. In the same way, the symbolic rituals and theatrical invocation of his ancestral gods with painted bodies in his shrines is a legacy recognised for bringing innovation of styles to performance tradition, world music and diaspora syncretic religion (Veal, 2000, p. 6). His ritual was used as a model to recreate my broken identity through symbolic ritual as a performance inspiration and production.

In this piece, one of my ideas was to embody and give value to African indigenous culture and art as a process to connect, reclaim my origin and identity and the greatness of my ancestors. In this process, one of my objectives was to indicate the Afrocentric method and voice as an ideological principal of an African worldview and orientation. (The Afrocentric or Afrocentricity is a distinct academic ideological method of research and study that reached its peak in the 1970s, 1980s and 1990s as part of the activism of African American intellectuals.) I wanted to express Afrocentricity in this piece as a theoretical and philosophical principle that emphasises the existence of Africans as leading subjects, not as objects. Moving and performing with my body painted, I took the central strand while I was communicating and navigating the cemetery and site-specific space. In doing this, I was highlighting Afrocentric information with self-determination of Pan-African agency and perceptions of culture and social reality. In other words, this Afrocentric piece was a self-conscious exploration of conceptual ideas to place the historical enterprise of my experiences in Britain in an organic relationship with Angolan history. It manifested my diaspora experience as an African-centred view and the portrayal of the characteristics of my black Britishness. The piece represented a documentation of African culture and diaspora history in the multicultural space of Hackney, and in the context of performance arts, dance and symbolic ritual. The Afrocentric study and research method is brilliantly championed by Asante in his text *The Principal Issues in Afrocentric Inquiry* (Asante, 1996, p. 256) where he gives characteristics to Afrocentric enterprise as an African-centred cosmology and a relationship with the spiritual existence between body, soul and the universe as a cultural manifestation and social reflection of the metaphysical dimensions.

Asante writes that, *Afrocentricity* is an African way of life and spiritual relationship with the cosmos as a form of religion and ancestral worship with nature. According to Asante "Afrocentricity" is directly connected with Kemet as Africalogy, which is generically known through the context of the ancient practice of the classical African civilization of Egypt (Asante, 1996, pp. 256–257). However, it is in this academic work *Afrocentricity: The Theory of Social Change* (2003) whereby Asante popularises the concept of Afrocentricity by relating with the influences of the Pan-African leaders of the twentieth century such as Marcus Garvey, W. E. B. Dubois, Kwame Nkrumah, Haile Selassie, Cheikh Anta Diop, Malcolm X, Martin Luther King, Frederick Douglas and John Henrik Clarke.

In my creative process with the use of body painting, I connected with his articulation about the need of an African person in the new world to look at Africa as the beginning and centre of one's existence and reflection. In other words, the world is a reflection of African cultural, philosophical and religious values. For me, through discovering Asante's works on *Afrocentricity* I began to install those values in my practice as imaginary and symbolic creative ideas in a form of ritual composition. Afrocentricity centres on ideas of unity and places black people at the forefront of decision-making processes and as the catalyst of their own destiny worldwide. Nonetheless, through the performance, I was aware that the physical presence of my body in the space was strange for the audience who were passing by that, for the most part, did not understand the meaning of me been at the cemetery painted and creating symbolic ritual as an expressive action and enactment of the evocation of dramatic arts. The performance ritual in itself was not done specifically for an audience, but there was an audience passing by that for few minutes wanted to glimpse and understand the performance and what we were doing in an environment where it is not normal to be half naked and painted during day light. In the end, I did realise that when they saw my collaborator and photographer, Vera Cruz, holding the camera, there was a shift in their gazing at the performance and the scenario. People seemed to accept an interpretation of the work as visual practice and aesthetic of the body in display in the public and site-specific space. The dichotomy of an open space of the cemetery contributed to the reception and perception of the piece, whereby the audience brought with them their personal burden while being captivated by the presence of my body as a stranger—what Tommy L. Lott called "black vernacular" (Lott, 1994, p. 230). In this context, I am using the term "black vernacular" to denote the communication of my performative body as a black dialect and culture. Here, I use the terminology to express and convey my ideas of my body as the medium of communication and speaker in the public space. As a black artist, my intention in using the term is to challenge the misperception of the black body as devalued subject on display and to empower its presence as an ideological art form.

The nature of the place, the choreography of the performance, generated and offered multiple postcolonial interpretations and experiences of the gazed body, presented as a live creative identity of a primitive and tribal exotic subject of desire. The reading of my body had a lot to do with the environment I was in and British history's recent encounters with the black body as a colonial subject, neo-colonialism and dictatorship.

I detected the latter in the audience understanding and reading of the African painted body in the cemetery open space as a site of the Western metropolis and power. In *Reading the Contemporary: African Art from Theory to the Marketplace* (1999), Okwui Enwezor explains that the Western metropolis is a site constructed "...as a plural environment in the contemporary imagination...", which displaces, diminishes and disintegrates the African performance arts and artists. The postcolonial condition of the black body in the Western environment makes difficult the reading and perception of African performance arts and artists. As a result of this, Enwezor points out, African artists are forced to

...Transgress the boundaries of 'otherness': a colonial condition that a reductive postmodernist thinking constantly attempts to refashion under the polite but alien banner of 'difference'. (Enwezor, 1999, p. 251)

The Haitian cultural tradition and ritual of Voodoo, healing and initiation is my diaspora influence and creative relation with my ancestral roots. I am arguing that, the Haitian ritual of Voodoo Gods, Loa and Legba actually has some pattern of relation in the religious practice in the west-central African region of Congo and in some parts of Angola. The French colonial legacy reinforces this point because some of the slaves transported to Haiti were taken from the Congo Kingdom, and both countries are still connected with France through the imperial legacy of French language and culture. Thompson in his text *Flash of the Spirit: African & Afro-American Art & Philosophy*, gives an outstanding account of the widespread signs and insights of the cosmographic symbol of "... spiritual renaissance and classical religion of the great Congo people of Zaire, Angola, Cabinda and Congo-Brazzaville" (Thompson, 1984, p. 167). Thompson presents an in-depth synthesis of the contribution of their

Fig. 10.12 Cuxima-Zwa, Abney Park Cemetery performance, London, 2015 (Aguinaldo Vera Cruz, 2015)

ritual and religion in the new world, whereby he contextualises Voodoo in Haiti with the Congo and Angolan civilization and visual tradition, as a means to retain a black cultural sense of origin (Thompson, 1984, p. 105).

In the Abney Park cemetery piece, the works of Hurston played an important part as a choreographic influence. This is because of Hurston's power and ability to write stories relating to African ritual tradition. Further, Hurston possessed a creative imagination as a writer of folklore, ceremony and superstition, a revealer of the Hoodoo mysticism and Voodoo of New Orleans and Haiti (Hurston, 1990, p. 183). In this context, I used the works of Hurston as a principal to engage my props with symbolic gestures, movements and the worship of nature, earth and cosmos with a kiss on the ground as a tribute to the creator. Her work inspired the open space of the performance and inference of religious ceremony and the revelation of my painted body half naked. In Hurston's literary work *Tell My Horse: Voodoo and Life in Haiti and Jamaica* (2009) she presents a series of pictures of ceremonies in Haiti and Jamaica, which visually influenced this piece in the way I created my symbolic Voodoo altar, with sacred and divine objects (Fig. 10.12).

Conclusion

One of the aims of this chapter was to create awareness of the context and background of the Angolan history and the value of its rich cultural tradition and creative practice, in relation to the black diasporic creative process and my identity in Britain. Angolan's brutal past historical experiences of slavery, colonialism and civil war impacted on my diasporic construction of identity and performance practice. For me body painting, symbolic ritual and dance as creative and aesthetic forms of identity have great value.

Thus, as a performance artist in my creation of live performances in London, I am impacted by the Angolan history of 27 years of civil war, instability and trauma. Growing up in Luanda in the 1980s, I am impacted by the dynamic of the experience of war. My neighbours were catalysts of raw sources; they introduced to me traditional and rural dance movements, gestures and African dress attire as narrative centred on body nativity and codes of knowledge. With the modernisation of Luanda and the migration and movement of people, my neighbours made me understand life and identity in rural areas, which as a result of this knowledge I can now exemplify in my creative performances and photographs.

References

Anderson, B. (2006). *Imagined Communities*. London: Verso.
Asante, M. (1988). *Afrocentricity*. Trenton, NJ: Africa World Press.
Asante, M. (1996). The Principal Issues in Afrocentric Inquiry. In M. K. Asante & A. S. Abarry (Eds.), *African Intellectual Heritage: A Book of Sources* (pp. 256–261). Philadelphia, PA: Temple University Press.
Asante, M. (2003). *Afrocentricity: The Theory of Social Change*. Chicago, IL: African American Images Press.
Birmingham, D. (1995). Language Is Power: Regional Politics in Angola. In J. Lewis & K. Hart (Eds.), *Why Angola Matters*. New York: James Currey.
Birmingham, D. (1999). *Portugal and African*. London: Palgrave Macmillan.
Birmingham, D. (2006). *Empire in Africa: Angola and Its Neighbors*. Athens, OH: Ohio University Press.
Bourgault, L. (2003). *Playing For Life: Performance in Africa in the Age of AIDS*. Durham, NC: Caroline Academic Press.
Braziel, J., & Anita, M. (2003). *Theorizing Diaspora*. Oxford, UK: Blackwell Press.
Chin, D. (1991). Interculturalism, Postmodernism, Pluralism. In B. Marranca & G. Dasgupta (Eds.), *Interculturalism & Performance* (pp. 83–95). New York: PAJ Publications.
Christian, M. (2002). Reflections of the 1997 European Year Against Racism: A Black British Perspective. In M. Christian (Ed.), *Black Identity in the 20th Century: Expressions of the US and UK African Diaspora* (pp. 59–77). London: Hansib Publications.
Cohen-Cruz, J. (1998). Notes Toward An Unwritten History of Anti-Apartheid Street Performance. In J. Cohen-Cruz (Ed.), *Radical Street Performance: An International Anthology* (pp. 282–287). London: Routledge.
Cordell, D. (2004). Oral Tradition: Classic Questions, New Answers. In T. Falola & C. Jennings (Eds.), *Sources and Methods in African History: Spoken Written, Unearthed* (pp. 239–248). Rochester, NY: University of Rochester Press.
Darwin, C. (1998). *The Origin of Species*. Hertfordshire, UK: Wordsworth Editions Limited.
Deren, M. (2004). *Divine Horsemen: The Living Gods of Haiti*. New York: McPherson & Company.
Doy, G. (2000). *Black Visual Culture: Modernity and Postmodernity*. London: I. B. Tauris Publishers.
Enwezor, O. (1999). Between Worlds: Postmodernism and African Artists in the Western Metropolis. In O. Oguibe & O. Enwezor (Eds.), *Reading the Contemporary: African Art from Theory to the Marketplace* (pp. 244–275). London: Institute of International Visual Arts (Iniva).

Gilroy, P. (1996). British Cultural Studies and the Pitfalls of Identity. In H. A. Baker Jr., M. Diawara, & R. H. Lindeborg (Eds.), *Black British Cultural Studies 'A Reader'* (pp. 223–239). Chicago: The University of Chicago Press.

Gilroy, P. (2000a). The Dialectics of Diaspora Identification. In L. Back & J. Solomos (Eds.), *Theories of Race and Racism: A Reader* (pp. 490–502). London: Routledge.

Gilroy, P. (2000b). Cruciality and the Frog's Perspective: An Agenda of Difficulties for the Black Arts Movement in Britain. In J. Procter (Ed.), *Writing Black Britain, 1948–1998: An Interdisciplinary Anthology* (pp. 307–320). Manchester, UK: Manchester University Press.

Hall, S. (1994). Cultural Identity and Diaspora. In P. Williams & L. Chrisman (Eds.), *Colonial Discourse and Post-Colonial Theory: A Reader* (pp. 392–403). London: Harvester Wheatsheaf.

Hall, S., & Sealy, M. (Eds.). (2001). *Different: A Historical Context*. London: Phaidon.

Hodges, T. (2004). *Angola: Anatomy of an Oil State* (2nd ed.). Oxford: James Currey.

Hurston, Z. (1990). *Mules and Men*. New York: Harper Perennial.

Hurston, Z. (2009). *Tell My Horse: Voodoo and Life in Haiti and Jamaica*. New York: Harper Perennial.

Lott, T. (1994). Black Vernacular Representation and Cultural Malpractice. In D. T. Goldberg (Ed.), *Multiculturalism: A Critical Reader* (pp. 230–258). Oxford: Blackwell.

Maier, K. (2007). *Angola: Promises and Lies*. London: Serif.

Matzke, C., & Okagbue, O. (2009). Introduction. In C. Matzke & O. Okagbue (Eds.), *African Theatre Diaspora* (pp. xvi–xxx). James Currey: Suffolk, UK.

Mbiti, J. (1991). *Introduction to African Religion* (2nd ed.). Oxford: Heinemann.

Moorman, M. (2008). *Intonations: A Social History of Music and Nation in Luanda, Angola, from 1945 to Recent Times*. Athens, OH: Ohio University Press.

Murphy, M. J. (1994). *Working the Spirit: Ceremonies of the African Diaspora*. Boston: Beacon Press.

Nicholson, H. (2009). Re-location Memory: Performance, Reminiscence and Communities of Diaspora. In T. Prentki & S. Preston (Eds.), *The Applied Theatre Reader* (pp. 268–275). London: Routledge.

Oyebade, A. (2007). *Culture and Customs of Angola*. London: Greenwood Press.

Picton, J. (2004). What to Wear in West Africa: Textile Design, Dress and Self-Representation. In C. Tulloch (Ed.), *Black Style* (pp. 22–47). London: Victoria and Albert Museum Publications.

Rug, J. (2010). *Exploring Site-Specific Art: Issues of Space and Internationalism*. London: I. B. Tauris & Co Ltd.

Somerville, K. (1986). *Angola: Politics, Economic and Society*. London: Pinter Publishers Limited.
Tenaille, F. (2002). *Music Is the Weapon of the Future: Fifty Years of African Popular Music*. Chicago: Lawrence Hill Books.
Thompson, R. (1984). *Flash of the Spirit: Afro-American Art and Philosophy*. New York: Vintage Books.
Tulloch, C. (2004a). *Check It: Back Style in Britain*. In C. Tulloch (Ed.), *Black Style* (pp. 84–121). London: Victoria and Albert Museum.
Tulloch, C. (2004b). *It's Good to Have the Feeling You're the Best*. In C. Tulloch (Ed.), *Black Style* (pp. 10–21). London: Victoria and Albert Museum.
Veal, M. (2000). *Fela: The Life and Times of an African Musical Icon*. Philadelphia: Temple University Press.
Welsing, F. (1991). *The Isis Papers: The Keys to the Colors*. Washington, DC: C. W. Publishing.

DVD Documentaries

Akomfrah, J. (2013). *The Stuart Hall Project*. London: British Film Institute.
Deren, M. (2004). *Divine Horsemen 'The Living Gods of Haiti*. New York: McPherson & Company.

CHAPTER 11

Dancehall: A Continuity of Spiritual, Corporeal Practice in Jamaican Dance

H. Patten

INTRODUCTION

The dancing reggae/dancehall body, its movement patterns and their social, political and historical significance in relation to African retentions within Jamaican ideology has been under-investigated. Being British born of Jamaican heritage and a participant in the reggae/dancehall space, many of the movements I performed socially over time have been recorded by various scholars. Most are recorded in name only with few detailed written descriptions readily available. A paucity of written descriptions of Jamaican African/neo-African[1] practices and their bodily manifestations also exists. 'Neo-African', meaning 'new African' (Ryman, 1984), is used here to negate the negative connotations attached to the colonial terms 'traditional' or 'folk' in Jamaica and in the British context, as I shall later expand upon. As a professional African and Caribbean performing artist for over 33 years I place centre-stage the 'corporeal dancing body', which I will explain shortly. This chapter therefore seeks to contest and move beyond the present slackness and violence 'trope', or conception ingrained within existing readings of the dancehall genre.

H. Patten (✉)
Canterbury Christ Church University, London, UK

Combining dance studies and theology, I suggest that aspects of the African spiritual cosmology retained in Jamaican religious dance practices may also be found within the 'corporeal dancing body' in the reggae/dancehall space. In contributing to reggae/dancehall discourse, in this chapter I further contend that reggae/dancehall is a contemporary continuum of African-derived spiritual cosmology. In doing so, in the first section I outline the notion of *The corporeal dancing body,* a concept I coin to foreground the body's engagement of history, dance, corporeality (fleshly physicality) and spirituality. I will then explain the importance of reggae/dancehall's *Alternative history of Jamaican cultural expression* incorporating an African/neo-African spiritual cosmology, which deserves serious attention, focus and engagement. A brief contextual overview of *Dancehall scholarship and discourses,* presents the key scholars and the dominant themes within reggae/dancehall.

Shifting focus, I then address *The dancehall phenomenon,* and *Dancehall participants.* I then explore *Reggae/dancehall as a continuum of African-derived spiritual cosmology,* laying the ground for the main African/neo-African dance practices to be discussed. *The body within the spiritual context* creates a focus against which the following section, *African/Jamaican cosmology,* illuminates dance and spiritual communication between the mortal and the spiritual worlds. The *Encoded knowledge within the dancehall space* section juxtaposes dancehall and African/neo-African dance movements within the dancehall context, while *Dancehall in Britain* foregrounds dancehall as a countercultural and subversive space. In conclusion, I bring together reggae/dancehall, the corporeal dancing body and spirituality in critical dialogue. Thereby, as a secular, popular, cultural form, reggae/dancehall is read through a sacred religious/spiritual lens employing dance and the body. Ultimately, this chapter aims to show how reggae/dancehall's subversive aesthetic provides a transformative survival and coping strategy through which many marginalised individuals attempt to make meaning of their lives.

The Corporeal Dancing Body

The 'corporeal dancing body' is a term I coin to intentionally emphasise the fleshly physicality of the African body and its corpse-like existence, which is symbolically re-animated, regaining visibility through the sustaining spirit embodied within African/neo-African dance. As I explain elsewhere (Patten, 2016), this signals the African body as being invested with historical references of 'otherness' (difference) connected to enslavement, oppression and inferiority, in relation to the white race. Dance is the public display of 'cultural memory', which consists of the symbolic gestures that emotionally link a community to its environment, handed down over generations (Buckland, 2001; Meusburger, Heffernan, & Wunder, 2011). The 'corporeal dancing body' triggers cultural memory linking the socio-political, historical and economic values encompassed in the physicality and cultural expression of formerly enslaved Africans. As an embodied idiom, dance is therefore part of a signifying system, communicating symbolic 'ancestral data' (Stines, 2005), encoded with 'cultural knowledge' (Sklar, 1991), the historically situated constructs that maintain cultural continuity both sacred and secular. This provides dancers with a consciousness of self that reaches way beyond 'outsider' (viewers outside of the culture) readings of the physicality of the 'corporeal dancing body'.

The 'corporeal dancing body' incorporates two aspects, firstly the 'lived body', which from a phenomenological perspective is concerned with the pre-reflective, kinesthetic movement of the body, integrating the senses and the physical limbs. Secondly, the 'corporeal body' enables a reflective engagement that manifests emotion. According to Thomas Fuchs (2003), it is when the automatic functioning of the 'lived body' is interrupted and one becomes conscious of the body and its objectification under the gaze of others that it becomes 'corporealized' (Fuchs, 2003, p. 225) and feelings of shame, guilt and/or performance are felt. I extend the duality of the *'lived'* and *'corporeal'* body through the black *'corporeal dancing body'* which within the reggae/dancehall space, I contend, serves to collapse time and space. Thereby, reggae/dancehall's 'corporeal dancing body' removes guilt and shame in enabling a temporal displacement of the conscious sensing body, in manifesting a historical engagement of the spiritual realm. In other words, within the secular reggae/dancehall space, the 'corporeal dancing body' in its continued embodiment of ancestral data, cultural knowledge and cultural memory, genealogically engages religious and spiritual practices.

ALTERNATIVE HISTORY OF JAMAICAN CULTURAL EXPRESSION

The global Jamaican reggae/dancehall phenomenon is a creative transnational space,[2] reflecting the socio-political and economic condition of its participants, as a site in which notions of identity are negotiated. A creative cultural form, reggae/dancehall emerges from the negotiation of cultural identity. In relation to Black artists in Britain, reggae/dancehall represents, in part, a subversive response to the marginalisation of African

People's dance[3] expression. Through performance and 'performativity' (Butler, 1988; Nash, 2000),[4] the behavioural actions of its participants, reggae/dancehall may be regarded as a conduit through which personhood and agency is played out, which has had a major impact on British urban youth culture. This agency is evident in the creative products of reggae/dancehall, in its dance, language, erotic styling and sartorial fashion as acknowledged by most (Hope, 2006; Bakare-Yusuf, 2006). Agency is developed within the ritual processes through which dancehall participants subvert or reject 'hegemony' (ruling class structures) in an attempt to gain 'smadditisation' also termed 'smadditizin', meaning to be recognised as somebody of worth. This self-actualisation permits the gaining of visibility and access denied by race in the construction and enactment of 'personhood' (Mills, 1997; Nettleford in Scott, 2006; Stanley-Niaah, 2010), as I argue through the corporeal dancing body.

However, what has escaped most scholars, I suggest here, is that reggae/dancehall has at its foundations an African/Jamaican spiritual cosmology that manifests genealogical retentions within the corporeal dancing body and the 'smadditisation' or agency it facilitates, as a contemporary continuum. These retentions originate from African/Jamaican religious dance practices such as, Jonkonnu masquerade,[5] the African-derived Revival dance[6] and the classical African Kumina dance ritual.[7] I aim to illustrate how these practices manifest in the performance and 'performative' actions displayed both consciously and unconsciously within contemporary reggae/dancehall culture.

Dancehall Scholarship and Discourses

Dancehall scholarship has often been presented through the lens of cultural studies, sociology, anthropology, philosophy, gender studies, geography and ethnomusicology. Attention has mainly focused on the historical development of the dancehall space, the sound systems and music (Stolzoff, 2000; Henriques, 2003; Manuel & Marshall, 2006; Hebdige, 2007), lyrical content and female rituals, (Cooper, 1993; Wright, 2004), social and political dynamics in Jamaican society and the dancehall space (Hope, 2006; Pinnock, 2007), the geographical mapping of the dancehall space (Stanley-Niaah, 2010), dancehall origins (Walker, 2008), issues of fashion, which have highlighted the corporeal body (Bakare-Yusuf, 2006), gender, identity, sex and sexuality (Sharpe, 2003; White, 2003; Gutzmore, 2004; Hebdige, 2007; Hope, 2010), slackness, violence and culture (Cooper, 2004; Ryman, 2004). However, besides Robert Beckford's (2006) musical exploration of dancehall and church hall, very little is written on reggae/dancehall in relation to religion or the alternative histories within the vocabulary of the dancing body, the focus of my research (Patten, 2016). Having presented reggae/dancehall's main discourses, it is necessary to outline what dancehall is.

The Dancehall Phenomenon

Transcending the dance hall venues from which it derives its name, the term 'reggae/dancehall' signals 'dancehall' as a distinct contemporary form within the 'reggae' genre, although the terms 'reggae' and 'dancehall' are often used interchangeably. Acknowledging this fact and for the sake of clarity, the term 'dancehall' will be used in this chapter in relation to the discrete music and dance genre emerging from the late 1970s onward as part of the genealogical line from Mento, Ska, (Blue Beat in Britain), Rocksteady, Reggae to Dancehall. This maintains its usage by most participants in the Jamaican context. The term 'reggae/dancehall', foregrounds dancehall's function as a phenomenon and historical space, incorporating its genealogical forerunners and African/neo-African antecedence.

Jamaican dancehall as a discrete form emerged out of reggae as a music and dance genre, before developing into a language, fashion, style, space, community, attitude, ritual, creative economy, a cultural and ideological phenomenon. Dancehall is rightly perceived as Jamaica's most popular indigenous cultural expression, as highlighted by leading dancehall scholars (such as Norman Stolzoff, 2000; Carolyn Cooper, 2004; Donna P. Hope, 2006 and Sonjah Stanley-Niaah, 2010), among others. Dancehall's development and growth in Britain follows a parallel path to that in Jamaica, albeit less high profile. Thereby, as a hybrid African/Caribbean dance practice dancehall in Britain is often linked to hip hop culture under the more globalised commercial classification of contemporary urban expression.

Dancehall Participants

Many Jamaican dancehall participants, like the dancehall phenomenon itself, emerge from the lower socio-economic inner city areas within Jamaica's capital city, Kingston (Stolzoff, 2003; Hope, 2006). Dancehall participants include the DJs such as Beenie Man, Bounty Killer, Elephant Man, Lady Saw, Mavado, Popcaan, Spice and Vybz Kartel among numerous others, commonly referred to as the artists. Dancehall participants also encompass the dancers (who choreograph and create the visual aesthetic through the dances), selectors (the people who choose and talk over the music to excite and encourage audience participation), the Dancehall Queens (important solo dancers who alongside the modellers, set dancehall's sartorial fashion and style) and the audience or dancehall 'massive', whom I term 'the adherents' as they actively participate within the dancehall space. Having established who dancehall's participants are and its function as both a distinct form and a phenomenon linking time and space, I now explore dancehall as a neo-African continuum.

DANCEHALL A CONTINUUM OF AFRICAN/NEO-AFRICAN SPIRITUAL COSMOLOGY

As I argue elsewhere, within the British context dance enables Black bodies to be (re)presented and (re)invented, thus initiating a (re)gaining of agency. Despite being produced and defined in relation to place and space where their agency is often negated by the dominant culture, many dancing bodies are empowered by their engagement in reggae/dancehall. Submerged in 'sonic dominance' (Henriques, 2003), reggae/dancehall's all-engulfing, penetrating 'riddim' (rhythm) and sound, participating bodies often transform during the intense dialogue between music and movement that takes place within the reggae/dancehall space. I personally have observed dancers who appear to almost transcend physical space. During semi-structured interviews, some dancers have shared experiences of feeling a sense of transcendence, or little consciousness of the 'corporeal dancing body', their personal physicality. A Jamaican scholar describes a female dancer who admits:

> ...*[She] loves "wining" her hips because when she does it feels like renewing energy radiating through her body, and when these "vibes" take over she steps out of her self.* (Stanley-Niaah, 2010, p. 130)

This clearly demonstrates the collision of the body, movement, music, time and space, in the creation of the 'vibe' (the energy, atmosphere, ambience and force) that crucially assists in facilitating reggae/dancehall's functioning as a transformative and transcendent space.

Some scholars contend that dancehall emerged out of 'a deliberate ideological shift from the cultural and spiritual philosophy of the Rastafarian associated *"roots reggae"'* (Patten, 2016, p. 100). Many ruling-class, Rastafarian and lower-class Christian members of Jamaican society condemn dancehall regarding it as being antithetical to any cultural or spiritual philosophy. It is often dismissed and its participants pathologised, regarded or treated as abnormal, due to dancehall's negative positioning within 'the dichotomous slackness [lewd, crude vulgarity] versus culture debate' (Hope, 2006, p. 125). Rastafarian dub-poet Mutabaruka, denounces dancehall for its 'lewdness, the downgrading of women, the slackness, materialism, [and] gun violence' (in Sharpe, 2003, p. 448). He asserts that reggae/dancehall is, '*the worst thing that ever happen* (sic) *to Jamaica* (sic) *culture*' (ibid). On the contrary, Carolyn Cooper (1993) and Beth Sarah Wright (2004) argue that dancehall provides a space within which female fertility, liberation and communication rituals take place. Extending the ritual concept I explore a spiritual dimension to dancehall. I contend that while slackness, that is, vulgarity and/or violence within dancehall's explicit content is undeniable, it may also be read as echoing the way that African forebears recognised and used dance as a resistant, transformative survival and coping strategy (Burton, 1997; Stewart, 2005). Thereby, dancehall becomes a subversive aesthetic, the rebellious inversion of hegemonic ruling-class structures and, as such, a transformative means through which many of its marginalised participants make meaning of their lives.

Dancehall must therefore be re-thought and re-read as part of the Jamaican continuum of religious and spiritual philosophies, by suspending the idea that religion is the only route or mode through which the divine is obtainable. In her religious and theological interrogation of hip hop, Monica R. Miller suggests that popular culture viewed through the lens of religion and theology, 'forces a rethinking of traditional religious and theological concepts' (Miller, 2009, p. 58). Thereby, the cosmologies within African/Jamaican religious dance practices such as Jonkonnu, Kumina and Revivalism, should be regarded as channelling ancestral data, providing encoded cultural knowledge, within cultural memory. This symbolically and physically manifests and can be read within dancehall's 'corporeal dancing bodies', representing the embodied genealogy of spiritual dance practices from slavery to the present-day, which I shall now explore.

The Body Within the Spiritual Context

To identify spiritual meaning within the corporeal dancing body in the dancehall space, it is first necessary to explore the corporeal expression of the dancing body within the spiritual context. African/neo-African dance practices such as Myal, Jonkonnu, Revivalism and Kumina dance rituals all serve to inform the African-centric ideologies that form part of the cultural memory of African/descent Jamaicans. I start by ascertaining how the corporeal dancing body functions within the Kumina religious dance ritual, identifying the Kumina 'worldview' and finally adopting it in examining the corporeal dancing body in relation to the dancehall genre. It is therefore important to 'overstand'[8] the centrality of the 'myal' (possession) state as a medium for transformation and transcendence.

Historically, most dances within the Jamaican context served a religious function and engaged the corporeal dancing body as the main conduit or vessel for spirit possession termed 'myal' (Stewart, 2005; Lewin, 2000). Many scholars initially recorded Myal as being a dance linked to the Gumbay dance and 'Obeah' spiritual practice. Myal is often referred to as good in relation to Obeah, regarded as dangerous and evil (Burton, 1997; Stewart, 2005). The two have historically been positioned in opposition as separate practices in Jamaica until recently. Dianne M. Stewart (2005) rightly identifies Myal and Obeah as being polar ends of one entity. Myal only emerged as oppositional to Obeah in 1842, following the moral criminalisation of Obeah by Euro-Christian theology. The polarisation of the forms leads to Myal's emergence as a spiritual dance practice in its own right. Myal was later subsumed into the possession state, in which ancestral spirits temporarily inhabit an individual during the process of dance in most African/neo-African spiritual practices, through the corporeal dancing body. The 'myal state' is attained by the 'call and response', the antiphonal or alternating interaction between a dancer and a musician (Lewin, 2000; Stewart, 2005). The corporeal dancing body is a central element to attaining the 'myal state' and, thus, receiving and conveying messages, healing, teaching and praise, between human beings and the ancestors, the main function that dance serves within most African/neo-African religious practices (Ryman, 1984; Lewin, 2000; Stewart, 2005), as the following section on African/Jamaican cosmology further explores.

African/Jamaican Cosmology

Kumina, as a post-slavery KiKongo religious dance tradition, is practised in the Jamaican parishes of St Thomas and St Catherine and is performed for both social and religious occasions. Kumina specialists regard themselves as Africans, not Jamaican Africans or African Caribbean people (Lewin, 2000; Stewart, 2005), hence my use of the inclusive term 'African/Jamaicans' is in respect to them. Kumina cosmology consists of the duality of the spiritual world, housing the spirits of departed ancestors, the fallen angels, the archangels and the 'Supreme Being', alongside the parallel material or mortal world of human beings. Dance, movement, music and songs, serve to connect these two worlds, while connecting Kumina practitioners to their African, cultural, linguistic and oral heritage, through the transcendental myal state (Stewart, 2005). Communication between the mortal and spirit worlds is the key purpose of the Kumina dance ritual and is heavily reliant on the corporeal dancing body functioning as the main spiritual conduit.[9] This is true not only in Kumina, but within most other African/neo-African religious practices; therefore a direct comparison between the performance of the corporeal dancing body in the spiritual and dancehall context is necessary. This will facilitate my identification of any symbolisms manifesting or signifying as spiritual within dancehall towards the end of this chapter.

Similarly to Kumina, the African-derived Revival movement is established on the duality of the spiritual and mortal worlds across which the spirits communicate with Revival members, offering healing, guidance and direction through the corporeal dancing body (Seaga, 1982; Stewart, 2005; Lewin, 2000). As a neo-African practice, Revivalism consists of three spiritual levels within the spirit world. First are the heavenly host, accommodating the 'Supreme Being' and the archangels; second are the earthbound spirits, including fallen angels and the prophets; and third are the ground spirits, being the ancestral spirits that once occupied the earth. The constraints of space do not permit me to delve deeper into Revivalism within this chapter.[10] Yet, I must include a brief outline of Jonkonnu masquerade, Jamaica's oldest traditional form, as it highlights the blurring of boundaries between the sacred and secular within African/Jamaican practices (Walker, 2008). Jonkonnu is commonly regarded as a secular form; however, the theologian Dianne M. Stewart challenges this classification, citing Martha Beckwith's (1928) early ethnographic text, 'Christmas Mummings in Jamaica', in which Beckwith asserts:

> The man Ewan [Jonkonnu dancer from Lacovia] (and very likely Swabe [of Prospect] as well) was a notorious myal man in Lacovia, that is, a man who held communication with the spirits of the dead ... Mary Campbell, his leading singing girl at that time, told me that he always took the cap [i.e., the Jonkonnu house headdress] out into the graveyard on the night before it was to be brought out upon the road, and performed the songs and dances there among the dead.
> – (Beckwith cited in Stewart, 2005, p. 52)

Anthropologist Kenneth Bilby (2007) has also shown Jonkonnu to maintain a spiritual/ritual aspect. In Jamaica's Rhoden Town and Brown Town in the parish of St Elizabeth, for example, Bilby highlights Jonkonnu's association with the Gumbay spiritual dance. He supports Beckwith's earlier findings, confirming that it is 'always a myal-man' (2007, p. 16) who is responsible for the construction or building of the Jonkonnu mask/headdress and its initial dance both for and among the ancestors. Close examination of the corporeal dancing body within the 'worldly', secular dancehall space provides evidence of Jonkonnu dance movements. This alongside the appearance of movements from other African/Jamaican practices such as Kumina and Revival suggests some transference of African-centric religious coding, as will now be explored.

Encoded Knowledge Within the Dancehall Space

Links between the dancehall genre and spiritual African/neo-African Jamaican practices are overtly apparent through dancehall songs such as 'Kumina to Kumina' (1985) by Lord Sassafrass, 'Kumina' (2008) by Sample Six and Guidance, or 'Pocomania Day' (1989), and 'Poco Party' (1989) by Lloyd Lovindeer. In performance of these songs, the artists visually display the symbolisms of African/neo-African practices. The music videos often employ dancers dressed in traditional attire specific to the practices the artists have drawn inspiration from. Dancers execute steps such as Kumina's—*basic 'inching step' (which involves toes clenching and opening/relaxing as the body rocks shifting the weight from side to side or with one foot flat and the other on the ball of the foot, whilst the pelvis rotates)*. Revivalism steps—*the 'Revival balance' (entailing stepping out with the leading leg, then bringing the other leg to meet it, with a slight twist of the body from side to side, shoulder leading the twist towards the side of the leading leg)* is combined with the basic *'female wining'* (common within dancehall dancing) to form visual signifiers of dancehall's genealogy.

Alternatively, spiritual links are more implicitly incorporated into the music in songs such as '100 Miles' (2003) by Beenie Man featuring Simma, or 'Nah Give Up' (2003) by Natural Black, which are both sung on the Kumina dancehall *riddim* (rhythm), based on the traditional Kumina drum pattern. Black's track speaks out against the injustices in Jamaican society, which he charges as being a 'system weh [that is] dutty [dirty] and corrup [corrupt]', which is punctuated by the actual Kumina ritual drum pattern and Kumina breaks at strategic musical moments. Through tracks such as these, African/neo-African practices of the past become part of the socio-political discourses of the present, playing an essential role, as Stewart asserts, 'in the chain of re-membering and linking African traditions from the past to the struggle for liberation' (2005, p. xvii). Spirituality in the secular space therefore becomes part of the decolonisation process of liberation struggle (Burton, 1997; Beckford, 2006).

The corporeal body became part of dancehall discourse with the emergence of the original Dancehall Queen Carlene Smith in the 1970s, whose 'provocative dancing in the "bare-as-you-dare" outfits she designs' (Stolzoff, 2000, p. 2) created great controversy. Bringing new levels of sensuality and sexuality into the dancehall space, the flesh of the corporeal dancing body became a central motif on multiple levels. Musically the lyrics became increasingly explicit as visually, female sartorial fashion increased the levels of flesh on display, while both the 'man-dem' (males') and the females' clothing got tighter and more fitted, sculpting corporeal bodies (Bakare-Yusuf, 2006). Dancers presently argue that this enables the optimum visibility of every movement performed within the highly competitive levels of dance within the dancehall space.

Through the expressive performance of dance movements and performative action, female dancers in particular, such as Dancehall Queen Stacey, extend the dance floor executing inspired, spontaneous and/or loosely choreographed movements on speaker boxes, lorry cabins and roof-tops, as scholars highlight (Stolzoff, 2000; Hope, 2006; Stanley-Niaah, 2010). This represents a challenge to society's moral coding in subverting Jamaican hegemonic structures according to Stanley-Niaah (2010). It also resonates with the gymnastic and acrobatic feats performed by corporeal dancing bodies in the spiritual/religious practices. I myself have witnessed Kumina participants scale trees in seconds and dance precariously positioned on a limb/branch.

Dancehall is an active and constantly shifting space, which both in the Jamaican and British context forces a reliance on corporeality. Donna

P. Hope aptly scribes how females employ 'erotic posing and gymnastic and erotic dancing to claim the status of Queens in the dancehall' (2010, p. 136). Yet, dancehall is also a countercultural space in which Carolyn Cooper (2004) contends, female sexuality, the erotic and liberatory fertility rites converge in celebrating femininity. This reflects for Cooper, a historically routed 'African diasporic discourse as a manifestation of the spirit of female fertility figures such as the Yoruba [orishas/deities] Oshun ... [and] Oya' (2004, pp. 103–104). Oshun represents the 'personification of the Erotic in Nature' (2004, p. 103), while Oya is a river goddess and *orisha* for the element of wind, masquerades and female power, as articulated by Bibi Bakare-Yusuf (in Cooper, 2004). This clearly demonstrates how dancehall's sartorial fashion and erotic nature, read beyond the slackness trope becomes a cathartic healing process and spiritual masquerade through which participants attain 'smadditisation'. Thereby dancehall, as Beth-Sarah White rightly claims, is 'intimately tied to a spiritual or godly presence in the quest for self-ownership, self-acceptance and self-love' (2003, pp. 81–82).

Dancehall's female corporeality is, in part, a response to the onslaught of male dancers now challenging for the dance floor, dancehall's centre-space. The erotic or sexual styling of the male body has been deliberately avoided within the dancehall genre. Rex Nettleford, former Director of the Jamaica National Dance Theatre Company (NDTC), clearly delineates the impact of class and gender vis-à-vis the divide between dance as 'high art versus [dancehall as] low culture' (2003, p. x). Male involvement in dance in Jamaica has historically been frowned upon apart from that taking place within African/neo-African forms such as Kumina and Revivalism (Hope, 2010). However, the *'legsman'* era of the 1960s and the later rise to prominence of Gerald 'Bogle' Levy in the 1990s as creator of the *'Bogle'* dance, made popular in song by Buju Banton,[11] paved the way for the male dancers, crews and squads that currently populate dancehall's transgressive space. This has enabled male corporeal engagement in dancehall to be relatively free of any perceived stigma in Jamaica (Sonjah Niaah, 2010). In Britain, the growth and spread of hip hop dance and the involvement of male dancers in African People's Dance, made male dancing within dancehall much less of an issue than in Jamaica, albeit females still dominate the British dancehall dance space.

It is within the lead up to and the early morning coupling section of the dancehall session that a real sense of spirituality or even spiritual frenzy takes over, as the man-dem and female dancers contest for the dancehall floor.

As the man-dem battle each other individually, with intricate footsteps and arm patterns, performing movements such as *'clouds'*, *'nuh lingah'* and *'gully creaper'*, male squads and crews perform increasingly complex choreographed routines. Dance movements such as 'clouds', featuring—*dancer's arms just above the head, swinging from side to side, in half circling 'air-pumping' windscreen action, as feet simultaneously touch-step, touch-step*—resonates with the Revival 'hallelu' (hallelujah) movement—*arms swing above the head from one side in an arc, as if reaching for the heavens in windscreen wiper action, while jumping up onto the balls of the feet, then repeating on the alternative side.*

The *'nuh lingah'* movement with its *circling torso action* resonates with Kumina's *'cork-screw' circling action*—as Cheryl Ryman details (in interview with Patten, R. Ryman, interview with author, August 24, 2010), the *'cork-screw action'* is a term generally used by Jamaican dance artists and myself. 'Nuh lingah' also connects through the circling action of the feet within the Haitian Vodou spiritual dance called Yanvalou. Marie-Jose Alcide Saint-Lot describes Yanvalou as, 'undulation from the shoulders to the hips imitat[ing] the movement of the serpent and the waves of the sea' (2003, p. 98). This reflects the island locations out of which these dances emerge.

'Gully creaper's' undercover—*walking action, pelvis pushing forward and back on each step*—has similarities to Jonkonnu's *'belly woman'* character, usually performed by a male dancer dressed as a heavily pregnant female, who dances by—*thrusting the pelvis and 'false belly' (stomach) forward, intermittently wining the waist/belly in a circular motion*. The focus of the dancehall steps, being upwards towards the heavens in *'clouds'*, neutral in *'nuh linga'* and downwards in *'gully creaper'*, may be read as connecting the heavens and the earth. This is a common motif in many African/neo-African spiritual practices, including Kumina, Yanvalou, Revival and Jonkonnu.

The male aggression, camaraderie and tensions within the dancehall space is contrasted, complimented and at times upstaged by the females' crowd mesmerising pelvic wining (winding) action. Their athletic performance of splits, gambols, rolling-splits and the female signature 'head-top' movement—*wining while upside-down in a head-stand*—enables them to challenge for control of dancehall's centre-spot. Regaining agency in displaying control of/over their own bodies through female liberation rituals, as earlier explained (Wright, 2004; Cooper, 2004), may be read corporeally as part of the liberation struggle against centuries of enslavement, colonisation, patriarchal governance and male oppression. Yet, as females lock pelvis with the man-dem, the energy of the two combine as pelvises clash, connect, bounce, *'Bump n" Grind'* (R. Kelly, 1993),[12] in the controversial 'daggering' (Hyman, 2012) action[13] both front and back. The excitement of the 'daggering' action across the dancehall space drives the energy to frenzied fever pitch. At this point, the boundaries between artists, performers and audiences become blurred, as hierarchies collapse. Spontaneously, dancehall becomes at once a transgressive, transformative and transcendent space in which individuals, 'step out of themselves', as Stanley-Niaah (2010) earlier illuminated. In that moment, reggae/dancehall maintains a deep significance, embodying a resistant African/neo-African spiritual cosmology and religious coding, as a countercultural space (Beckford, 2006).

Dancehall in Britain

In the British setting, dancehall is represented within the context of stage shows and festivals, including the Notting Hill Carnival (Europe's biggest street event) and various club nights and special promotions, such as Dancehall Queen competitions. In contrast, Jamaican dancehall discourse is played out within the many outdoor and club events that constitute the dancehall space every night of the week. However, as I argue elsewhere (Patten in 2016), countercultural spaces such as the 'Me'Lange Hair Salon' in Peckham, South London, played a crucial role in dancehall's development and continuance in Britain. Run by Adrian 'Ashdon' Smith, a Jamaican-born dancehall dancer, within the confines of the 'Me'Lange' dancehall artists, crews and squads shared ancestral data, cultural knowledge and memory as they danced, rehearsed and collaborated. Together, these artists corporeally formed an important part of dancehall's contemporary resistant 'genealogy', in Beckford's (2006) sense of non-linear connections of historical moments and events.

Dancehall in Britain provides an important subversive aesthetic for (dis)advantaged, (dis)located and (dis)empowered Black youth to gain personhood and visibility. African and Caribbean dance in Britain, particularly classical/traditional forms within the Dance of the African Diaspora sector, are often marginalised and negatively perceived as culturally specific museum pieces and therefore irrelevant to today's hi-tech, multi-media, urban societies by venue holders, policymakers and funders, as Ramdhanie (2005) supports. However, dancehall as a hybrid African Caribbean dance practice integrating digital techniques from the early 1980s, is (re)positioned within the more desirable and culturally homogenous category of contemporary urban expression. This creates a tension between dancehall's informal and formal, or professional development, as dancehall dancing was introduced within the professional African People's dance sector by Patsy Ricketts, as part of the 'Black Dance Development Trust Summer School' in Wolverhampton, back in 1987. Ricketts' classes included reggae and nyabinghi dance vocabulary with dancehall movements such as 'dela move', 'bogle', 'jockey', 'butterfly' and 'water pumping'. Importantly, she also incorporated her Rastafarian ethos and aspects of Jamaican African/neo-African spiritual and cultural practices. Thereby, even within British secular spaces, reggae/dancehall maintains a deep symbolic and significant embodiment of Jamaican spiritual cosmology and religious coding, providing modern transformative rituals of renewal and transcendence.

Conclusion

This chapter set out to explore whether reggae/dancehall has any spiritual and/or religious signification within its performance. I have shown that African/Jamaican practices such as Jonkonnu, Kumina and Revivalism manifests in the performance and 'performative' actions displayed both consciously and unconsciously within contemporary reggae/dancehall culture. In doing so, I also established that ancestral data and encoded cultural knowledge is manifested through the corporeal dancing body as a conduit of embodied 'cultural memory' (Stines, 2005; Walker, 2008). I have demonstrated that spiritual communication is the main function of African/Jamaican dance ritual practices such as Kumina, Revivalism and Jonkonnu, which are reliant on the corporeal dancing body as the mode of communication through the myal state, to the ancestors and the divine. Thereby, I contend that the dancehall space enables the corporeal dancing body to function as a contemporary conduit or vessel, to transcend and expose for interrogation an embodied historical symbolism, representing a cathartic healing process and connection to the divine (Cooper, 2004; White, 2003). As I hope to have shown, the corporeal dancing body transforms the dancehall space, making healing and resistance part of the 'chain of re-membering' (Stewart, 2005, p. xvii). Moreover, as a symbolic, cathartic enactment of resistance, dancehall forms part of the ritual process through which many participants attempt and many (re)gain 'smadditisation', the recognition and visibility denied them by racism (Mills, 1997; Stanley-Niaah, 2010).

Many aspects of the African spiritual cosmology retained in African/Jamaican religious dance traditions have been shown to regularly manifest within the corporeal dancing body in the dancehall space, both within the Jamaican and British context. From Dancehall Queen competitions to its representation within the Nottinghill Carnival, dancehall creates and occupies countercultural spaces (Beckford, 2006) in which artists and adherents engage and participate together corporeally. As part of Jamaica's African/neo-African contemporary 'genealogy', reggae/dancehall's transformative rituals of renewal maintain a deep significance. Embodying Jamaican spiritual cosmology and religious coding, reggae/dancehall remains – *a continuity of Spiritual, Corporeal Practice in Jamaican Dance.*

NOTES

1. Meaning, or as a coming again and a present establishment of an object, concept, meaning and so on, foregrounding the fact that layered meanings may be differently comprehended from a Western and/or indigenous perspective.
2. The terms 'place' and 'space' refer to real or imagined locations that can be material or spiritual/metaphysical but are contingent on the body's physical or ideological engagement of or with it (Cresswell, 2006; Noxolo, 2015). Place often specifically references a physical location, while space exists in relation to the body and 'its material objects and agents' (Nash, 2000, p. 661).
3. African People's Dance (APD), formerly and still commonly termed 'Black Dance' is a term originally coined to address black bodies performing and working within African and Caribbean dance forms, excluding black bodies performing Western and other dance forms. Over the years it has shifted definition becoming more inclusive, referencing all bodies practising within African and Caribbean forms. Hence, it now covers black bodies working in Western forms.
4. Human action, particularly gendered behaviour is regarded by some as being constructed, learned behaviour and therefore performative, rather than a biological fact (nature versus nurture). For a more detailed analysis, see: Butler, J (1988) or Nash, C. (2000).
5. Jonkonnu, also spelt John Canoe, Junkanoo and John Kuner or as the anthropologist and historian Kenneth Bilby (2010) phonetically terms it Jankunu, is a masquerade tradition performed across the Caribbean and Central America. It is one of Jamaica's earliest surviving music and dance traditions of African descent.

6. Revivalism is a neo-African religious movement influenced by the Native Baptist movement and the Great Revival, which took place in Jamaica during 1860 and 1861. For a deeper exploration, see: Lewin, O. (2000).
7. Kumina is one of Jamaica's strongest classical African religious rituals and is practised in the parishes of St Thomas and St Catherine. It is performed to give reverence to the spirits and/or to service specific social issues or needs. Cheryl Ryman (1984) provides a detailed account of Kumina.
8. 'Overstand' is a Rastafarian term signalling increased comprehension, subverting the English word 'understand', which taken literally they argue represents less comprehension.
9. Lewin, O. (2000) provides a detailed analysis of Kumina ideology, including an overview of its African cosmology.
10. Edward Seaga (1982), Olive Lewin (2000) and Dianne M. Stewart (2005) all provide extensive details of Revivalism.
11. Gerald 'Bogle' Levy has since been credited with creating a succession of popular dancehall dances including: *'Urkel,' 'World-a-Dance,'* and *'Row Like a Boat'* (Stolzoff, 2000, p. 271.n.9; Hope, 2006, p. 30; Stanley Niaah, 2010, p. 124).
12. *'Bump n" Grind'* was a popular R&B hit by R Kelly in 1993, that featured within the slower more intimate section of the dancehall dance scene, particularly in Britain.
13. Hyman, R. D. (2012) provides an insightful interrogation of the 'daggering' movement, its possible readings and signification.

References

Bakare-Yusuf, B. (2006). Fabricating Identities: Survival and the Imagination in Jamaican Dancehall Culture. *Fashion Theory, 10*(3), 1–24.

Beckford, R. (2006). *Jesus Dub: Theology, Music and Social Change*. London: Routledge.

Bilby, K. (2007). Masking the Spirit in the South Atlantic World: Jankunu's Partially Hidden History. In *The Legacies of Slavery and Emancipation: Jamaica in the Atlantic World* (pp. 1–24). Proceedings of the Ninth Annual Gilder Lehrman Center International Conference at Yale University, Co-sponsored by the Yale Center for British Art.

Bilby, K. (2010). Surviving Secularization: Masking the Spirit in the Jankunu (John Canoe) Festivals of the Caribbean. *New West Indian Guide, 84*(3–4), 179–223.

Buckland, T. J. (2001). Dance, Authenticity and Cultural Memory: The Politics of Embodiment. *Yearbook for Traditional Music, 33*, 1–16. Published by: International Council for Traditional Music Stable. URL: http://www.jstor.org/stable/1519626. Accessed 02 Nov 2010, 02:57.

Burton, R. D. E. (1997). *Afro-Creole: Power, Opposition, and Play in the Caribbean.* Ithaca, NY: Cornell University Press.

Butler, J. (1988, December). Performative Acts and Gender Constitution: An Essay in Phenomenology and Feminist Theory. *Theatre Journal, 40*(4), 519–531.

Cooper, C. (1993). *Noises in the Blood: Gender and the "Vulgar" Body of Jamaican Popular Culture.* London: Macmillan Caribbean.

Cooper, C. (2004). *Sound Clash: Jamaican Dancehall Culture at Large.* New York: Palgrave Macmillan.

Cresswell, T. (2006). You Cannot Shake that Shimmie Here': Producing Mobility on the Dance Floor. *Cultural Geographies, 13,* 55.

Fuchs, T. (2003). The Phenomenology of Shame, Guilt and the Body in Body Dysmorphic Disorder and Depression. *Journal of Phenomenological Psychology, 33,* 223–243.

Gutzmore, C. (2004). Casting the First Stone!: Policing of Homo/Sexuality in Jamaican Popular Culture, Interventions. *International Journal of Postcolonial Studies, 6*(1), 118–134.

Hebdige, D. (1987, 2007). *Cut 'N' Mix: Culture, Identity and Caribbean Music.* A Comedia Book. London: Routledge.

Henriques, J. F. (2003). Sonic Dominance and the Reggae Sound System Session. In M. Bull & L. Back (Eds.), *The Auditory Culture Reader* (pp. 451–480). Oxford: Berg. ISBN 1859736130 [Book Section]: Goldsmiths Research Online.

Hope, D. P. (2006). *Inna Di Dancehall: Popular Culture and the Politics of Identity in Jamaica.* Mona: University of the West Indies Press.

Hope, D. P. (2010). *Man Vibes: Masculinities in the Jamaican Dancehall.* Kingston, Jamaica: Ian Randle Publishers.

Hyman, R.-D. (2012). *Daggering Inna Di Dancehall: Kierkegaard's Conceptualization of Subjectivity and Nietzsche's Dionysus in Relation to Jamaican Dance.* Simon Fraser University PhD.

Lewin, O. (2000). *Rock It Come Over: The Folk Music of Jamaica.* Kingston: The University of the West Indies Press.

Manuel, P., & Marshall, W. (2006). The Riddim Method: Aesthetics, Practice, and Ownership in Jamaican Dancehall. *Popular Music, 25*(3), 447–470. Cambridge University Press.

Meusburger, P., Heffernan, M., & Wunder, E. (2011). Cultural Memories: The Geographical Point of View. In *Knowledge and Space* (Vol. 4, Part 1, pp. 3–14). Dordrecht: Springer.

Miller, M. R. (2009). 'The Promiscuous Gospel': The Religious Complexity and Theological Multiplicity of Rap Music. *Culture and Religion, 10*(1), 39–61.

Mills, C. (1997). Smadditizin. *Caribbean Quarterly, 43*(2), 54–68.

Nash, C. (2000). Performativity in Practice: Some Recent Work in Cultural Geography. *Progress in Human Geography, 24*(4), 653–664.

Nettleford, R. (2003). *Caribbean Cultural Identity: The Case of Jamaica – An Essay in Cultural Dynamics.* Kingston: Ian Randle Publishers/Markus Wiener Publishers.

Noxolo, P. (2015). Moving Maps: African-Caribbean Dance as Embodied Mapping. In S. Barbour, T. Lacroix, D. Howard & J. Misrahi-Barak (Eds.), *PocoPages Diasporas and Cultures of Mobilities, Vol 2 Diaspora, Memory and Intimacy* (Series PoCoPages, Coll. "Horizons Anglophones"). Montpellier: Presses universitaires de la Méditerranée.

Patten, H. (2016). Feel De Riddim, Feel De Vibes: Dance as a Transcendent Act of Survival and Upliftment. In C. Adair & R. Burt (Eds.), *British Dance: Black Routes.* Oxon/New York: Routledge.

Pinnock, A. M. N. (2007). "A Ghetto Education Is Basic": (Jamaican) Dancehall Masculinities as Counter-Culture. *The Journal of Pan African Studies, 1*(9), 47–84.

Ramdhanie, R. (2005). *African Dance in England: Spirituality and Continuity* (2 Vols., Vol. 1). Coventry, England: University of Warwick, Centre for British and Comparative Cultural Studies.

Ryman, C. (1984). Jonkonnu: A Neo-African Form. *Jamaica Journal, 17*(1), 13–27.

Ryman, C. (2004). Bouyaka (Boo-Yah-Kah) a Salute to Dancehall. *Discourses in Dance, 2*(2), 5–8.

Saint-Lot, M.-J. A. (2003). *Vodou, a Sacred Theatre: The African Heritage in Haiti.* Florida: Educa Vision Inc.

Scott, D. (2006, June). 'To Be Liberated from the Obscurity of Themselves': An Interview with Rex Nettleford in *Small Axe,* Number 20, *10*(2), 97–246. Published by Indiana University Press.

Seaga, E. (1969, 1982). Revival Cults of Jamaica: Notes Towards a Sociology of Religion. The Institute of Jamaica Publications. Reprinted from *Jamaica Journal, 3*(2), 3–13.

Sharpe, J. (2003, November). Cartographies of Globalisation, Technologies of Gendered Subjectivities: The Dub Poetry of Jean "Binta" Breeze. *Gender & History, 15*(3), 440–459. Accessed 17 Aug 2011.

Sklar, D. (1991, Spring). On Dance Ethnography. *Dance Research Journal, 23*(1), 6–10. Published by: University of Illinois Press on behalf of Congress on Research in DanceStable URL: http://www.jstor.org/stable/1478692. Accessed 18 Nov 2010, 16:59.

Stanley-Niaah, S. (2010). *Dancehall: From Slave Ship to Ghetto.* Ottawa: University of Ottawa Press.

Stewart, D. M. (2005). *Three Eyes for the Journey: African Dimensions of the Jamaican Religious Experience.* Oxford: Oxford University Press.

Stines, L. (2005). Does the Caribbean Body Daaance or Daunce? An exploration of Modern Contemporary Dance from a Caribbean Perspective. In *Caribbean Quarterly, 51*(3/4), 35–54, Cultural Studies: A New Generation of Scholars.

Stolzoff, N. C. (2000). *Wake the Town and Tell the People: Dancehall Culture in Jamaica*. Durham: Duke University Press.

Walker, C. A. (2008). Dance Inna Dancehall: Roots of Jamaica's Popular Dance Expressions. In S. B. Shapiro (Ed.), *Dance in a World of Change: Reflections on Globalization and Cultural Difference*. Champaign: Human Kinetics Publishers.

White, B. S. (2003). Latter-Day Emancipation! Woman, Dance and Healing in Jamaican Dancehall Culture. *Agenda: Empowering Women for Gender Equity*, 43(58), 77–83. Retrieved from http://www.jstor.org/stable/4548100

Wright, B. S. (2004). Speaking the Unspeakable: Politics of the Vagina in Dancehall Docu-Videos. *Discourses in Dance*, 2(2), 45–60.

CHAPTER 12

Our Ethiopian Connection: Embodied Ethiopian Culture as a Tool in Urban-Contemporary Choreography

Ras Mikey (Michael) Courtney

INTRODUCTION

I was employed as a guest lecturer at the University of Limerick in Ireland, and work trans-nationally in Britain, USA, and Ethiopia. I was born in the United States as a child of the Civil Rights movement and grew up in the urban Hip hop culture movement. I have been extensively educated in contemporary dance and many other movement forms in the USA, Ireland, Great Britain, and Ethiopia. I am a part of the Pan-African movement. I am also Rastafarian, devoted to the teachings and the divine prophecy of His Imperial Majesty Emperor Haile Selassie I, who was the last of 225 Kings of Ethiopia's Kingdom of Abyssinia. With this "embodied corporal and cerebral knowledge" (Royce, 1977, 2002) I have developed a unique sense of movement, physically and philosophically. I repatriated to Ethiopia in 2006 and began to see Ethiopia's connections to our global socio-cultural community, through many aspects including the dances. Some of these connections I will exemplify in this chapter.

R. M. Courtney (✉)
Wayne State University, Detroit, MI, USA

I pursued my PhD in Arts Practice Research at the University of Limerick. My doctoral research focused on the use of what I termed Ethio-Modern Dance, as a medium for cultural knowledge exchange. Ethio-Modern Dance is a movement study based on my amalgamated *embodiment* (Csordas, 1990) of global cultures, emphasising Ethiopia, used as tools in my creative process as an urban contemporary performing artist and dance researcher from the West. In this chapter, I explore my embodied understanding of Ethiopian culture and her traditional dances while articulating how Ethiopia influences my creative process. I draw on my own personal experiences as part of the African Diaspora, raised and educated in the USA, Ireland, and Great Britain, but now residing in Ethiopia. I use my embodied knowledge to illustrate some of the theoretical and physical correlations I have discovered between Ethiopian dances and popular social dances of the West. In the conclusion of this chapter, I also express an necessity for a broader inclusion of Ethiopia's cultural diversity in our global understanding of African heritage.

Backstory

Although I was not born in Ethiopia, my wife and my first son were and I have been a resident of Addis Ababa, the capital city of Ethiopia, since 2006. Through my family and my spiritual faith Rastafari, I have developed an outside as well as an inside perspective on Ethiopian culture. With this unique connection, I have taken on the responsibility to increase the general understanding of African and African diaspora culture by planting seeds of Ethiopia's influential legacy in the hearts and minds of those who don't know the many contributions that Ethiopia has made to humanity. The depth in our story of African culture and her contributions to our human existence is oftentimes forgotten by the mainstream world. At most, when African dance is mentioned, we generally hear nothing of Eastern Africa and more specifically Ethiopia. It is my objective, as an ethnochoreologist and dance practitioner/educator, to shed light on the diversity of Ethiopia's culture and its unique dance traditions.

Ethiopia is a nation whose history stretches back to the time of the earliest hominids[1] and the establishment of traditional Judeo-Christian[2] as well as Islamic[3] religious values. Known to many observers as 'the Hidden Empire', Ethiopia is often referred to as the Kingdom of Abyssinia (Adejumobi, 2007, p. 3). This historical nation entered the twentieth century as a symbol of colonial resistance[4] and a leader in the liberation.[5]

Now in the twenty-first century, as the Federal Democratic Republic of Ethiopia, the legacy of 225 Kings[6] who sat upon the throne of this sovereign Christian nation has almost been forgotten by the mainstream world and her popular image has been reduced to associations with famine, disease, and political turmoil. Yet still today Ethiopia is one of the fastest developing nations in the world and its people are making big strides in changing the public image of their nation while redefining its national identity. Dance and other performing arts such as theatre and music have played a major role in redefining the image of Ethiopia, by being cultural commodities commonly performed on various platforms as a way of promoting the cultural diversity and historical legacy of this progressive African nation.

Ethiopia is bordered by Sudan and South Sudan to the west, Eritrea[7] and Djibouti to the north, Kenya to south and Somalia on the east. These surrounding countries influence and are influenced by this culturally diverse landlocked nation with a population of over 85 million people in nine regions[8] and more than 80 nationalities. Each nationality of Ethiopia has its own cultural nuances including different music and dance characteristics. Some of which are *eskista,* a shoulder dance of the *Amhara* region in low-highlands of the Semien Mountains, the hip isolations of the *Wolaita* people of the south-west and the full bodied dynamic movement of the *Guragé* dances in the south-eastern part of the country. Many of these characteristics influence my embodied understanding of Ethio-Modern Dance. I have also seen how the migration of many Ethiopians to countries like the USA, Ireland, and Great Britain has influenced the social and contemporary dance cultures of the African Diaspora communities in these and other countries. Although I grew up in Hip hop culture and studied contemporary dance in the West, it is my experiences of living, working, and exploring the Ethiopian ways of life that have endowed me with an embodied knowledge of the culture. With my development and presentation of Ethio-Modern Dance, I have assisted in the promotion of Ethiopia's cultural heritage to our global dance community.

Ethio-Modern Dance

'Ethio' is my African heritage and 'Modern' is my urban contemporary perception of the world I exist in now and am influenced by. (Courtney, 2013)

The Hip hop culture of the 1980s–1990s would be my "urban" cultural foundation from which I view the world I live in. I graduated with a

Bachelor of Fine Arts in Modern Dance Performance in 2001, giving me a very "contemporary" approach towards my creative process. For this reason, I classify my work and myself as urban contemporary. My philosophical approach towards movement as a lifestyle has guided me in my professional work with my own company *Fore I'm a Versatile Entertainer* (F.I.V.E.) Productions LLC, as well as with my ten years of working with Pilobolus Dance Theatre. I have always sought after a deeper meaning to movement and its connection to my life and discovered that, from a somatic perspective, there is no life without movement. As Ethiopia has been considered the birthplace of modern civilization, from where all human movement flowed, it was only natural that my journey through life as a movement led me there.

After moving to Addis Ababa, Ethiopia in 2006 I began to embody different aspects of the cultural traditions, languages, and daily life of the country and its people. In 2008 I started teaching jazz, contemporary/ballet, Hip hop, and capoeira dance classes. During this time I was the dance director of the newly founded Eallaz International Dance Studio. It was here that I would begin to incorporate aspects of Ethiopia into my movement vocabulary, which I would later develop into what I now call Ethio-Modern Dance. I eventually began to create new choreographic projects for the Eallaz Dance Group and I found it imperative that I draw on the folklore and unique stylization of the Ethiopian traditional dances for these projects. This included highlighting the usage of shoulder, neck, and torso isolations commonly found in one of Ethiopia's most popular traditional dances *eskista*. Through creating and performing works while in Ethiopia, my embodied cultural knowledge became another tool in my creative processes, I found myself attempting to steer away from the Afro-Modern dance umbrella that I had been associated with before my repatriation to Ethiopia. In knowing that the community of dance I had encountered in the West had very little information about the diverse cultural dances of Ethiopia and also understanding that I did not wish to create traditional Ethiopian dance choreography, I developed the name Ethio-Modern Dance and began to teach my understanding of this movement study at studios, schools, and universities. These early Ethio-Modern Dance classes had a unique format in that I would teach my embodied understanding of certain traditional dances such as *eskista*, *Guragé*, and *Wolaita* as part of the warm up. Following this, I would illustrate how the characteristics of these dances were used in my urban contemporary dance process through a taught choreographed phrase. I began to realise the importance of contributing my knowledge of Ethiopia to the dance communities I encountered and made this the focus of my research when I decided to pursue my Masters of Arts degree in Ethnochoreology at the University of Limerick, Ireland in 2011.

Through the completions of my MA in Ethnochoreology and my pursuit of my PhD in Arts Practice Research at the University of Limerick's Irish World Academy of Music and Dance, I refined my understanding of this new movement study, Ethio-Modern Dance, through *autoethnographic* (Chang, 2008) research methods to investigate my embodied *lived experiences* (Dewey, 1958) and *habitus* (Bourdieu, 1977). In essence, I have turned the lens of ethnographic research onto myself and attribute what I have experienced and learned from my past to how I understand who I am and what I am doing with dance in the present time. This would include, but not be limited to, my experiences of growing up as part of the African diaspora in the West and becoming a professional contemporary performing artist having pursued a doctoral degree in Ireland. I create Ethio-Modern Dances for performance as well as for educational purposes and I use the medium of movement to express how these ideas represent aspects of my personal identity. It is the Irish World Academy of Music and Dance that has given me a platform to research, create, and perform Ethio-Modern Dance globally, while lecturing and presenting on the topic as well. I have also played a major role in connecting the University of Limerick with the higher educational institutions of Ethiopia, specifically Addis Ababa University's Yared School of Music. With my relations to both countries, I was selected to facilitate cultural and academic collaboration between these two institutions by the Ethiopian Ambassador to Ireland, Her Excellency Lela-Alem Gebreyohannes, who has shown her support for my Ethio-Modern Dance works since 2012. The directors of both institutions recently came together in Addis Ababa at the Yared School of Music's 1st International Music Conference: Promoting Ethiopian Indigenous Music in Higher Education Institutions. Both parties agreed that there is much to be shared between the two universities through academic and cultural exchange as well as in research collaborations.

I did not grow up within Ethiopian culture so it is through my embodied knowledge or what I have learned physically and mentally from living in the country that I am able to share my understandings of the culture with communities in Ireland, Great Britain, and beyond. I am well aware of other Ethiopian artists and dance groups who are doing works similar to my own, such as the Destino, whose directors Addisu Demissie and Juniad Jemal were a part of the Adugna Community Dance Group, that was funded by a Gemini Trust and supported by the governments of Ethiopia and Great Britain. Both of these Ethiopian-born contemporary dance artists have travelled the world, sharing what they call Ethiopian Contemporary dance with the global dance community. There is also the HaHu Dance Entertainment, known as a *zeminawi* or "modern" dance group, which like Destino is based in Addis Ababa and uses the Ethiopian folklore and traditional dance vocabulary as a part of their choreographic compositions. There are other groups that I have encountered abroad such as the *Jaivah* Dance Troupe of Toronto, who refer to their works as Ethio-Fusion dance, and the Beta-Israel Dance Company of Haifa, who create contemporary dance works that are influenced by the Ethiopian Jew community of Israel. I have a personal relationship with all these groups and have worked with some of these artists as well. I support their endeavours with dance in and out of Ethiopia and am inspired by the works they create. I hope that my understanding of Ethio-Modern Dance will inspire them as well. I feel that all of our works are original in their own right and I developed an original term to describe my Ethiopian-influenced works. I do not feel as though I own the term "Ethio-Modern Dance" and I encourage others to use the term to describe their works if they see fit. To my knowledge I am the only person using the term "Ethio-Modern Dance" to describe this type of work at this time.

It is because of my particular career path and professional network that I have become the "cultural broker" of Ethio-Modern Dance, which for me takes on a different dimension when I am in Ethiopia and outside the country. In essence there are two sides to my metaphorical Ethio-Modern Dance coin. On the "Ethio" side, I share my embodied knowledge of Ethiopian culture with my global community. On the "Modern" side, I am also able to expose my knowledge and expertise of Western contemporary performing arts with the Ethiopian community. My doctoral research investigated these ideas in my thesis entitled "Bridging Horizons: Embodied Cultural Knowledge through the Development and Presentation of Ethio-Modern Dance". I used the medium of movement as a conduit for intercultural knowledge exchange between communities. This was very evident in my Ethio-Modern Dance production *YeBuna Alem/A Coffee World*,[9] which premiered at the Irish World Academy of Music and Dance in May of 2015. This intercultural performance experience included thirteen performers from more than six countries, who under the Ethio-Modern Dance theme integrated their own lived experiences into the choreographic and musical compositions that expressed my embodied understandings of Ethiopian culture in a contemporary performance setting. *YeBuna Alem/A Coffee World* interpretively explored the narratives associated with the origins of Ethiopia's Arabica coffee (*buna*) culture and the phenomenology of coffee's integration into world culture. My role in the performance was not only as cultural conduit but also as the metaphorical embodiment of *buna* and its journey from *Kaffa*, a Southern Ethiopian province, to the world. This production was an anthropology of the senses as the theatre was adorned with Ethiopian iconography, and the aromatic scent of roasted Arabica coffee mixed with frankincense provided more than just a visually stimulating atmosphere. All of this was set to the soundtrack of recorded Ethiopian contemporary music. Following the show, the audience was able to participate in a traditional Ethiopian *buna* ceremony in the foyer of the Tower Theatre. This performance was a part of Limerick City's Africa Day 2015 events, and brought together a culturally diverse and intergenerational audience.

As I have mentioned above, it is my lived experiences that have allowed me to develop this understanding of Ethio-Modern Dance. With this embodied knowledge, not only have I been able to connect Ethiopian culture to Ireland, Great Britain, and other countries through sharing Ethio-Modern Dance, I have also developed my own theoretical connections between Ethiopian cultural dances to other dance cultures around the globe.

Ethiopian Cultural Dance and the Pop-Culture Connection

Ethiopia's contribution of Arabica coffee to the world is just one example of the many connections I have discovered and am attempting to share with our global community through Ethio-Modern Dance. Some others would include Ethiopia's national food *injera be wot*[10] and national language, *Amharic* or *Amarignya*.[11] As an ethnochoreologist and dance practitioner, I am compelled to use the performing arts as my medium to share these as well as the cultural (*bahelawi*) music (*muzika*), dance (*chefera*), and song (*zefin*) of Ethiopia, which also play major roles in the Ethiopian way of life. Some if not all of these aspects influenced my Ethio-Modern Dance production *YeBuna Alem/A Coffee World*. As you can see in the title of this work and many of my other Ethio-Modern Dance works, I used *Amarignya*. I also teach some basic words, like those mentioned above, in my workshops, presentations, and master classes, while emphasising that the Ethiopian alphabet known as the *fidel*[12] is one of the only known African scripts still used today.

I have often stressed the fact that it is more than the traditional dances that influence my Ethio-Modern Dance works as I am also influenced by the many other aspects of Ethiopian life. As one Hungarian researcher Dr. György Martin stated, "Air, music, and dance as well as singer, musician, and dancer, are interwoven in an inseparable unity" (Martin, 1967, p. 23). I also attempt to use this integrative perspective in my own Ethiopian-influenced works. Traditionally, dance is directed by rhythmic hand clapping (*chebeta*), drums (*kabero*), a single stringed violin (*masinko*), and a melodic vocal element. These elements are still evident in many Ethiopian cultural clubs and restaurants of today. This rhythmic hand-clapping technique is a method that I employ when I am introducing the traditional dances in my Ethio-Modern Dance projects, to those unfamiliar with the different rhythmic nuances of particular Ethiopian dances. Martin divided Ethiopian dances into "*three large categories,*"[13] arguing that within the Ethiopian context,

> *The dances are not divided according to their functions into categories showing formal differences, as is the case in Europe generally, but a single dance species is used with different functions.* (Martin, 1967, p. 23)

Although I do not completely agree with how Martin categorises the dances, to some extent I do agree with his perspective on the functionality of the movement. From my experience the function of Ethiopian dances is not as defined as in other cultural dances of the African continent and the origins of where the movement has derived is generally theoretical. I have plans to do more research on the origins and functionality of Ethiopian traditional dances and hope to update some of the previous research on this topic. This will give me more to add to my own understanding of these dances and how they influence my understanding of Ethio-Modern Dance. For now, I will discuss how I have connected my current embodied understanding of the some of these Ethiopian dances to my *habitus* as an urban contemporary performing artist.

When I began developing Ethio-Modern Dance in Addis Ababa's Eallaz Dance Studio, back in 2008, I also began to relate certain regional dances of Ethiopia like *eskista, Wolaita,* and *Guragé* to other cultural dances of the African countries such as Senegal shoulder angulations and South Africa rhythmic foot steps. As I was born in the West, it was natural that I connected the Ethiopian dances to popular social dances of the Hip hop culture I grew up being a part of. Relating the Ethiopian dances to other cultures of my lived experiences is what helped me embody the different nuances of some of these unique traditional dances. One of Ethiopia's most popular traditional dances, *eskista,* which is said to have originated from the lower highlands of Ethiopia's Amhara region, exemplifies the type of multi-functionality that Martin (1967) acknowledges as it is performed in many different settings of the Ethiopian community. It is common to see *eskista* at Ethiopian weddings, birthdays, popular nightclubs, and performed to handclapping, drumming, or even to traditional and contemporary music. *Eskista* was the focus of my ethnochoreological research for my Master of Arts written thesis and choreographic work. As I mentioned above, *eskista* is a traditional shoulder, neck, and torso dance with characteristics that are easily identifiable by the sharp isolated movements of the upper body (Martin, 1967). I used the characteristics of *eskista,* which I related to popping and locking in Hip hop, as part of my contemporary movement vocabulary to create *Kerb Gen Ruk/Close But Far,*[14] a choreographed Ethio-Modern Dance work. I then analysed my use of *eskista* as a tool in my urban contemporary dance process for the written portion of this Masters thesis.

These types of dynamic vibrating upper-body movements found in *eskista* are also seen in various dances of Senegal, Afro-Haitian, Indian, and many other cultures globally. With my background in Hip hop culture, it was no surprise when I discovered that *eskista* is known to have inspired popular dances such as 'The Harlem Shake' of New York and the 'Bankhead Bounce' of Atlanta. This revelation is one I often express to my students who are familiar with these dances, in order for them to see *eskista's* characteristics in a different cultural context. I also mention that a variation of *eskista* type movement was seen in the choreography of Beyoncé's music video "Run the World."[15] My knowledge and exposure to Ethiopian and other world cultures has allowed me to see these correlations of *eskista* and as I discover my findings I do not hesitate to share them with those involved in my Ethio-Modern Dance works. This helps to provide a broader context of the movement and further illustrates

Ethiopia's connection to popular dance culture. I have made similar correlations with other traditional Ethiopian dances as well.

From my lived experiences in Ethiopia, I have discovered that the *Wolaita* and the *Agew* dances, which originate from the people of Ethiopia's Southern region, are two of the only Ethiopian cultural dances involving, but not limited to, isolated movements of the hips. These hip isolations resemble "rites of passage" or maternity dances of other indigenous practices found in many parts of the world, although the meanings of the movement may differ depending on the culture. (Welsh-Asante, 2010) For me, these hip movements also reference the "Dancehall" culture of the Caribbean islands as well as the more popular social dance phenomenon known as "twerking." These correlations again make it easier for me to teach my embodiment of these Ethiopian dances as I can illustrate how they relate to pop-culture social dances. In some of my Ethio-Modern Dance classes, I have even gone so far as to teach these Ethiopian traditional hip movements to Caribbean Dancehall music, as well as to Afro-beat music that has now gained popularity all over the African continent and abroad. Knowing that most traditional African dance movements are driven by the rhythm, connecting the rhythms of other cultures to my Ethio-Modern Dance works illustrates a broader cross-cultural connection.

Guragé is a nation of people in the southwestern region of Ethiopia with dances that commonly incorporate the whole body of the performer, not just the upper body as in *eskista*. Within certain *Guragé* dances, there is a lot of quick stepping footwork motifs, and small rhythmic hops (Vadasy, 1971). For myself, as a product of Hip hop culture, I have connected this stylized footwork motifs of the *Guragé* people to top-rock steps of Hip hop's breakdancing culture. This correlation is one that I often share in workshops with the Ethiopian community. I will play music that is based in the *Guragé* rhythm, illustrate my embodied understanding of basic *Guragé* footwork and bodily movements, and then begin to incorporate more top-rocking steps from my Hip hop knowledge that links in with the *Guragé* rhythm. This is just scratching the surface of the over 80 different cultures that exist in Ethiopia and I plan to do more research, in the direction of my embodied correlations.

After discussing these few correlations, it is imperative that I mention that my second major Ethio-Modern Dance production required for the completion of my PhD in Arts Practice Research was titled *Common Threads* and premiered in Addis Ababa, July 2016 in collaboration with the National Theatre of Ethiopia. This production was a community engagement-based project that uses Ethio-Modern Dance as a medium for cultural exchange and youth empowerment. The Addis Ababa dance community is well-versed in their own cultural traditions, but many young artists aspire to know more about and engage with the Hip hop and contemporary dance cultures from which I stem. Through cultural exchange and community-based Ethio-Modern Dance collaborations, I produced a professional-level choreographed dance show that illuminates the depth of Ethiopia's dance culture and illustrates *Common Threads* with other world dance cultures. *Common Threads* further exemplifies my expertise in the contemporary performing arts and explores my embodied connections of Ethiopian traditional dances with other world dance cultures. This performance incorporated choreographic collaborations with artists of European, American, and African backgrounds and featured prominent traditional as well as contemporary dance groups and artists of the Addis Ababa community. *Common Threads* further illustrates my understanding of Ethiopia's cultural influence on the world and the world's influence on Ethiopia. With this and other Ethio-Modern Dance projects, I continue to bridge the gaps of cultural understanding in our global community, while changing the scope of dance as a profession in Ethiopia.

Conclusion

The reasons why I have been able to make these types of correlations between movements and cultures is all based on my embodied corporal and cerebral knowledge stemming from my lived experiences. I have been a student of institutions for more than 20 years, but most importantly I am a student of life. Although I have multiple academic degrees, philosophically I am a master of nothing and a student of everything. I seek such connections because I believe that as human beings we cling to our understanding of our cultural identity, which can divide us. I believe that the way to unify our existence as human beings in this universe is through an understanding that we have more in common than in difference. Movement is something that is basic and innate to life everywhere. It is in many ways primal. If we as humanity stem from one source, then naturally so does our movement. This movement is a language of its own and has communicated messages without words for eons. As people we should live, move, and experience life as it relates to the space we inhabit, and to the others we encounter. I study the movement of life and seek to understand how it all connects physically, mentally, and spiritually.

I am often asked why I am so driven to develop Ethio-Modern Dance and why I am promoting aspects of Ethiopian culture as someone who did not grow up in Ethiopia. My reply generally is "Why not me?" As an artist and academic with a deep-rooted spiritual and family connection to Ethiopia, I feel it is my responsibility to educate the communities I encounter on how I see Ethiopia and her legacy woven into the fabric of our global culture. Through Ethio-Modern Dance, I have strived to illustrate the connections that I have embodied in my dance classes, presentations, and creative compositions. I would encourage artists and academics of any discipline to be passionate about and develop personal connections to the material that they learn, create, teach, or research. This will help foster a well-rounded perception of one's self as a professional in one's respective field. If we share what we have learned through lived experiences, we may further bridge the gaps of cultural knowledge and understanding in our global community.

In closing, it is my feeling that further development of Ethio-Modern Dance coupled with my continuous presentations on related topics, will broaden the perspective of African dance and its Diaspora, as it relates to world culture and African studies. These social and cultural connections between traditional and contemporary performing arts can help younger generations to see how popular social norms may have an origin in indigenous traditions. With regards to Ethiopia, more scholarly research is necessary in order for the depth of this country's vast culture to be expressed. I am committed to the pursuit of Ethiopia's inclusion as a part of the African continental dance perspective. I have created and performed Ethio-Modern Dance as well as given master classes and lectures on my research, with the aim of bringing awareness of the importance of Ethiopian cultural dances studies in Higher Education Institutions of Ethiopia, Ireland, Great Britain, USA, and other countries worldwide. The Ethiopian Ambassador to Ireland has regarded me as a cultural Ambassador for Ethiopia because of my endeavours and it is my hope that someday I can assist in the development of a Dance Major programme at Addis Ababa University's SkundernBoghossian College of Performing and Visual Arts. With Ethio-Modern Dance, I aspire to further bridge the gaps of movement and cultural understanding by connecting my vast global dance network to that of Ethiopia and that of Ethiopia's to the world.

NOTES

1. An *Australopithecus afarensis,* founded in 1974, is known to foreigners as "Lucy" and to Ethiopians as "Deqenash". She was discovered in Hadar in the Afar desert and is the female ancestor of the human race, who lived 3.5 million years ago (Adejumobi, 2007).
2. Fourth century AD Coptic Christianity is introduced via Egypt (ibid).
3. The first Muslims arrived in the Axumite Empire as early as the seventh century, migrating from Mecca. They were instructed by the Prophet to protect Axum and live in peace with the Christian natives.
4. Ethiopia was never colonised although there was an Italian invasion in 1935–1941 (the second Ethio-Italian War) (ibid).
5. Emperor Haile Selassie I, along with other African leaders, founded the Organization of African Unity charter of 1963 in Addis Ababa, now known as the African Union (ibid).
6. The Ethiopian Monarchy dates back to the time of King Solomon of Israel and the Queen of Sheba of the Axumite Empire (approximately100–940 AD). Their love child David (Menelik I) was the first king of the Solomonic Dynasty (Kingdom of Abyssinia), which ended with the deposition of Emperor Haile Selassie I (formerly Rastafari) in 1974 (Brooks, 1995).
7. Before the late 1800s, it was part of the northern region of Ethiopia. It was controlled by Italy after the first Ethio-Italian War 1895–1896 (Adejumobi, 2007).
8. The Amhara; Tigray; Oromia; Afar; Somali; Southern Nations, Nationalities, and People (SNNPR); Gambela; Benishangal-Gumaz Regions.
9. This was the first of two major performances that must be produced as a requirement for the completion of the PhD in Arts Practice Research at the University of Limerick. See YouTube video https://youtu.be/LRveDhYJUMg
10. A fermented flat bread served with a variety of stewed meat and vegetable sauces.
11. A language from Ethiopia's Amhara region, which is derived from Ge'ez, a Semtic language of the Ethiopian Orthodox Church (Adejumobi, 2007).
12. The Ethiopic syllabic script that is used to notate most languages of Ethiopia and Eritrea (ibid).
13. I. *Group dances with segregated sexes;* II. *Eskista;* III. *Couple dances.*
14. See Courtney, M. 2013. View the recorded performance at http://youtu.be/neOe_wgkTHo
15. Choreography directed by Jeffery Page, an African American who uses the African traditions as a tool in his urban contemporary dance style.

Bibliography

Adejumobi, S. A. (2007). In F. W. Thackeray & J. E. Findling (Eds.), *The History of Ethiopia* (pp. xv–19). Westport, CT/London: Greenwood Press.

Bourdieu, P. (1977). *Outline of a Theory of Practice*. New York: Cambridge University Press.

Bourdieu, P. (2001). *Masculine Domination*. Cambridge: Polity Press.

Brooks, M. F. (Ed. and Trans.). (1995). *Kebra Nagast (The Glory of Kings): The True Ark of the Covenant*. Trenton, NJ/Asmara: Red Sea Press.

Campbell, H. (1987). *Rasta and Resistance: From Marcus Garvey to Walter Rodney*. Trenton, NJ: Africa World Press, Inc.

Chang, H. (2008). *Autoethnography as Method*. Walnut Creek: Left Coast Press.

Courtney, M. (2013). *Kerb Gen Ruk: An Autoethnographic Investigation into Choreographing an Ethio-Modern Dance Work*. Unpublished Thesis (M.A.), University of Limerick.

Csordas, T. (1990). Embodiment as a Paradigm for Anthropology. *American Anthropology Association, 18*(1), 5–47.

Dewey, J. (1958). *Experience and Nature*. New York: Dover Publications Inc.

Martin, G. (1967). Dance Types in Ethiopia. *Journal of the International Folk Music Council, 19,* 23–27. International Council for Traditional Music.

Royce, A. P. (1977, 2002). From Body as Artifact to Embodied Knowledge: An Introduction to the Reprint Edition. In *The Anthropology of Dance* (2nd ed., pp. xv–xxvi). London: Dance Books.

Shusterman, R. (2000). Somaesthetics and the Body/Media Issue. In *Performing Live: Aesthetic Alternatives for the Ends of Art* (pp. 137–153). Ithaca: Cornell University Press.

Vadasy, T. (1971). Ethiopian Folk – Dance II: Tegré and Guragé. *Journal of Ethiopian Studies, IX*(2), 191–217. Addis Ababa University.

Welsh-Asante, K. (2010). In E. Hanley (Ed.), *World of Dance: African Dance* (2nd ed.). New York: Chelsea House Publishers.

CHAPTER 13

Reflections: Snapshots of Dancing Home, 1985, 2010 and 2012

Hopal Romans

Home "*is a place, space, feeling, practices or an active state of being in the world highlighting how much "home" is a multidimensional and, sometimes, contradictory concept...*" (Shelley Mallet, 2004)

Every time I visit this statement, my response is 'yes!' *Home* is all of the above in terms of place, space and practices with all its complexities. A lot of the time, *home* has been physical and geographical, but then also my mindset, state of being and feeling. Over my dance career, *home* has been *in* my body and *in* my dance technique as well as the places I have left the dance studio to return to in order to sleep. The choices I made to travel out of UK (my birth home) for my career have meant that *home* is often the place I have left behind as I root down somewhere I temporarily call *home*, only to uproot again. My career began in the UK, at the age of 16, where I was on a mission of discovery of 'me the dancer', 'me the artist', 'me the discoverer of my own movement language' and 'me the person'. Somehow, and for whatever reason, I had to dance. My moving body was the reference point for my life. This need for the discovery and investigation of movement and a series of experiences as a young person led to me leaving the UK to find environments that celebrated my movement language and style.

H. Romans (✉)
Independent artist, London, UK

In 1985, I had to find home in the activity of dance itself rather than in a place. This was largely because I left the UK to take up opportunities in the USA that were closed to me in the UK. In the United States, I worked as a dancer in small companies and took on projects internationally. I later moved back to the United Kingdom to have a family and, after a period of time, re-entered the performing arts sector as a dancing-mother, arts manager and now, arts educator. By then, I had returned to UK, but the sacrifice I made to return to my place of home was in the lack of opportunity to dance that continued to dog my career in the UK. Attending the Association of Dance of the African Diaspora (ADAD) Re:Generations conferences in London, both in 2010 and 2012, became reflective mirrors and snapshots of my life. This was because after all my travelling, I was finally having conversations about the experiences of my career in the very place where my career began—at home in London. For the first time, I felt at home on a multidimensional level: through a state of shared memories with other dancers; through a mind-set of expressing myself as a dancer; and physically in the place where I grew-up and started to discover my artistic voice. My perceptions along the way have shifted through the many experiences of learning, engaging and reflecting. These reflections and emergent questions led to a need to ponder on my journey and a route back home to dance mentally, physically and experientially. In writing this chapter, I forced myself to confront and re-think my journey through dance up to now and look back at my journeying for 'home' to the authentic self and ask why I (and other dancers) had to uproot to the other side of the world after finishing the first part of my initial training as a dancer and young apprentice.

Determined to be a part of the arts and with a career history in dance for over 25 years, in this chapter I consider 'where is *home* now?'.

At Home as an Emerging Dancer

While I had a good foundational training with some inspirational teachers along the way, I was not satisfied as a young dancer because I knew there was something more out there for me to explore the self. I also wanted to shake off negative perceptions of me as a young black female dancer in British contemporary culture, which at that time had very limited opportunities; I had a strong sense that I did not feel at home despite being exposed to amazing experiences, and I felt limited. My initial professional training as a dance student exposed me to some American teachers and choreographers who introduced me to a new and intriguing world of dance, opening up my eyes to new and different possibilities. It agitated me in a positive way and set the idea in motion that I wanted more from my developing career in England. By now I had graduated from dance college, and had completed an apprenticeship as a dancer with *Extemporary Dance Theatre*. I had nothing to lose, was young and curious and my new home became the United States. Prior to and by moving across the Atlantic, I had to confront and shake off the constructs of my race and blackness I had grown-up with in Britain. I examined my experiences in Britain, comparing them to training in the USA as a dancer in a predominately African American culture and environment that included diverse training methods and strict discipline and traditions.

Peter Brinson (1991) acknowledged that through dance education and the curriculum, schools are training more and more British dancers from backgrounds '*outside*' of Britain. Also, that 'they deserve a place in existing British dance companies alongside their white compatriots because of the quality of what they can contribute'. It is interesting to think how relevant it was then a long time ago, for me growing up in the mid to late 1970s and 1980s and now. I experienced as a youngster a disparity between concert dance (contemporary) and commercial dance opportunities for black and 'minority' artists then and currently now in my mature years. Those experiences prompted me to leave the UK. Now, I would argue that while there are opportunities which exist for black and 'minority' ethnic dancers to train and perform, the number of opportunities for artists accessing major and established dance companies in a contemporary context is still limited and as a result some dancers either never fully develop their dance careers or in some cases vote with their feet and opt for a more commercial experience abroad. The issue for me then, as now, was a lack of accessibility for black dancers, and for me, particularly, as a female. Another issue to shake off was the stereotyping me as a black dancer only fit for African dance. African dance in all its forms and permutations from the diaspora contributed to my dance experiences but as a person I was more than dancing purely African dance. I wanted to move and not be typecast to move a certain way. It reminds me of something I read about the late, great Katherine Dunham who, in the 1930s and 1940s, created and performed contemporary modern dance works only to be told by critics that she should stick to more traditional, African diaspora forms for which she was credited. Her contemporary works were not critically acclaimed or favoured, unlike her white contemporaries at the time in modern dance. There was, and is, more to me than that.

At Home in a Foreign Land

My route to my temporary 'home' in the United States, was the Lester Horton Technique. It was a modern dance training fit for my purpose. I felt that the training enabled dancers from all disciplines, cultures (particularly black, 'minority' or ethnic dancers) to develop skills that bridged the gap between the contemporary concert stage, commercial and theatrical enterprises. The training, as I experienced it, increased my entrepreneurial skills, flexibility and transferability to other genres not only in what the technique presents but also in Lester Horton's philosophy of total theatre. The technique itself was relevant for me because of its simple (though challenging) form and function; its cultural representation. Ethnically, Horton in the 1940s and 1950s had a very diverse company of dancers and he saw difference as a positive. The techniques like the other modern techniques and particularly Graham included many elements of drama and storytelling. Horton himself was influenced by traditional cultures of the African diaspora, Native American, Indigenous culture and practice and theatre from Asia (particularly Japanese art, theatre and architecture) and the environment in which he inhabited. Alvin Ailey was a former student and company member of the Lester Horton Company and, following the death of Horton in 1953, Ailey developed his legacy through the creation of the Alvin Ailey Company and subsequent school where many years later I trained in this modern tradition. Woven into the mix was black modernism as part of American history and culture. The above ingredients and influences whetted my British appetite and energy to experience and find out more and not be seen as an 'other' dancer within British culture. Within all of that, I was beginning to find a sense of 'home'.

My training abroad added to preparations for the wider dance world but also, importantly, the feeling that I could be me and not be defined by my colour—I felt I had found a 'home' to prepare me to own who I was and not have to constantly justify my existence, and also to not experience the challenges of my body type. In the UK, there were too many occasions when I received negative comments, such as that anatomically my body type was not suited to some particular Western dance art forms and highlighting physical weaknesses. I picked up strong hints that my career would be shortened had I continued—unlike my experiences in America where I was encouraged to seize all opportunities and *go for it*. Had I not taken the plunge to leave and decided to remain in the UK, would my career have been different? Would I have had or been opened to opportunities to help me grow and develop the way I wanted to? I feel that had I stayed in the UK, I would have moved from job to job but would never have been fulfilled in my quest for my sense of self and vocabulary. The experiences, therefore, would have been limited. Being the type of person that I am, I had no choice but to leave. The mental and emotional barriers experienced at the time necessitated that I continue my mission to find my 'self' elsewhere and not be compromised. While in New York, I was encouraged to go out there and dance. I remember going to auditions for the larger companies (e.g. Martha Graham company, Philadanco and of course The Alvin Ailey). There were also opportunities for exploring other movement vocabularies downtown, through release techniques and trying out for other types of companies. The competition to dance for those companies was intense, but I was able to measure my own achievements and success by being on a level playing field with a sea of dancers from different disciplines. Undeterred, the auditioning process and experience propelled me into working on different dance projects with companies. I worked for a brief time with the Joyce Trisler Company. This experience was special as it was through a recommendation by the Horton teacher Milton Myers who found in me a movement language that best suited my career at that time. The company founded by the late Joyce Trisler was choreographically relevant for me within a Horton style that I was most familiar with. I worked with other dance companies that allowed for my training and vocabulary to evolve.

Returning Home to Being 'Other'

Returning home to the UK began another chapter as a working mother. I had a renewed sense of purpose and responsibility as a mother but, importantly, also as a dancer. The landscape had changed and for a number of black British artists including myself there were discussions for years about the contributions of black British artists and a need to acknowledge their contributions to British dance history. There was a sense and feeling of invisibility. Discussions about the validity of the terminology 'black dance' suggested to me that any dance I did fell under the umbrella term *black dance*, representative of all artists who, like myself, were black. I was extremely frustrated at the separation of me as 'other' in my home of British contemporary dance. My place was seemingly defined by the colour of my skin. I felt a lack of validity that also affirmed a lack of opportunity that I had always felt, prompting the move abroad in 1985. It made me feel that any 'black dance' I did as an artist and/or teacher suggested a genre of dance separate from contemporary dance generally in the UK. As if I could not contribute as a British dancer, to British contemporary dance, but instead contributed to some form called 'black' dance. Coming back to the UK, the saving grace for me was working for Union Dance Company, which as a racially and experientially diverse company that allowed for the exploration of themes and concepts through contemporary dance.

Finding a Home in Dance Again

In 2010 I returned back to the dance sector after a long break of 15 years. During this break I had spent time retraining in the wider Arts sector, blending and bridging the world of arts management/policy/and education. As a dancer, the transferability of skills, training and discipline had contributed to my work in the wider sector giving me a unique perspective on arts practice. Upon my return to dance I found a lot had changed, which for the outsider looking in was a positive step but after settling back into the culture from which I had left, I felt there was still a long way to go. I was able to further re-connect with the dance culture through the first Re:Generations conferences in 2010 & 2012. These had a home-style environment, which had the familiarity of being a child of dance returning back to the community all grown up!

The personal backdrop of my re-emergence into dance in 2010 was the loss of my father, whose legacy encouraged me to be defiantly me and not allow myself to be defined or determined by others' perception: 'You will always be you!' He and my mother had a sense of adventure and like a lot of their contemporaries from the Caribbean took the plunge across the Atlantic Ocean to UK shores to find their sense of 'home' and a better life. Although extremely painful, numbing and devastating, his death called into my consciousness the opportunity to reflect on the legacy of his life as a man, father and grandfather, who made me laugh, was childlike, curious with a vulnerable spirit that was open, free to express by the way he moved, not defined by anyone. It was the way he moved which sparked my curiosity and wondered about our epic memory of dance; its ritual of movement and connections with our ancestors from the Caribbean and distant African heritage; the feeling and sensing of life in any situation or experience, a dance of life deeply rooted and connected to the earth or some kind of lineage. I wondered whether that lineage was in fact a way of handing on life and experience through movement and whether that was through teaching, pedagogy and expression of movement contributing the rhythm of life through movement back to the sector. I have a short video of my father dancing to a reggae track which had the lyrics '…*you never know what you've got till its gone…*'—deeply ironic but in that video footage he left behind my musical and movement legacy—'never knowing what I had until it was gone' prompted me to keep on moving, being present, expressing and remembering through some form of dance practice, be it professionally or not, embracing the nuances, essence, physicality of moving my body as a measure of my experiences. His passing (his 'transition') caused me to ask deeper questions about myself, my life, my experiences and potential contribution to the world. At the same time, I reconnected with close friends I grew up with both in England and abroad who had a shared passion for dance. We had shared experiences and reasons for moving, coming from a place of common experience, living life as a young person wanting to find a voice, make sense of the world and all seeing dance as (for want of a better word) 'saving' us. I had a shared 'community of practice' with these friends through dance and moving as part of my identity. In their company, I did not in any way feel 'other'.

Added to personal developments and my re-emergence was the loss of key individuals, mentors and supporters. The first was Denise Jefferson, Principal of the Ailey School, who supported my training and did not compromise on professionalism and standards. Then, Eduardo Rivero Walker, Artistic Director, choreographer and teacher of Compañía Teatro de la Danza del Caribe, Cuba. His death was devastating for me as he had been a long-time mentor, professional and personal friend, and had influenced my thinking and embracing of my sense of pride as a black woman and dancer. He is part of the canon of influential people in my life that contributed to the fabric of my experiences, learning and development as a dancer and, now, a teacher. It was always a pleasure to watch him move and teach and his rhythm was deeply rooted to his Caribbean roots, and African lineage—it was his movement poetry that contributed also to a sense of emotional and spiritual home and had a contemporary flavour that worked within his surroundings. Eduardo empowered me to raise the bar high and challenged me to be myself with dignity, grace and sense of purpose, to experience dance as the ritual of movement and life emanating from our ancestors. There also was a sense of giving back to the community in the presence of Eduardo when he supported me. Reflecting back on these instances in my life, I realised I was sitting on an unrealised potential to contribute to the sector by teaching as a former performing 'artist-as-educator' and contributing to the legacy of dance in some way, albeit small.

The 2010 Re:Generations conference was a route to reconnect and get back onto the path towards teaching as an artist-as-educator—this was my re-entry through the route of dance education rather than that of a choreographer. Themes emerging from the conversations I had with peers at the conference highlighted dance from the African diaspora as a diverse arts practice in terms of excellence, innovation and leadership. I fully embrace the practice of dance from the diaspora being diverse because for a long time I viewed myself as more than just a dancer versed in modern dance principles—I was also very much influenced by my Caribbean background through retraining and transferring my skills as artist and manager into the wider cultural sector. This supports my own stance from an Africanist paradigm as it helped to shape my identity and how exploring and experiencing modern dance was specific to my lived experience. For me, the lived experience exists in movement, expression and performance. I was excited at the thought of debating about dance and arts as an innovative practice that can transform perspective and engagement in the world and leadership. I also mused on the idea of diaspora and came to the conclusion that diaspora for me was fluid and rooted to where you were physically and the community into which you engaged. When teaching young people contemporary dance, I have a modern dance style to offer; although practically relevant and meaningful to my current situation as a dance teacher, it became more than the teaching of dance as a subject. What was revealed to me was my own philosophical and interpretive stance and how and where I orientate myself—the home for me in this was the use of the technique that gave me hope and permission to understand young people in their situation and their engagement in dance and performance. I had exposure to and learning of and about their lives socially, culturally and artistically in their community. I was able to acknowledge their culture, which is global, and a diaspora for them that was immediate through social media and accessible in a variety of formats.

I have started to develop and be sensitive to work that gives emphasis to young people and the emergence of young artists and choreographers.

It is a good focus to think about as my role as a teacher and mentor. However, I couldn't help but wonder what was available for the older more mature artist and the career paths and opportunities available for those with a bank of knowledge and experiences to pass on. It may be about recognition and value of those older dancers who sidestepped the limelight of dance but nonetheless diligently kept their practice alive in other areas of dance.

During the 2012 Re:Generations conference, I found once again that it was great to engage in the debate and bear witness to the number of dancers and educators and academics exploring and interrogating the richness of dance and the impact on contemporary culture. I was impressed by the energy of the conference, which contained lots of interesting papers and talks presented. It opened up a new way for me to reflect, engage and debate about dance from the perspective of the African diaspora and what that meant for me. Had I not left the UK for the United States, I feel that my thinking and experience would not have evolved or been as open. Engaging in a number of discussions and listening affirmed my belief about the concept of diaspora being fluid and how, through dance touching many different cultures and perspectives, of dance can be modern or be more culturally specific dance experiences.

Evolving discussions emerged about definitions, acknowledging that the sector comprises a variety of related dance practices of or influenced by theatre that have emerged from a global network of institutions and performance traditions: a vision of dance practice rather than technical formality that defines the work of the sector as artists; Africa and blackness that is conceptualised in different ways within artistic vision; and practitioners that cater for different audiences. This resonates with my own history when I think about my belief system of having lots of different experiences that all are relevant and that diversity of experience is a good thing. It was refreshing to be a part of a debate and realise that these types of conversations were happening during my roaming years abroad and outside of the dance sector and engagement through other art forms. The conference also flagged up critical dialogues that recognised the range of style and aesthetics in dance and a need to reshape the term 'contemporary dance'. 'Contemporary' is as broad, as long, as deep and as relevant as you want it to be within the influence of trends that we experience in the society at any given time. There was a lot of discussion to recognise and support the profile of black dancers and choreographers at all stages of their careers. It was interesting to listen and take part in that discussion because for me going through my initial dance training and career, it was lonely and I had to do the majority of it myself, find and map my own route to develop professionally mostly through a network of contacts and opportunities. Embarking on this solo journey, I had no choice but to create little pockets of home so that I could develop my practice and my voice in dance.

For me, the 2012 conference also awakened my sense of space and perception with other dancers and practitioners with an emphasis on the circle as an inclusive way of participating, experiencing, sensing, watching dance not as a spectator but as a participator. I was struck by the idea that 'seeing' one another within a circle contributes to a sense of valuing different perspectives as enriching dance. It reminded me how we see our lives as a continuum or circle of experiences.

Both the 2010 and 2012 conferences made me think deeply about my transition and movements in my career as a dancer and now a dance teacher and what that means. The conference in a way encouraged possibilities to move and transition into areas that support my continual growth, the idea of dance and movement in the area of teaching pedagogy plus thinking about the legacy I have inherited from my father and mentors, the need to continue and move on throughout life.

This draws me to my impulse for writing this chapter to articulate the process of my journeying towards 'home' and where I position myself within that. My journeying abroad initially started out as passion for more training in a modern dance technique, it also led me to having the feeling of being accepted for who I was, and not be pigeon-holed, with the freedom to explore and evolve. Home became an interpretation of my circumstances and definition of who I am, and an acceptance that I will always evolve and learn. The triggers were experience, the environment. I naturally have a love for a modern dance form and its pedagogy which, although codified, is still organic with room for more exploration. Within that code is a framework I can use as a 'home' base and explore lots of different rooms or component parts.

I referred to Shelley Mallet (2004) tracing the relevant theories, which suggested another interpretation of home. She suggests another way of visioning 'home'—to see it as the footprint of our inner self and asks 'What are the environmental triggers that constitute home or mimics the internal processes we associate with home?' For me, it is myriad of disciplines and experiences and I am a dancer versed with a vocabulary framed within an Africanist paradigm of a lived and embodied experience.

REFERENCES

Brinson, P. (1991). *Dance as Education Towards a National Dance Culture.* London/New York: Falmer.

Mallet, S. (2004). Understanding Home: A Critical Review of the Literature. *The Sociological Review,* 52(1), 62–89.

PART III

Products

For *Black* peoples and cultures around the world, part of the aftermath of colonialism has been a continuing struggle to address and re-articulate how they are represented. For artists, mis-representation is particularly harrowing because their drive and life's work is about communication of ideas, feelings and thoughts (see discussion in Chap. 1). Part of the goal of this book is to engage in the struggle to gain control over how dance artists from within the spectrums of Blackness and Britishness represent themselves as artists in general, and within the scholarship of dance. This is the struggle to capture the somatic in text and at the same time the art of bravely inhabiting the ambiguity of an embodied existence. The embodied lived experience itself creates responses to situations, and these responses are the phenomena of 'being' in that situation. Therefore it is important to note that there are particular phenomena that arise out of being in the spectrums of Black, British and dance.

In this section I am asking what the phenomena are that arise from the situation of Black, British and dance. Seeing the making of dance and dance scholarship as a process (some processes of which were presented in Part II), Part III is not about seeing the art works themselves as products. Rather, the section looks at the consequences and manifestations produced when the spectrums of Black, British, and dance are experienced together. These by-products of working as an artist within the spectrums of Black, British and dance demonstrate how artists have found sophisticated and innovative responses to marginalisation, in order to keep engaging with dance. This section recognises how some artists have had to track new paths in order to begin, to develop or to continue their dance practices. These new pathways (that are created 'despite…' rather than 'because of…')

become the *products* of resistance. Resistance not necessarily depicted in the art work itself, but in how the artist has survived and continued to advance their work.

I feel that these phenomena, which have been forged in the fire of necessity, offer methods, histories and approaches that are significant to dance practice in general. This section suggests that, in a sustained determination to follow their artistic development, artists within the Black, British, dance spectrums have also contributed beyond their individual work to larger developments in dance practice.

In Chap. 14 '*Battling Under Britannia's Shadow: UK Jazz Dancing in the 1970s and 1980s*' Carr suggests a re-remembrance of Jazz history to include the many dancers who developed dance styles in the nightclubs of Britain in 1970s and 1980s. Set against the backdrop of political upheaval that aimed to focus blame for financial problems on Britain's post-colonial immigration policy, the sons and daughters of the recently immigrated found spaces for expressing themselves on nightclub floors, creating new movement fusions.

In Chap. 15 '*Caribfunk Technique: A New Feminist/Womanist Futuristic Technology in Black Dance Studies in Higher Education*', Carey proposes that Afro-Caribbean fusions of dance floor improvisation with codified technique create focus on movement that can empower female bodies. Taking the *Hip Wine* as an example, Carey suggests that rather than misogynistic inference projected onto the movement, for the female dancer, these dance forms give an embodied language to her agency in her own pleasure and expression. Working in a university setting, Carey has seen how for herself and her female students the agency gained from these dance forms has spread beyond their dance studio experience to a more general celebration and acceptance of the sensing female body.

Glean and Lehan further discuss the breadth and role that dance education can have in Higher Education when it is presented within a diverse curriculum offer. In Chap. 16 '*More Similarities than Differences: Searching for New Pathways*', Glean and Lehan describe the second phase of research they have been undertaking as they create a dance curriculum that mirrors the cultural backgrounds and multi-cultural needs of students in Britain in the twenty-first century. They discuss research trips to observe good dance teaching practice in the USA, Jamaica, Cuba and Ghana and analyse how this good practice can be translated to their own curriculum, which has emerged out of the necessity of meeting the needs of their students.

In Chap. 17 '*Epistemology of the Weekend: Youth Dance Theatre*', Romans, Joseph and I re-witness the youth dance groups we attended at the beginning of our dance careers. Perhaps a response to violence and raising tensions around immigration (see Barnes, Chap. 7; Carr, Chap. 14), perhaps a response to the influx of exciting new contemporary dance styles (see Namron, Chap. 2) Youth dance clubs were set-up in the late 1970s and 1980s that seemed to have a focus on the '*Black*' youth. It could be argued that support for Youth Dance companies emerged as a product of addressing a perceived need to keep the urban and black youth busy. Groups from around Britain gathered in Leicester at the first and second Youth Dance Festivals in 1980 and 1981. Many of the young dancers who attended these festivals went onto have extensive careers in different elements of the Performing Arts and so doing blazed new and non-traditional trails for dance access and training.

Lastly, in acknowledging the journeys that many British artists have made leaving UK in order to find acceptance as a dance artist, *Gonzalez* traces the transatlantic arts exchange of Afro-Caribbean performers. In Chap. 18 '*Transatlantic Voyages: Then and Now*', *Gonzalez* reflects on the artists who have pursued international performance opportunities between the UK and USA over the past two hundred years. She explores the phenomena of artists from the African Diaspora voyaging across the Atlantic, pointing out that it is not just a 'thing of the past' but continues to be a necessity for many today. She then gives a short commentary on the interviews she undertook with British artists for the web-site accompanying this book.

Throughout the book I have asked the reader to rethink, re-remember and reimagine dance in general through taking a closer look at the narratives from within the spectrums of Black, British, and dance. As this last section suggests, this is partly to be proactive within the construct for what dance can be. It is also to acknowledge that dance is an embodied practice that is realised through the lived narratives of the people who manifest it in their lives. Always an act of resistance in the face of dualism, dance is the medium through which we can begin to bridge the gap of separation constructed between *them and us, mind and body, sensation and reality*. The role of dance is not to be constantly inwardly defining itself and who can participate in it but to move beyond the dance studio to give voice to a way of being, and connecting with the world.

CHAPTER 14

Battling Under Britannia's Shadow: UK Jazz Dancing in the 1970s and 1980s

Jane Carr

New styles of dancing, termed UK, Underground or, more recently, Old Skool Jazz, that emerged in British clubs during the late 1970s are still practised and taught today and have influenced choreography for the theatre. The evidence from recordings of this dancing attest to the high levels of technical and performance skills the dancers attained. Yet these dancers received limited recognition in this country beyond their immediate circle of fellow dancers and jazz enthusiasts. As I have argued elsewhere, consideration of these dance styles is important to gaining a fuller understanding of the history of dance in Britain in the last quarter of the twentieth century. Moreover, an acknowledgement of their significance may contribute to a shift in the historical narratives through which that history is shared (Carr, 2012). Writing with the dancer Irven Lewis, I have also previously suggested that, through their improvised intercorporeal transactions on the dance floor, the dancers brought into being new styles of British identities (Lewis & Carr, forthcoming). While African diasporic cultural influences were key to the development of this jazz dancing, not all those involved in what was an underground 'scene' were Black. In relation to this

J. Carr (✉)
University of Bedfordshire, Luton, UK

period of British history, the cultural theorist Paul Gilroy has explored how Black expressive cultures 'spring up at the intersection of 'race' and class' (Gilroy, 2002/1987). What I think is worth starting to consider is how this youthful, subcultural development of jazz dancing moved through the intersections of 'race', class and gender. As a previous ballet and 'contemporary' dancer who never witnessed this dancing until it crossed over into theatre, I am ill-equipped to write about it. My aim is to raise awareness of its significance so as to encourage those with more direct experience to document and reflect upon the styles they developed. It is in this spirit that I raise questions as to how this dancing may be interpreted within its historical context by drawing upon perspectives from (British) cultural studies while also referring to the more recent framework of intersectional theory.

Intersectional theory is usually associated with Black feminist theory because it is generally accepted to have been identified by Kimberle Crenshaw, an American law professor who became frustrated with the polarisation of the different identity politics of 'race' and gender. She recognised that:

Although racism and sexism readily intersect in the lives of real people, they seldom do in feminist and anti-racist practices. And so when practices expound identity as woman or person of colour as an either/or proposition they relegate the identity of women of color to a location that resists telling. (Crenshaw, 1993)

Crenshaw, in describing the struggles of the women she encounters, also includes class in her analysis. While Crenshaw is more concerned with combating the combination of racism and sexism experienced by women, the consideration of the interplay of different aspects of identities may prove a fruitful approach to start to consider the different ways in which jazz dancing negotiated notions of gender, 'race' and class that were prevalent at that time.

In relation to the significance of difference to the visual arts, Amelia Jones proposes:

Identifications...profoundly shape and inform meaning and value, thus interpretive frameworks are part of the picture, not invisible apparatuses...through which a single correct meaning will reveal itself to the appropriately situated interpreter. (Jones, 2012, p. 225)

Jones is critical of intersectional theories, arguing that, like the single identity politics they aimed to replace, they rely on oppositional identifications that depend on fixed boundaries between terms. However, in relation to dancing during an era in which the politics of class, 'race' and gender were bitterly contested, differences in the ways they were experienced and embodied can be understood as related to shifting, but necessary, categories used by people to understand their positional relationship to others. Hence my approach to interpreting this dancing is framed within a conceptualisation of 'difference' that is described within the framework of (British) cultural studies by Stuart Hall:

> There is the *'difference'* that makes a radical and unbridgeable separation: and there is a *'difference'* which is positional, conditional and conjunctural, closer to Derrida's notion of *differance*, although if we are concerned to maintain a politics it cannot be defined exclusively in terms of an infinite sliding of the signifier. (Hall, 1992/1989, pp. 446–447)

It is because of the limited recognition that so far has been accorded to this dancing, that I propose it is interpreted within a framework that acknowledges how, at this time, UK Jazz dancing negotiated the dynamics of class, 'race' and, to some extent, gender. Due to the complexities of how all of these might be theorised, what follows is presented as an initial indication of some of the themes that such an approach might bring to the surface with the aim of encouraging their further consideration.

UK Jazz dancing can be understood as having developed within a club-orientated youth subculture that was dynamically related to both Black and working-class cultures. It is important here to recognise that not only were each of the parent cultures from which the subculture was formed subject to internal differences and changes but, as with any subculture, UK Jazz would not be experienced by all those participating in the same ways. However, those involved recognise themselves as belonging to a distinct group, even while also being very aware of differences in the various 'scenes'. UK Jazz dancing emerged as a response to music that itself was a complex fusion of different influences. While the introduction of electronic instruments and funky beats infuriated jazz 'purists', when, from the mid-1970s, DJs started to play music that combined elements of funk, Latin or rock, with jazz in clubs in Britain, they inspired new dance styles. Dancers may have initially drawn on the moves they already knew, but developing as a jazz dancer depended on responding to different rhythms, absorbing different influences and learning new moves which were incorporated into a coherent, innovative style. Jazz dancers experienced their dance style as key to their sense of belonging to both a group and a locality. Both the DJ and dancer Seymour Nurse (n.d. a) and the DJ Mark 'Snowboy' Cotgrove (2009) document the lineage of dancers who influenced the development of the fusion style in London, but the suggestion that London-based dancers were the 'originators' of this jazz dancing would be strongly contested by dancers from other parts of Great Britain. It is perhaps more appropriate to this particular dance history to consider that scenes developed around clubs in different parts of the country. Invested as it was with their personal and local histories, dancers are adamant that, while their dancing might draw on many different influences, their dancing was also uniquely British. Hence, while they may refer to their dancing as a form of street dance, they emphasise its distinctness from the American street dance forms of hip hop and house (Cotgrove, 2009; Lewis, 2010).

The development of this dancing coincides with a period of often turbulent political, social and economic changes in Britain. When the DJs first introduced jazz funk and jazz fusion to the dance floors in the mid-1970s, the country was governed by a Labour government. Their policies followed in, what it has been argued, was a general political consensus established after the Second World War that was held together by 'a belief in the state's capacity to reduce social injustice and, by expanding the economy, to create a better life for the whole population' (Dutton, 1997, p. 13). However, what had been a relatively secure environment for workers was to change. As the prosperity and optimism of the 1960s gave way to industrial decline and rising unemployment, high inflation fuelled public sector workers' demands for better pay that were not met by a government struggling to manage the economy. The resulting strikes and a general sense of decline led to frustration with the Labour government who were replaced in 1979 by Margaret Thatcher's Conservative government. Thatcher's leadership lasted 11 years, during which time the Conservatives introduced many measures that overturned the previous consensus. Their policies limited the power of trades unions to protect their workers, promoted a free market economy and emphasised the value of individual enterprise. Inevitably, the government clashed with the unions, the miners' strikes becoming a key focus for opposition. As the old consensus gave way to the new 'neo-liberalism', it destabilised the structures of British society (Hall & Jefferson, 2006). The new economic order undermined previous class distinctions, including the political association of Labour with the working classes. However, it also brought in a new kind of class politics that recognised an 'underclass', 'new poverty' and the 'widening inequalities that accompanied de-industrialization' (Hall & Jefferson, 2006, p. xvi). For young people reaching adulthood in the late 1970s, the most immediate impact of the change in the political climate in the first years of Thatcher's leadership was a dramatic rise in unemployment. This particularly affected young people and those among the working classes who had been employed in the 'old' heavy industries such as mining and steel manufacturing. Many Black and white youths thus found themselves part of this 'underclass' and at odds with 'Thatcherism'. For the jazz dancers, however, this did mean they had time, energy and motivation to invest in their dancing, which was practised not just in clubs but at home, in the streets and the halls belonging to local schools, colleges or community centres.

This period was also one during which immigration from Commonwealth countries was a subject of much tension. During the period of sustained decolonisation in the decades following the Second World War, the rights of peoples from the countries of Africa and the African Caribbean, and from India and Pakistan, to reside in the United Kingdom became a source of much controversy that was fuelled by the 'new racism' that reworked the negative attitudes to Black people of the colonial period (Lawrence, 1982, p. 45). The founding of the National Front in 1967 established the political organisation of antagonism to Black immigrants. The National Front's policies aimed not only at prohibiting immigration of Black people, but at enforcing the repatriation of those already settled. When these attitudes were voiced by the Conservative MP Enoch Powell in 1968, in his now infamous 'Rivers of Blood' speech (2007/1968), he was sacked from his position in the Conservative shadow cabinet. Nevertheless limitations were imposed upon immigration. Legislation in 1962, 1968 and 1971 increased restrictions on who could settle permanently in the United Kingdom until this right was limited to those who could establish a prior link, usually a British-born parent or grandparent. While seeking to minimise immigration, during this period these measures also worked to distinguish between Black and white immigrants, reinforcing a sense that British identity was defined by 'race' (Joppke, 1999). The thinking behind such a distinction is evident in Margaret Thatcher's comments made on television in the year before she led the Conservative party to election victory. Emphasising the growth in numbers of immigrants, she proposed that: 'People are really rather afraid that this country might be rather swamped by people with a different culture' (Margaret Thatcher, 1978, cited by Margaret Thatcher Foundation, n.d.).

Margaret Thatcher's appeal to those with (white) nationalist sentiments was strengthened by her determination to go to war to protect one of the last overseas British territories, The Falkland Islands. It was this conflict that led to Mrs. Thatcher being cast in the popular imagination as 'Britannia', the symbolic female protector of a Britain that, in the words of a Victorian rendition of a patriotic song, 'rules the waves'. Some caricatures of Mrs. Thatcher as Britannia were rather negative; Chris Madden (n.d.) revealed her an as anachronism, sitting adrift on a tiny island that might not only represent the Falklands but the small size of a Britain that no longer ruled over a vast Empire (1988). Others revelled in her symbolic status: On 9 June 1983, the front page of the Sun newspaper urged its readers to vote for Margaret Thatcher's second term of leadership by featuring an image of her as a smiling Britannia sitting on a tamed lion (Jones, 2015).

This optimistic image of Britannia was perhaps reassuring to those inhabitants of post-colonial Britain suffering from what the cultural theorist Paul Gilroy describes as:

> ...*acute bouts of racial and national anxiety that are the products of a chronic inability to adjust to changes brought about by a changing global position manifest in melancholic responses to the loss of imperial pre-eminence and the painful demand to adjust the life of a national collective to a severely reduced sense of itself as a global power.* (Gilroy, 2002, p. xxxvii)

One such bout of anxiety over questions of 'race' and nation is captured in the Conservative party's 1983 election poster that, alongside the image of a young Black male dressed in a suit, proclaims 'Labour says he's Black. Tories say he's British' (cited in Gilroy, 2002/1987, p. 64). This message, which Gilroy has described as coherent with a policy of assimilation, was criticised by representatives of Black British communities at the time for its seeming unwillingness to countenance the dual identity of being both Black and British. Yet, as Gilroy argues, during this period young Black British citizens experienced their identities as belonging to both the African diaspora and to the country of their birth:

> *Black Britain defines itself crucially as part of diaspora. Its unique cultures draw inspiration from those developed by black populations elsewhere. In*

> *particular the cultures and politics of black America and the Caribbean have become raw materials for creative processes that redefine what it means to be black, adapting it to distinctively British experiences and meanings. Black culture is actively made and remade.* (Gilroy, 2002/1987, p. 202)

Where more formal dance activities engaged with British institutions, the anxieties over questions of identity can be seen underlying constant interrogations of how the dance activities of Black British artists should be identified and supported. For example, in 1984 the Arts Council England, along with two regional arts organisations, a city council and a private trust, funded the Black Dance Development Trust to support African dance forms. Bob Ramdhanie states that the Trust

> *…clearly differentiated between black people in dance (whether African, Contemporary, Ballet e.t.c.) and the development of African dance in England, focussing on the development of the form and introducing theory and spiritual guidance into the infrastructure for development.* (Ramdhanie, 2013, p. 27)

Used in this way, the label 'Black' emphasised the continuation of diasporic traditions. This raised some anxieties regarding the status of Black dancers in other styles particularly because, at this time, Black dancers struggled to be accepted in ballet companies and even the experience of inclusion in 'contemporary' dance was not always positive. Greta Mendez, who started MAAS Movers in 1977, commented later that 'there was no vehicle for black contemporary dancers; they were voiceless at that time' (Mendez, 2003, cited in Claid, 2006, p. 105).

While Kenneth Tharp (2013) is concerned that 'Black' as a category of dance was too limiting, Peter Badejo argued that the term 'Black dance' made 'the colour of the practitioner more important than the content of their art' (cited in Claid, 2006, p. 107). Yet for some artists at this time, issues of Black identities may have been central to the content of their art. Inspired by the cultural theory of Stuart Hall and similar arts movements in the USA, the British Black Arts Movement was established in 1982 to raise awareness of issues of representation (Bailey, Baucom, & Boyce, 2005). Beyond the formal arts sector, during the 1970s, many ethnic minorities in Britain started to identify under the label 'Black' to develop a cohesive approach to combatting racism. (For a time, along with Asians, the term also included Irish immigrants.) More generally, Black expressive culture embraced the influence of African-American activism, for example celebrating the words of Martin Luther King's speech 'Black is Beautiful' (1967) or the words and music of James Brown's 'Say it Loud I'm Black and Proud' (1968). Hence, in the 1980's 'Black' gained political connotations associated with resistance to racism. For artists, in this sense, the term might be applied to their work to signify an expectation that the content of their art challenged the hegemonic representational systems that reinforced European assumptions subordinating Black peoples and cultures to Western standards. However, Emilyn Claid (2006) recognises how the label 'Black', used as a catch-all category by established arts institutions, became used by 'white' institutions to suppress the complex identities of Black artists.

Not surprisingly, for many young people, how to conceptualise Black British identities in the period of decolonisation led to confusion as much as anxiety:

The whole Black and British thing was happening in the mid 70s – back then it was a confusing concept. We didn't really know exactly where we fit. It was a weird social experiment that had no previous blueprint. We were looking to America but weren't American – we are of Jamaica but we weren't Jamaican. (Letts cited by Adoo, 2015, para.2.)

This mix of anxiety and confusion, along with the tensions associated with the experiences of unemployment and racism, was part of the jazz dancers' daily lives. Dancing was an outlet and the clubs somewhere to escape. That a large proportion of dancers in many of the clubs playing jazz music in the later 1970s and early 1980s were young people of African or African-Caribbean heritage meant that this dancing was influenced by range of traditions learned from families and friends at house parties and community events (Lewis, 2010; Nurse, n.d. a). Ska, and 'shufflin' may have been particular influences on some early jazz scenes, but elements of jazz dancing may also have already been experienced within African and African-Caribbean communities. Seymour Nurse reveals that when he and his brother demonstrated their jazz moves, his mother recognised them from her youth in Barbados (n.d. a). Another dancer, Steve Edwards, recalls:

When my Mum and Dad knew I liked jazz they played me all this African jazz they'd bought from as far back as the 50's. They told me that I would dance to it when I was a little boy! (cited in Cotgrove, 2009, p. 257)

In an interview with Seymour Nurse, Harris Berlin also reveals that, when he came to Britain from Jamaica in 1962, there was a thriving scene of house parties and underground clubs at which Berlin danced to a wide range of music including imported jazz records (Nurse, n.d. b). This not only accords with Nurse's account of how the jazz scene grew out of 'Blues' parties but also Paul Gilroy's analysis of how, in Britain in the 1950s and '60s, African and African-Caribbean immigrants shared in the development of an expressive culture through a range of social events at which people danced to imported records from America, Africa, Latin America and the Caribbean (Gilroy, 2002).

However, as the new generation of jazz dancers ventured out to clubs, they also drew on movements seen on television or in films. Nurse emphasises the influence of 'Top of the Pops' and 'Soul Train' on the London scene (n.d. a) while Cotgrove (2009) and Lewis (2010) also refer to steps seen in dance sequences in televised musicals and ballet and the actions in martial arts films. Some dancers, including Edward Lynch, one of the members of Phoenix Dance Company and RJC, were inspired by both jazz and the 'contemporary' dance that was taught at school (Cotgrove, 2009). However, there is little mention of the jazz dancers seeing the developing African and African-Caribbean theatre companies, perhaps because for poorer youths, film and television were more likely forms of entertainment and, as Nurse points out, these forms of dance were rarely programmed on television (n.d. a.)

With so many influences, different styles of jazz dancing emerged in different areas, but due to dancers travelling to clubs in different cities, the various scenes influenced one another. Cotgrove identifies that by the late 1970s there were three key styles: contemporary (or ballet) style jazz, jazz funk and fusion (2009, pp. 40–41). The first drew heavily on influences from dancing seen on television, mainly in musicals; jazz funk developed from the rhythmic twists and turns of funk; while fusion also developed out of funk but with more emphasis on fast rhythmic footwork interspersed with drops to the floor that emphasise the dancers' strength. From the late 1970s these styles, and combinations of them, were utilised by groups of dancers who not only danced together but also began to perform. Through the work of groups such as Brothers in Jazz, Bubble and Squeak, Expansions, Foot Patrol, IDJ, the Jazz Defektors (who also became established as a pop group), Mahogany and The Untouchable Force, jazz dancers appeared as guest acts in clubs, theatre shows and in pop videos and film.

While there are evident differences in their involvement, jazz dancers shared in the experience of going out to clubs to test their jazz dancing against one another, often through dance challenges or 'battles'. This practice, in which two dancers compete against each other within a circle of dancers, is an element of this jazz dancing that draws upon African diasporic traditions. During the early 1980s, as if caught up in the drive of neo-liberalism, the challenges in jazz dancing increased in their competitiveness (Paul Anderson cited in Cotgrove, 2009, p. 252). Within an acknowledged hierarchy, dancers would study potential opponents in preparation for the opportunity to battle them, Irven Lewis remembers:

> *You go to a club it was like a football pitch. It was like 1000's of pitches in one club. It was like hip hop today if everyone was into it.... Before you couldn't get a job because there was a lot of racism going on....So dancing was the only thing they had.* (Lewis, 2010)

Lewis' testimony makes clear both the intensity of the scene (that could at times provoke heated antagonism) and the impact of racism experienced by Black youths. In Britain at this time, racist attitudes continued negative stereotypes of Black people constructed during the colonial expansion of the British Empire (Lawrence, 1982). Black people were disproportionately affected by unemployment (Mohan, 1997), while young Black men were the focus of negative representation in the media (Gilroy, 2002). In the 1970s and early '80s some clubs still operated racist door policies (Nurse, n.d. a); hence much of this jazz dancing emerged in underground venues. While the focus in jazz dance battles was on individual and area pride – on beating the opposition – dancers also recognised a shared sensibility. Upon seeing IDJ dance, Lewis states that he knew 'where they came from' (Lewis, Nurse, & Nurse, 2011). Although battling was approached very competitively, there was also a sense that the intensity of their interactions drove the dancers to develop both their skills and their ability to respond creatively to each other's dancing. Jazz dancing is at heart an improvised form and, while the dancers rely on a palette of well-practised steps, it's the moment of creative inspiration that is the ultimate goal. Such instants are the result of a shared encounter, not just between dancers but emanating from the 'energy' of all those involved (Lewis & Carr, forthcoming). Absorbed in the intense action of their dancing, there is little evidence to suggest that these dancers were consciously intending for their movements to represent their struggles beyond the confines of the club. Yet because their dancing 'was all they had', the intensity with which it was practised meant that it might well embody all that these young people were.

Viewed from the perspective of cultural studies, this subculture was significant by virtue of groups of largely working-class young people working out new styles of dancing by drawing on a complex fusion of traditions that embodied different cultural heritages. Of the styles Cotgroves acknowledges, in fusion the emphasis on rhythmic footwork performed with a low centre of gravity strongly suggests a sense of African heritage that Seymour Nurse, who documents this style, situates in relation to 'West Indian' culture (Nurse, n.d. a). Contemporary jazz, and later Bebop, also drew on adaptations of steps from Western theatre genres. These included some ballet vocabulary, adding turns and leaps into the air which I have suggested previously may be seen as an example of syncretic adaptation of dominant cultural codes (Carr, 2016). Yet whichever style the dancers practised, their dancing may be interpreted as embodying new British identities that resisted inequalities between Black and white, while beginning to dismantle essentialist notions of authentic Black and white identities.

Although dancers themselves comment little on differences in terms of 'race', a number of the DJs interviewed by Mark Cotgrove (2009) discuss the proportions of Black and white people at various clubs. In contrast to the short-lived attraction of working-class, white youths to ska and reggae in the late 1960s (Hebdidge, 1976), the jazz scene does seem, at least on the surface, to have been a less transient point of engagement for Black and white youths. More analysis and historical research would be needed to understand the dynamic interplay of (white) working-class and Black cultures. While Black youths were most affected by high levels of unemployment, the lack of a job was an issue for many youths from working-class families. Did this experience engender a shared antagonism to 'Thatcherism'? Were ties to local areas a means of establishing a sense of collective identity when at a national level the issue of identity was so fraught and confusing? Did the creative act of dancing help young people negotiate 'difference' through practices not confined by the binaries of the language of 'race'? In contrast to reggae that maintained roots in Rastafarian African-centric ideals (Hebdidge, 1976), perhaps the jazz scene intuitively grasped the beginning of an anti-essentialist approach to identity that, in the terms of cultural studies, was identified by Stuart Hall as 'new ethnicities' (1992/1989). Alternatively, as the jazz scene developed, did it become another instance of Black people's dance skills being appropriated, with canny jazz club owners and DJs recognising the dancers' value as entertainment? Certainly, some DJs seem to have been worried that while paying club goers liked to watch the dancers, sometimes the jazz dancers' requirement for space for the 'circle' for a dance challenge inhibited the more casual club goers from dancing (Cotgrove, 2009).

For men involved in this scene in the 1970s and 1980s, a passion for dancing went against conventional, western, gender stereotypes (Burt, 2007). However, this stereotype was not shared within Black cultures in which young men grew up dancing among their families and friends (Lewis, 2010). For the white male dancers, disco and Northern soul had already begun to popularise social dancing as a male activity. The evident strength required for jazz dancing and the frame of the dance battle provided an arena in which to pursue a passion for dancing while not straying too far from Western gender norms. Not every young man enjoyed it when the dancing became more competitive (Cotgrove, 2009, p. 257). Yet for some men, dancing could be a means to assert dominance in clearly defined hierarchies in an era in which more traditional routes to achieving status were thwarted by the combination of high unemployment and, for Black men, racism. Significantly, it was young male Black British dancers who were 'rated' and who took positions of leadership in developing the dancing to provide performance opportunities. For some, their status as dancers was a form of 'subcultural capital' (Thornton, 1995) that could be transformed into tangible financial capital, employment and the opportunity of being on stage or television. The video made for the pop group Working Week's *Venceremos* (Temple, 1984), that features some of the fusion dancers who would form IDJ, captures elements of the interplay between poor Black men, an affluent, fashionable set and the media. The video also suggests the dancers' connections to a wider African diaspora through the dancing of African-American tap legend Will Gaines and clips of the Nicholas Brothers.

Some young men also seem to have been concerned about how their dancing might attract female attention. For example, Trevor Miller, in recounting his unease when the Jazz Defektors 'took over' the dance floor, mentions their 'getting attention from the ladies' (cited in Cotgrove, 2009, p. 268). He also seems to have enjoyed that, as part of Brothers in Jazz, the dancers' new-found status in Japan led to their 'being chased down the road by screaming girls' (cited in Cotgrove, 2009, p. 269). Yet on the whole many young men attending jazz clubs were largely focused on the music and the dancing, something that the many interviews with jazz dancers undertaken by Mark Cotgrove (2009) also reveal. The desire to learn new steps would take some dancers to gay clubs for inspiration. This cross-over between different subcultures may also demonstrate the weakening of boundaries that would be a part of the more fluid 'postmodern' clubbing scenes that would follow (Hall & Jefferson, 2006).[1]

Much of the dancing, and particularly fusion, in its emphasis on strong dynamics and virtuosic display of physical power may seem to emphasise what are stereotypically often viewed as masculine qualities. Yet it is notable that where women are recorded dancing, they dance in similar style to the men and dress in the same manner (Jazz fusion battle part one; Jazzcotech, International Weekender, part 2). Further, Lewis reports that women danced competitively against men (Lewis, 2010). While in the field of postmodern dance, choreographers were challenging gender stereotypes (Burt, 2007), in more 'mainstream' dance gender roles were often differentiated following stereotypical (Western) assumptions. This is particularly evident in the mainstream styles of jazz exemplified in Bob Fosse's *Dancin'* 1978: Men wear jackets and trousers but women dance in heels and skimpy dresses; and although at times men and women dance in unison, at others the women pose in ways that draw the eye to their bodies while it is the men who demonstrate their strength through knee turns. It is not evident whether a more liberated approach to gender was always practised in the clubs. Very few females are shown in the available video examples of UK Jazz and an article for *New Dance*, that surveyed dancing in clubs in the early 1980s, suggested that generally women's place was secondary (Tolley & Burt, 1983). However, drawing on discussions prevalent at that time regarding the position of the female body as the object of the 'male gaze', the authors point out that the Black male dancer is similarly susceptible to becoming its object:

> *By thus emphasising the potency of the black body, its image becomes the object of comparable social processes as those that affect the image of women.* (Tolley & Burt, 1983, p. 11)

While within the European hegemony of the late twentieth century Black men were likely to be positioned in subordinate positions, UK Jazz provides dancers with opportunities to demonstrate a sense of agency that works against the dancers being viewed as passive objects of desire. In video recordings of the all-male group IDJ (e.g. Thorburn, 1988; Scratchworx, n.d.) the dancers hardly stop moving long enough for the eyes to rest on them and their bodies are rarely opened out fully towards the audience's gaze—which is also often deflected by their very stylish suits. In battles, focused as the dancers were on beating an opponent, their actions and postures were more likely to be aimed at putting those looking at them in a subordinate position. When the dance styles were transformed for stage or film, there was an emphasis on celebrating the sense of camaraderie between the dancers. Hence Jane Thorburn's (1988) film of the fusion dancers IDJ starts with the dancers meeting and greeting one another to establish the positive social relations between them and to emphasise that they are dancing for their own enjoyment. IDJ dancer Gary Nurse's admission 'I don't really dance for the audience I dance for myself...and us' (cited by Scratchworx, n.d.) accords with an often inwards focus on steps interspersed with looks and gestures towards the other dancers. Footage of IDJ dancing on stage again shows the close relationship between the dancers (Scratchworx, n.d.). However, in live performance their gaze is more focused outwards, alternating between watching each other and looking confidently at the audience. An element of play is introduced when they pull back, away from the audience, and pose briefly, looking quizzically at their audience with their hands in their pockets, in a manner that subverts conventions as to who is positioned to look and who to be looked at.

In many ways, UK Jazz dancing may be seen as a form of artistic expression through which young people were able to foster identities in terms that were important to them and their peers. Many jazz dancers would echo dancer Michael Brown's words: 'I was proud of the Jazz scene; the dance; the integration of colours; the innovations; the dancing' (cited in Cotgrove, 2009, p. 253). Yet this youth subculture was not impervious to the harsh social, political and economic realities of the period. Financial and social uncertainties and, for many dancers, the impact of racism, cast a shadow under which dance battles took on an intensity fuelled by the sense that dancing was the young people's primary means of self-fulfilment. For some, jazz could be a route to participate in the new entrepreneurial society. However, wider social attitudes to women may have impinged on their opportunities to take on positions of leadership within the dance-based hierarchies. There is more research needed to identify in detail how this dancing negotiated the interplay of class, 'race' and gender during a period in which Britain, as a nation, struggled with what its post-imperial identity might be. In a context in which British society still finds it difficult to come to terms with the histories and aspirations of all its citizens, such analysis is surely worthwhile.

Note

1. It could be noted that the dancers are careful to emphasise their identity as 'not gay' (cited in Cotgrove, 2009, pp. 249–251).

References

Adoo, E. (2015). Don Letts: I Didn't Feel Accepted as Black and British Until Soul II Soul Came Through. *Huffington Post* [On Line]. Available at URL: http://www.huffingtonpost.co.uk/edward-adoo/don-letts-i-didnt-feel-accepted_b_8083064.html. Accessed 1 July 2016.

Bailey, D., Baucom, I., & Boyce, S. (Eds.). (2005). *Shades of Black: Assembling Black Art in 1980s Britain*. Durham, NC: Duke University Press.

Burt, R. (2007). *The Male Dancer: Bodies, Spectacle, Sexualities* (2nd ed.). London/New York: Routledge.

Carr, J. (2012). Re-remembering the (Almost) Lost Jazz Dances of 1980s Britain. *Dance Chronicle, 35*(3), 315–337.

Carr, J. (2016). Researching British (Underground) Jazz Dancing c1979–1990. In C. Adair & R. Burt (Eds.), *British Dance: Black Routes*. London: Routledge.

Claid, E. (2006). *Yes? No! Maybe… Seductive Ambiguity in Dance*. London/New York: Routledge.

Cotgrove, M. (2009). *From Jazz Funk and Fusion to Acid Jazz*. London: Chaser Publications.

Crenshaw, K. (1993). Mapping the Margins, Intersectionality, Identity Politics and Violence Against Women of Color. *Stanford Law Review, 43*, 1241–1299.

Dutton, D. (1997). *British Politics Since 1945 Second Edition: The Rise, Fall and Rebirth of Consensus*. Oxford: Blackwell.

Gilroy, P. (2002). *There Ain't No Black in the Union Jack: The Cultural Politics of Race and Nation*. London/New York: Routledge (First Published 1987).

Hall, S. (1992). New Ethnicities. In D. Morley & K. Chen (Eds.), *Stuart Hall: Critical Dialogues in Cultural Studies* (pp. 442–451). London/New York: Routledge (First Published 1989).

Hall, S., & Jefferson, T. (Eds.). (2006). *Resistance Through Rituals. Youth Subcultures in Post-War Britain* (2nd ed.). London: Routledge.

Hebdidge, D. (1976). Reggae, Rastas and Rudies. In S. Hall & T. Jefferson (Eds.), *Resistance Through Rituals* (pp. 135–156). London: Hutchinson.

Jazz Fusion Battle Part One [On Line]. Available at URL: http://www.youtube.com/watch?v=v5DZo1ptSCc. Accessed 10 May 2010.

Jazzcotech International Dance Weekender, Part 2 [On Line]. Available at URL: https://www.youtube.com/watch?v=oIeaJ_H0rHI

Jones, A. (2012). *Seeing Differently, a History and Theory of Identification and the Visual Arts*. London/New York: Routledge.

Jones, A. (2015). The Sun Wot Done It: Relive Our Amazing Election Coverage Through the Years. *Sun Nation* [On Line]. Available at URL: http://www.sunnation.co.uk/the-sun-wot-done-it/. Accessed 1 July 2016.

Joppke, C. (1999). The Zero Immigration Country: Great Britain. In *Immigration and the Nation State: The United States, Germany and Great Britain* (pp. 100–140). Oxford: Oxford University Press.

Lawrence, E. (1982). Just Plain Common Sense: The Roots of Racism. In P. Gilroy (Ed.), *The Empire Strikes Back: Race and Racism in 70s Britain* (pp. 45–92). London: Hutchinson.

Lewis, I. (2010). Heritage Highlight: British Jazz Dance 1979–1990. *Hotfoot* [On Line]. Available at URL http://www.adad.org.uk/metadot/index.pl?id=24050&isa= Category&op=show. Accessed 1 June 2012.

Lewis, I., & Carr, J. (forthcoming). Disrupting the Habitus: Improvisational Practices in Jazz Dance Battles. In V. Midgelow (Ed.), *The Oxford Handbook of Improvisation in Dance*. Oxford: Oxford University Press.

Lewis, I., Nurse, G., & Nurse, S. (2011, May 2). In Discussion with Jane Carr, *Sadler's Wells Theatre*.

Maddon, C. (n.d.). *Waiving the Rules,* Chris Maddon Cartoons [On Line]. Available at URL http://www.chrismadden.co.uk/caricature/thatcher-caricature.html Accessed 1 July 2016.

Margaret Thatcher Foundation. (n.d.). *1978 Jan 27 Margaret Thatcher TV Interview for Granada World in Action ("rather swamped")* [On-Line]. Available at: URL: http://www.margaretthatcher.org/document/103485. Accessed 1 July 2016.

Mohan, L. (1997). *Britain's Black Population: Social Change, Public Policy and Agenda*. London: 717 Arena.

Nurse, S. (n.d.-a). *Seymour Nurse's Jazzifunk Club Jazz History* [On Line]. Available at: URL: http://www.thebottomend.co.uk/Seymour_Nurses Jazzifunk_Club_ Jazz_Chart.php. Accessed 1 June 2011.

Nurse, S. (n.d.-b). *Harris Berlin* [On Line]. Available at URL: http://www.thebottomend.co.uk/Harris_Berlin.php Acessed 26 June 2011.

Powell, E. (2007, November). Enoch Powell's Rivers of Blood Speech. *The Telegraph* (Speech First Given to Conservative Association Meeting in Birmingham 20th April 1968).

Ramdhanie, B. (2013). The Black Dance Development Trust (BDTT) 1984–1990. In P. Brookes (Ed.), *Hidden Movement: Contemporary Voices of Black British Dance*. Leicester: Serendipity Artists Movement.

Scratchworx. (n.d.). *IDJ Dance and Interview* [On Line]. Available at URL: https://www.youtube.com/watch?v=s8XVIyVfgiM

Temple J. (1984). *Venceremos* [Motion Picture] Working Week: Great Britain.

Tharp, K. (2013). Do We Need the Term 'Black Dance'? In P. Brookes (Ed.), *Hidden Movement: Contemporary Voices of Black British Dance*. Leicester: Serendipity Artists Movement.

Thorburn, J. (1988, July 5). IDJ: Dancing to The Peanut Vendor. *Alter Image* [Television Broadcast] Channel 4.

Thornton, S. (1995). *Club Cultures: Music, Media and Subcultural Capital*. Middletown, CT: Wesleyan University Press.

Tolley, J., & Burt, R. (1983). Strut Your Funky Stuff, Body Popping, Jazz and Funk in the North of England. *New Dance, 26*(Autumn), 8–11.

CHAPTER 15

Caribfunk Technique: A New Feminist/Womanist Futuristic Technology in Black Dance Studies in Higher Education

A'Keitha Carey

Theorising the hip wine through a Black feminist lens, I engage in a storytelling/narrative with the hope that by sharing my own story questions are raised concerning the black (female) body examining our place and history in society. This chapter is informed by my growing up in the Bahamas, a former British colony. In the chapter I define CaribFunk™, a fusion dance technology that incorporates traditional and social Afro-Caribbean, classical ballet, modern, and fitness elements that I developed, a dance technology that identifies that the body is a site of knowledge, illuminating the transformative performances of the pelvis. Lastly, I discuss the exclusion of Afro-Diasporic movements and aesthetics in dance curriculum and the future of dance studies.

> *She dances*
> *Slow earth-shaking motions*
> *That suddenly alter*
> *and lighten*

A. Carey (✉)
Dance Teacher at Indian Ridge Middle School and Adjunct Professor at Miami Dade College-Kendall Campus, FL, USA

© The Author(s) 2018
A. Akinleye (ed.), *Narratives in Black British Dance*,
https://doi.org/10.1007/978-3-319-70314-5_15

> *as she whirls laughing*
> *the tooled metal over her hips*
> *comes to an end*
> *and at the shiny edge*
> *an astonishment*
> *of soft black curly hair*
>> an excerpt from "Scar" in Audre Lorde's The Black Unicorn: Poems.
>> (Lorde, 2015, "Scar" paragraph 7)

Audre Lorde's writings are ripe with kinesthetic overtones of euphonious expressions of love, freedom, bodily references, and sensuality capturing a power that is erotic and rooted in pleasure and liberation. Lorde defines this expression as the "erotic as power" in terms that are counter to the Western masculinist definition, which solely references the sexual and is absorbed in the pornographic (Lorde, 1984):

> *Lorde's understanding of the erotic moves beyond the sexual as a purely physical relationship to encompass a wider realm of feeling and the sensual.* (Sheller, 2012, "Theorizing Erotic Agency," 1st paragraph)

Sociologist Mimi Sheller theorises the erotic, affirming that erotic agency functions as the converse of slavery and oppression. It focuses on the empowered and liberated self through efforts that include the spiritual and sensual (Sheller, 2012). A woman who is conscious of her power and performs this virtue is potent. This embodied freedom is pleasurable, natural, and inviting—drawing those in who are seeking the same type of liberation. A woman who recognises this endowment is powerful and a threat to some.

Women's bodies, specifically the bodies of women of colour have been ridiculed, marginalised, oppressed, and victimised for centuries. This has impacted the ways in which women of colour express their desire, sexuality, and sensuality, and in how these performances are read. Lorde's revised definition and Sheller's expanded theory encourages women to reclaim their power and energy. This energy is a sustenance that is fertile and innovative "*a life force ... of creative energy*" empowering women to investigate all parts of their existence, heritage, and experience(s) (Lorde, 1984). Lorde's work celebrates this power—this power is found in the hips. Performances of the pelvis deemed as vulgar (by some) are reclaimed as a body politic of pleasure, subjectivity, and erotic agency, a politic that Hip Hop feminist Joan Morgan refers to as the "politics of pleasure" (2015). Morgan declares that "pleasure politics is a liberatory, black feminist project" (Morgan, 2015, p. 39). It consists of heightening the desire for sexual sovereignty and erotic agency without "shame to the level of black feminist imperative ... Black women's erotic maps exist on an expansive spectrum, which could include non-heteronormative submissiveness, hypermasculinity, aggression, exhibitionism, and voyeurism" (Morgan, 2015, p. 39). Morgan introduces an expanded theory on Black feminism, one that is a new ideology; one which I incorporate in my praxis.

Thought 1

All of me is present and involved when I am experiencing the sexual, sensual, and the erotic power of the hip wine
Lift ya leg and wine, wine, wine, wine—this is my mantra
I enter the dance floor with my signature move leading with my pelvis, summoning a spirit that provides an abysmal power
I am captured in the wave of the spiritual eroticism of both the wicked beats and the rotation of my pelvis
My back arches
I feel the sweat on my skin and taste the salt of my body on my lips
This produces a syncopated thrust of my waist—poppin' and isolating my pelvis
Hands on my hips as I figure eight—slow winin'
Look how she winin' gal! She nasty eh?
Yes, she slack[1] and dutty[2]!

While growing up in the Bahamas, I encountered several incidents in which my too sexy moves were criticised. I was shamed, left questioning my self-worth, morals, value, and how I may have contributed to the constant reprimand for a performance that seemed so natural to me. I was grieving and depressed; unable to express who I was as an uninhibited mover. At a young age, I was cognizant that rotating my pelvis felt familiar—it was home. I was visible, projecting and articulating a narrative that is considered taboo in colonial cultures focused on respectability politics. Evelyn Brooks Higginbotham first coined the term "politics of respectability" to describe the work of the Women's Convention of the Black Baptist Church during the Progressive Era. She specifically referred to African Americans' promotion of temperance, cleanliness of person and property, thrift, polite manners, and sexual purity. I am associating this term with the policing of behaviour and bodies in the Caribbean.

Those that performed with sexual agency were rebelling against colonial infractions of policing, reserved primarily for bodies of colour. Respectability and Puritanism were expected of all women, particularly those of a particular social status. Women that performed erotic power without shame expressed erotic agency. I realised that many were driven in their attempts to tame this power.

Winin'... Historical Implications

Colonial notions concerning respectability are pervasive in much of the Caribbean, particularly as it relates to Black women's bodies, which lead to the abhorrent policing that took place in the Dancehall and during Carnival (Noel, 2010). Women that performed wining were labelled indecent and immoral:

> *The policing of sexuality is a colonial infraction, one which bears witness to the shaping and demonstration of corporeal associations and practices of liberation and agency throughout the Caribbean.* (Carey, 2016, p. 132)

Sheller discusses the connections to embodied freedom and practices and its constraints and potentiality that are associated with the "aftermath of slavery" (Sheller, 2012). Bodies that performed and talked back to the rhythmic percussion of the drum, articulating a sensuous carnality that evoked spontaneous and/or lyrical gyrations of the pelvis were deemed indecent—contemptible bodies that needed to be tamed per Victorian puritan standards. These bodies that were demonised and sexualized and understood to be immoral engaged in a protest, a survival of sorts, performing the wine as a decolonial expression of agency and rebellion, one which redresses the politics of the body, sexuality, and respectability through the lens of the abject and marginalised body.

Thought 2

'You does dance, eh?' This was the common question asked when I was at home in the Bahamas getting on bad, rolling, twerking, and winin' up. I realise now that there must have been something striking, stimulating and maybe even su generis in the way that I fused my ballet and jazz training with the rhythmic isolations and grounded movement associated with the African Diaspora. When the beat dropped and the music (most likely reggae)

summoned me to the dance floor, I hit the position—a deep second position turned out, hips open to the earth. I often began most movement arias in this stance. I reflect on my first Dancehall experience and the virtuosity of the movement that I witnessed and often participated in—it was blissful and cathartic. I remember being mesmerised at how one was able to balance on one leg while the body undulates at various tempos. I remember the smells of sweating bodies, alcohol, cigarettes, and ganja. I was intrigued with my power and how I was able to captivate the audience with a nuanced performance of the hip wine but also how electrified I was from witnessing the ways in which bodies interacted and responded to da riddim'. This was an example of the 'erotic as power.' This energy was very empowering for me, producing a level of consciousness that I did not understand at the time. It produced a confidence that was expressed in the multifarious and sinuous ways that I moved my body commanding and owning the space. I was aware of my body and accepted the freedom that flowed with each flick of the hip and roll of my torso. I was at home. There was an unspoken history; bodies performed celebrating their freedom—my freedom. I kinesthetically protested against colonial restrictions and the politics of respectability, reclaiming what was policed and taking ownership of my history and my body. I knew that moment would remain with me for a lifetime—as an educator, performer, and scholar.'

A woman who performs the hip wine is confident, she performs erotic agency. Sheller states:

> *Erotic agency, in sum, is the antithesis of enslavement. It appears not only in the context of sexual relations, but also in other forms of creativity, including all kinds of work.* (Sheller, 2012, *"Theorizing Erotic Agency,"* 3rd paragraph)

This agency is premised on a freedom of the body, one that complicates the colonial narrative that seeks to constrain, silence, and police bodies of colour. It is important to note that slavery has had a tremendous impact on the ways in which Caribbean societies interpret and engage with the corporeal:

> *When slavery ended, techniques and practices of sexual domination and biopolitical power remained entrenched.* (Sheller, 2012, *"Overview of the Book,"* 1st paragraph)

As a teenager in the Bahamas, I was often policed when I performed the hip wine and any movements that illustrated an embodied freedom. Those in positions of power revoked my citizenship as a Black woman, disallowing me to articulate my African and Afro-Caribbean heritage. This erotic agency refutes the "politics of silence" shifting the centre to include a "politic of articulation." The "politics of silence" suggests that Black women's sexuality should be concealed; it includes repugnant performances and was most often placed in "binary opposition to white women" (Morgan, 2015, p. 37).

The hip wine is an articulation and expression of Black female pleasure—a "politic of articulation." This is a resistance against the meta narrative that limits Black female sexuality. Black feminist Joan Morgan reframes the existing narrative of Black female sexuality, "positioning desire, agency and black women's engagements with pleasure as a viable theoretical paradigm" (Morgan, 2015, p. 36). She terms this expression as "pleasure politics." Pleasure politics redresses the tropes of the Jezebel, asexual Mammy, and the hyper sexual, animalistic, lascivious (Black) woman providing a counter-narrative, complicating the very restrictive ways in which Black female sexuality is perceived, shaped, and consumed (Morgan, 2015).

THOUGHT 3

My interest in the body, particularly the hip has been long-standing due to my specialized interest in Caribbean music and dance and popular culture. Researching movement for CaribFunk,™ I observed similarities between the movements performed in Jamaican Dancehall, wining at Carnival in Trinidad, and movements that are performed to Congolese Soukous and Mutuashi. Through this discovery, I had an "aha" moment, deciding that this needed further exploration not only within the context of movement derivation, but for my own interest in cultural identity, citizenship, and commonalities and how these ideas also ground CaribFunk™ technique. (Carey, 2015, *an excerpt from E-misferica article*)

My research "call[s] for Caribbean women's erotic autonomy to become a benchmark of our citizenship, dismantling 'the colonial connection between property and ownership, respectability, and citizenship'" (Sheller, 2012, *"New Voices," 4th paragraph*) explored through the pelvis. This suggests a modern discussion on a dance technique/movement vocabulary that supports "embodied freedom and erotic agency in wider contemporary contexts of the neocolonial restructuring of citizenship, sovereignty, and power across both national and transnational terrains"

(Sheller, 2012, *"Imagining Citizenship From Below,"* 2nd paragraph). This new technique is CaribFunk™. CaribFunk™ encourages a "reimagining [of] black feminist sexuality theory that is inclusive of pleasure and the erotic" (Morgan, 2015, p. 38).

CaribFunk™…The Foundation

CaribFunk™ is a dance technique that I developed in response to systems of marginalisation and oppression that I experienced growing up in the former British colony of the Bahamas. It is a fusion technique that:

> *Encourages exploration of self while investigating identity, citizenship, and culture through a kinesthetic expression of the rhythmic gestures of the pelvis. It fuses Afro-Caribbean (traditional and social dance forms), classical ballet, modern (Lester Horton, Martha Graham, and José Limón) and fitness elements that have inspired me, such as kickboxing, aerobics, and dance fitness philosophies and constructs.* (Carey, 2016, p. 130)

CaribFunk™ provides the dancers with a Caribglobal experience; encouraging a journey that recognises a creolized movement vocabulary and philosophy. I consider this concept a framework for de/re-constructing current dance curriculum. Caribbeanist scholar Rosamond S. King introduced the term Caribglobal in her seminal text *Island Bodies: Transgressive Sexualities in the Caribbean Imagination*, which captures concisely how I interact with Caribbean identity and precepts within a Diasporic paradigm that recognises the complexities of such an identity relationally from a "local, regional, and global" (King, 2014, p. 5) perspective.

King defines a Caribglobal perspective as being:

> *Pan African; it recognizes and takes seriously the linguistic, ethnic, racial, cultural, political, and economic differences within these areas, yet remains convinced that there is enough shared history and experience among Caribbean people who warrant an inclusive approach.* (King, 2014, p. 5)

My goal is to propose a differential curriculum that expounds on current Eurocentric ideals and aesthetics as it relates to dance studies, offering a distinctive praxis recognising Black Feminist/womanist ideology and Afro-Diasporic aesthetics and precepts in dance curriculum in higher education.

This praxis attends to the culture of the African Diaspora through multiple vehicles: history, music, and dance. This educational ideology articulates heterogeneity, eliciting an edifying cultural experience with multiple foci: inter/transdisciplinary, integration, and inclusion. Students that participate in CaribFunk™ on the university level, learn my educational system titled C.E.L. C.E.L. is an ideology that is premised on three themes 1. preserving the Culture 2. embarking on a new Experience and 3. speaking a new Language. This philosophy promotes self-reflection through the exploration of identity, citizenship, and culture. This investigation is grounded in the articulation of the hips and rhythmic gesticulations of the pelvis. The technique envisions Caribbean performance (Jamaican Dancehall and Trinidadian Carnival in particular) as a celebration of bodily truths, history, and desire culminating in a dance technique and praxis.

CaribFunk™ is influenced by the African-derived principles and practices of Jamaican Dancehall and Trinidadian Carnival. Both of these Afro-Caribbean practices encourage a liberty of freedom inclusive of identity and sexuality; they also entails exploring the colonial effects of enslavement through performances of resistance. Bridges connecting communities are established through inclusion and plurality. These celebrations provide opportunities to interface communities, ethnic and racial groups allowing citizens to maintain their identity through the recognition and celebrating of one's history and culture—this creates a sense of home in transnational spaces—affirming the "other." One method for maintaining and performing identity is through storytelling.

Black feminist scholar Brittany Cooper states that people of colour engage in narrative as a form of theory:

> *Our theorizing …is often in narrative forms, in the stories we create, in riddles and proverbs, in the play with language, since dynamic rather than fixed ideas seem more to our liking.* (Cooper, 2015, p. 8)

This methodology stands in direct contrast to the "Western form of abstract logic" (Cooper, 2015, p. 8). This unorthodox praxis serves as the cornerstone within CaribFunk™. Narrative/storytelling—similar to the work of dance anthropologist Katherine Dunham and folklorist and novelist Zora Neal Hurston are embedded in CaribFunk™ praxis. Through the use of narrative, students participate in critical ethnography, bringing to the classroom, studio, and stage the culture, behaviour, concerns, and histories of the lives of women and men globally, aiming to create a social framework engendering social justice and activism. Through social justice initiatives, students are encouraged to critically query systems of power, race, gender, sexuality, and womanhood from a global perspective. Students are asked to "recall, remember, and represent" (Durham, 2014, pp. 126–127) systems of oppression—race, gender, class, sexuality, and ability— through choreography/performance. When I speak of my personal experience, I look into the eyes of my students and I see how they respond to my discussions concerning marginalisation and oppression; they seem to desire an opportunity to engage in a corporeal protest against such systems of injustice. This praxis focuses on Black feminist author Audre Lorde's "biomythography" that connects and weaves narrative, autobiography, fiction, and myth to depict materiality. The technique is a representation of my negotiation with, a struggle against, and a threat to both the oppressed and the oppressor. CaribFunk™ technique is an embodied practice of freedom, erotic agency, and citizenship. It is transformational:

> Performers and observers feel glimpses of the human/spirit connection and are inevitably affected; they are consequently transported to a realm of extreme fascination, engagement, and rapture. (Daniel, 2011, p. 190)

My student's statements concerning the transformational experiences that they encounter oftentimes move me. I am delighted in the discussions that I have with students in my community classes, residencies, workshops, and in various dance programmes testifying about their transformative experience. They claim to have a new self-awareness and appreciation of their bodies, expressing confidence and how they perform a new level of power in their daily lives. Some of them speak of the connections that they make to the African Diaspora through movement, music, and/or ideologies/principles and the healing that takes place—physically, emotionally, and spiritually. They offer rich analysis of the release that they feel in their spines provided by the rotation and articulation of the pelvis.

Womanism and CaribFunk™

CaribFunk™ offers a vocabulary and language for women's stories to be expressed, (re)telling their bodily truths, kinesthetically serving as an embodied protest falling within womanist praxis ideals. Layli Maparyan defines womanist methodology as a "transmutation of energy—mental, emotional, physical, material, social, and environmental" (Maparyan, 2012, p. 51). This transmutation of energy that Maparyan alludes to is presented in the performances of the hip wine, which serves as a conscious exchange and transference of notions and representations of power, confidence, and agency. This transmutation is evidenced in the "mental, emotional, physical, material, social, and environmental" aspects of her embodied practice—"the body [is] a vessel of divine revelation" (Maparyan, 2012, p. 53). I advocate that the body is the vehicle used to transfer this energy and knowledge. The insight that CaribFunk™ imparts on students, audiences of women of divergent ethnicities, cultures, class, and body types is profound. I impart "vitality" in my students: "Vitality … comes from a deep-rooted sense of rest, poise, awareness and strength to make one feel 'on top of the world' and that life is truly worth living every waking moment" (Maparyan, 2012, p. 53)—this is an expression of the erotic as power and erotic agency.

Final Thought (4)

I recall an experience when I attended boarding school in Eleuthera, Bahamas. On one of my weekend trips home, I took the opportunity to visit with my roommate's family that lived in Harbour Island, one of the neighbouring islands in the chain of Bahamian isles. We went to the club—this was my first time hanging out! I was excited. I didn't know what to expect. It was dark and the bass was thumping in competition with my heartbeat. I wondered what was the correct protocol. Do I dance by myself or do I dance with a partner? As the music played, my body took over. It knew exactly what to do. I had no questions yet my body responded to multiple emotions. I had a visceral experience with the dancehall. I was bombarded with rhythms, sensations, and aromas that overwhelmed my body. In this space I was able to perform not only my erotic power but I was able to showcase my fusion of the dance techniques that I studied in the U.S. (ballet, modern, and jazz) and the Afro-Diasporic social dances that included pelvic thrusts and undulations. In this environment these elements were pervasive. I was in my element! Wooeeii!!

I had never experienced this type of sensation before. I felt like I entered another dimension, one that allowed me to express myself as a dancer and a woman, free from ridicule and judgement. In the dancehall, there were no castigating comments or shaming stares that would be expressed by certain church folk and bourgeoisie who were preaching the politics of respectability. It seemed that everyone in this space embodied the same freedom and erotic power that I performed. In this space, I was queen of the dance, exercising agency, sensuality and an unknown sensibility (at the time) of the erotic as power. In that moment, I felt powerful. There was a force permeating from within. The power within me was transcendental; my hips breathed life into the atmosphere. The circularity of my hips and torso felt spiritual. Maparyan surmises "Spirituality is a combination of consciousness, ethos, lifestyle, and discourse that privileges spirit—that is life force—as a primary aspect of self that defines and determines health and well-being (Maparyan, 2012, p. 90). This is spiritual eroticism. In this instance, I embodied my culture as a Bahamian woman, embracing this power and my new moniker, "Dancin' Queen." I realised in that moment, this was profound. Caught in the embrace of "di riddim", "ya wicked gal" is what I heard, felt, or maybe even imagined. I was entranced by the pulsations of the music and my heartbeat, not realising that I would someday be teaching and developing a praxis that demonstrated such profound consciousness, one that performs and practises an embodied freedom that is not only political but is also a spiritual and sensual regime resurrecting ancestral memories and bodily practices. This was an embodied freedom that I articulated through my body, reinforced in my pelvis.

Research/Observations

Through my experience as a student and educator in higher education, I observed students engage in dance techniques that oppressed and constrained the pelvis and lower region of the body. Based on class discussions and reflections, many of the students revealed that they were led to believe that movements that included the pelvis (rotations, isolations, and pulsations) were sexual, inappropriate, and vulgar. It appeared that dance curriculum covertly/overtly assumed the same position as many of the Western-European techniques taught that excluded this area of the body. I was of the opinion that the pelvis was oppressed and that Afro-Diasporic aesthetics that emphasised this area of the body did not serve the current curriculum, which maintained white Western dance as a primary epistemological model. I also observed students of colour struggle to maintain their identity within structures that do not represent who they are as people of colour, their areas of interest, how they wanted to move, and what they identified with culturally. These pedagogical experiences along with the ridicule of my *"vulgar"* expressions influenced the birth of CaribFunk™.

It was my attempt to demonstrate the legitimacy and advantages of the inclusion of a non-Western dance form as a core course of study and conditioning technique at the university level, one that privileges the body particularly the hips, advocating that the body is a site for knowledge that encourages the (re)imagining of life experiences, allowing students to explore their authentic selves through an empowering and transformative performance of the pelvis. I realised that a feminist/womanist praxis was necessary in attempting to teach such a powerful movement form.

In doing so, I explored more deeply why such practices have not been included in dance curriculum. My research revealed that racist stereotypes concerning body, respectability politics, and the policing of bodies of colour were impacting how particular movements were interpreted, such as the hip wine (the circular rotation of the hip). Through the development of CaribFunk™, I attempt to "reclaim the disavowed realms of the vulgar, including the lower regions of the body politic and the excluded realms of the bodily, the sexual, and the spiritual" (Sheller, 2012, *"Chapter 1: History From the Bottom(s) Up," 2nd paragraph*).

Conclusion

I know why the caged bird sings. She sings to hear her own voice, validating her existence, reassuring herself that she does indeed have a voice, a story—my story. Black woman, girl child, the young miss with the starry eye. Her eyes gleam so bright when she looks at herself in the mirror. In her reflection she sees a light that projects the imagined reality of a free brown skin gal. The woman in the mirror is glamorous and confident, entitled to her own freedom with hips that don't lie. She is sex positive and conscious, reclaiming her space in the world, performing an embodied freedom. She masterfully acknowledges her past and rewrites her future with the radical deviant expression of her erotic agency. Her identity is fluid like her hips. I know why the caged bird sings. She sings to tell the world that she is free.

CaribFunk™ gave me a voice, acknowledged who I was as Caribbean woman, a woman who performed an embodied freedom. I recognised that CaribFunk™ could proffer hope for many of my students, offering a counter-narrative to the issues of shaming and policing and/or body politics that they revealed they had experienced. As an educator, one focused on erotic agency, I went into my research with the strong belief that the voices of women and people of colour have been erased in higher education and bodies were not engaging with "pleasure politics." I realised that this was an area that needed examining and that CaribFunk™ was ideal in this investigation. CaribFunk™ "Encourages performers to become totally one with the movement such that the corporeal becomes ecstatic, so that the ancestral world joins the present and transformational states" (Daniel, 2011, p. 190); this metamorphosis should be a normal occurrence.

CaribFunk™ is transgressive and transformative, serving as a conduit for evoking a change in perception of self, encouraging a shift in how one interprets and perceives the body, specifically the hip wine. I desire to place the stories of women at the centre of my praxis, discussing embodied freedom and erotic agency in their prescribed places of interest and existence. I encourage you to think of CaribFunk™ as a futuristic technology, one which encourages women to freely perform our complex and complicated identity, history, and desires, one which has the potential to transform the abject body, placing her at the centre of her own life, performing her story with agency and freedom (Sheller, 2012).

I am suggesting that CaribFunk™ as an expression of Caribglobalism is a technology that illustrates a feminist/womanist praxis that can be taught in dance studies, one that illuminates feminist/womanist and African Diasporic practices, histories, and theories in purposeful and relevant ways, serving to enhance the students' dance studies: kinesthetically, culturally, critically, historically, and philosophically. This framework allows for a (re) imagining of dance studies in an undergraduate curriculum, one that applies feminist/womanist and Afro-Diasporic principles to "actively resist and transform the pervasiveness of white cultural hegemony within dance in the academy" (Amin, 2015).

Notes

1. Meaning 'loose morals'.
2. Meaning 'dirty behaviour', 'raunchy'.

References

Amin, T. (2015). *Beyond Hierarchy: Re-imagining African Diaspora in Dance Education Curricula*. Paper Presented at Congress on Research and Dance.

Carey, A. (2015). CaribFunk: A Melangé of Caribbean Expressions in a New Dance Technique. Caribbean Rasanblaj. *Hemispheric Institute E-misferica 12*(1). http://hemisphericinstitute.org/hemi/en/emisferica-121-caribbean-rasanblaj/carey.

Carey, A. (2016). Visualizing Caribbean Performance (Jamaican Dancehall and Trinidadian Carnival) as Praxis: An Autohistoria of KiKi's Journey. *National Dance Education Journal, 16*(4), 129–138.

Cooper, B. (2015). Love No Limit: Towards a Black Feminist Futurist Future (in Theory). *The Black Scholar: Journal of Black Studies and Research, 45*(4), 7–21.

Daniel, Y. (2011). *Caribbean and Atlantic Diaspora Dance: Igniting Citizenship* (Kindle ed.). Urbana: University of Illinois Press.

Durham, A. S. (2014). *Home with Hip Hop Feminism: Performances in Communication and Culture*. New York: Peter Lang.

King, R. S. (2014). *Island Bodies: Transgressive Sexualities in the Caribbean Imagination*. Gainesville, FL: University Press of Florida.

Lorde, A. (1984). Uses of the Erotic: The Erotic as Power. In *Sister Outsider* (pp. 53–59). Berkley, CA: Crossing Press.

Lorde, A. (2015). Scar. In *The Black Unicorn Poems* (Kindle ed.). New York: W.W. Norton and Company.

Morgan, J. (2015). Why We Get Off. Moving Towards a Black Feminist Politics of Pleasure. *The Black Scholar: Journal of Black Studies and Research, 45*(4), 36–46.

Noel, S. A. (2010). De Jamette in We. Redefining Performance in Contemporary Trinidad Carnival. *Small Axe, 14*(1), 60–78.

Phillips-Maparyan, L. (2012). *The Womanist Idea*. New York: Routledge.

Sheller, M. (2012). *Citizenship from Below: Erotic Agency and Caribbean Freedom* (Kindle ed.). Durham, NC: Duke University Press.

CHAPTER 16

More Similarities than Differences: Searching for New Pathways

Beverley Glean and Rosie Lehan

Dance and Diversity is an action-based research project that has looked at the place of cultural diversity in dance education and practice with particular reference to African and Caribbean dance forms. The project was designed to take place in three phases and was directed by Beverley Glean, the Artistic Director of IRIE! dance theatre and Rosie Lehan, Dance Lecturer at City and Islington College. Phase One (2004–2005, funded by NESTA) of the research focused on practice in the UK and is summarised in the report 'Taking Stock and Making it Happen' produced by IRIE! dance theatre and accompanied by a DVD. Phase Two 2006–2008, funded by Arts Council England (ACE) looked at cultural diversity in an international context and aimed to broaden the appeal of the work. Phase Three (2009 onwards) has focused on disseminating the findings of Phase Two by collaborating with strategic partners such as Association of Dance of the African Diaspora (now a part of One Dance UK) to debate material at national and international events, celebrating the work of artists, educators and young people promoting cultural diversity in dance.

This chapter concerns Phase Two, focusing on a research trip we made in 2007 to the USA, Jamaica, Cuba and Ghana in order to view examples

B. Glean (✉) • R. Lehan
IRIE! dance theatre, London, UK

of good practice in dance education and performance. Representing very different levels of resources and political engagement with the arts, we felt that each country would be able to offer an insight into the development and survival of African and Caribbean dance forms in a multitude of arenas. Our intention was to then look at and develop how we delivered dance education from an Africanist perspective within the institutions we work from in the UK. For this purpose, this chapter also includes our work with former and current students on the Foundation Degree in Dance, one of the enterprises to come out of our research trip.

The USA, with its extremes of wealth and poverty, home to large numbers of the Diaspora who define themselves as African Americans, has carved out its own history of dance. Within this context, we thought it would be interesting to research how this manifested itself in terms of an equality of dance forms. Jamaica, with its focus on the development of the traditional and contemporary within Caribbean forms, appears to struggle with resources and political commitment; however, as we were to discover, there are many moves afoot to change perceptions of the arts. Cuba, politically committed to celebrating the status of its unique cultural mix, uses dance and the arts to define its identity, making a strong statement that defies levels of resources. Ghana celebrated 50 years of independence in 2007; with its strong tradition of African dance, it became an interesting year to look at the development of forms within education and performance.

PREPARATION FOR THE TRAVEL OF PHASE TWO

Taking the research forward into Phase Two necessitated us returning to the dominant findings of Phase One, which had revealed a lack of African and Caribbean dance forms within formal education in the UK, particularly in higher education. The main reasons cited for the lack of presence include the absence of discourse on the forms, and a lack of participants and teaching expertise. Therefore, the most crucial element in the research of Phase One seemed to concern training, in order to build a viable infrastructure for the development of African and Caribbean dance as an art form in practice and theory.

Before we embarked on our travels, it became crucial at the end of Phase One to connect with other higher education (HE) institutions in the UK. This took the form of a focus group held in October 2006, attended by key representatives from higher education, facilitated by Dr

Vivien Freakley, the external evaluator and a strategic voice behind the organisation of Phase One. The focus group set the tone for the research in Phase Two allowing the two phases to naturally follow on from each other. Priorities highlighted by the Focus Group included the idea of partnerships in the UK and abroad, combined with the development of significant training in African and Caribbean dance following on from ideas developed by IRIE! dance theatre in their African and Caribbean Diploma Course, (validated by Birbeck College, London University (1998–2001) and franchised to City and Islington College). Since the Focus Group was established, there have been some interesting developments regarding the course, which has been developed into a Foundation Degree in Dance, working as a three-way partnership between IRIE! dance theatre, City and Islington College and London Metropolitan University. The course has become the strategic base for the practical realisation of ideas germinated during this research.

Internationally, the work of university departments, individual artists and dance companies became central to the second phase of our research. Each country provided a very different perspective, providing an interesting arena for debate; however issues of funding, gender, status and survival dominated the agenda and found common links throughout the world. However, links were made with many remarkable individuals who have resolutely built up departments, companies, designed courses and individual performance programmes. These people have trailblazed, acting as linchpins for their organisations, without whom much of the work would still be in its infancy.

Practitioners Across the Diaspora

Within this broad spectrum of the research, it becomes useful to focus on practitioners who in the context of this chapter demonstrate good practice and innovative work.

USA

Barbara Bashaw
When we first interviewed Barbara Bashaw in 2007, she was the Coordinator of PK-12 Teacher Certification Dance Education Programme at the Steinhardt School of Education, New York University. She has since become the Coordinator at Rutgers University, Mason Gross School of

the Arts/Graduate School of Education, responsible for developing the EdM in Dance Education with PK-12 Certification degree.

Bashaw, in developing her work at New York University, fostered an innovative approach to teacher training. One of the most interesting things about the work was the evident commitment to working with the cultural forms that the students brought with them, rather than imposing a standard contemporary training that must then be replicated in the schools. This demonstrates a change of emphasis from teacher training in the UK, where codified contemporary techniques are represented as the dominant form with cultural dance forms being seen as advantageous but not essential.

> *The schools are diverse so it's very important that the teachers are embedded in cultural practice, which tends to change their teaching and learning practice even if they are modern dancers. You are creating culture and community when you teach which has to be understood. We are interested in offering diverse forms.* (Bashaw, 2007, p. 10)

Bashaw's philosophy is geared towards the promotion of individual voices, which works towards the empowerment of teachers with ultimate ownership of their own practice. This in turn will filter through to students as they find their own voice within different dance forms.

With regards to contemporary urban culture, Bashaw recognised the need to provide resources that would help the trainees to connect with their students. In bringing in Hip Hop, Bashaw was also concerned to address the cultural history and take the students beyond what they know; challenging perceptions that it is a form without a significant history. By connecting with current trends, Bashaw provided the students with valuable communication tools, giving them a starting point for their work with young people. Students also had to complete one hundred hours of fieldwork, examples of which include an outreach dance group and a three-week project in Uganda.

> *In New York we have thirty-two languages in a single school so we have to cater for a diverse population. Some undergraduate students come with no experience of cultural practice[s] which needs to be addressed.* (Bashaw, 2007, p. 10)

Returning to Bashaw, in 2010 it was interesting to see that her concern for the practical application of cultural diversity in dance education appears to have followed her to her new position at Rutgers, from an examination of established dance theories to the practical interaction with diverse communities in New Jersey. If dance is to be seen as a progressive art form, then it needs to constantly re-examine established training methodologies, particularly if it wants to nurture a wider spectrum of society to participate and contribute as practitioners. The broad training of dance educators is therefore vital to this quest and evident with the EdM dance programme. Within the curriculum, 'cultural receptivity' is presented from several perspectives from courses run at the Graduate School of Education, where dancers participate with students from other subjects, to the dance education courses at Mason Gross School of the Arts.

> *In additional courses, students will take educational ethnographic stances in several classes as they make inquiry or practice research methodology; they will consider the different learning values, styles and preferences students may bring with them from their family/community culture; they will examine dance as a poly-cultural phenomena and will examine their own inherited dance beliefs; they will examine issues of race, class, gender, etc.* (Bashaw 2007, pg 11)

Practically, during their first year of study, students work on placement for the entire year with different schools, community centres and cultural institutions, an aspect of which is linked to a project with the New Jersey Department of Education and NJ Network Television to develop units of study based on the choreographic work of two diverse artists, NaNi Chen (Chinese American artist) and Carolyn Dorfman (Jewish heritage). Future projects include engagement with the Latino Community in 2011 through the Latino Community Symposium and with East Asian artists, a high proportion of which are present in the surrounding community and teach at the Mason Gross Extension Division.

It appears to be evident from this programme that teacher training is being designed to cater for a diverse twenty-first century society, which must lead to the examination of cultural philosophy and the entrenched views that often exist within dance education.

Teacher Training in the UK

With regards to teacher training in the UK, there appears to be much to be learnt from Bashaw, which may involve a re-framing of ideas. Catering for culturally diverse populations of young people involves developing their voice through the inclusion of a range of dance styles, which does not necessarily assume that Western contemporary codified dance is the dominant form. This brings us to the subject of our own students on the Foundation Degree in Dance and their progression in light of the knowledge gained on the research trip. It is not our intention here to analyse teacher training in the UK but to examine several examples where the landscape appears to be shifting.

We returned to the UK with a renewed sense of optimism and energy and, as stated in the introduction, we were invited to set up a Foundation Degree in Dance as a three-way partnership between City and Islington College, IRIE! dance theatre and London Metropolitan University. The venture was not without its challenges as education is notoriously bureaucratic and does not normally favour the risk-takers! However, challenges aside, after seven years we are able to reflect on the impact of our initial research and the further development of what is still a fledging course as we strive to stay ahead in terms of training. Like our course, Dance as an art form is constantly evolving and by following the careers of our graduates it becomes possible to see whether the landscape in terms of diversity has truly shifted.

Shermaine Seaman completed the Foundation Degree (2009–11), continued for a third year at London Metropolitan University (2012–13) and completed a PGCE in Dance at Brighton University gaining Outstanding Teacher status with MA Credits (2014–15). Originally from a traditional dance studio background, Shermaine studied Ballet, Tap and Modern before choosing to focus on music, only to return to dance as an adult. She stated that coming back to dance, she remained unclear as to her direction, which she was only able to clarify as she progressed on the course.

> *I found my pathway when I came here and I knew it wasn't just contemporary dance… Studying African and Caribbean dance made me find where I was comfortable and what I wanted to do because I was lost, I didn't know what I wanted to do but when I came here I thought this is what I want to do and what I am familiar with…. I had actually found a sector in dance that I really liked and that's what I wanted to do.* (Seaman, 2015)

Shermaine walked into her first job teaching Dance at Langdon Academy in September 2015; as researchers and her former teachers, it has been exciting for us to follow her journey. It appears that the PGCE course at Brighton is indeed forward thinking, encouraging their cohorts to use diverse dance styles; in Shermaine's case, she was able to utilise her training in African and Caribbean dance. Change is not only brought about by institutions but often by the young people themselves, as dance has become a popular subject.

> *I think Brighton wanted versatile teachers because when you go into a School the young people don't want to just do contemporary, especially the boys they want to do House, they want to do African and Hip Hop etc.* (Seaman, 2015)

Returning to Bashaw and her analysis of New York schools, it remains true that London is a very diverse city and for many young people their first experience of dance will be at school, so it is important that dance education is positive. Dance needs to take account of cultural history and creativity, so that students are able to bring themselves to the work. This was a factor that we discovered at City and Islington College in the 1990s, when it became apparent that the best work came from encouraging cultural and creative engagement. Shermaine echoes this as she starts out on her career.

> *Particularly in my second placement the majority of girls were from Asian, African and Caribbean backgrounds so having the training from the FD course allowed me to transfer what I loved to them.* (Seaman, 2015)

Shermaine feels that she was able to utilise her background in her development as a teacher, which is encouraging, particularly in light of our initial research. The new General Certificate of Secondary Education (GCSE) syllabus currently being finalised advocates a greater range of styles and a diverse selection of set works, which again is a positive move. However, it remains to be seen whether these changes will be fully adopted by the majority or left to a handful of teachers to move forward. Throughout our travels, it was common to find dedicated practitioners bringing about change through their individual vision.

During Phase 1 of the research in 2005, we ran a Saturday School for 14–19 year olds with weekly workshops in African dances, Ballet, Urban, Contemporary and Choreography. We have always advocated that the traditional core forms of Ballet and Contemporary are part of a larger offer of diverse dance styles, thus preparing young people for a broader range of work. African and Caribbean dance forms suffer from a popular misconception that they are not technical but social, a myth that the Foundation Degree aims to dispel.

The ethos of the Saturday School has followed through into the Foundation Degree, which encourages students to experiment with the studied dance genres of African, Caribbean, Contemporary and Urban with supporting workshops in Ballet. The aim is to prepare potential dance practitioners for employment, so flexibility and entrepreneurship is encouraged. Students take on a variety of roles as freelancers, which is common practice for dancers.

Stevie Brown completed the Foundation Degree (2010–12) with a work placement at the London Hospital with Green Candle Dance Company, before working for IRIE! dance theatre as the Education Officer (2012–14). She recently completed her third year in Education at Southbank University, gaining a First Class Honours Degree (2014–15). Throughout her training and career, she has been involved with a diverse range of projects in community centres, schools and colleges. Reflecting on the FdA Course, she recognises the value of a diverse training.

> *I think it's really important to have that level of diversity in your training – it's a full course -there's a lot to take in but its all relative and I think you are in a much better position rather than just studying one form.* (Brown, 2015)

The hope is that diversity in dance will become part of a collective vision particularly within training, as practitioners like Shermaine and Stevie depart from the traditional presentation of dance; the ambition is that this will soon become common practice.

Jamaica

Maria Smith and the Jamaican Cultural Development Commission (JCDC)

Maria Smith is the Performing and Visual Arts Coordinator of The Jamaican Cultural Development Commission (JCDC). The commission is government-supported with a vision to unearth, to train, to preserve and to showcase the best of Jamaica's culture and heritage. JCDC appears to be the chief advocator for the preservation of Jamaican folk forms. Alongside the folk form, there is a drive to include and embrace the wealth of other dances and dance cultures that presented itself on the island.

The essence of Jamaica's national culture is rooted in the ceremonies and traditions of their folk forms. These forms are sustained through the commission's annual festival of performing arts. Each district has an opportunity to showcase forms such as the British-influenced Quadrille and Maypole and the African-influenced Dinki-Mini, Gerreh and Kumina. The festival lends a sense of value, importance and dignity to these traditional folk dances, affording them a rightful place in the consciousness of Jamaican society.

Smith feels that it is essential to have full representation from all performing/professional dance companies to support this process. This is mainly through senior representatives or the Artistic Directors. The School of Dance and the University of the West Indies is also involved. This has proved to be a very effective way of working as the profession becomes involved in a variety of creative, social and community events, keeping them informed of dance within the community and vice versa. This team also takes the shape of an advisory body for the JCDC dance department, supporting and advising Smith on policies, training needs and development.

> *We have a body of people who understand dance...they help to train people in the zones and parishes for the festival...the network also provides employment and ensures that the dance will always be there. To me that is the strongest part of the JCDC.* (Smith, 2007, p. 18)

Smith admits that her job is both challenging and rewarding. From what we witnessed, initiatives and programmes that are in place are there through consultation, need and preservation. She is aware that there is still much to do but we believe that the JCDC is a vital component in the development and survival of dance in Jamaica. Interestingly, each person interviewed in Jamaica mentioned the JCDC and the work of Maria Smith.

Cuba

Adrian Wanliss
While in Havana, we were shown around by 18-year old student Adrian Wanliss, a Jamaican studying dance at La Escuela Nacional de Art because he believed, alongside many other international students, that he would receive the best training in Cuba. Battling with a lack of Spanish and

money, he had developed survival tactics to help him get through what seemed to be a very confusing landscape. The strength of his determination enabled him to learn Spanish and orientate himself within a few months; all guided by his belief in the training which he was able to enthuse about at length, explaining the value of diversity:

> *Dancers need to be versatile, dance tells a story and has a history. If you become a diverse dancer you are able to face many challenges.* (Wanliss, 2007, p. 21)

Adrian was determined and ambitious, at 18 he was acutely aware that he was competing with dancers who had been training from a young age to reach an advanced level of technical proficiency. He valued the seriousness of the training and had formulated a number of career paths, influenced by strong role models, such as Alvin Ailey. He also reflected a desire to return home and make a contribution through the arts:

> *I am hoping to open my own school and company in Jamaica and build a brand new theatre for the performing arts. In returning to Jamaica I want to bring a larger pride to the arts, in Jamaica people think of the arts as a second choice it is not considered as a profession.* (Wanliss, 2007, p. 18)

Reflections from Dance Students in the UK

We found Adrian's drive and strong-minded approach both refreshing and exciting. However, set against the level of access to opportunities open to his contemporaries in the UK the challenges are very similar. The lack of serious diverse training opportunities in the UK today is still a concern for young artists wishing to use, in particular, African and Caribbean movement language/cultural expression to inform their creativity. One could argue that over the past eight to ten years, there has been more exposure to the forms through initiatives, such as the Re:Generations Conferences, the Foundation Degree in Dance with its associated performance company Connectingvibes, alongside others who are seeking to formalise, engage and encourage discourse.

Through the Foundation Degree, we have observed many gifted, interesting and sometimes challenging young people on their journey through the course. They have engaged with performance projects, an array of guest artists, seminars and lectures while being introduced to what we hope is a worldview of dance that champions equality. Like the course led by Bashaw at Rutgers, students engage with many diverse work placements and have the opportunity to join Connectingvibes. These two avenues introduce them to dance as a community tool, alongside aspects of the wider industry. Bearing in mind the equal emphasis on African, Caribbean, Contemporary and Urban, the audition process is open to students proficient in any one of those techniques with the ability to adapt to new forms. Our ambition has been for diversity in the dance curriculum to become a consistent part of the landscape. Consequently the different cohorts have contained a range of nationalities: from Black British students of African and Caribbean descent; to EU students from countries such as Bulgaria, France, Lithuania, Poland, Romania and Spain; and with international representation from Namibia, South Korea and Antigua. With the majority of students being from 18 to 25 years, we have also been joined by mature students in their thirties and forties. The diversity of the student population has made for exciting debates on dance, as students work to decipher their pathways and contemplate the broader picture of dance. Considering the diversity of the student body, which is what we actively try to encourage, it is important that the curriculum represents this diversity and welcomes the skills that students bring to the table.

Among young people auditioning for the Foundation Degree, when asked where they see themselves in the future the vast majority share the vision of either teaching, choreographing, performing and/or starting their own company. When asked why they chose the course, the consensus is that a cross-cultural understanding is increasingly essential to their career development. These ambitions have followed students through their engagement with the work, as recent interviews appear to demonstrate their enthusiasm for the ethos of the course. Despite the challenges of surviving in the dance world, they appear keen to reflect diversity in their chosen pathways. They are all second year students who will finish their studies in June 2016.

Kita Butler is a British student who grew up in Antigua. Finding the course on a family visit to London, she auditioned and interviewed before returning to Antigua. Convinced that the course was a perfect 'fit' for her, she returned to enrol on the course. Her journey has not been without its difficulties, as funding from the government of Antigua has been minimal. Therefore, she has had to balance her study commitments with work, thus providing her with an added incentive to succeed.

> *I never really wanted to just study Ballet or Contemporary. I wanted to study Ballet for technique but it wasn't really my forte- I preferred to do African and Caribbean dance. So I applied for the course and I was very happy when I got in.* (Butler, 2016)

Despite all the challenges of being away from her home, she feels that the diverse curriculum will enable her to develop and utilise her skills in Antigua, thus carving out a career for herself.

> *Long term I would like to go to Jamaica to complete my third year. I really want to develop my African and Caribbean within myself so that I can teach because I think that in Antigua Caribbean dance is a part of our history but it's not pushed forward enough. For the arts I think it's very important for a culture to make sure that it's seen by the world and for oneself – I hope to really study that and develop that in Antigua.* (Butler, 2016)

Listening to Kita's plans brings us back to Adrian (studying in Cuba) and his desire to establish work and use his training in Jamaica, where Caribbean dance is part of the cultural landscape but not necessarily seen as a viable profession. Again we will follow Kita's progress with interest to see whether she accomplishes her goals.

Mactaly Nyamusole is orginally from the Republic of the Congo and came to the UK at the age of nine. She came to the course with a background in Afro-Beats, a fusion of African Dance and Hip Hop. She was mainly self-taught in groups, rather than through formal dance classes. Throughout the course, she has worked very hard to acquire different techniques and make the most of her training. With African and Caribbean dance, in particular, she has valued learning the technique and history behind the forms.

> *When I started African and Caribbean wasn't completely new, I knew the general moves, the basics but not the techniques or the grounding, the techniques are something I really wanted to learn, so it was very exciting. I am in everyday getting into the classes, always ready and warming up. We learn the traditional language of the drums; the history of the movement, all of that was pretty new and it was really exciting to learn.* (Nyamusole, 2016)

Choreographically, students are encouraged to develop their own language, which often becomes a fusion of different genres combined with their own innovations. On the question of choreography and the fusion, Mactaly also had this to say about her creative work.

I can now choreograph a piece where I can put together all these different elements that I learnt...learning different styles and techniques is good because you know the history but you can also bring in your own work. (Nyamusole, 2016)

In terms of her pathway she is quite clear that she wants to use the forms to work with young people, as well as to create performance work. Indeed, on the course she has acted as a mentor to first-year students and within her group she demonstrates positive qualities of leadership. Another aim of the course is to nurture and introduce students to what can be a very challenging industry, particularly in terms of employment.

I want to train myself a bit more in African and Caribbean and develop my knowledge and techniques and then open up an academy giving young people opportunities to learn the basics of African, Caribbean and Urban. I have started teaching, which is going really well. (Nyamusole, 2016)

Calvin Etten-Forbes came to the course with a background in Drama and Urban dance with minimal contemporary training. He had never studied African and Caribbean dance before and despite finding the forms very challenging, he has become a more confident and committed dancer, keen to take part in all additional projects. He reflected on how his diverse training had impacted on his choreography.

I believe that every genre is beneficial for our training and future career because dance is evolving. I am thinking about using Contemporary in my Hip Hop or using elements of African or Caribbean in my choreography. I do feel it benefits me as a person and it will benefit my career. (Etten-Forbes, 2016)

In terms of his career pathway, he has developed an interest in teaching as demonstrated through recent workshops in schools with Connectingvibes and through projects for young people run by IRIE! dance theatre. Eventually he wants to complete a third year, and then go on to establish independent projects, performing and teaching.

Ghana

Dr Isaac Amuah

When interviewing Dr Isaac Amuah, Head of the Department of Music at the University of Cape Coast, his initial response to the first question put our general thinking of the culture of dance education in Ghana and perhaps the rest of Africa into perspective.

> *We have a wealth of dance materials left to us by our forefathers, which have been overlooked by the colonial educators. The colonial educators were largely missionaries who felt that the dances were pagan in origin and they did not want them mixed with academia. All of those teachers were educated in Europe in Western dances.* (Amuah, 2007, p. 25)

Not dissimilar to our approach in the UK, there is a struggle to integrate diverse dance styles, particularly African and Caribbean traditional forms, into the structure of existing courses. Nevertheless, there are a number of dance and music specialists working to address this concern. Dr Richard Amuah himself studied at Cape Coast University, where his music professor, whom he describes as an Africanist, proved to be a great influence on him as he attempted to incorporate African traditional forms into the programme.

Returning to the university after furthering his training in the USA, Amuah reviewed the departments' study of African materials. He was aware that music holds the dominant position and acknowledges that this will probably remain the case. In spite of this, he believes that he is capable of ensuring that at least 70 per cent of the courses will be devoted to the integration of African music and dance, although realistically he thought this would be a five to ten-year plan.

Joined up local, national and international initiatives have to take place for this plan to be realised. He mentioned the need for a shift in parental attitudes, training in schools, the call for Ghanaian professionals abroad and government support. For example, Panafest is a biennial festival that takes place in Ghana promoting Pan Africanism through arts and culture. The festival first took place in 1992 and in recent years the hub of the festival has moved from the capital Accra to Cape Coast. The Centre for National Culture (CNC) is situated opposite the University of Cape Coast and houses The Centre for National Culture Folkloric Company (CNCFC) an 18-member resident dance company. Panafest has had an important impact on both the profile of the company and dance in the region. The festival has encouraged the development of a number of smaller dance troupes, which Amuah feels will benefit students studying dance as part of their music degree as involvement will add to their professional development. The developing culture of thriving dance projects would encourage a greater intake at the university, as potential students would begin to see the developing opportunities in the subject.

Conclusion: The Way Forward

Taking the Dance and Diversity research forward to Phase Two was exciting on many levels as it gave us the opportunity for comparative reflection on UK and international practice. The research has confirmed that the potential for developing equality through the promotion of cultural diversity is infinitely possible, providing that strategic contacts in education and performance are willing to actively engage in the research.

The key issue appears to be the status of dance, in particular African and Caribbean derived forms, how they are perceived as art forms by governments with implications for funding and resources. This impacts on the recognition of the forms among educators, artists, managers and those in positions of influence who have the authority to determine the future directions of dance.

Returning to the question of training and the presence of African and Caribbean dance forms, a greater number of HE institutions in the UK need to be persuaded of the value of including the forms within the core curriculum, which may manifest itself as modules in the beginning stages of curriculum development.

Partnerships between dance companies and universities also aid the quest for survival as people join together to pool resources in the pursuit of common goals. This is evident with the Foundation Degree in Dance as it is a strategic partnership between a dance company, and a further and higher education institution. Graduating students have begun since 2010 to address the lack of skilled practitioners as identified in Phase One of our research. Other innovative partnerships include the University of East London and the BA in Urban Dance Practice with East London Dance at Stratford Circus.

With regards to teacher training, innovation in the UK seems to have moved on as cited in the above example of Brighton University and the encouragement of diverse dance forms within the curriculum. Following on from that, the emergence of a greater range of diversity within the new GCSE syllabus would appear to suggest that dance is indeed becoming more progressive.

Increased focus on training both practical and academic, mutually beneficial partnerships and the visibility of African and Caribbean forms through performance appear to be the vital ingredients for moving the questions of Dance and Diversity forwards. The research demonstrated that good practice can be found across the Diaspora, with many practitioners willing to share their knowledge; the skill lies in the ability to disseminate information and provide persuasive arguments for change.

Moving forward to our practice since returning from our travels with the formation of the Foundation Degree, it would appear that although these are challenging times with many cuts in funding, the signs for an increase in diverse dance practice are good. Reflecting on the commitment and work of the current students was encouraging. The ambition was to create a course that catered for different pathways, while simultaneously broadening the appeal of dance, and presenting different employment options. As the course develops, more and more young people will be contributing to the debate. However, in order to have the required effect a political call to action is necessary to recognise the cultural and economic value afforded by investing in earnest training and development in cultural diversity in the arts in the modern world.

Will our graduating students make a difference by including African and Caribbean dance in their practice? Will more courses come on line with a dedicated interest in diversity? Will we be able to expand the course and perhaps offer a third year to allow for more in depth training? All of these questions remain at the forefront of our practice, as we attempt to continually build on the findings of our research.

REFERENCES

This chapter is taken from the full report produced for the Re:Generations conference.

Amuah, R., Bashaw, B., Smith, M., Wanliss, A. (2007) Interviews by Glean, B., Lehan, R. (2010) More Similarities Than Differences – Dance and Diversity Phase Two (Full Report) IRIE! dance theatre, Re:generations Conference, London, November 5–6, 2010

Bashaw, B., Smith, M., Wanliss, A. (2007) Interviews by Glean, B., Lehan, R. (2010) *More Similarities Than Differences – Dance and Diversity Phase Two* (Full Report) IRIE! dance theatre, Re:generations Conference, London, November 5–6, 2010

Brown, S., Seaman, S. (2015) *Case Study*, Interview by Beverley Glean, Rosie Lehan, London, September 14, 2015

Butler, K., Etten-Forbes, C., Nyamusole, N. (2016) *Case Study*, Interview by Beverley Glean, Rosie Lehan, London, January 5, 2016.

CHAPTER 17

Epistemology of the Weekend: Youth Dance Theatre

Hopal Romans, Adesola Akinleye, and Michael Joseph

The three of us (along with Leonora Stapleton) first met in 1980 and again in 1981 at the first and second Youth Dance Festivals. These festivals brought together youth groups from around UK. In the 1970s and 1980s, a time of disharmony and political unrest, the youth seemed to be a focus point. For us, dancing kept us busy within the turmoil of being a Black young person in Britain, and within the exciting new voices that were emerging around us in trans-Atlantic contemporary dance arts. At the festivals, youth dance companies came together and many of their members were of African or Caribbean descent. Marginalised from auditioning for

---

The first National Festival of Youth Dance was held in Leicester from 14th to 21st September 1980 at De Montfort Campus and performances shown at The Haymarket and Phoenix Theatres, Dame Ninette de Valois was the Guest of Honour.

H. Romans (✉)
Independent artist, London, UK

A. Akinleye
Middlesex University, London, UK

M. Joseph
Independent artist-researcher, Leicester, UK

performing arts schools by cost and lack of access, as well as the openly racist aesthetic criteria for entry, our dance training formed intense weekends of technique classes and rehearsals, often working with world renowned guest dance artists. So many young people from these early youth companies went on to have distinguished careers in dance. In this chapter, the three of us each describe the landscape of our early dance training in these youth companies.

Day in the Life of a Youngster in Dance

Making the journey from South London to Euston station and then towards The Place, my entry into the building is always marked by the sound of the bell of the church across from Dukes Road. Provoking my memory, the resonate sound chimes every quarter of an hour. I am transported back to a memory of my life as a teenager taking those formative steps, which signalled my life-long love for and career in dance, movement and the performing arts. Like a wave, the chimes drew me back to when I was a teenager and my association with The Place when I auditioned for the Inner London Education Authority (ILEA) special ability classes, where I had to audition in order to be selected to take contemporary classes with Kay Andrews, who taught Graham technique. These were challenging and exhilarating classes which I relished despite the pain and very often against the backdrop of the bell chiming outside in what was Studio 3, now the Founders Studio.

The bell once again tolls another quarter of an hour and again I am immediately transported back to a memory of myself at 16 years old walking into the building on a Sunday morning, where it was cold and damp, and rehearsing with the youth group Contemporary Youth Dance (CYD). Led by Todryk Danuta and Jackie Vallin, this group evolved after a successful collaboration between the London Schools Symphony Orchestra (LSSO) and London Schools Dance. I was part of a group of young dancers from across London boroughs brought together to take part in a large production of a piece called *Persephone*. The project was such a success that a number of us stayed together to form CYD to continue dancing, create work, develop our technique and tour locally and further afield out of London. I am pretty sure we had CYD t-shirts with a designed logo on them. We usually met at the weekend and particularly on Sundays at the Place in the studio just to the bottom of the stairs (which today is the café). I vividly remember a payphone directly outside the studio where dancers who were students at the Place (LSCD) as well as us teenagers congregated. Outside the studio dancers could be found stretching on the stairs, hanging out by the payphone, legs in splits, or sporting oversized rucksacks bigger than we could manage of 'stuff' and paraphernalia associated with being a dancer, whether professionally or not.

The usual schedule for a Sunday involved me flying downstairs into the changing room in the morning, rushing back upstairs and doing my own warm-up before the class began, led by Danuta. She usually gave a general contemporary class, which, was dominated by a combination of popular and eclectic music—quite contemporary and unlike what I was used to at home. I remember that each tune had a purpose for a particular exercise. A short break would follow and then rehearsal for a new piece or choreography previously performed. There was a lunch-break and then more rehearsals followed by a de-briefing of the day, which ended in the late afternoon. I do remember sometimes lounging against the mirrors as I watched sections danced and being aware of my surroundings in the studio again, against the backdrop of the bell tolling the quarter hour.

The studio was quite long (for the countless sparkles steps and leaps across the diagonal) and also quite dark with a small window at one end of the studio. The flooring was wooden with the potential to rip your feet and constantly smelled of ingrained sweat of the bodies of other dancers previously using the studio, plus resin from the use of ballet shoes, which I remember dipping my feet into on those occasions when the floor was like an ice-rink.

Magic for me happened in the studio; it was the one place for me to be myself moving, rehearsing, lounging and stretching. In those classes and rehearsal settings, there was always a healthy banter between the dancers and there was always an atmosphere of friendly competition to see who could jump or leap the highest or furthest. After a long day, a few of us religiously congregated at the McDonalds on the Charing Cross Road, right beside the entrance, which linked both Charing Cross and Embankment stations. My staple then (before having rice and peas at home later) was a Filet'o Fish and Strawberry milkshake topped off with a hot apple pie. The reason for meeting there was its central location for everybody to get home from, regardless of where we lived in London at the time. Journeying as a group from The Place, getting onto the Northern Line from Euston to Charing Cross was always eventful and, especially with a group of young people, rowdy but not outrageous. After spending at least an hour in McDonalds and to the point that I thought on many occasions the management would kick us out, I usually walked down towards Trafalgar Square and caught the number 12 bus back south.

Reflecting on the consistent sound of the bell tolling, I remembered how it faded into the background against the drone of our voices when in the company of the other young dancers, but I always remember how much the sound, when it caught my attention, quickened my heart and I could feel the beating in my chest in anticipation of moving, dancing, auditioning or rehearsing, watching shows in the building, it was a kind of nervous energy that I was embarking on something so special, …

– Hopal Romans

Walking Home from London Youth Dance Theatre

I've 'done' a ballet class and a Horton class and rehearsal. *Done* them until I can barely drag myself home late on a Saturday afternoon. But the feeling of exhilaration from moving, devouring the space of the big gyms where we practise feels as if the world has opened up to be *my* creation as I start home. I start writing poems in my head: my feelings, my words and movement of my steps constitute the rhythm and lines of the poems as I walk. Each line is an infinite moment from the day.

Line one is: In ballet today I did a double turn, my ballet teacher had said 'before you start decide how many you will do and do them. Don't start to negotiate with yourself about how many you will do in the middle of doing them.' I decided and did them.

Line two is: I race across the floor when we do jumps. I am the youngest in the company and feel so small as we do travelling steps in Horton class. Sometimes I cry, I get so frustrated. Me moving through that big space is where I belong.

Line three is: Nobody has confirmed it but I am sure the National Front[1] meet in the school playground near my launderette.

Line four is: I love the dance Albie is choreographing on me. He brings in music I have never heard before. He shows me his small drawings: all the dance movements worked out in his note book, then translated through him to my body.

On week days I would take the number 5 bus down Commercial Street and then Commercial Road or the 67 bus and walk through, past Cable Street. But the Cable Street route meant entering the school from the back gate and on a Saturday, when it was only us in Dance club, that back gate was locked. Saturday mornings meant the 5 bus or walk. On the way back, I often walked because a lot of people from the company walked up to Whitechapel Station to get the tube. My friend Alice and I chat about class and rehearsal as we walk through the London

Hospital—short cut to the station. After buying a sticky bun at Percy Ingles, we'd all say goodbye and I walked alone on through Weavers Fields across Bethnal Green Road and then through to my flats. My world: shedding the dancer and becoming a young 'mixed race' girl walking through the East End. 1980s: the National Front, 'Blacks go home' 'Rivers of blood': tomorrow at Brick Lane's Sunday market, they will be handing out leaflets. Flyers I will step over as I head off to school again on Monday morning.

Take wide turns as you walk round corners, walk against the flow of traffic so cars can't curb crawl you so easily. Thinking about the double pirouette I did today, cross the road as a group of white boys approach. 4 5 6 7...and 8: going over the counts of the last phrase we just learned for Albie's dance. Look down at the pavement so as not to catch the boys' eyes. The pavement begins to melt—could it be? Enormous splashes of colour explode around me. I feel a drop down my back. Could it be so sudden, rain—luscious drops exploding onto the paving, turning the colour of the ground—pale to dark—releasing the smell of rain—the fresh hope to quench the streets. Drops on my face and hands and I think 'great that will clean the street'—clear the streets if it's a downpour and I'll have my world to myself as I hurry home. I turn into the road before my block of flats and the rain is already stopping. A man on the other side of our courtyard is washing a car defiant of the rain shower.

Almost at our door. Saturday afternoon my dad would have been down the Ridley Road Market collecting food for tomorrow's Sunday dinner (rice, plantain, tomato stew). Feeling plantains, picking-up big yams and using the flat side of his hand on to the palm of the other hand in order to indicate where he wants the yam to be cut. He enjoys picking his way through the market, gathering, collecting, re-creating Nigeria for Sunday dinner. My mum with my baby sister would have been cleaning the house. Gone for a walk to the corner shop, buying Manor House cake, and orange squash maybe—English food.

I look at the multi-coloured pavement painted with light dry and with dark wet. And for a moment, that unique moment, I am the daughter of this place. I am suspended in now—here in East London for a moment I will, and I have, and I am.

Reciting the names of those who were around me, like the ancestors called by my Yoruba Grandmothers as the rain pours libations, I go over the day's dancing one more time in my head. Pedro, Steve, Trevor, Perry, Alison, Mohamed, Darshan, Gurmit, Algenon, Dee Dee, Helen, Albie, Stuart, Micheal, Deirdre, Chris, Deborah, Linda, Hillary, Colin,

Philip, Bunty, Anthony, Verde, Juliette, Teresa, Paulette, Lesley, Kathryne, Beverley, Alice, …

Five years later, I will leave them: fly away to join the Dance Theatre of Harlem. 'No place for you here': *London is a place for everyone who comes from somewhere else. That way there is always someone to hate you for being here*, my friend says. But 13 years old on Saturday afternoons after dance, London belongs to me.

– Adesola Akinleye

Early Dance Days

1980: I am 17 at *Scamps* nightclub on a Saturday night. Dark dank walls dripping with condensation from so many bodies dancing to the hypnotic music of *Chick Corea's Tap Step*, eight minutes and nineteen seconds long. A circle has formed; you have to be brave to enter or at least an accomplished freestyle dancer to battle the likes of Norman Spence. This is the Jazz, Funk, Soul era and the music dictates the movement of the body and feet with such clarity that would render 'Mickey Mousing' simple by comparison. Any dancer holding their own in the circle would have spent hours practising, honing their skills, to unleash on the dance floor, to battle, to win. No drugs, no alcohol, just a pint of *lemonade* and *black* (blackcurrant cordial) was the chosen refreshment, you needed a clear mind to dance your heart out. Choosing the right time to go in to the circle was paramount; you don't want to get tired too early. That introduction, I hear the repeating bassline, I *know* this track very well, *Summer's Ended* by *Incognito*, it starts slow and then speeds up… my turn to battle. My heart is racing, I step in regardless, a smile slips on to my face, I lose myself to music, the bass, the drums, that flute, that pied piper flute leading us to dance. Battle is on.

I need more.

1981: The crackling sound of the needle on the vinyl summoned the beginning of the Jazz class. The dance studios were located at Leicestershire County School of Dance on Herrick Road in Knighton Fields. The album being played on the record player was *The Dude* by Quincy Jones. Warming up with *body isolations, travelling steps* and *Matt Mattox* arms, then moving on to *Razzmatazz* for the routine taught by Rachel. She was dressed in a long-sleeved leotard, with a ballet wrap skirt, leg warmers and Jazz shoes. Nervousness, excitement, exhilaration, sweat and leg warmers, this was all new to me… I was there to learn new moves for the discothèque, *my* battling ground. However, I entered a whole new world that I did not know existed. The studio was an old, large hall with large windows, the wooden floor worn in by thousands of steps danced, on a weekly basis. The next class next door, was Contemporary Dance taught by Peter W Kyle, the man who opened my eyes to a strange new world. I had never heard of *contractions, flexed foot* or even a *plié*. I soon learned the new words to describe movement at an old age of 18, 'way too old to start dance training' some said. I remember Peter trying to teach me a *tour en l'air*, holding out his hand for me to *'spot'*. The hall was a huge space, much bigger than the discothèque floors I was used to dancing on. I was very comfortable on the night club floor, now I was frustrated unable to jump in the air, turn two times, and land facing Peter's hand. Everyone had stopped to watch me, on the third attempt I did it. It was Peter's encouragement that made me do it and my stubbornness to achieve it. I learned a valuable lesson, never give up.

1981: Summer and one whole week to learn new choreography for the second National Festival of Youth Dance taking place at Solihull. Peter W Kyle had chosen *Jeff Wayne's War of The Worlds* as our musical soundtrack. Being away from home for week was a strange and new sensation even at 18. Luckily for me, my identical twin brother Stephen was there with me for support. We both were dancers in the studio and the discothèque, now we shared the thrill of dancing all day, learning new movements, partnering, all of it outweighing the aches and pains of our bodies. The excitement of meeting new friends, the hunger to learn choreography and to improve my skills fuelled me. Being with dancers all day and then chatting in the early hours was heaven on earth for me. Building strong bonds of friendship, foundations for my future began right there, Peter W Kyle at the helm and we his eager students. The end of the week we had technical rehearsals at Phoenix Arts Centre in Leicester, the smell of the theatre, the bright lights, wings for entrances and exits again was all a new experience for me. Adrenalin pumping through my body as we performed in front of friends and family that very same evening of rehearsals. There was more to come…

Arriving at the second National Festival of Youth Dance taking place at Solihull, my excitement was overwhelming, seeing so many dancers from around UK in one place sent my feelings into the stratosphere! Learning new dance styles, taught by new teachers, experiencing new emotions was so exhilarating for me. Watching so many different performances from different youth groups and of course battling in the evenings in my free time combined my love of freestyle dancing in the discothèque and performing set choreography. I had found my future profession and love of movement—dance.

– Michael Joseph

of the final school year.

The group performing in the Festival is a newly formed group of past and present pupils whose ages range from 12 to 15 years. The group meets for one evening each week, to provide the participants with an opportunity to work at a higher level and to continue their dance training after they have left Harehills School.

HAREHILLS MIDDLE SCHOOL CONTEMPORARY DANCE GROUP will present 'Paradise Lost', based on the poem by John Milton with choreography by the dancers.

"Of man's first disobedience, and the fruit of that forbidden tree, whose mortal taste brought death into the world, and all our woe, with loss of Eden . . . ."

Book 1-4

Inner London Schools Dance Group

Ade Bola, Dylan Brown, Sophia Clarke, Siobhan Collins, Sarah Dove, Marva Dyer, Sadie Frost, Joanna Hines, Ali Jones, Lorrine Joseph, Brenda Lamont, Linda Morris, Natasha Neale, Mandy Odutole, Rosalin Dorcas, Lloyd Roberts, Sasha Roubicek, Colete Samuel, Jackie Samuel, Tania Vaughan

Group Leaders

Jill Henderson, Fiona Wheat

Pianist

Philip Taylor

This group, selected from many ILEA Schools, was formed in October 1979. Several members joined in the Summer of 1980 and so have only been with the group for one term. The dancers' ages rang efrom 14 to 16 years.

The group meets every Saturday afternoon in term time at the College of Physical Education, and works for 2½ hours doing a class and a choreographic workshop.

Our first small performance was in the spring of 1980 and our first major public performances were in the Queen Elizabeth Hall in July 1980 where we contributed to the 'Schools on the South Bank' festival.

THE INNER LONDON SCHOOLS DANCE GROUP will present three pieces:

1. 'For Those that Walk in Darkness'
Choreography: Jill Henderson. Music: Handel.
A suite of three dances.
2. 'The Dance of the Snowflakes'
Choreography: Ann Mogndge. Music: Tomita.
A duet.
3. 'Nanchaku'. Choreography: Lloyd Roberts. Music composed and played by Philip Taylor.
A suite of five dances: (i) 'Nose to the Grindstone' (ii) 'Over my Dead Body' (iii) 'Heart on my Sleeve' (iv) 'Backs against the Wall' (v) 'All Hands on Deck'

a Junior School for … Senior School for those aged 14 or over. Training is given in classical ballet, contemporary dance, creative dance, folk dance and mime. The school has two centres, one in Leicester, which has over 100 students, and one in Loughborough, which has over 50.

Entrance to the school is by audition and is open to every young person in Leicestershire, whether or not they have previous dance experience. Through performances to schools and to the general public, the County School of Dance hopes to show the possibilities of dance and the standard of work which can be achieved; it is planned to develop further centres of the County School in other parts of Leicestershire. Past productions have been greeted with widespread acclaim both in this country and abroad; last October a production of classical ballet and contemporary dance was taken to Leicestershire's twin area in Germany, the Saarland.

LEICESTERSHIRE COUNTY SCHOOL OF DANCE will present 'Fair Chance'. The piece is divided into four sections and the action takes place in:
an astrologer's den; a fairground; a house of horrors and a tunnel of love.

The ballet focuses on a central character who is trying to bring the varied elements of his personality into order. These are portrayed by the signs of the zodiac. He discovers, however, that trying to order people's lives brings complications.

London Youth Dance Theatre

Adesola Akinleye, Philip Christian, Perry Douglin, Dee Dee Evans, Lesley Fearon, Kathryn Goodson, Teresa Hall, Verdi Hall, Beverley Jones, Trevor Mbatha, Helen McGhee, Deborah Nixon, Julietta Norde, Albert Ollivierre, Michael Pratt, Stephen Reid, Pedro Sandiford, Paulette Stephens, Alvina Volney, Algernon Williams

Directors

Hilary Ball, Linda Robinson, Clive Whitburn

Technical Assistants

Lesley Fearon, Teresa Hall

The London Youth Dance Theatre was formed in 1976 under the direction of Hilary Ball and Linda Robinson, teachers from Tower Hamlets School in London. The group's members come from many backgrounds, but all live, work or study in London.

Some of the company members are at present studying dance full-time at, for example, the London School of Contemporary Dance, the Laban Centre and the Arts Educational School; but all company members receive a regular training in contemporary dance, classical and neo-classical ballet, and guest classes in

10

Fig. 17.1 Romans' private collection: Pages from the first National Festival of Youth Dance programme, held in Leicester 14–21 September 1980 at De Montford Campus and performances shown at the Haymarket and Phoenix Theatres. Dame Ninette de Valois was the Guest of Honour (Hopal Romans, 2017)

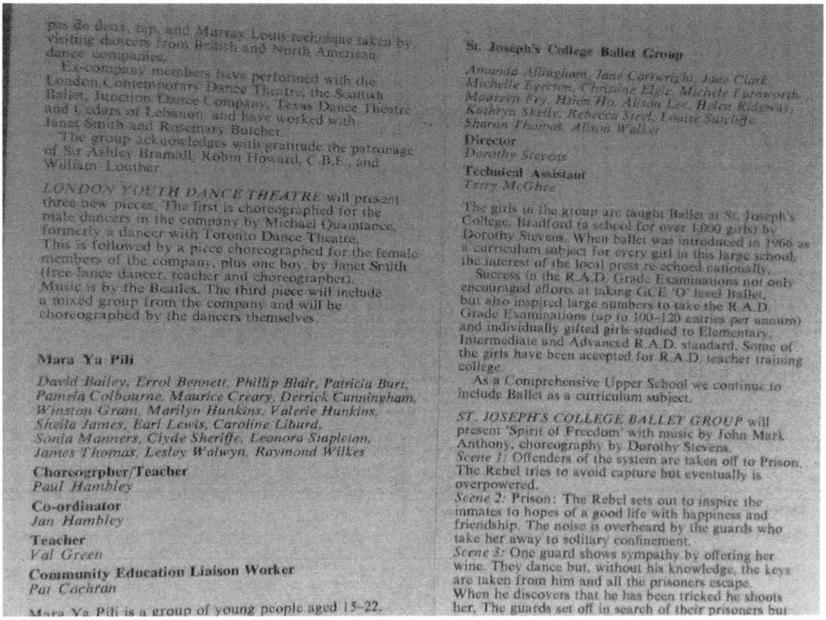

pas de deux, tap, and Murray Louis technique taken by visiting dancers from British and North American dance companies.

Ex-company members have performed with the London Contemporary Dance Theatre, the Scottish Ballet, Junction Dance Company, Texas Dance Theatre and Cedars of Lebanon, and have worked with Janet Smith and Rosemary Butcher.

The group acknowledges with gratitude the patronage of Sir Ashley Bramall, Robin Howard, C.B.E., and William Louther.

LONDON YOUTH DANCE THEATRE will present three new pieces. The first is choreographed for the male dancers in the company by Michael Quaintance, formerly a dancer with Toronto Dance Theatre. This is followed by a piece choreographed for the female members of the company, plus one boy, by Janet Smith (free-lance dancer, teacher and choreographer). Music is by the Beatles. The third piece will include a mixed group from the company and will be choreographed by the dancers themselves.

Mara Ya Pili

David Bailey, Errol Bennett, Phillip Blair, Patricia Burt, Pamela Colbourne, Maurice Creary, Derrick Cunningham, Winston Grant, Marilyn Hunkins, Valerie Hunkins, Sheila James, Earl Lewis, Caroline Liburd, Sonia Manners, Clyde Sheriffe, Leonora Stapleton, James Thomas, Lesley Walwyn, Raymond Wilkes

Choreogrpher/Teacher
Paul Hambley

Co-ordinator
Jan Hambley

Teacher
Val Green

Community Education Liaison Worker
Pat Cochran

Mara Ya Pili is a group of young people aged 15–22,

St. Joseph's College Ballet Group

Amanda Allingham, Jane Cartwright, Jane Clark, Michelle Egerton, Christine Elgie, Michele Farnworth, Maureen Fry, Helen Ho, Alison Lee, Helen Ridgway, Kathryn Skelly, Rebecca Steel, Louise Sutcliffe, Sharon Thomas, Alison Walker

Director
Dorothy Stevens

Technical Assistant
Terry McGhee

The girls in the group are taught Ballet at St. Joseph's College, Bradford (a school for over 1,000 girls) by Dorothy Stevens. When ballet was introduced in 1966 as a curriculum subject for every girl in this large school, the interest of the local press re-echoed nationally.

Success in the R.A.D. Grade Examinations not only encouraged efforts at taking GCE 'O' level Ballet, but also inspired large numbers to take the R.A.D. Grade Examinations (up to 100–120 entries per annum) and individually gifted girls studied to Elementary, Intermediate and Advanced R.A.D. standard. Some of the girls have been accepted for R.A.D. teacher training college.

As a Comprehensive Upper School we continue to include Ballet as a curriculum subject.

ST. JOSEPH'S COLLEGE BALLET GROUP will present 'Spirit of Freedom' with music by John Mark Anthony, choreography by Dorothy Stevens.
Scene 1: Offenders of the system are taken off to Prison. The Rebel tries to avoid capture but eventually is overpowered.
Scene 2: Prison: The Rebel sets out to inspire the inmates to hopes of a good life with happiness and friendship. The noise is overheard by the guards who take her away to solitary confinement.
Scene 3: One guard shows sympathy by offering her wine. They dance but, without his knowledge, the keys are taken from him and all the prisoners escape. When he discovers that he has been tricked he shoots her. The guards set off in search of their prisoners but

Fig. 17.2 Romans' private collection: Pages from the first National Festival of Youth Dance programme, held in Leicester 14–21 September 1980 at De Montford Campus and performances shown at the Haymarket and Phoenix Theatres. Dame Ninette de Valois was the Guest of Honour (Hopal Romans, 2017)

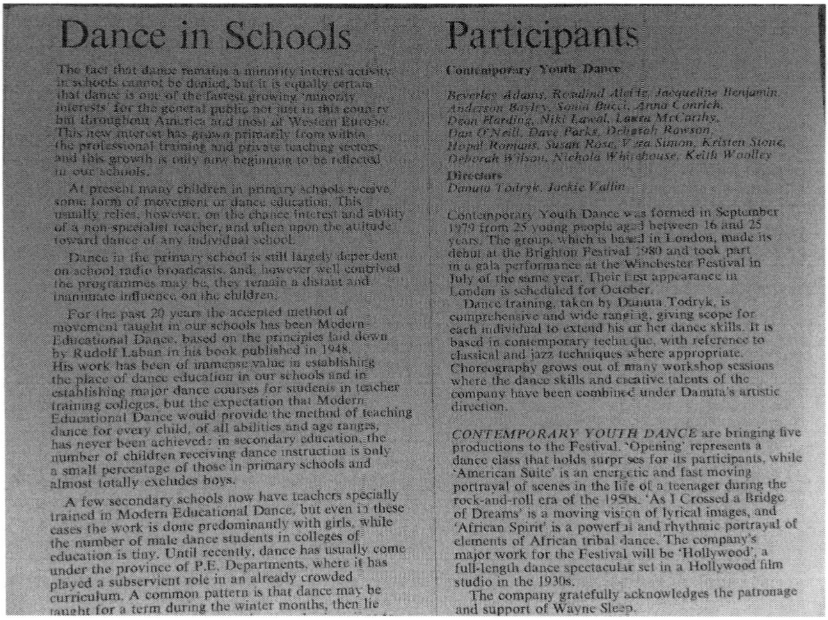

Dance in Schools

The fact that dance remains a minority interest activity in schools cannot be denied, but it is equally certain that dance is one of the fastest growing 'minority interests' for the general public, not just in this country but throughout America and most of Western Europe. This new interest has grown primarily from within the professional training and private teaching sectors, and this growth is only now beginning to be reflected in our schools.

At present many children in primary schools receive some form of movement or dance education. This usually relies, however, on the chance interest and ability of a non-specialist teacher, and often upon the attitude toward dance of any individual school.

Dance in the primary school is still largely dependent on school radio broadcasts, and, however well contrived the programmes may be, they remain a distant and inanimate influence on the children.

For the past 20 years the accepted method of movement taught in our schools has been Modern Educational Dance, based on the principles laid down by Rudolf Laban in his book published in 1948. His work has been of immense value in establishing the place of dance education in our schools and in establishing major dance courses for students in teacher training colleges, but the expectation that Modern Educational Dance would provide the method of teaching dance for every child, of all abilities and age ranges, has never been achieved: in secondary education, the number of children receiving dance instruction is only a small percentage of those in primary schools and almost totally excludes boys.

A few secondary schools now have teachers specially trained in Modern Educational Dance, but even in these cases the work is done predominantly with girls, while the number of male dance students in colleges of education is tiny. Until recently, dance has usually come under the province of P.E. Departments, where it has played a subservient role in an already crowded curriculum. A common pattern is that dance may be taught for a term during the winter months, then lie

Participants

Contemporary Youth Dance

Beverley Adams, Rosalind Alcriss, Jacqueline Benjamin, Anderson Bayley, Sonia Bucci, Anna Conrick, Dean Harding, Niki Lawal, Laura McCarthy, Dan O'Neill, Dave Parks, Deborah Rawson, Hopal Romans, Susan Rose, Virga Simon, Kristen Stone, Deborah Wilson, Nichola Whitehouse, Keith Woolley

Directors
Danuta Todryk, Jackie Vallin

Contemporary Youth Dance was formed in September 1979 from 25 young people aged between 16 and 25 years. The group, which is based in London, made its debut at the Brighton Festival 1980 and took part in a gala performance at the Winchester Festival in July of the same year. Their first appearance in London is scheduled for October.

Dance training, taken by Danuta Todryk, is comprehensive and wide ranging, giving scope for each individual to extend his or her dance skills. It is based in contemporary technique, with reference to classical and jazz techniques where appropriate. Choreography grows out of many workshop sessions where the dance skills and creative talents of the company have been combined under Danuta's artistic direction.

CONTEMPORARY YOUTH DANCE are bringing five productions to the Festival. 'Opening' represents a dance class that holds surprises for its participants, while 'American Suite' is an energetic and fast moving portrayal of scenes in the life of a teenager during the rock-and-roll era of the 1950s. 'As I Crossed a Bridge of Dreams' is a moving vision of lyrical images, and 'African Spirit' is a powerful and rhythmic portrayal of elements of African tribal dance. The company's major work for the Festival will be 'Hollywood', a full-length dance spectacular set in a Hollywood film studio in the 1930s.

The company gratefully acknowledges the patronage and support of Wayne Sleep.

Fig. 17.3 Romans' private collection: Pages from the first National Festival of Youth Dance programme, held in Leicester 14–21 September 1980 at De Montford Campus and performances shown at the Haymarket and Phoenix Theatres. Dame Ninette de Valois was the Guest of Honour (Hopal Romans, 2017)

Fig. 17.4 Romans' private collection: Pages from the first National Festival of Youth Dance programme, held in Leicester 14–21 September 1980 at De Montford Campus and performances shown at the Haymarket and Phoenix Theatres, Dame Ninette de Valois was the Guest of Honour (Hopal Romans, 2017)

Note

1. National Front was a far-right wing party for 'whites' only, that advocated violence and hostility toward black people.

CHAPTER 18

Transatlantic Voyages: Then and Now

Anita Gonzalez

Almost 200 years ago, Afro-Caribbean performers took jobs as stewards on sailing vessels to pursue international performance opportunities in the United Kingdom and the United States. These early adventurers began a trend of transatlantic arts exchange that continues in present-day artistry.

Overseas opportunities lure African Diaspora dancers to travel abroad. Atlantic world scholars often write about Africans voyaging between the United Kingdom and the Americas as if it were a thing of the past, yet performance Diasporas continue to invigorate professional dance practice. Dancers cross Atlantic and other waters as they learn techniques, make acquaintances and experience the cultural currency that will activate their careers.

Professor Jay Cook shared this information with me during an interview in Ann Arbor on October 3, 2013.

The photograph documenting this aspect of the Blackbirds tour comes from the University of Bristol Mander and Mitchenson Collection.

A. Gonzalez (✉)
Professor of Theatre and Drama, University of Michigan,
Ann Arbor, MI, USA

Historical Black British/American/Caribbean Arts Exchange

Legacies of slavery overlay academic histories of transatlantic exchange—dancing the slaves, plantation dances, performers dancing like slaves or in minstrel shows.[1] Why is slavery the marker of the Black experience? Some of these dancing travellers were free men making a buck, a pound or a shilling. One early and renowned transatlantic voyager was the actor Ira Aldridge. His travels to England in the early nineteenth century introduced a range of characters played by a Black man to a cross-section of European audiences. Over the course of decades, he was able to maintain an active professional career by travelling and touring.

Yet his 1829 voyage from New York to London was not the first American/United Kingdom exchange. Even earlier his mentor, James Hewlett was working on the ocean—travelling on Liverpool packet ships where he made garments and served shipmasters. Whenever he landed in UK ports, he attended theatrical performances of Shakespeare. James was from the Caribbean, probably St. Vincent's island. Whenever he headed back to the New York port, he collaborated with his fellow stewards to create an entertainment garden where he sang and performed for free 'coloured' audiences. Can we consider James Hewlett to be a first model for international cooperative exchange? (Dewberry, 1982; Lindfors, 2007; MacAllister, 2003; Marshall & Stock, 1993).

One early Black dance artist in the transatlantic exchange record is Juba. Some people think of the 'juba' as a plantation dance or an African foot pattern. Juba was, however, also a man named William Henry Lane who took the name of the dance to mark his talent. As James Cook indicates in his lengthy article about Juba, William Lane figured out how to navigate and negotiate his way not only to England but also away from his white managers. His decision to spend some time in the United Kingdom did not advance his career as much as he might have believed. There is some evidence that after several years in Manchester he encountered race resistance. Eventually he decided to abandon his manager and strike out on his own. He was not able to achieve his goals and he never returned to his homeland. Historian Jay Cook has recently ascertained that Juba died in poverty in Liverpool.

A trend of seeking autonomy from White producers begins in the nineteenth century, continues into the twentieth century and even demonstrates its efficacy in the new millennium. African descendent performers looking to profit from their work historically depend upon white patronage to buy their 'dances'. Even though artists want to manage their own enterprises of embodied practice, access to venues requires liaisons with managers. When artists find their own markets and audiences, they break free by self-producing or establishing independent companies.

In 1903, 50 years after Juba's astonishing dance career ended, Williams and Walker brought the musical *In Dahomey* to the Shaftsbury Stage. At this moment in time, dancing the cakewalk was an international craze, and Ada Walker headlined the show's cakewalk dance act. Her high-kicking brown legs and her lifted skirts were a precursor to Auntie Mame's Broadway strut. Ada Walker's fellow dancers, Mattie Edwards and Lizzie Avery also achieved notoriety. *In Dahomey* was self-produced. The African American artists wrote and directed their project, assembling a creative team to skillfully execute Africanist comedic song and dance. Some numbers in the show such as 'Emancipation Day' were tongue-in-cheek displays of Black double consciousness; the audience saw Blacks happily cavorting onstage while the actors celebrated the freedom of dancing while emancipated. This production demonstrated how Black American dancers and actors, performing well-costumed and well-executed plantation dances, could earn enough to finance a passenger berth for a troupe of performers. (Hatch & Hill, 2003)

In Dahomey achieved a financial success that escapes many of today's dance/theatre companies as they attempt to travel overseas. Getting ticket sales to generate enough income for housing overseas remains a challenge for small dance proprietors who want to promote their choreographic works. Travelling overseas increases recognition and inspires brainstorming about how to reach new audiences. Generally, it enhances the mind and expands an artist's network of venues. Often, it adds little to the artists' financial profile.

The twentieth century and the expansion of Black employment on Broadway brought more United States artists to London stages. Some were skilled vaudevillians such Brookins and Van (Tommy Brookins and Sammy Van), a duo team who spent two glorious years in London circulating their tap and comedy act. Once they left the United States and returned home in 1937, they split up. (Brookins & Van Split, 1935)

Florence Mills came to London with *Blackbirds of 1926*, a fully staged musical show. In one picture, the photographer captures the 'Blackbird' ladies as they pause for a tourist jaunt at Euston station. They lean against the backdrop, reclining within a typically British scenario. Florence needed to rest up. When she returned home, she died from the exhaustion of the tour.

Staying in one place has its advantages. Building a cohesive ensemble and a strong audience base is smart administrative choice. Producing as well as performing becomes an important part of a Black dance artist's 'tool kit'. In 1946, Jamaican-born dancer Berto Pasuka formed the first European Black dance company in London with dancers from Trinidad, Nigeria, Ghana. *Ballet Negres* was a uniquely multi-cultural dance company that brought African traditional dances and theatrical storytelling to British audiences.

Katherine Dunham crossed the Atlantic in 1948 with a troupe of performers who played the stages of Prince of Wales Theatre. Dunham and her dancers then travelled to the Theatre Royal in Birmingham. It was a company tour. John Barer described her collective as 'elegance and ecstasy, mystery and magnetism'. Ironically she returned to this Diaspora United Kingdom home with dances of the Americas and the Caribbean: street scenes of Havana, dances honouring Shango, dockyard stories of a woman with a cigar, even a Brazilian quadrille. Her 'Ragtime and Blues' suites presented hybrid forms: foxtrot, tango, Charleston, Mooch and turkey trot, distinctively American forms in distinctively American styles. Photographer Wood captured beautiful photos of the company's works, many of which remain in the archives of the Mander and Mitchenson collection at the University of Bristol.

When Eartha Kitt, then a Dunham company member, reflected upon travelling to London, she wrote: 'every theatre in London contains a royal box, so it was natural for our eyes to glance there first on entering the stage. We were terribly disappointed when kings and queens did not look down on us.' For Kitt, the exotic notion of travelling to perform in a foreign country brought unrealised expectations about how her performance would be received overseas.

In 1954 Ward Flemyng and Thelma Hill founded the New York Negro Ballet, the first of its kind. Later, they merged with the Joseph Rickard's California-based First Negro Classic Ballet. The collective then validated their dance expertise with a trip to Britain the following year. Their programme with choreography by Joseph Rickard, Graham Johnson and Louis Johnson premiered in Liverpool with an orchestra on October 7, 1957. When Hill's New York Negro Ballet appeared in Liverpool, they danced excerpts of Americana. 'Raisin' Cane', 'Folk Impressions', and 'Harlots House'. Dolores Brown and Bernard Johnson also performed the Bluebird pas de deux from Petipa's Sleeping Beauty. The eclectic repertoire harkened back to the aesthetics of Pasuka, albeit with a touch of the Russian classical ballet.

Continued Crossings

The journeys continue. I first came to London with Urban Bush Women in 1987. It feels like a long time ago. Black dance immigrants and migrants are seldom upper crust. More likely they are working-class talent who bring with them the will to make performances lucrative wherever they are. *The Place* and *London Contemporary Dance Theatre* sponsored our Urban Bush Women tour. We learned that there were other Black dance artists working in London who were pursuing Africanist aesthetics within contemporary dance. At the time that was important to the company as we strove to carve out a niche for validation and exposure of contemporary Black dance artistry. Today, I see similar needs and desires in young artists seeking to make their mark on the world.

Today's transatlantic journeys serve multiple purposes. Many Black British artists hail from Afro-Caribbean or African lineages so venturing out may actually be travelling back to reconnect with family. While nineteenth-century voyagers followed maritime currents from African to the Caribbean to New York to the United Kingdom, contemporary British citizens reverse the journey. New York (or Toronto or Boston or Philadelphia) offers classes and venues where dancers can learn technique. Exchanging corporeal practices with other Black dancers enriches possibilities for creative growth. Socialising in training spaces inevitably leads to comparative discussions of race, identity and opportunity. In some ways, we press against the tide of oppressions looking for indentations or a shift in cultural flows where there may be a chance for a new gig or an unexpected patron. And we travel back again. Homelands, especially Caribbean or African homelands, unearth familiar languages and rhythms. The backwards journey can offer family connections or spiritual rejuvenation. Circling against the maritime currents ends in Africa, a source of aesthetic inspiration for many practitioners. Transatlantic journeys press against and leap beyond tropes of slavery or minstrelsy. Exchanges between Africans in the Diaspora fertilise the genre. Dancers and choreographers, looking for artistic cauldrons and the opportunity to affirm connections across national boundaries, bring dances home, wherever that may be, promoting dance work through exchanges because within varying economic and historical climates, social systems can limit Black artistry.

Circling Back Through Interviews

This book, *Narratives in Black British Dance: Embodied Practices*, has offered me an opportunity to speak with dancers about their practices and their passions.[2] I interviewed seven artists, now based in the United Kingdom, who draw upon their international origins and experiences to define their practice. Their work crosses disciplinary and geographic boundaries as they locate themselves through embodied engagement in professional practice. Collectively, their professional practices reach across proscenium stages, touch down at community sites, and take off, exciting and inciting audiences to respond.

These profiles were developed in conversation with choreographers and resulted in a series of written interviews. My experiences of dialogic learning, coupled with somatic writing, influenced my approach to interviewing the choreographers about their work. I want to know less about the studio choreography, and more about each dancer's reason for continuing to pursue art in a sometimes adversarial landscape. I found that artists, through the process of remembering key influences on their practice, reconnected to their passions.

Through the process, I connected with dance artists through different pathways as I listened to them describe their inner reasons for doing the work that they do. In the interviewing process, I sought to capture emotive patterns of the speakers: the breath, the pauses, the hesitations and even the tears as artists remembered their impetus for dancing. In general, talking releases physical responses that spur memories, and I hoped to see how specific memories might reveal why the dancer chose to follow their specific career path. The interview sessions allowed repetitive thought. The speakers could loop back and revisit what happened before. Each time we talked about the memory, something new would emerge. What follows are three interview excerpts which exemplify the type of responses the interviewees shared.

In the first, H Patten uses his breath and memories to connect to how choreography emerges for him. As he speaks, you feel his movement through the circular patterns of the dance.

> my work is about squaring the circle, circling the square and building new communications. In a circle there are physical partners, the one in front and the one behind and you can turn and face the one in front and then the one behind. You can also face the musicians in the center and you get the musicians from anywhere. Proscenium makes them not a third partner anymore and you only communicate when you pass them or when you turn to them. You are getting the information from behind.

As he describes his practice, I find myself wanting to participate in the community he sees in his mind as he (re)members choreographies of encounter. His words help the reader to feel the ritual of connecting with and then disengaging from each face in the circle. There is a sense of geospatial locations siphoned through human memories of the circle. Another artist, Sandra Golding, finds metaphysical connections through somatic practices as she works with students. Here, she describes how she transforms within her practice and draws down a spiritual portal that allows her to share work with those in the room.

> What I feel I do in performance is like creating a portal, creating a space and inviting people in.... It's no longer about me, Sandra. It's about wherever those individuals are at any given point in time and what release they get from it.

Sometimes the process of talking about dance evoked very specific historical memories. With Maxine Brown, we began by talking about her process, and discovered, through the interview process, how deeply her practice is imbedded in cultural history.

> Outside of the house I was in England, but once you stepped over the door you were in Jamaica. The smells were in Jamaica, the food was in Jamaica the music and language was in Jamaica. My brothers and sisters were actually born in Jamaica. My mum was a singer and she used to sing us folk songs and dances around the house. I had that strong influence about Jamaica all the time and I still do.

As I interviewed artists for this *Embodied Practices* volume and web-site, I found that dancers and choreographers speak through their bodies, remembering their life experiences in a holistic manner. They bring self, to life, to artistry. My dance writing wants to capture this breath.

Each of the artists I interviewed came to their practice through transition and travel. Some were born elsewhere and arrived in England to begin their dance career. Others enhanced their artistry by travelling out of the country to participate in African Diaspora art practices, to connect with their families, or to learn more about the wide array of cultural arts found in other countries. In all cases, the process of moving from one location to another, learning to adapt and adjust to different ideas about artistry and ethnicity, changed the artists' approach to art-making. The interviews provided an opportunity for contemporary Black British choreographers and administrators to reflect upon how the process of journeying, implicit in the reality of working as an artist of the African Diaspora, shapes their process and practice.

Notes

1. "Dancing the slaves" was a practice used on slave ships where the captives were forced to dance on the deck on the ship for exercise when they were brought out of the hold. citation (Mustakeem, Sowandie, Slavery At Sea: Terror, Sex and Sickness in the Middle Passage, Urbana: University of Illinois Press, 2016 p. 71).
2. Full documentation of the interviews carried out are posted on the book's accompanying web site http://narrativesindance.com.

References

Brookins and Van Split, But Sammy Refuses to Talk. *The Afro American*. (1935, April 13).

Cook, James W. (2006). Master Juba, The King of All Dancers: A Story of Stardom and Struggle from the Dawn of the Transatlantic Culture Industry. *Discourses in Dance (Volume 3, Issue 2)*. London: Laban Dance Center.

Dewberry, J. (1982). The African Grove Theatre and Company. *Black American Literature Forum, 16*, 128–131.

Hatch, J. V., & Hill, E. (2003). *A History of African American Theatre (Cambridge Studies in American Theatre and Drama)*. New York: Cambridge University Press.

Lindfors, B. (Ed.). (2007). *Ira Aldridge: The African Roscius*. Rochester: University of Rochester Press.

Marshall, H., & Stock, M. (1993). *Ira Aldridge: The Negro Tragedian*. Washington, DC: Howard University Press.

McAllister, M. (2003). *White People Do Not Know How to Behave at Entertainments Designed for Ladies & Gentlemen of Colour: Williiam Brown's African & American Theater*. Chapel Hill: The University of North Carolina Press.

Index[1]

NUMBERS AND SYMBOLS
1820s, 278
1900s, 279
1920s, 55
1930s, 57, 203
1940s, 57, 204, 279
1950s, 76n2, 102, 204, 225, 280
1960s, 25, 26, 28, 138, 178, 220, 227
1970s, 32, 51, 54, 58–60, 88, 138, 140, 159, 171, 177, 214, 215, 217–231, 265
1980s, 29, 32, 33, 58–60, 86, 89, 99, 102, 132, 134–140, 159, 163, 181, 189, 203, 214, 215, 217–231, 265, 269, 280
1990s, 32, 45, 60, 159, 178, 189, 255
21st century, 2, 4, 68, 74, 76, 81, 106, 154, 214

A
Acogny, Germaine, 44
Acogny, Patrick, 90
Adair, Christy, 31

Adzido Dance Company, 28, 32
Aesthetic
  aesthetic of whiteness, 1
  black aesthetic, 34, 35, 95, 120, 137, 180, 235, 241, 245, 281
African American, 2, 34, 35, 56, 57, 61, 71, 112, 134, 157, 159, 199n15, 203, 237, 250, 279
African-Caribbean, 107
African dance
  conflation with Black dance, 79, 115–127
  drumming, 34, 103, 106, 107, 195
  homogenisation of, 28, 32, 79, 115–127
African Diaspora, 2
African Healing Dance, 107–109
Africanist, 7
  Africanist quality, 36
  Afrocentricity, 133, 134, 159, 160
  Afro-Diasporic aesthetics, 241, 245
  diasporic, 33, 37–50, 82, 89, 116, 145, 178, 217

[1]Note: Page number followed by 'n' refer to notes.

INDEX

Afro-Caribbean, 28, 90, 214, 215, 235, 240–242, 277, 281
Agency, 88, 92, 98, 144, 159, 170, 172, 179, 214, 229, 236–240, 243–247
Ailey, Alvin
  company, 204, 205
  school, 204, 207
Akinleye, Adesola, 1–14, 59, 60, 65–76, 265–276
Ancestors, 6, 7, 92, 96, 103, 104, 106, 107, 110, 134, 137, 140, 149, 157, 159, 174–176, 181, 199n1, 207, 208, 269
  ancestral, 93–96, 98, 106, 134, 145, 148, 157, 159, 161, 169, 173–175, 180, 181, 247
Anderson, Derrick, 90, 92, 104
Angol, Francis, 33, 36
Angola, 82, 121, 131, 134, 137–139, 141, 143, 145, 161
Antigua, 259, 260
Apartheid, 27, 118, 122
Appropriation, 116, 121, 124, 144
Arts Council, 32, 58, 59, 106, 223, 249
Association of Dance of the African Diaspora (ADAD), 202, 249, 258
Atlantic, 141
  travel across, 203, 206, 215, 277, 280
Audience, 4, 6, 8, 10, 26, 27, 33, 44, 47, 48, 79, 80, 97, 98, 105, 117, 119, 121, 133, 144, 148, 160, 161, 172, 180, 193, 209, 230, 239, 244, 278–280, 282
Authenticity, 74, 80, 82, 84, 92, 97, 98, 105
  authentic, 25, 81, 84, 86, 87, 89, 90, 96–99, 121, 202, 227, 246

B

Baartman, Saartjie, 8
Badejo, Peter OBE, 32, 223
Bahamas, 235, 237–239, 241, 244
Bailey, Paul, 59
Balance, 9, 75, 93, 106, 123, 239, 259
Ballet, 102, 104, 116, 223, 238, 254
  Australian Dance Theatre, 27
  Balanchine, 56
  Ballet Black Company, 57–61
  Ballet Nacional de Cuba, 58
  Ballet Russes, 52, 54–56
  Black ballerinas, 5
  Black British ballet, 51–61
  English National Ballet (*see* London Festival Ballet)
  King Louis XIV, 52
  London Festival Ballet, 58, 59
  'The Moor's Room', (*Petrouchka*), 53
  New York City Ballet, 57
  Petipa's Sleeping Beauty, 280
  Royal Ballet & Royal Birmingham Ballet, 57–61
  See also Dance Theatre of Harlem
Banda, Isaac, 104
Barbados, 224
Barefoot, 25, 27, 93
Barnes, Thea, 3, 84
Beginnings, 40, 43, 46, 89, 101, 102, 104, 110, 112, 127, 152, 160, 204, 215, 227, 263, 270
Benin, 145
Berlin, Harris, 225
Binary, 69, 76, 122, 123, 227, 240
  See also Dualism, Mind/body
Birmingham, 32, 86, 102
  Handsworth Community Centre (HCC), 88, 89
  Handsworth Cultural Centre, 102–103
  Theatre Royal in Birmingham, 280
Blackbirds of 1926/Florence Mills, 227, 279
Black community, 33, 59, 89, 105
Black (cultural), 26, 29, 30, 42, 68, 163
Black Dance Development Trust (BDDT), 92, 105, 181, 223

INDEX

Black dancer/Black dance (discussed), 1, 20, 23, 28, 33, 51, 79, 121, 122, 203
Blacked-up, 52, 53
  See also Blackface
Blackface, 52
Black feminism, 237
Blackness, 4, 8, 12, 28, 76
  black, 1–3, 68, 122, 123, 223, 229
  black dancers '*vs.*' black dance, 23, 51
  black female body, 8, 11
  black male body, 8, 132, 158
  black women's body, 8, 237, 238
Black (skin colour), 25, 28, 34, 46, 52, 57–59, 61, 221, 223, 227
Bodily
  corporeal, 170, 177
  corporeal dancing body, 167–170, 172–177, 181, 182
  lived body, 169
  mind-ful-body, 13
  somatic, 6, 7, 72, 80, 81, 107–110, 112, 190, 213, 282, 283
  writing about, 7
Body, 101, 132, 148, 149
  black bodies, 2, 8, 9, 144, 150, 160, 161, 172, 229
  black female body, 235
  black women's bodies, 238
  bodies of women, 236
  body type, 11, 104, 204, 244
  dancing bodies, 2, 4, 7, 70, 74–76, 85, 97, 172
  painting, 82, 131–163
  performativity, 82, 131–163
  policing of, 237, 238, 246
  sensing body, 10, 11, 69, 169
Bougard, Corrine, 32
Bourne, Sandie, 5, 51
Brazil, 145
British, 76, 96, 150
  Black Britain, 222
  Britannia, 21, 31, 217–231

British-based, 31–33, 35, 90
British Black Arts Movement, 223
British dance industry, 4, 21, 37–50
commonwealth, 1, 28
National Front (The British Movement), 221, 268, 269, 276n1
Brixton, 60, 86
Brothers in Jazz, 225, 228
Brown, Maxine, 283
Brown, Michael, 230
Bubble and Squeak (Jazz dance group), 225
Burt, Ramsay, 31

C

Carey, A'Keitha, 8, 235–247
Caribbean, 87, 91, 96, 102
Caribbean dance, African/Caribbean dance
  Burru Masquerade, 95
  CaribFunk™, 214, 235–247
  Gerreh, 90, 94, 95, 257
  Jonkonnu, 90, 95, 170, 173–176, 179, 181
  Kumina, 90, 95, 103, 108, 170, 173–179, 181, 257
  Myal, 174
  Obeah, 174
  Revivalism, 175
CaribFunk™, 240
Carnival, 140–143, 180, 182, 238, 240, 242
Carr, Jane, 217
Castelyn, Sarahleigh, 81, 115
Cemetery, 134
Choreography, 3, 28, 32–34, 38, 55, 66, 82, 86, 90, 91, 97, 106, 138, 161, 187–198, 217, 243, 255, 261, 271, 280, 282
Circle, 9, 93, 94, 107, 109, 148, 210, 217, 226, 228, 270, 282, 283

Clubs
  battling, 226
  disco, 228
  nightclubs, 195, 214, 270
  See also Dancehall
Cobson, Felix, 32
Cohan, Robert, 26
Collaboration
  collaborating together, 66, 278
  knowledge sharing, 180
Colonialism, 1, 8, 10, 118, 122, 136, 139, 145, 153, 163, 213
  colonization, 66
  neo-colonialism, 161
  pre-colonial, 139
  respectability, 237–239
Community dance, 68, 69, 104, 282
  community development, 88
  outreach, 106, 252
  participatory performance, 73
Compañía Teatro de la Danza del Caribe
  Walker, Eduardo River, 207
Congo, 103, 134, 139–141, 145, 161, 163, 260
Connection, 1, 6, 23, 30, 35, 72, 82, 93, 98, 103, 105, 108–111, 123, 131, 134, 140, 141, 145, 148, 149, 157, 180, 181, 187–198, 207, 228, 238, 243, 281, 283
  connecting, 79
  interconnectedness, 71, 151
Contemporary dance
  African contemporary dance, 120, 121, 223
  urban contemporary dance, 5, 188–190, 194, 195, 199n15, 255
Continuum, 108
Corporeal body, 169, 170
Cosmology, 137
  African, 133, 137, 159, 168, 170, 172–176, 180, 182

  cosmos, 109, 112
  Jamaican, 168, 170, 174–176, 181, 182
  neo-African, 168, 172, 173, 180
Courtney, RAS Mikey (Michael), 187
Cuba, 145, 207, 214, 249, 250, 257, 258
Cultural self defence, 84–86, 99
Cultural '*vs.*' high art, 2, 5, 9, 178
Cunningham, Merce, 25, 46
Curriculum/dance curriculum, 121, 127, 203, 214, 235, 241, 245–247, 253, 259, 260, 263
Cuxima-Zwa, Chikukwango, 5, 131

D
Dahomey, In, 279
Dance
  academy, the, 13, 68, 71
  studio, the, 6, 10, 13, 66, 67, 71, 75, 103, 116, 120, 201, 214, 215, 254, 270
  western dance canon, 73
Dancehall, 8, 35, 82, 167–182, 196, 238–240, 242, 244
  subversive space, 168
Dance Theatre of Harlem, 58
  Mitchell, Arthur, 57, 60
  Shook, Karel, 57
Dance training
  Brighton University, 263
  City and Islington College, 249
  codified dance, 4, 254
  diverse training, 203, 256, 258, 261
  London Contemporary Dance School/The Place, 24, 26, 27, 266, 267, 281
  London Metropolitan University, 254
  Max Rivers Studios, 25
  Middlesex University, xvi, xxiii, xxiv, xxvi, xxix, xxx

Northern School of Contemporary Dance, 24
Rambert School/Rambert Academy, 58
University of East London, 263
University of Limerick, 187, 188, 191
Urban Dance Practice with East London Dance, 263
Urdang academy, 58
Willesden Jazz Ballet, 24
Danse de L'Afrique, 87
Darwin, Charles, 10, 11, 54, 136
Dasein, 69, 70
See also Heidegger, Martin; Improvisation
Death/to transition, 123, 206, 207
cemetery, 154–162
Death/to transition, 94
Dinki Mini dance, 94
funeral, 139
Decolonisation, 67, 68, 75, 104, 136, 177, 221
DeFrantz, Thomas, 8, 39
Defying, 71, 76
defiant, 206
Dewey, John, 13, 67, 69–71, 74, 76n1, 76n2, 191
Diasporic, 33, 37–50, 131–163, 178, 217, 223, 226, 235, 241, 247
Difference, 11, 12, 24, 34, 45, 67, 68, 73, 124, 125, 135, 139, 144, 161, 168, 194, 197, 204, 214, 218, 219, 226, 227, 241, 249–264
Diversity
cultural, 116, 188, 189, 249, 252, 263, 264
practice, 121, 125
Dixon Gottschild, Brenda, 34, 35, 56, 120
DJ, 172, 220, 227, 228

Dominican Republic, 145
Donaldson, Patricia, 93
Double consciousness, 39, 88, 279
Dress
costume, 141, 142, 279
fabric, 103, 132, 137, 207
textile materials, 137
Dualism, 2
subject/object, 2, 9–14, 68, 75, 215
See also Mind/body
Dubois, W.E.B., 39, 87, 88, 160
Dunham, Katherine, 203, 242, 280
Dynott, Shevelle, 60
Dzikunu, George, 32

E
Earth
earth mother, 110
grounded movement, 110
Edwards, Brenda MBE, 32, 59
Egypt, 111, 160
Egyptian mythology, 108, 109
Elders, 6, 7, 20, 24, 30, 106
Elie, Mark, 58
Embodiment/embody, 7, 13, 21, 66, 69, 70, 74, 84, 87, 90, 92, 96, 101, 102, 108, 133, 159, 169, 181, 188, 190, 193, 195, 227
Emerging, xiii, 1, 19, 26, 171, 202–204, 208, 265
Enough
not African enough, 44, 121
not Black enough, 45
Environment, 9, 28, 46, 61, 66, 69, 70, 72, 74, 80, 96, 102, 109, 112, 135, 137, 139, 142, 151, 153, 154, 157, 160, 161, 169, 201, 203, 204, 206, 210, 220, 244

Eroticism, 237, 245
  erotic, 170, 178, 236–241, 243–247
Ethio-Modern Dance, 190, 192, 193
Ethiopia, 187
Ethiopian dance, including Ethiopian Contemporary dance
  Agew, 196
  eskista, 189, 195
  Ethio-Modern dance, 194
  Guragé, 189, 195, 196
  Wolaita, 195, 196
Ethnography, xv, 7, 126, 242
European, 7, 8, 10–12, 34, 38, 39, 45, 52, 54–56, 85, 110, 111, 121, 123, 126, 136, 141, 197, 224, 229, 278, 279
Exchange, 6, 26, 66, 88, 118, 127, 150, 191, 197, 215, 244, 277–283
Expansions (Jazz dance group), 225
Exploration, 30, 65, 66, 69, 80, 81, 116, 132, 144, 145, 149, 158, 159, 171, 206, 210, 240–242
Extemporary Dance Theatre, 203

F
Family, 281
  christenings, 102
  wakes, 94
  weddings, 102, 139, 195
Felix, Julie, 58
Femininity, 53, 178
  asexual Mammy, 240
  belly woman, 179
  hyper-sexualisation, 8
  slackness, 173, 237
Feminist, xv, 8, 214, 218, 235–247
First generation, 101, 102, 118, 122
Food, 26, 91, 140, 193, 267, 269, 283
Foot Patrol, 225
Forbes, Cecelin, 93
Forbes, Doreen, 87

Freedom, 55, 92, 141, 157, 210, 236, 238–240, 242, 243, 245–247, 279
  agency, 239, 240, 243, 247
Funding, 33, 58, 106, 117, 126, 180, 250, 251, 259, 263, 264

G
Garrett-Glassman, Brenda, 58, 59
Gaze, 73, 121, 169, 229, 230
Gender, 12, 67, 118, 124, 170, 178, 218, 219, 228–230, 243, 251, 253
  male, 228
Ghana, 32, 34, 214, 249, 250, 262, 263, 280
Ghanaian, 39, 89, 90, 111
Glean, Beverley, 32, 33, 214, 249–264
Golding, Sandra, 101
Gonzalez, Anita, 277
Graham, Martha, 23, 25, 92, 205, 241
  technique, 266
Grandfather, 206
Grandmas & Grandmothers, 5, 6, 269
Greater London Council, 58, 59
Grounded, to be, 45, 95, 110, 111, 126, 242
  See also Earth
Guy, Jackie MBE, CD, 83, 84, 89–94, 96, 97, 99, 105

H
Haiti, 107, 134, 145, 148, 149, 161, 163
Healing, 82, 102, 105, 106, 108, 111, 112, 148, 161, 174, 175, 178, 181, 243
Heidegger, Martin, 69–71, 76n1
Heightened awareness, 72, 103
  See also Out of body experience
Hemsley, Alexandrina, 37, 40, 42, 44, 48

Heritage, 26, 38–40, 42–46, 50, 73, 84, 88–91, 96, 99, 104, 106, 139, 152, 167, 175, 188, 189, 207, 224, 227, 236, 240, 256
Hewlett, James, 278
Higher education (HE), 81, 115–127, 214, 250, 263
Hip hop, 28, 30, 32, 112, 117, 171, 173, 178, 187, 189, 190, 195–197, 220, 226, 236, 252, 255, 260, 261
Hips, *see* Pelvis
History
   alternative histories, 168–171
   historical injury, 8
Home, 68, 150, 152, 201, 202, 237, 242
   artistic voice, 202
   belonging, 152
   coming to, 152
   leaving, 201
hooks, bell, 126
Horton, Lester, 204, 205, 241, 268
   technique, 204
House
   music, 225
   parties, 224, 225
Howard, Robin, 24, 27
Hybridity, 118–127, 143, 144, 152, 154
   See also In-betweenness
Hylton, Robert, 32

I
Identity, 43, 76, 98, 119, 131, 150, 163, 242
   African Diasporic identities, 38, 40, 47, 50
   black idenitiy, 82, 135, 154, 159
   post imperial, 231
   as a women, 42, 247
IDJ, 225, 228, 230

Igbokwe, Vicki, 37, 39, 40, 42, 43, 49
Immigration, 214, 221
Improvisation, 44, 71–73, 214
   improvised, 9, 73, 93, 217, 226
In-betweenness, 65, 69, 70, 72
   between-ness, 69, 70, 73, 75
In-between spaces, 39, 45, 46, 49
Indigenous, xiv, 5, 7, 9, 10, 66, 68, 71, 80, 111, 112, 135, 139, 141, 159, 171, 196, 198, 204
Invisibility, 61, 72, 122, 205
Ireland, 187–189, 191, 193, 198
IRIE! dance theatre, 249

J
Jamaica, 86, 93, 102, 145, 163, 167, 249, 250
   Cultural Development Commission (JCDC), 256, 257
   National Dance Theatre Company (NDTC), 90, 178
James, Adam, 59
James, Gregory, 59
Jazz, 104, 190
   jazz dancing, 217, 218, 220, 224–226, 228
   jazz funk, 220, 225
   jazz fusion, 220, 229
   Old Skool, 217
   UK jazz dancing, 219
   underground Jazz movement, 56
Jazz Defektors, 225, 228
Johnson, Cecelin, 87, 88, 91
Johnson-Small, Jamila, 37, 40, 42, 44, 48
Jones, Merville, 29, 35
Jonzi D, 29, 32
Joseph, Michael, 271
Journey, 210
   journeying, 82, 202, 210, 267, 283
   voyaging, 215

K

Kindred, Helen, 10, 65
Kokuma Dance Company, 3, 87, 89, 104
Kokuma Performing Arts, *see* Kokuma Dance Company
Kyle, Peter, W., 271

L

Lakota, 5, 6
Lane, William Henry ('Juba'), 278
Language, 2, 6, 8, 10, 20, 21, 34, 38, 40, 44, 48–50, 65–76, 80, 105, 107, 112, 113, 161, 170, 171, 190, 193, 197, 201, 205, 214, 227, 242, 243, 252, 258, 260, 281, 283
Last, Brenda, 27
Leeds, 29, 32, 33, 35, 86
Lehan, Rosie, 249
Leicester, Phoenix Arts Centre, 271
Les Ballet Nègres, 5, 18
Lewis, Cathy, 33
Lewis, Irvin, 217
Libations, 140, 269
Limón, José, 241
Liverpool, 32, 33, 36, 86, 278, 280
London, 1, 24, 26, 37, 74, 82, 86, 115, 131, 202, 220, 255, 266
London Contemporary Dance Theatre, 24–27, 29
Lorde, Audre, 236, 243
Love, 23–25, 53, 102, 110, 172, 210, 236, 266, 268, 271
Lynch, Edward, 35, 225

M

MAAS Movers Dance Company, 32, 223
Mahogany (Jazz dance company), 225
Mainstream, 1–5, 12, 13, 20, 57–61, 66, 67, 69, 71–73, 79, 82, 89, 116, 188, 189, 229
Manchester, 278
Matthais, Bunty, 33
Mendez, Greta, 32, 33, 223
Migration, 59, 110, 122, 132, 149, 163, 189
migrants, 138
Miller, Trevor, 228
Mind/Body dualism
  Cartesian dualism, 9
  Rene Descartes, 9, 10, 12
Moors, 52, 53, 61
Movement, 4, 24, 32, 79, 101, 122, 131, 167, 201, 238, 266, 282
  no life without movement, 190
Moving Tu Balance (African Healing Dance/Ankh Ku Maat), 81, 101–113
Multiple consciousnesses, 40
  multitude of consciousnesses., 45
Mystic and the Israelites (M&I), 87–89
  See also Kokuma Dance Company

N

Namron, OBE, 9, 23, 33
Narrative, 132
  inquiry method, xiv–xvi, 7
  oral history, 7
  stories through movement, 107
  storytelling, 99, 235, 242
National Front, 221, 268, 269, 276n1
Neo-African, 167, 168, 171–182
Neo-Liberalism, 220, 226
New York, 26, 37, 74, 195, 205, 251, 252, 255, 278, 280, 281
Nigeria, x, 39, 145, 280
  See also Yoruba
Nightclubs
  battle, 270

battling, 226
clubs, 219, 224
discothèque, 270
gay clubs, 229
underground venues, 226
See also Clubs
Northern soul, 228
Nurse, Gary, 230
Nurse, Seymour, 220, 224–227

O

Oceanic philosophies, 75
See also Ta-Va
Opoku-Addaie, Freddie, 37, 40, 41, 45–47
Orisha, 178
Otherness, viii, 2–4, 73, 74, 161, 168
orientalism, 125
other, viii, 2–4, 42, 73, 74, 123, 149, 161, 168, 204
othered, 2, 38, 41, 47
Out of body experience, 105

P

Palmer, Judith, 33
Pancho, Cassa, 60
Parmell, Gail, 33
Pasuka, Berto, 57, 279, 280
Patten, H, 8, 35, 82, 167–182, 282
Pedagogy, 68, 118, 119, 124–126, 207, 210, 245
Pelvis, 9, 95, 235–238, 243, 245
hips, 242, 246 (*see also* Wining)
pelvic wining, 179
Performance
access to venues, 279
Prince of Wales Theatre, 25, 280
Theatre Royal Birmingham, 280
touring, 27, 278
Phenomenology, 69, 73, 76n1, 193

Phoenix Dance Company, 29, 35, 265
See also Phoenix Dance Theatre
Phoenix Dance Theatre, 29, 265
Photography, 132, 133, 157
Portuguese, 52, 134–137, 139, 141, 143
Post-Apartheid, 118, 151
Postcolonial, 132, 133, 135, 139–142, 144, 145, 149, 151, 152, 159, 161
Powell, Enoch, 221
Rivers of Blood speech, 221, 269
Practice, viii, xi, xiii, 5, 20, 25, 33, 43, 59, 66, 81, 82, 103, 115, 131, 167, 188, 201, 213, 217, 238, 249, 277
Pragmatism, *see* John Dewey's
Primitivism, 54–57, 61, 136, 149
primitive, 9, 54–56, 144, 149, 152, 161
Project O, 37
See also Johnson-Small, Jamila; Hemsley, Alexandrina

Q

Queen, 140, 245
dancehall Queens, 172, 177, 180, 182
Queen Nancy, 93, 95

R

Rambert, Marie, 24, 58
Ramdhanie, Bob, 88–92, 102, 104, 180, 223
Rastafarian, 103, 173, 181, 187, 227
Refugee, 82, 131, 135, 143, 144, 149
Re:Generations conferences, 206, 209, 258
Reggae, 167–173, 180–182, 207, 227, 238
roots reggae, 173

Reid, Nicki, 92
Religious
  practices, 95, 134, 145, 157, 161, 168–170, 174, 175, 177
  revivalism, 173, 181
Representation, xv, xvi, 7–9, 21, 28, 33, 38, 40–45, 51–61, 74, 121, 125, 135, 137, 141, 144, 146, 150, 182, 204, 213, 223, 224, 226, 243, 244, 257, 259
  audienced, 2
Resistance, xiii, 10, 89, 93, 137, 181, 188, 214, 215, 224, 240, 242, 278
  anansi, 93
Rhythm, 48, 72, 93, 105, 107, 196, 244, 281
  Guragé rhythm, 196
  of life, 207
  polyrhythm, 34–36
  riddim, 172, 177
Riley, Richard, 57
Ritual, 73, 82, 95, 103, 105–109, 112, 116, 131–163, 170, 171, 173–177, 181, 206, 208, 282
Romans, Hopal, 33, 82, 201–210, 215, 265, 268
Royal Birmingham Ballet, 60, 61

S

St Thomas, 103
Sekyi, Rachel, 59
Self, 144
  personhood /smadditisation, 170
  self-actualisation, 109, 170
  self defence, 84–86, 99
  self-realisation, 79, 80, 84, 85
  sense of self, 87, 90, 99, 205
Senegal, 32, 145, 195
Senior, Nadine, 29, 88, 121, 257
Seutin, Alesandra, 37, 39, 40, 42, 44, 49
Sexualise, 53, 238
Sexuality, 67, 118, 158, 170, 177, 178, 236, 238, 240–243
  agency, 240
Shame, 169, 237, 238
  shaming, 244, 246
Singleton, Tyrone, 61
Ska (Blue Beat), 171, 224, 227
Skin
  brown bodies, 37–50
  brown skin, 246
  flesh, 168, 177
Slavery / slave trade, 111, 153, 163, 236, 238, 239, 278
  enslavement, 106, 168
  the Middle Passage, 111
  post-slavery, 133, 175
Social, viii, ix, xv, 8, 12, 24, 33, 47, 55, 80, 84–90, 105, 112, 113, 115–118, 120, 124, 125, 132, 135–139, 144, 149, 151, 152, 154, 159, 167, 170, 175, 188, 189, 196, 198, 208, 220, 224, 225, 228–230, 235, 238, 241, 242, 244, 256, 257, 281
  fabric, 135, 198
  social justice, 243
Solihull, 271
South Africa, 27, 48, 116
  teaching of, 45, 48, 102–109, 115–127, 250, 255
South African
  cape Jazz Social dance, 117
  dance, 8, 81, 115–127
  ingoma, 116
  langarm, 116, 117
Spiritual, ix, 5, 13, 35, 79, 81, 82, 84, 85, 94–96, 105, 109, 111, 112, 132, 134, 137, 140, 149, 157,

159, 161, 168–170, 172–182, 188, 198, 207, 223, 236, 245, 246, 281, 283
  myal state, 174, 175, 181
  spirit, 93, 94, 105
  spirituality, 35
Stapleton, Leonora, 265, 266
Stereotypes, xv, 20, 51, 53, 74, 81, 120, 124, 125, 127, 226, 228, 229, 246
Straker, Carol, 33, 58
Students, dance, xi, 34, 81, 124, 247, 258–261
Subculture, 219, 227, 229, 230
Survival, 85, 93, 95, 101, 168, 173, 238, 250, 251, 257, 258, 263

T
Tap dance, 254
Ta-Va, 75
Tharp, Kenneth OBE, 223
Thatcher, Margret, 220–222
Therapeutic, 81, 102, 105, 107, 111, 112
Thorpe, Dougie, 35, 57
Time, 7, 24, 32, 39, 54, 67, 80, 84, 103, 117, 133, 167, 169, 201, 213, 239, 264, 265, 278
  and space, viii, 7, 70, 72, 74, 75, 172
Todryk, Danuta, 266
Trails of Ado, 84
  See also Kokuma Dance Company
Transaction, 13, 65, 69–72, 74, 75, 217
  See also In-betweeness, John Dewey
Transatlantic, 215, 277–283
Transcend, 38, 49, 85, 86, 172, 181
Transformation
  transformational experiences, 243
    (*see also* Aesthetic)
  transformative, 82, 125, 157, 168, 172, 173, 180–182, 235, 243, 246, 247
Transnationally
  transatlantic arts exchange, 215, 277
Travel, 59, 60, 115, 124, 201, 202, 250, 251, 255, 264, 277–281, 283
  arrived in Britain, 102
  journeying abroad, 210
  movement of communities, 122
  touring, 27

U
Uchenna Dance, *see* Vicki Igbokwe
Uganda, 252
Unemployment, 220, 221, 224, 226–228
Union Dance company, 206
United States of America (USA), 68, 202, 203
The Untouchable Force (Jazz dance group), 225
Urban
  urbanization, 132
Urban Bush women, 280, 281
Urban Contemporary, *see* Contemporary dance
USA, vii–x, 20, 58, 105, 187, 214, 215, 249–253, 262
Uzor, Tia-Monique, 37

V
Vallin, Jackie, 266
Visibility/ invisibility, 61, 74, 148, 150, 168, 170, 177, 180, 181, 263
  visible, voices can be heard, 48
Vocab Dance Company, *see* Alesandra Seutin

W

Wallace, Noel, 59
Water, 103, 141
  ocean, 141
  See also Libations
Watson, Hugh, 89
Watson, Sharon, 32
Watu Wazuri, 90
Webb, Samantha, 59
Western
  culture, 10, 68, 73, 144
  dance canon, 73
  framework, 66, 69, 73
White (cultural identifier), 21, 26, 30, 42, 68, 227
Whiteness, viii, 1, 3, 76
White (skin colour), 3, 11, 12, 25, 28, 34, 40, 42, 44, 46, 52, 58, 61, 87, 93, 136, 169, 221, 227, 228, 240, 269
Williams, Evan, 60, 279
Wining, 8, 176, 179, 238, 246, 247
  hip wine, 235, 237
Womanist, 247
  See also Feminist
Working Class, 80, 219–221, 227, 281
Wray, Sheron, 32, 33

Y

Yoruba, 6, 11, 73, 158, 178, 269
  Orisha, 11, 178
Youth and young people, 112
  Black youth, 180
  probation / policing, 86, 88
  recreation centres, 138
  subculture, 230
  youth clubs, 215, 219, 227, 268
  youth culture, 170
  youth empowerment, 197
  youths, 221, 226, 227
  youth subculture, 219
Youth Dance, 208
  Contemporary Youth Dance (CYD), 266
  Leicestershire County School of Dance, 270
  London Youth Dance Theatre (LYDT), 268–270
  Mara Ya Pili, 272, 273
  National Festival of Youth Dance, 265, 271
  Saturday afternoon, 268
  Saturday School, 256
  Sunday mornings, 266

MIX

Papier aus ver-
antwortungsvollen
Quellen
Paper from
responsible sources
FSC® C141904

Druck:
Customized Business Services GmbH
im Auftrag der KNV-Gruppe
Ferdinand-Jühlke-Str. 7
99095 Erfurt